Frontispiece: Donato Bramante, *I due filosofi*, Fresco. (Chapter XI).

CYNTHIA M. PYLE

# MILAN AND LOMBARDY IN THE RENAISSANCE: ESSAYS IN CULTURAL HISTORY

*Presentation by Paolo Bongrani*

LA FENICE EDIZIONI

UNIVERSITÀ DEGLI STUDI - PARMA
Istituto di Filologia Moderna

*TESTI E STUDI*
Collana fondata da FRANCA BRAMBILLA AGENO
Nuova serie. Studi 1

Finito di stampare nel mese di Maggio 1997
Presso la Tipografia Litografica Iride s.r.l. - Via della Bufalotta, 224 - 00139 Roma

© 1997 La Fenice Edizioni
Via Adolfo Prasso 5 - 00149 Roma (Italia). Tel.-Fax 06/5565954

ISBN 88-86171-34-X

TO  MY  HUSBAND

RICHARD  S.  KAYNE

# TABLE OF CONTENTS

# PRESENTAZIONE

### di Paolo Bongrani

Cynthia M. Pyle, allieva del grande Paul Oskar Kristeller alla Columbia University e poi docente in varie Università americane (tra cui la Graduate School della City University di New York, dove ha fondato il "Renaissance Studies Program" e diretto il "Renaissance Forum"), è nota da tempo agli studiosi per le sue ricerche sul Quattrocento letterario italiano, e in particolare sulla produzione teatrale delle corti settentrionali; un campo questo (quasi inesplorato fino ai nostri giorni), in cui la Pyle ha esordito nel 1976 con una tesi di dottorato ricca di novità (*Politian's "Orfeo" and Other "Favole mitologiche" in the Context of Late Quattrocento Northern Italy*), a cui hanno fatto seguito altri contributi significativi.

Ora, sette di tali contributi (affiancati da tre studi inediti e da una introduzione generale) sono stati raccolti in questo volume, che ho caldeggiato e che mi pare rappresenti un'iniziativa doppiamente positiva: innanzi tutto perché ci permette di avere a disposizione tutti i principali lavori dedicati dalla Pyle alla cultura 'lombarda' e milanese del Quattrocento; e poi perché offre l'occasione a noi, studiosi italiani che operiamo sugli stessi temi (o su temi analoghi e vicini), di confrontarci con i metodi di ricerca di una studiosa americana, e di apprezzare meglio alcune delle qualità che sono proprie della sua scuola; qui ne voglio ricordare almeno tre: la vasta erudizione (che si traduce in una attenzione speciale per i dati biografici e bibliografici relativi agli autori e ai testi esaminati, e in una esplorazione assidua dei fondi antichi delle principali biblioteche europee e americane, a contatto diretto con i manoscritti e le prime stampe); la conoscenza delle lingue classiche e delle lingue volgari, e la capacità (e il gusto) di lavorare contemporaneamente sia sul versante delle letterature romanze sia su quello della produzione umanistica; e inoltre (e soprattutto) la raffinata e vivace esperienza multidisciplinare, aperta così alla letteratura (varia e plurilingue, come si è detto), come alla filosofia, all'arte, alla musica e alle scienze.

Questi metodi di ricerca hanno trovato un campo privilegiato di applicazione nello studio degli ambienti culturali sforzeschi del secondo Quattrocento, per i quali, prima dei rapidi progressi di questi ultimi anni (un punto di svolta si può forse indicare nel convegno internazionale del 1982 su "Milano nell'età di Ludovico il Moro"), si era sostanzialmente fermi ai dati offerti dall'ormai vecchio *Quattrocento* di Vittorio Rossi; e ciò (come ebbe a sottolineare Carlo Dionisotti), anche a proposito dei dati fondamentali e di base relativi al riconoscimento del profilo biografico (oltreché del percorso letterario e intellettuale) di molti 'attori' di quella stagione, e non solo dei minori. E pertanto non è un caso che la Pyle abbia lavorato alla ricostruzione di due biografie 'eccellenti' della Milano sforzesca: quella di Gasparo Visconti (resa particolarmente problematica dalla presenza di un alto numero di omonimi coevi, o quasi coevi), e quella dell'alessandrino (di origine) Baldassarre Taccone; mentre un altro personaggio (fin qui quasi indistinto) è stato riconosciuto, grazie alla Pyle, nel folto coro dei letterati cortigiani degli Sforza: Giovanni II Tolentino.

Anche il personale e particolare *iter italicum* che la studiosa ha compiuto attraverso la produzione libraria lombarda (dissodata solo da poco da ricerche sistematiche come quella della Pellegrin sui codici visconteo-sforzeschi, e quelle della Rogledi Manni e del Sandal sugli incunaboli milanesi e sugli editori e tipografi operanti a Milano nel corso del Cinquecento), è risultato assai fruttuoso, consentendole di recuperare alcuni 'pezzi', manoscritti e a stampa, di notevole interesse bibliografico e culturale: penso, per esempio, alla rara edizione milanese (stampata da Giovanni da Castiglione nel 1512) delle epistole latine e degli epigrammi del già citato Giovanni II Tolentino, utilizzati e in gran parte editi nei capitoli VI e VII di questo volume.

Ma è soprattutto nello studio delle opere teatrali di Milano e delle altre corti padane (opere intese in un'accezione giustamente ampia, comprensiva di feste nuziali e conviviali), che la Pyle ha saputo mostrare le sue doti migliori ed offrire gli stimoli più vivi; e anche questa volta non a caso, perché la spiccata propensione alla ricerca interdisciplinare che, come si è detto, è tipica della sua scuola (ed è stata raffinata dalla studiosa nella sua esperienza internazionale), trova un'applicazione quanto mai felice in questo 'genere' particolare, che nasce quasi miracolosamente, negli ultimi decenni del Quattrocento, alla confluenza di letteratura (insieme umanistica e volgare) e di musica, di filosofia (soprattutto neoplatonica) e di arte e tecnica scenografica. È nell'esperienza teatrale (fragile ma vivace, composita e ideologicamente sempre più rasserenante), che pare specchiarsi più che nelle altre manifestazioni artistiche coeve (la Pyle parla di *Theater as Mirror*), quella libertà creativa e insieme quella ricerca di una superiore *concordia discors* morale e intellettuale (oltreché estetica), che sono proprie del nostro tardo Quattrocento.

Questo discorso sul teatro, come genere felicemente rappresentativo di una cultura 'mondana' e mescidata, memore dell'antico e curiosa di esperimenti e sincretismi nuovi, vale per quasi tutte le corti italiane di quell'età; ma vale soprattutto per Milano che, sia per la sua situazione geo-politica, sia per l'esplicita volontà dei suoi Signori (*newcomers*, '*upstarts*', e quindi desiderosi di fondare una tradizione culturale originale e legata al proprio nome), appare singolarmente aperta alle più varie presenze, alle più varie suggestioni e ai più diversi innesti; grazie ai quali (e la Pyle ha occasione di mostrarlo non solo nei capitoli sul teatro ma anche in quello finale sul riso di Democrito e il pianto di Eraclito: un altro tema al centro di letteratura, filosofia ed arte), germogliano e 'rinascono' nuovi generi letterari, nuovi miti, nuovi *tòpoi* e simboli, che in seguito, pur attraverso ininterrotte metamorfosi, diverranno patrimonio comune della cultura italiana ed europea.

# PREFACE

In our search for the Renaissance, both for its own character and for what we today can learn from such a fertile period, it is both inspiring and useful to attempt to reconstruct the attitudes and the culture to be found in that era of scholarship and creation. To understand how people of the Renaissance thought, what were the terms of their perception of the world, requires approaching their lives and their age from many different directions: it requires studying their literature, science, political history, education, music and art. Only in this way can we hope to even glimpse what we may call by the term adopted by Werner Jaeger for his study of Greek culture, the «paideia» of the Italian Renaissance.

This is what I have attempted to do in my research on fifteenth century Italian culture. The curiosity to pursue this approach is born of my own backgrounds in the arts and in life science, neither of which did I eschew for the study of the Renaissance, both of which have afforded me insight into the material of, and the methods for pursuing, my vocation.

Of the Italian Renaissance the English-speaking world is aware principally of Florentine culture, with some acquaintance with Venice and Rome added for good measure. But the significant and powerful state of Milan is often overlooked, despite its aesthetically rich and even fascinating culture. Milan and Lombardy, as will be made clear from a perusal of the studies collected here, inherited a different cultural mix, in great part due to their diplomatic and cultural ties with France and Savoy, dating from at least the fourteenth century. Gothic inspiration is thus important, and lends a different grace to the art of the area, and even to its handwriting, as can be seen here in the hand and the manuscript miniatures discussed in chapters II and III. In music too, the Northern connection was important, as we know from the work of Edward Lowinsky and others on the choir of the Duomo in Milan. The decoration of the Duomo itself, along with that of the Certosa of Pavia, unique monuments of Gothic architecture, unite, in Lombard Quattrocento fashion, the art of the late Middle Ages with the new perspectival and humanistic interests of the Renaissance. One of the major proponents of the use of that perspective, Donato Bramante, also drew on intellectual themes in the air at the time, as we see in chapter XI. In the native poetry and literature, we find a preponderance of vernacular works with a patina of Milanese and Lombard dialects. Theatrical trends take their lead from a seminal secular play by Angelo Poliziano, veering off in interesting ways, determined by the Lombard and other courtly audiences for which they were created, to create a small genre containing the seeds of nothing less than the theatrical future of Italy and Europe (including opera).

To facilitate an acquaintance with these currents among the English-speaking public, I have left a number of these essays, especially the Introduction, in English, the language they were written in. The others are in Italian either because they were written and published in that language, or (chapter IX, at the editors' request) to make the volume more accessible to the Italian-speaking audience in its host country. The volume is directed at both the scholarly public and those with interests in adjacent areas such as collecting, bibliophilia and the culture of the Renaissance in general. To these ends, I am particularly pleased to be able to print the footnotes in a conveniently accessible place in these versions of all the articles, at the same time noting that they may of course be skipped in reading.

Upon embarking on this project a year and a half ago, I intended to leave the published essays as they had appeared. Likewise, those essays that seemed finished but had not yet seen print. Needless to say, the temptation, first to correct oversights or other deficiencies in the published works, and then even to turn a footnote to chapter IV into an appendix and finally into a chapter (XI), overcame the exigencies of rapid publication. I have also attempted to bring many references up to date and to make uniform the bibliographical citations. (Bibliographical references can be found through the Index of Names and, in some cases, through the Index of Mythological and Fictional Characters; there is also an Index of Manuscripts; early printed editions, while not indexed separately, can in most cases be found through references to their printers [so labelled] or to Ludwig Hain [H] and other bibliographers, such as G. W. Panzer and L. Polain).

Rather than keep the (somewhat repetitious) headnotes with the chapters to which they pertain, I here acknowledge the venues in which some papers were aired and special help received. Chapters IV, VI, VIII and IX, as well as elements of chapters V and X, have their roots (if not their branches) in my Columbia University Ph.D. dissertation. Chapter I began life as part of an unpublished catalogue to Andrea Norris's Sforza exhibition of 1988-1989. Chapter II was begun when I was a fellow of the American Academy in Rome and had the great pleasure and privilege of working with Augusto Campana and Luigi Michelini Tocci; it also benefitted from talks with Albinia de la Mare, Paul Gehl, Elisabeth Pellegrin and Paola Scarcia Piacentini; I have made my arguments for dating Decembrio's birth at 1399 more explicit in the text, though their basis remains exactly the same as when I announced this finding in 1981. Chapter III was written during the first year of my thoroughly enjoyable term as an Associate in the Department of the History of Science, Harvard University. The text published in the appendix of Chapter V was kindly read by Antonia Tissoni Benvenuti. Chapter VI profited at different stages from the linguistic acuity of Carole Boggs, Lucrezia Campus, Thomas Cerbu and Maria Grazia Pernis. I am happy to have the chance to publish chapter VII in revised form, overcoming the happenstance of not having seen proof for the first version. Chapter IX was read in earlier versions at the Renaissance Society of America annual meeting, Tempe, Arizona and the Columbia University Seminar in the Renaissance (1987), at the Harvard University Seminar in Renaissance Studies (1988), and at the Congresso Internazionale in onore di Eugenio Battisti, Milano (1991), and it was shared thanks to the generosity of Robert Erenstein with the participants in the Theatre Iconography Symposium at the Netherlands Institute for Advanced Study (Wassenaar, 1995); a preliminary version was kindly read by Thomas Greene. Chapter X was presented at the Renaissance Society of America annual meeting, Kansas City (1993) and benefitted from the lively discussion during a reading before the Society for the Study of Women in the Renaissance in October, 1993, including helpful comments by Beatrice Gottlieb, Dorothy Latz, Paula Loscocco, Margaret Mikesell, Joyce Miller, Phyllis Roberts, Rinaldina Russell, Susan Senneff, Betty Travitsky and Elizabeth Welles; I owe an early bibliographical suggestion in this area to Albert Rabil; John R. Clarke deserves special thanks for a focussed and perceptive reading at a late stage. Chapter XI grew out of note 25 to chapter IV, spurred in part by correspondence with Creighton Gilbert and Carlo Pedretti, in part by a question posed by Pietro Marani; the chapter was drafted at the Warburg Institute in London, in New York and in Oquossoc, Maine, and was finished at the American Academy in Rome; it has benefitted from readings by Philipp Fehl and Raina Fehl, and from iconographical recognitions by Andrea Cavaggioni and Karin Einaudi; it is on the Fall, 1996 schedule of the Columbia University Seminar in the Renaissance, whose chairman, Richard Harrier, and whose members have always provided intelligent, informed and fruitful comments on my work.

So many predecessors, professors, colleagues and friends have contributed over the years to my research, beginning with Professor Camillo P. Merlino who suggested Middlebury's Italian School as a locus for transitional studies. Professor Oscar Büdel directed me to Paul Oskar Kristeller, from whom I was to derive my basic training. My principal guide and stimulus in Italian literature during my years of study at Columbia University was Maristella de Panizza Lorch. The other colleagues and friends from whom I have learned so much and for whose support at crucial moments I am exceptionally grateful make an imposing list, stretching from the 1960s to the present (with the exception of several deeply felt losses): Maria Ines Aliverti, Michael Allen, Paola Benincà, Giuseppe Billanovich, Constance Taylor Blackwell, Uta-Renate Blumenthal, Phyllis Pray Bober, Leonard Boyle, Vittore Branca, Howard Mayer Brown, André Chastel, Diskin Clay, Louise George Clubb, Sebastian De Grazia, Carlo Dionisotti, William Elton, Mirella Ferrari, Gabriella Ferri Piccaluga, Gianfranco Folena, Giuseppe Frasso, Marc Fumaroli, Claudio Gallico, Ernst Gamillscheg, Eugenio Garin, Silvia Gavuzzo Stewart, Cecil Grayson, Marcel Gutwirth, Vincent Ilardi, Jean Jacquot, Isaías Lerner, Lewis Lockwood, Ida Maïer, Angelo Mazzocco, Philip McNair, Alain Michel, Nino Pirrotta, Paul Renucci, Ingrid D. Rowland, José

Ruysschaert, Charles B. Schmitt, Anne Schnoebelen, Giovannangiola Secchi Tarugi, Michael Shank, Sandra and David Sider, Nancy Siraisi, Frederick Sternfeld, Alfons M. Stickler, Joachim Stieber, Edith Sylla, Liba Taub, Gary Tomlinson, Charles Trinkaus, D. P. Walker and Mark and Phoebe Weil.

To Paolo Bongrani, whose work in Milanese studies I greatly appreciate, I express particular gratitude for having presented this project to his colleagues at the Istituto di Filologia Moderna of the Università di Parma, and for having acted as editor for this volume. The benefit of his eye, especially in reworking the Italian essays, has been indispensable.

My faithful assistants at the City University of New York Graduate School also deserve thanks: Francisco Ordoñez, George Ouwendijk, Carol Pedersen, John Pilsner, William Rednour and Louis Waldman.

The work of forging this book was done in large part at the American Academy in Rome. The project has also benefitted greatly from work done in Milan at the Biblioteca Trivulziana and the Biblioteca Ambrosiana (when that library, so crucial to research on Milan's cultural and intellectual history, was accessible, as it must become again); the Biblioteca Apostolica Vaticana, the Biblioteca Nazionale Centrale Vittorio Emanuele II, and the Biblioteca Hertziana, Rome; the Warburg Institute, London; and my working libraries for many years, the Bibliothèque Nationale, Paris, and Butler and Avery Libraries at Columbia University. The other libraries and institutions I have worked in with deep satisfaction include the: Archivi di Stato of Mantua, Milan and Modena, Archivio Segreto Vaticano, Biblioteca dell'Archiginnasio (Bologna), Biblioteca Casanatense (Rome), Biblioteca Nazionale Braidense (Milan), Biblioteca Nazionale Marciana (Venice), Biblioteca dell'Università Cattolica del Sacro Cuore (Milan), Biblioteca Universitaria di Bologna, British Library (London), Harvard University Libraries (Cambridge, Mass.), Pierpont Morgan Library (New York), and the revered institution where I first tasted of research on primary sources, the New York Public Library.

The final recognition, inexpressibly the greatest, is to the dedicatee of this book, my husband, Richard S. Kayne, who has witnessed the birth of its entire contents, and of all my work, from the beginnings of my second training in philology, literature and history, and who has supported and inspired my work and me unstintingly.

New York, August, 1996

# LIST OF ILLUSTRATIONS

Cover: *The Two Philosophers: Democritus and Heracleitus,* from A. Campofregoso, *Il riso de Democrito,* Milano, 1506. Woodcut. Courtesy of the Biblioteca Trivulziana, Milano (Chapter XI).

Frontispiece: Donato Bramante, *I due filosofi.* Fresco. Courtesy of the Pinacoteca di Brera, Milano (Chapter XI).

# ACKNOWLEDGEMENTS

Grateful acknowledgement is made to the following publications for permission to reprint:

Chapter II from *Umanesimo a Roma nel Quattrocento*: Acts of the Congress (New York, December, 1981), Istituto di Studi Romani, Roma - Barnard College, New York, 1984, pp. 295-307.

Chapter III from *Scriptorium*, XLII (1988), pp. 191-198.

Chapter IV from *Bibliothèque d'Humanisme et Renaissance*, LV (1993), pp. 565-582.

Chapter V from *Supplementum Festivum. Studies in Honor of Paul Oskar Kristeller*, Binghamton, NY, Medieval and Renaissance Texts and Studies, 1987, pp. 457-467.

Chapter VI from *Archivio Storico Lombardo*, CXVII (1991), pp. 391-413.

Chapter VII from *Libri & Documenti*, XVIII, 3 (1993), pp. 20-26.

Chapter VIII from *Il teatro italiano del Rinascimento*: Acts of the Congress, «Renaissance Theater in Northern Italy: The Court and the City 1400-1600» (New York, November, 1978), Milano, Edizioni di Comunità, 1980, pp. 349-360.

Portions of Chapter IX from Acts of the Conference: «Metodologia della ricerca. Orientamenti attuali. Congresso Internazionale in onore di Eugenio Battisti» (Milano, 27-31 May, 1991), in *Arte Lombarda*, 105-107 (1993), pp. 84-87.

# PART I
*Introduction*

# CHAPTER I

## Literary and Intellectual Currents
## in the Sforza Court (1450-1535)

The Sforzas were newcomers, «upstarts» in the minds of many, when Francesco was invited into the city to take charge of the faltering Ambrosian Republic and save Milan from its own civil violence in 1450. Francesco had had the acumen to wed Filippo Maria Visconti's daughter Bianca Maria, which lent him a vicarious legitimacy, though imperial recognition of this was not to come until 1493 in the reign of his son Ludovico il Moro. But Francesco Sforza was also keen enough to recognize the value of continuing the cultural tone of the duchy established by the Visconti, especially Gian Galeazzo, founder of the Visconti library at Pavia, and Filippo Maria, who were enthusiastic collectors and curious to learn from the discoveries of humanists and to meet and read the works of contemporary writers, from Francesco Petrarca on.[1] The tone was not as intellectual as that of Florence,

---

[1] On Milanese culture during the fifteenth century, see E. GARIN, «La cultura milanese nella prima metà del XV secolo» and «La cultura milanese nella seconda metà del XV secolo», in *Storia di Milano*, ed. G. Treccani degli Alfieri, vol. VI, pp. 545-608 and vol. VII, pp. 539-597, Milano, 1955 and 1956; G. L. BARNI, «La vita culturale a Milano dal 1500 alla scomparsa dell'ultimo duca Sforza», and F. GIANNESSI, «Gli inizi della tradizione poetica milanese», *Ibid.*, vol. VIII, Milano, 1957, pp. 421-453, 455-484. The richly illustrated volume, *Gli Sforza a Milano*, Milano, 1978, includes four synthetic articles by G. LOPEZ, G. A. DELL'ACQUA, L. GRASSI and G. BOLOGNA. The article by G. FERRI PICCALUGA, «Gli affreschi di casa Panigarola e la cultura milanese tra Quattro e Cinquecento», *Arte lombar-*

especially the Florence of Cosimo and Lorenzo de' Medici, who were philo-
sophically oriented, nearly scholarly men. It was a tone affected by French
aesthetic currents, owing to close relations with the Orléanais and, by prox-
imity, with Provence and Savoy. Manuscripts for the library were embellished in styles combining the austere classically oriented forms of Florence
with playful contemporary French ornamentation.

Unlike Florence, where the Medici had what must be called their circle,
Milan's cultural center was the court. There, the humanist (teacher, scholar,
writer), like the historian and the poet, was also a courtier, subject to and
patronized by a monarchic ruler who wished not only to learn, but to be
flattered and immortalized in letters and in art as well (not that the Medici
were free of these desires, but the republican form of government gave consi-
derably more intellectual freedom to the writers of Florence and dictated re-
straint to her rulers). The sponsoring of the Studio (to become the University) of Pavia and the building of the Visconti library in that city[2] seem to

----

*da*, n.s. 86-87 (1988, nn. 3-4), pp. 14-25, exhibits a broad vision of Renaissance Milanese
culture and its significance. See also the articles in the two-volume *Florence and Milan: Com-
parisons and Relations. Acts of Two Conferences at Villa I Tatti in 1982-1984*, org. S. Bertelli,
N. Rubinstein, C. H. Smyth; eds. C. H. Smyth, G. C. Garfagnini, Florence, 1989, especially
those by E. GARIN, C. TRINKAUS, A. TISSONI BENVENUTI, G. IANZITI, V. ILARDI, G. LUB-
KIN, E. GARBERO ZORZI. There is now a multi-volume *Storia illustrata di Milano*, ed. F. Della
Peruta, Milano, Sellino, 1992-; vols. 3 and 4 (1993) include articles relevant to particular facets
of the period under study. Most recently, we have the valuable contribution of P. BONGRANI,
«Novità sulla letteratura volgare nella Milano di fine Quattrocento», in *Politica, cultura e
lingua nell'età sforzesca. Incontro di Studio n. 4*, Milano, 1995, pp. 61-75.

   The essential works for the reign of Ludovico il Moro (1480-1499) are the classic F. MALA-
GUZZI VALERI, *La corte di Lodovico il Moro*, 4 volumes, Milano, 1913-23 (for subjects under
discussion, esp. M. PESENTI VILLA, «I letterati e i poeti», vol. IV) and the recent *Milano
nell'età di Ludovico il Moro. Atti del convegno internazionale, 28 febbraio-4 marzo 1983*, 2
vols., contin. pagin., Milano, 1983 (henceforth *Milano*; for subjects under discussion, esp.
articles by E. GARIN, G. RESTA, P. BONGRANI, A. TISSONI BENVENUTI, A. C. DE LA
MARE, C. GRAYSON). For the happily numerous individuals active in Milan under the Sforza
whose names fall in the early part of the alphabet (including Lavagna = Cavagni, Montano =
Capponi, Pistoia = Cammelli and Filarete = Averlino), see *Dizionario Biografico degli Italiani*, vols. I-, Roma, 1960- (henceforth, *DBI*, now up to vol. 44 (1994): «Farina»).

   Covering the currents discussed here, in the broader context of Italy, is the ever-valuable
*Storia della letteratura italiana* of G. TIRABOSCHI, 10 vols. in 13, Napoli, 1777-1786 and
many later editions.

[2] On the university, see P. VACCARI, *Storia della Università di Pavia*, Pavia, 1957. On the
library, E. PELLEGRIN, *La bibliothèque des Visconti et des Sforza ducs de Milan, au XVᵉ
siècle*, Paris, 1955; Eadem, *La bibliothèque des Visconti et des Sforza ducs de Milan. Supplément*, Firenze, Paris, 1969; A. C. DE LA MARE, «Scrittura e manoscritti a Milano al tempo
degli Sforza», in *Milano* (n. 1), pp. 397-408.

have stemmed from a real understanding of the intellectual satisfaction and value of learning, but were from an early stage socially (and in the broader sense of socially: politically) and aesthetically motivated as well.

When Francesco Sforza came to power, then, preoccupied as he was with consolidating his power and bringing order to the duchy, he did not aspire to leave his own mark on the cultural life, but followed instead in the tradition of his wife's family, simultaneously thereby enhancing his claims to legitimacy. Scholarship and letters were patronized, and at Pavia the Library was furnished with books and the Studio kept alive with eminent professors. This conservative policy was continued by his son, Galeazzo Maria, but after the latter's assassination (1476) and the interim rule by his widow, Bona of Savoy, and his secretary, Cicco Simonetta, another son of Francesco, Ludovico il Moro, usurped the power of his nephew and Galeazzo Maria's son, Gian Galeazzo, and, while remaining within the Franco-Lombard tradition, impressed his own lavish style on the court, nurturing its particularly Milanese flavor. Especially after his marriage to Beatrice d'Este in 1491 the court blossomed with popularesque and classically inspired vernacular poetry and spectacle. The fruits of the humanists' classical studies were reborn in the Italian tongue, with strong Milanese overtones. Also manifest in this flowering were the Neoplatonic tendencies which had been growing and spreading from Medicean Florence since Cosimo's interest in and sponsorship of Marsilio Ficino's studies and translations of Plato and the Hermetic Corpus, furthered by Lorenzo. After the flight of Ludovico il Moro in 1499, the duchy was dominated by the French, whose enlightened governor, Charles d'Amboise, Seigneur de Chaumont (1473-1511;[3] later to become patron of Leonardo da Vinci), saw the advantage in continuity of culture and kept many humanists, poets and men of science on in their positions. But the unifying effect of a court centered on an Italian duke was present only sporadically, with the returns of Ludovico's sons, Massimiliano (1512-1515) and Francesco II (1521-1525, 1529-1535), and then in times of war and plague which further unsettled the cultural life of Milan and Pavia.

## Milanese Humanists

Francesco Sforza's entry into Milan in 1450 meant the departure of Lombardy's native humanist, Pier Candido Decembrio (1399-1477) for Rome and

---

[3] *Biographie universelle ancienne et moderne* (Michaud), vol. VIII, Paris, s.d., pp. 43-44.

the Papal court of Nicholas V. Decembrio, for twenty-eight years ducal
secretary to Filippo Maria Visconti, had participated in the short-lived
Republic and made his position against inviting Francesco Sforza to defend
Milan clear. During the first year of the Republic, Decembrio had furthermore written a relatively uncompromising portrait of the ruler he had served
so closely for so long, who was also Francesco's father-in-law and of necessity
one of his models. Decembrio's funeral oration of 1444 honoring Niccolò
Piccinino, against whom Francesco had been pitted in battle in his days as a
*condottiere*, was even more likely to have been a factor, although there had
been a reconciliation of the two. For his stands on all or some of these
matters, Decembrio was forced to give way to his politically able rival, Francesco Filelfo (1398-1481), a native of Tolentino.

Pier Candido Decembrio and his father Uberto represented the Lombard
tradition of the humanistic movement. Humanists were teachers, editors,
translators, perforce historians and philologists, and sometimes, like poets of
the time, statesmen or bureaucrats as well. They worked on the manuscripts
of classical texts recently unearthed by themselves or others like them. [4] Petrarca and Boccaccio in the fourteenth century had begun this exciting endea-
vor; now it was up to their followers to develop methods to ascertain the
particular value to the culture of each manuscript: to see how close it could
bring them to the author of the text. They studied the handwriting found in
these manuscripts, and, thinking it was truly ancient rather than Carolingian
as was the case, they imitated it lovingly, and much to our present benefit,
for it is their humanistic hand that we imitate in script and print today. Both
Decembrios had translated works of Plato and other Greeks into Latin, and
Pier Candido had written historical works and encomia while participating in
the government of Milan, as was frequently the case with these *érudits en-
gagés*. He was instrumental in diffusing humanist culture to the distant shores

---

[4] For the accepted definition of Renaissance humanism (based on the *studia humanitatis*), see P.
O. KRISTELLER, «The Humanist Movement», in *Renaissance Thought. The Classic, Scholastic
and Humanist Strains*, New York, 1961, pp. 3-23 (esp. pp. 8-10); A. CAMPANA, «The Origin
of the Word 'Humanist'», *Journal of the Warburg and Courtauld Institutes*, IX (1946), pp.
60-73. See also: R. SABBADINI, *Il metodo degli umanisti*, Firenze, 1922; R. WEISS, *The
Renaissance Discovery of Classical Antiquity*, Oxford, 1969; *Two Renaissance Book Hunters:
The Letters of Poggius Bracciolini to Nicolaus de Niccolis*, trans. and ed. by P. W. G. Gordan,
New York and London, 1974; W. ULLMANN, *Medieval Origins of Renaissance Humanism*,
Ithaca, 1977; C. TRINKAUS, *The Scope of Renaissance Humanism*, Ann Arbor, 1983. Human-
ism in Milan is surveyed by A. Rabil, Jr. in *Renaissance Humanism. Foundations, Forms and
Legacies*, vol. I: *Humanism in Italy*, Philadelphia, 1988, pp. 235-263.

of England, corresponding with Duke Humfrey of Gloucester and helping him to establish his rich library (later left to the University of Oxford, but then dispersed). He would go on to broaden his interests in the directions of philosophy and natural history as well as other subjects.[5]

But for the moment, Decembrio was suffering the lot of those who depend on patronage for their livelihood. Not until the last year of his long life would he be recalled to the Sforza court. This suited Filelfo perfectly.[6] Being by nature more suited to the life of a courtier in post-republican Milan, while flirting with other patronage and obtaining, briefly, that of his pupil Aeneas Sylvius Piccolomini as Pope Pius II, he nevertheless clung to his position with the Sforza for three more decades until, upon the advent to power of Ludovico il Moro, he departed for Florence at the invitation of Lorenzo de' Medici, only to die two weeks after his arrival. Filelfo had arrived in Milan during the reign of Filippo Maria Visconti in 1439. He was then already a mature scholar of 41, and his choice of Milan implied, significantly, a commitment to the composition of Latin and Greek panegyric poetry, and

---

[5] On Decembrio and English humanism, see R. WEISS, *Humanism in England during the Fifteenth Century*, Oxford, 1967; A. SAMMUT, *Unfredo duca di Gloucester e gli umanisti italiani*, Padova, 1980, esp. pp. 29-53, 180-215; A.C. DE LA MARE, in *Duke Humfrey's Library and the Divinity School, 1488-1988* (exhibition catalogue), Oxford, 1988. For his life and works, M. BORSA, «P. C. D. e l'Umanesimo in Lombardia», *Archivio storico lombardo*, XX (1893), pp. 5-75, 358-441; E. DITT, «P. C. D. Contributo alla storia dell'Umanesimo italiano», *Memorie del R. Istituto Lombardo di Scienze e Lettere*, XXIV (XV of Ser. III), fasc. 2 (1931), pp. 21-108; V. ZACCARIA, «Sulle opere di P. C. D.», *Rinascimento*, VII (1956), pp. 13-74; C. M. PYLE, *Das Tierbuch des Petrus Candidus. Codex Urbinas latinus 276. Eine Einführung*, Zürich, 1984; P. O. KRISTELLER, «P. C. D. and his Unpublished Treatise on the Immortality of the Soul», in *Studies in Renaissance Thought and Letters, II*, Roma, 1985, pp. 281-300, 567-584; J. HANKINS, *Plato in the Italian Renaissance*, Leiden and New York, 1990, pp. 105-154 and chapters II and III, below.

[6] On Filelfo, C. DE' ROSMINI, *Vita di Francesco Filelfo da Tolentino*, 3 vols., Milano, 1808; R. G. ADAM, *Francesco Filelfo at the Court of Milan (1439-1481). A Contribution to the Study of Humanism in Northern Italy*, Ph.D. Thesis, Brasenose College, Oxford, 1974 (the publication of a revised version in the «Bibliothek des Deutschen Historischen Instituts in Rom» is announced by H. GOLDBRUNNER at pp. 597-608 of the following work); *Francesco Filelfo nel quinto centenario della morte. Atti del XVII Convegno di Studi Maceratesi* (Tolentino, 27-30 settembre, 1981), Padova, 1986, especially, in the present context, articles by G. RESTA, F. TATEO, V. FERA, C. BIANCA, V. R. GIUSTINIANI, G. ALBANESE, G. BOTTARI; D. ROBIN, *Filelfo in Milan. Writings 1451-1477*, Princeton, 1991 provides an interesting corrective to previous assessments of his work and character; F. RUGGERI, «Il testamento del Filelfo», *Italia medioevale e umanistica*, XXXV (1992), pp. 345-366 (with information on his library, pp. 347-349).

one might say to the diffusion of humanism rather than to its practice (in the sense of the practice of historical and philological restoration of texts). It also implied subjecting himself to the Francophilic tastes of the court, and to its taste for the vernacular tradition. Thus, in 1443 he was ordered to prepare a commentary on Petrarca's *Canzoniere*, which he left unfinished at Filippo Maria's death four years later (though it was one of the works printed several times in the reign of Ludovico il Moro, when the flowering of vernacular culture reached a high point).

Filelfo, clearly most at home in the courtly environment, while active in giving orations during the Ambrosian Republic, was, unlike Decembrio, relieved when Francesco Sforza established his rule in Milan. He offered his services in the form of an epic poem, the *Sphortias* (in imitation of the *Iliad*, with gods descending, and heroes and ancestors appearing to aid Sforza in his struggle to obtain dominion over Milan and Lombardy) of which he eventually completed ten and a half books. The complexity and ambiguity of the poem has recently been recognized, attributing to Filelfo a more sophisticated, and less sycophantic, attitude towards his patron than had previously been accorded him.[7]

Another humanist, Antonio Cornazzano (or Cornazano) of Piacenza (post-1430 - post-1487), finished a *Sforziade* in 1460, midway through his residence in the court of Francesco Sforza. Cornazzano's versatility renders him hard to classify, for besides undertaking typical humanistic projects for his patrons (*De mulieribus admirandis* for Bianca Maria Visconti Sforza; *De proverbiorum origine* for Cicco Simonetta; *De re militari* for Ercole d'Este), he also wrote a Latin comedy, *Fraudiphila*, and vernacular poetry and is perhaps best known today as the author of *Il libro dell'arte del danzare*, dedicated to Ippolita Sforza (whom he would later follow to Naples) on the occasion of her engagement to Alfonso II d'Aragona in 1455.[8]

---

[7] The work as a whole is unpublished to date; there is a summary (through Book VIII) in DE' ROSMINI (n. 6), II, pp.158-174, and D. ROBIN, *Filelfo in Milan* (n. 6), publishes Book III at pp. 177-196. On the autograph manuscript containing Books IX, XI and part of X, see G. GIRI, «Il codice autografo della *Sforziade* di F. F.», *Atti e memorie della R. Deputazione di Storia Patria per le Provincie delle Marche*, V (1901), pp. 421-457. The relatively unrestrained descriptions of even negative aspects of Sforza policies and actions, highlighted by Robin (ch. II), taken along with the recent article by Vincent ILARDI («The Banker-Statesman and the Condottiere-Prince: Cosimo de' Medici and Francesco Sforza [1450-1464]», in *Florence and Milan* [n. 1] vol. II, pp. 217-239) oblige a revision of our portrait, not only of Filelfo but also of Francesco Sforza, whose close adviser and ambassador to Florence, Nicodemo Tranchedini, was shown portions of the work in the course of its composition.

[8] P. FARENGA, «A. C.», *DBI* 29, Roma, 1983, pp. 123-132; N. DE VECCHI PELLATI, «Sulla

Thus it was that humanism could show its material value: by creating a literature in the service of legitimizing a ruling family and immortalizing its members, as well as ornamenting and contributing to the quality of life in its court (and thereby affecting a large number of people[9]). And this was to be the face of humanism in Milan throughout the Sforza dominion. More than training their students in the science of philology, or developing its techniques as men like Angelo Poliziano were doing in Florence, the Milanese humanists under the Sforza would teach the classical languages and literatures and, as often as not, put their rhetorical talents and training to the practical end of persuasion: not the noble civic persuasion of the republic, but that of the tyranny.

Ostensibly against that tyranny, but in reality as part of a larger political plot, three young men were inspired to act, by assassinating Galeazzo Maria Sforza the day after Christmas, 1476, as he arrived at church. Their teacher had been the Emilian humanist Cola Montano (Nicola Capponi, pre-1450-1482). Montano was in Milan from 1462 to 1475, and held the chair of Latin letters there from 1468, besides engaging in the earliest printing activities in 1472 with Antonio Zarotto, Gabriele Paveri Fontana and others, and in 1473 with Filippo Lavagna. From his chair, the activist Montano inveighed against tyranny, invoking the examples of Brutus and other tyrannicides of antiquity. Whether or not his students, Girolamo Olgiati, Gian Andrea De' Lampugnani and Carlo Visconti, were urged directly by him (in turn at the urging of forces sympathetic to other tyrants, but who could have been made to look sympathetic to a republican form of government), or whether the youthful enthusiasm he inspired in them for freedom was exploited by those other forces, is not known, but his own career is peppered with «anti-tyrannical» activities, including those against Ercole d'Este of Ferrara and Lorenzo de' Medici, and his death came at the gallows of Florence. The humanism of the Italian Renaissance was far from being an «ivory tower» movement, any more than scholarship is today: from the *otium* required for deep study and

---

vita e sulle opere di A. C.», *Rendiconti dell'Istituto Lombardo, Accademia di Scienze e Lettere. Classe di Lettere e Scienze Morali e Storiche*, 115 (1981 [but 1984]), pp. 345-370; R. BRUNI, D. ZANCANI, *A. C. La tradizione testuale*, Firenze, 1992. On his dance manual, see A. PONTREMOLI and P. LA ROCCA, *Il ballare lombardo. Teoria e prassi coreutica nella festa di corte del XV secolo*, Milano, 1987 (esp. A. PONTREMOLI, pp. 29-44, 100-124 *passim*); G. EBREO OF PESARO, *De pratica seu arte tripudii. On the Practice or art of Dancing*, ed., tr. and intro. by B. Sparti, Oxford, 1993.

[9] See, on the court of Galeazzo Maria Sforza, G. LUBKIN, *A Renaissance Court: Milan under Galeazzo Maria Sforza*, Berkeley, 1994; also S. BERTELLI, F. CARDONI, E. GARBERO ZORZI, *The Courts of the Italian Renaissance*, New York and Oxford, 1986.

thought are born important cultural, social and political currents, which in turn affect the later ideas of their inventors (sometimes in unexpected ways).

Piattino Piatti (ca. 1442-post 1508[10]), who with Giovanni Vincenzo Biffi and Lancino Curti formed the triad of Milanese Latin poets in the Sforza court (to borrow Simioni's phrase), was in close touch with the Tuscans Cristoforo Landino, Marsilio Ficino, Angelo Poliziano and Giovanni Pico della Mirandola. Besides being the author of epigrams, Piatti is best known for the moving tale of his ill-explained imprisonment by his former employer, Galeazzo Maria Sforza, in the dungeons of Monza (1469-1470), *Libellus de carcere* (printed by Antonio Zarotto in 1483 and 1485). Giovanni Vincenzo Biffi (1464-1516[11]) was drawn to the religious life, and his works include two long poems in honor of the Virgin Mary. He retained close contacts with such Milanese courtiers as Niccolò da Correggio and Gaspare Visconti, as well as his contemporary humanists at the court. Lancino Curti (or Curzio, 1462-1512[12]) was an eccentric figure, especially in his later years, after the downfall of Ludovico il Moro. His Latin verse too is unusual for its use of Italian rhyme schemes, and he is known to have composed at least one vernacular burlesque poem in a dialect compounded of Bergamasque and Milanese.

Filelfo's successor, and Curti's mentor, Giorgio Merula of Alessandria (1430/31-1494),[13] arrived in Milan in 1482 from his philological activities in Venice. Much the same fate as that of his former teacher, though perhaps more extreme, awaited him. Ludovico Sforza immediately put him to the

---

[10] A. SIMIONI, «Un umanista milanese, P. P.», *Archivio storico lombardo*, XXXI (1904), pp. 5-50, 227-301; A. MONTANARI, «Le Elegie ed Epigrammi di Piattino Piatti: contributo al censimento dei testimoni», *Libri e documenti*, XIV, 2 (1988), pp. 56-82.

[11] R. NEGRI, «G. V. B.», *DBI*, X, Roma, 1968, pp. 383-385.

[12] E. MELFI, «L. C.», *DBI*, XXXI, Roma, 1985, pp. 487-488; but more reliable data in F. MARRI, «L. C. a Gaspare Visconti», *Studi filologici letterari e storici in memoria di Guido Favati*, 2 vols., Padova, 1977, vol. II, pp. 397-423; Idem, «Lingua e dialetto nella poesia giocosa ai tempi del Moro», in *Milano* (n. 1), I, pp. 231-292 (the poems are edited, commented and translated at pp. 255-270); cf. R. MARCHI, «Rime volgari di Lancino Curti», *Studi di letteratura italiana offerti a Dante Isella*, Napoli, 1983, pp. 33-52; see too M. PESENTI VILLA in *La corte* (n. 1); relevant articles in *Storia di Milano* (n. 1); G. FERRI PICCALUGA, «Gli affreschi» (n. 1), p. 16 and nn. 22-28; and the recent article by A. GANDA, «La biblioteca latina del poeta milanese Lancino Corte», *La Bibliofilia*, XCIII (1991), pp. 221-277.

[13] Besides the relevant portions of essays in the works cited in note 1 (and their recent sources), see F. GABOTTO and A. BADINI CONFALONIERI, «Vita di Giorgio Merula», *Rivista di storia, arte, archeologia della provincia di Alessandria*, II (1893), pp. 7-66, 279-356; III (1894), pp. 5-69, 151-173, 227-350.

task of writing a hagiography of the Visconti and Sforza families. As one accustomed to dealing with original materials, he was given access to the archives in Pavia, and his *Historia Vicecomitum*, unlike many of the humanists' endeavors, was accorded the highest priority and reward by il Moro. Despite this, the *Historia* remained incomplete at Merula's death in March of 1494, and a successor, Tristano Calco, was appointed to continue the work.

The last year of Merula's life was both rich and frustrating (and the late polemics with other humanists such as Poliziano – reminiscent of those between Filelfo and Merula himself at the end of the Tolentinian's life – must have been the result, at least in part, of a frustration of longer duration), for his assistant, Giorgio Galbiate, whom he had sent to the monastery of San Colombano in Bobbio in search of documents relevant to his history, returned instead with the last great humanist «find» of manuscripts containing a number of hitherto unknown classical and late classical texts, largely metrical, grammatical and gromatical, and including some commentaries and poetry as well: texts by Probus, Fortunatianus, Terentianus, Prudentius and others.[14] Unfortunately, such were the priorities of Ludovico's court that during his rule the texts were kept from the eyes of other, greater humanists such as Angelo Poliziano[15] who might have profited more from their study, and the manuscripts themselves were in the end dispersed, some being found today as far afield as Naples and Wolfenbüttel. But the respected Calabrian humanist Aulo Giano Parrasio (1470-1521/22) copied and edited (even in print) a number of the texts during his residence in Milan, 1499-1506, when he was also able to impart something of the scholarly tradition to which he was heir – that of Lorenzo Valla, Angelo Poliziano and Pomponio Leto – to the young Andrea Alciato (1492-1550).[16]

Alciato, widely known for his collection of emblems,[17] was in his own day famous as a jurist, and still holds a prominent place in the history of that

---

[14] On the discovery and the codices' significance and fortune, see R. SABBADINI, *Le scoperte dei codici latini e greci ne' secoli XIV e XV*, Firenze, 1905, pp. 156-164; M. FERRARI, «Le scoperte a Bobbio nel 1493: vicende di codici e fortuna di testi», *Italia medioevale e umanistica*, XIII (1980) pp. 139-180.

[15] Who requested to see them in 1494 and was refused access by Ludovico, probably owing to the polemic initiated by Merula after publication of Poliziano's *Miscellanea* in 1489. See F. GABOTTO, *Una relazione sconosciuta di A. P. colla Corte di Milano*, Torino, 1889; L. PEROTTO SALI, «L'opuscolo inedito di G. M. contro i *Miscellanea* di A. P.», *Interpres*, I (1978), pp. 146-183.

[16] SABBADINI (n. 14), p. 158; FERRARI (n. 14), pp. 156-162. F. LO PARCO, «A. G. P. e Andrea Alciato (con documenti inediti)», *Archivio storico lombardo*, XXXIV (1907), pp. 160-197.

[17] See the publication of the Latin and several vernacular versions: *Andreas Alciatus*, ed. P. M.

field. As a student at Milan, his mentors included Johannes Lascaris and
Demetrio Calcondila; when he moved on to Pavia in 1507, he came under the
tutelage of the great jurist Giasone del Maino (1435-1519). [18] His early interest in emblems and monuments resulted in a treatise on epigraphy (1508) and
in a history of Milan (unpublished until 1625), in both of which his humanistic historical method shines through, as would the humanistic philological
methods in his juridical works. Attention to detail and to history – possibly
even direct acquaintance with the gromatic treatises found in Bobbio – must
account for his interest in the weights, measures and monies of the ancients,
evident in his *Libellus de ponderibus et mensuris*, published in Hagenau in
1530. His late friendship with Gerolamo Cardano, on the chair of medicine
at Pavia sporadically from 1536, attests further to what we today would term
a scientific bent, closely akin to the philological and historical penchants
which occupied most of his life. [19]

Francesco Filelfo, having spent six years of his youth in Greece, and
returning with important Greek manuscripts, scientific as well as literary and
philosophical, could boast of being one of the few really fluent non-Greek
humanists. He greatly furthered the study of Greek learning, language and
literature in Italy and Milan. Although his own candidate in 1462 for the
chair of Greek letters, Demetrio Castreno, was overruled by a petition
(signed, among others, by Decembrio), his presence, his enthusiasm for
Greek and his correspondence with important Greek scholars of the day (Ar-
giropolus, Bessarion, Gaza, Trapezunzio and others) kept interest alive.
Constantine Lascaris was named to the chair, remaining only two years before following Ippolita Sforza, Francesco's learned daughter and Lascaris'
pupil, to Naples in 1465 when she wed Alfonso II of Aragon, Duke of
Calabria, then moving on to found his own famous school of Greek studies in
Messina. In 1475, Milan attracted Andronico Callisto from Florence, although this too proved a brief tenure, for he was quickly lured by Paris, and
then London. Demetrio Calcondila, called from his post in the Studio of

---

Daly and V. W. Callahan, with S. Cuttler, 2 vols., Toronto, 1985. On his life and works, R.
ABBONDANZA in *DBI*, II, Roma, 1960, pp. 69-77, and see chapter XI, below.

[18] On whom, F. GABOTTO, *Giason del Maino e gli scandali universitari nel Quattrocento*, Torino, 1888.

[19] On this question, see my «Renaissance Humanism and Science», *Studi umanistici piceni*, XI (1991),
pp. 197-202, and my «Historical and Philological Method in Angelo Poliziano and Method in
Science: Practice and Theory», in the Acts of the VI° Convegno Internazionale «Poliziano nel suo
tempo» (Chianciano-Montepulciano, Italy, 18-21 July, 1994), Firenze, Cesati, in press.

Florence by Ludovico il Moro, remained to impart the love of Greek language and letters to colleagues and students from 1491 until his death in 1511, being recalled by Charles d'Amboise to Milan from Ferrara where he had gone after the French occupation in 1501.

## Printing in Milan

Calcondila's role was enriched by his participation in the flourishing Milanese printing enterprise.[20] His edition of the *Suidas Lexicon*, the great Greek encyclopedia of the tenth century, was the first printed, appearing in Milan in November, 1499 (Hain *15135), despite the political upheavals of the moment. As early as 1469 an attempt was made by Antonio Caccia di Ceresole d'Asti to establish a printing concern with Galeazzo Crivelli, a Milanese noble, and on September 7, 1470 Galeazzo Maria Sforza granted permission to publish in Milan for five years to an Antonio Pianella, although no evidence survives of his work. Our first material evidence for the beginning of printing in Milan is Panfilo Castaldi's publication on August 3, 1471 of Sextus Pompeius Festus' *De verborum significatione* (Hain *7038). On September 25 of the same year Castaldi[21] printed Pomponio Mela's *Cosmographia* (Hain 11014), and prior to March 29, 1472 he directed the publication of Cicero's letters, edited by Giuliano de' Merli and printed by Antonio and Fortunato Zarotto and Gabriele Orsoni (Hain 5161). Antonio Zarotto then

---

[20] Besides the relevant portions of the works cited in note 1, see G. A. SASSI, *Historia Literario-Tipographica Mediolanensis ab anno MCDLXV ad annum MD* in *Philippi Argelati ... Bibliotheca Scriptorum Mediolanensium*, vol. I, part 1, Milano, 1745; T. ROGLEDI MANNI, *La tipografia a Milano nel XV secolo*, Firenze, 1980; *Editori e tipografi a Milano nel Cinquecento*, ed. E. Sandal, 3 vols., Baden-Baden, 1977, 1978, 1981; and specifically on Calcondila, E. MOTTA, «D. C. editore», *Archivio storico lombardo*, XX (1893), pp. 143-166. There is an English survey of the fifteenth century situation in Milan, though printed virtually without notes: V. SCHOLDERER, «Printing at Milan in the XV Century», in his *Fifty Essays in Fifteenth- and Sixteenth-Century Bibliography*, ed. D. E. Rhodes, Amsterdam, 1966, pp. 96-105, and see his Introduction (with notes) to the *Catalogue of Books Printed in the XVth Century now in the British Museum*, vol. VI (henceforth, *BMC* VI), London, 1930, pp. ix-l, esp. pp. xix-xxx; the 1963 reprint reproduces manuscript notes which add to the documentation; now see C. DI FILIPPO BAREGGI, «Tipografie, accademie, biblioteche (secoli XVI-XVII)» in *Storia illustrata di Milano* (n. 1), 4, 1993. Reference is made throughout to L. F. T. HAIN, *Repertorium Bibliographicum*, 2 vols. in 4, Milano, 1948.

[21] It is now known that this was not Antonio Zarotto as in PESENTI VILLA (n. 1), p. 128 and HAIN: cf. *BMC* VI, p. 699; ROGLEDI MANNI (n. 20), pp. 20, 166.

went on to print and publish on his own (fl. 1472-1507[22]), and with the support of humanists such as Cola Montano and Gabriele Paveri Fontana many works were published, including, of the classics, Cicero, Terence, Vergil, Ovid, Quintilian, Livy, Horace; of the humanists, Francesco Filelfo, Niccolò Perotti, Piattino Piatti; of the vernacular writers, Petrarca and Gaspare Visconti, as well as liturgical works. The other printer of note in the first months of printing in Milan was Filippo Cavagni da Lavagna (pre-1450-post-1499[23]). His repertory, beginning also in 1471 and extending to 1493, includes classical (Cicero, Vergil, Ovid, Juvenal, Martial) and humanistic works (Lorenzo Valla, George of Trebizond or Trapezuntius) and some medieval scientific and literary works as well (Avicenna, Boccaccio). His rival edition of Cicero's letters (Hain *5171) appeared on the 25th of March, 1472, thus possibly even preceding that of Castaldi.

After 1477, two German printers played a dominant role in Milanese typographical history: Leonhard Pachel and Ulrich Scinzenzeler, the former continuing on into the sixteenth century. They worked alone and together, printing more than half the books printed in Milan between 1478 and 1500, such that the term «mass production» has been applied to them.[24] Their production, geared to commercial success, concentrated on the law and classics, with some vernacular and theological works. Filippo Mantegazza (fl. 1490-1497) and his sons, Pietro Martire and his brothers (fl. 1499-1512)[25] published works of a more popular nature, including the vernacular works of several of the poets we will encounter, and religious works, but also including the important *Theorica musicae* of Franchino Gaffurio (1492). Also bridging the artificial chasm between incunabula (to 1501) and other early printed editions was the typographical career of the Pugliese humanist Alessandro Minuziano (ca. 1450-1532?[26]), whose fifteenth century works, however,

---

[22] See A. GANDA, *I primordi della tipografia milanese. Antonio Zarotto da Parma (1471-1507)*, pref. L. Balsamo, Firenze, 1984.

[23] L. FERRO, «F. C.», *DBI*, XXII, Roma, 1979, pp. 571-574; ROGLEDI MANNI (n. 20), pp. 229-231, and passim; C. GALLAZZI, *L'editoria milanese nel primo cinquantennio della stampa: i da Legnano*, Busto Arsizio, 1980.

[24] SCHOLDERER, «Printing at Milan» (n. 20), p. 102. See also L. BALSAMO, *Giovann'Angelo Scinzenzeler tipografo in Milano (1500-1526). Annali e bio-bibliografia*, Firenze, 1959 (Biblioteca Bibliografica Italica, 20); Idem, «Annali di Giovann'Angelo Scinzenzeler stampatore in Milano (1500-1526). Supplemento», *La Bibliofilia*, XCV (1993), pp. 199-270.

[25] ROGLEDI MANNI (n. 20), pp. 232-233; SANDAL (n. 20), III, pp. 31-46.

[26] C. DIONISOTTI, «Notizie di Alessandro Minuziano», *Miscellanea Giovanni Mercati*, IV, Città del Vaticano, 1946, pp. 327-372 (Studi e Testi, 124); SANDAL (n. 20), II, pp. 13-51; ROGLEDI MANNI (n. 20), p. 234.

number only four or five. Having been active as a humanist from the time of his arrival in Milan by 1484, he worked on as a printer until 1525, publishing some classical, but primarily contemporary humanist and vernacular texts, including works by Andrea Alciato, Lancino Curti and Galeotto del Carretto. His publication of Bernardino Corio's *Storia di Milano* in 1503 brings us to a consideration of Milanese historiography under the Sforza.

### Milanese Historiography

Pier Candido Decembrio's posthumous portrait of his employer in *Vita Philippi Mariae Tertij Ligurum Ducis*[27] (1447) gives us an early example of Milanese humanist historiography, of interest precisely for its candor and for the fact that it is based on the first-hand experience of this longtime ducal secretary. We find Decembrio even intervening, as he does in other works, with his own eye-witness account, bearing testimony to a growing emphasis on experience as a basis for argument. The Florentine humanist Leonardo Bruni had, as always following in the footsteps of Petrarca, established new criteria for the writing of history, based in part on classical sources, in part on new demands made by the writer and by his public. These included firmer grounding in contemporary sources and sources whose reliability could be questioned and thus be subjected to critical examination, and the demand that history itself provide models for the practical arts of government and war.[28]

---

[27] In *Rerum Italicarum Scriptores*, XX, 1, eds. A. Butti, F. Fossati, G. Petraglione, Bologna, 1925-1958, pp. 3-438; Italian translation with introduction and notes by E. Bartolini: P. C. DECEMBRIO, *Vita di Filippo Maria Visconti*, Milano, 1983. This work is not within the scope of the recent study by G. IANZITI, *Humanist Historiography under the Sforzas. Politics and Propaganda in Fifteenth-Century Milan*, Oxford, Clarendon, 1988 (p. 18). On Milanese historiography (which has been termed «the literary aspect of the chancellery culture» by G. M. PIAZZA: «Appunti sulla lingua di Bernardino Corio», *Libri & documenti*, 1, 1975, pp. 28-38, p. 28) see too E. COCHRANE, *Historians and Historiography in the Italian Renaissance*, Chicago and London, 1981, pp. 108-118.

[28] E. FUETER, *Histoire de l'historiographie moderne*, tr. E. Jeanmaire, Paris, 1914, pp. 19-31; G. IANZITI, «From Flavio Biondo to Lodrisio Crivelli. The Beginnings of Humanistic Historiography in Sforza Milan», *Rinascimento*, ser. II, vol. XX (1980), pp. 3-39; E. B. FRYDE, *Humanism and Renaissance Historiography*, London, 1983. A contemporary work similar in approach and dealing with the years 1402-1431 is A. BIGLIA, *Rerum mediolanensium historiae*, in L. A. MURATORI, *Rerum Italicarum Scriptores*, XIX, Milano, 1731, cols. 9-158: cf. «A. B.», *DBI*, X, Roma, 1968, pp. 413-415; IANZITI, *Humanist Historiography* (n. 27), pp. 17-18.

Biondo Biondi (or Blondus Flavius as he signed himself in Latin;[29] 1392-1463) continued this tradition and, being appreciated by Francesco Sforza for painting a realistic (or at least not an adulatory) picture of events, he was encouraged to pursue his *Historiarum ab inclinatione Romani imperii decades tres* with the telling of Sforza's taking of Milan in 1450.[30] At about the same time, Lodrisio Crivelli (1412?-pre-1488) took up his pen, dipped in the ink of Biondi's method, to write what has been called the «first full-scale humanistic history to emerge in Milan», *De vita rebusque gestis Francisci Sforciae Vicecomitis Mediolanensium Ducis Illustrissimi*.[31] This marks the combining of the humanists' attempts at critical handling of sources and interpretation with the requirements of courtly historiography. Crivelli's could not be the independent handling of either Bruni (working within a republic) or Biondi (wilfully remaining independent of a single patron), for he was writing in the context of his own *patria* and commissioned by its lord. Yet it is significant that his and Biondi's realism was appreciated and even sought by Francesco.

By the early 1460s Sforza had received portions of Francesco Filelfo's poem *Sphortias*. He had also received Decembrio's attempt to win his good graces and patronage, *Annotatio rerum gestarum in vita ill[ustrissi]mi Francisci Sfortie, quarti Mediolanensium Ducis*.[32] But this work inspired purely by need had little effect on its target and certainly did nothing to contribute to the tone of humanist historiography. After Francesco's death, Giovanni Simonetta, brother of the ill-fated Cicco, approached the same topic with both sympathy and intimate knowledge, having been attached to Sforza as secretary since 1444. His *De rebus gestis Francisci Sfortiae commentarii* was

---

[29] The name of Biondi has suffered a distortion throughout the literature. His family name is Biondi (Lat. *de Blondis*), his given name Biondo. He took the Latin translation of *biondo, flavus*, to create his Latin pen-name, *Flavius*, which he appended to his signature. He also signs himself *Blondus Antonii Blondi de Forlivio* (his father's name being Antonio, his birthplace Forlì). See B. NOGARA, *Introduzione* to *Scritti inediti e rari di Biondo Flavio*, Roma, 1927 (Studi e Testi, 48), pp. XIX-XXI and Plates II and III. See too A. Campana's remarks in his review of the edition: «Biondo Flavio da Forlì», in *La Romagna*, XVI (1927), pp. 487-498. Biography by R. FUBINI in *DBI*, X, Roma, 1968, pp. 536-559.

[30] IANZITI, «From Flavio Biondo» (n. 28), pp. 21-22; Idem, *Humanistic Historiography* (n. 27), pp. 64-65; FUBINI (n. 29), pp. 554-555, where he announces a 16th century Italian translation, possibly including the continuation of Biondi's fourth *Decade*.

[31] IANZITI, «From Flavio Biondo» (n. 28), p. 23; cf. Idem, *Humanistic Historiography* (n. 27), pp. 35-49. The text is edited in L. A. MURATORI, *Rerum Italicarum Scriptores*, XIX, Milano, 1731, cols. 628-732.

[32] In *Rerum Italicarum Scriptores*, XX, 1, eds. A. Butti, F. Fossati, G. Petraglione, Bologna, 1925-1958, pp. 439-989.

printed in 1483 with prefaces by Filelfo and Francesco dal Pozzo, and emendations by the latter bringing it in line with Ludovico's political stance. [33] Dal Pozzo, also called Il Puteolano (pre-1450-1490[34]), was the editor of Ovid and Tacitus, residing in Milan since 1477 at the invitation of the influential and learned protector of humanists, Jacopo Antiquari (1444/5-1512[35]).

In the last decade of the century, after the failure of Filelfo's successor, Giorgio Merula, to complete a hagiographic history of the Visconti-Sforza family (albeit one based on archival and epigraphic research), the picture again changed, with the work of Tristano Calco (mid-15th century-1516 ca.) whose *Historia patria*, infused with the critical use of archival and epigraphic sources, would however not see print until 1627. [36] We are given a marvelous, and plausible, picture of Calco in the archives, peering over the shoulder of his contemporary and friend, Bernardino Corio (1459-15??), also commissioned by Ludovico Sforza in the 1490s to write a history (more of a vernacular compilation of chronicles with humanistic overtones) to offer bits of erudition from the newly discovered Bobbio codices. [37] Paolo Giovio of Como (later bishop of Nocera; 1483-1552[38]), carried on the less proud Lom-

---

[33] Ianziti determines the date in *Humanistic Historiography* (n. 27), pp. 211-219; he discusses the political significance of the different versions at pp. 220-231. This work and its propagandistic ramifications are the principal topic of much of his book: pp. 127-231. Cf. FUETER (n. 28), pp. 50-52. The text is in MURATORI, *Rerum Italicarum Scriptores*, XXI, 1732, cols. 165-782; a newer edition by G. Soranzo in *R.I.S.*, XXI, 2, Bologna, 1932-1934 takes into account Simonetta's original text. It was translated into Italian as *La Sforziada* (with further politically correct emendations) by Cristoforo Landino in 1489 (first printed in Milan, 1490 [HAIN 14756], and again in Venice, 1543, 1544): cf. DIONISOTTI, «Leonardo» (n. 39 below) p. 209, and R. M. COMANDUCCI, «Nota sulla versione landiniana della *Sforziade* di G. S.», *Interpres*, XII (1992), pp. 306-316.

[34] On whom, R. CONTARINO, «F. D. P.», *DBI*, XXXII, Roma, 1986, pp. 213-216.

[35] On the sympathetic figure of Antiquari, see E. BIGI, «I. A.», *DBI*, III, Roma, 1961, pp. 470-472. Bandello describes him (III, 26; cf. n. 61, below) thus: «Era l'Antiquario uomo di buonissime lettere e di vita integerrima e appo tutti per i castigatissimi costumi in grandissima stimazione».

[36] *Tristani Calchi mediolanensis Historiae patriae libri viginti*, Milano, 1627. His valuable chronicles of contemporary weddings were published in *Tristani Calchi mediolanensis historiographi Residua*, Milano, 1644. Both are in J. G. GRAEVIUS, *Thesaurus Antiquitatum et Historiarum Italiae*, vol. II, pt. 1, Lugduni Batavorum (Leiden), 1704. Historiography under Il Moro is briefly treated in IANZITI, *Humanistic Historiography* (n. 27), pp. 232-238.

[37] FERRARI (n. 14), pp. 150-151; on Corio's history: P. BONGRANI, «Gli storici sforzeschi e il volgarizzamento landiniano dei *Commentarii* del Simonetta», *Lingua Nostra*, XLVII (1986), pp. 40-50.

[38] L. LACOUR, «P. G.», in *Nouvelle biographie générale*, ed. Hoefer, vol. XX, Paris, 1858, cols. 634-638; FUETER (n. 28), pp. 60-66.

bard tradition in his work, reputedly selective on the basis of return, *Historiarum sui temporis, ab anno 1494 ad annum 1547, libri XLV* (Florence, 1550-1552). Giovio had completed his medical education at Pavia, but he was already writing his history when in 1512 he reached Rome, where he was to spend half of his life. His journalistic approach can be seen in his various *Elogiae*, catalogues of famous men (scholars, warriors and writers) complete with portraits, real or fictitious, which certainly contributed to the works' popularity.

### Vernacular Letters and Theater

As has been intimated, the literary flowering of the Sforza court took place under Ludovico il Moro, and in the vernacular. This might have been expected from the long-standing Visconti-Sforza patronage of vernacular works beginning with those of Petrarca, a patronage stemming from the palpable influence of French tastes on the court, from the ease of reception by the court and its subjects of works in Italian, and from the clear political advantages that these implied. As in the closely related courts of Mantua and Ferrara, the rulers and the court were comfortable with their native tongue, and translations into Italian of classical works were not uncommon, even in the days of Pier Candido Decembrio's and Francesco Filelfo's work for Filippo Maria Visconti. The unabashed use of the vernacular in Milan, however, awaited the ascendency of Il Moro, and indeed is but one manifestation of the passage of humanistic learning into the more popular, albeit refined, culture general in the last quarter of the fifteenth century in Italy. Even in Florence, Angelo Poliziano was as adept at writing vernacular poetry as he was at Latin, and was instrumental in transposing the high culture of Greek and Latin into the more accessible language of the present, as in his *Fabula di Orfeo* and *Stanze per la Giostra*; indeed, his general fame today rests primarily on these two works and their influence on the theater and art of his time. [39]

Two poets, Bernardo Bellincioni (1452-1492) and Antonio Cammelli, il Pistoia (1436-1502), brought from Tuscany the form of the vernacular the Milanese poets had chosen as their model, largely because of the influence of Dante's and Petrarca's commitment to their native (Tuscan) language. Bel-

---

[39] On the vernacular question generally, see C. DIONISOTTI, «Leonardo uomo di lettere», *Italia medioevale e umanistica*, V (1962), pp. 183-216. A picture of the interactions of the Sforza poets in R. RENIER, «Gaspare Visconti», *Archivio storico lombardo*, XIII (1886), pp. 509-562, 776-824; and see BONGRANI, «Novità» (n. 1), and this volume, *passim*.

lincioni,[40] a poetic correspondent of Lorenzo de' Medici while still in Florence, was probably the first of the two to arrive in Milan, and the only one to reside there in a fixed manner, from 1485 to his death. Pistoia, who seems to have long been in close touch with other poets of Ludovico's court, especially Niccolò da Correggio, may have spent time there before then, as he certainly did while holding the position of Capitano in Reggio (Emilia) from 1485 on (with interruptions after 1497). While Bellincioni was the more successful courtier, there is little doubt that Pistoia was the more interesting poet, preferring to create his own images in the burlesque tradition of Luigi Pulci rather than to write in the prevalent Petrarchist vein. He possessed the realism and humor required for burlesque and satire,[41] which he did not hesitate to use in verses of a political nature, and his poetic forms, such as the extended sonnet in dialogue, were imitated by other poets of the court.

Bellincioni, whom Ludovico virtually appointed companion and confidant to Gian Galeazzo Sforza, the rightful heir to the duchy, also filled diplomatic missions, being one of the company (with Galeotto del Carretto and probably the poet Gaspare Visconti) sent to Naples in 1488-1489 to fetch Isabella d'Aragona, Gian Galeazzo's bride. He was thus doubtless present at the banquet in Tortona hosted by Orpheus and other mythological figures organized and choreographed by Bergonzio Botta in his residence and described in detail by Tristano Calco in his *Nuptiae Mediolanensium Ducum*.[42] He was himself also the author of two or three of il Moro's fabulous spectacles, one of which, the *Festa del Paradiso*, was staged by Leonardo

---

[40] Biography by R. SCRIVANO in *DBI*, VII, Roma, 1965, pp. 687-689. There is a 1493 edition of his poems printed by Filippo Mantegazza (HAIN 2754); see ROGLEDI MANNI (n. 20, above), no. 152, p. 116. The poems were republished uncritically by P. Fanfani: *Le rime di B. B. riscontrate sui manoscritti*, Bologna, 1876-1878; cf. A. LUZIO, R. RENIER, «Del Bellincioni», *Archivio storico lombardo*, XVI (1889), pp. 703-720, esp. p. 716. A thesis on the poet was written by P. Cozzi at the University of Pavia.

[41] As in the description of a walk to Carpi in winter: «L'aqua era in gelatina e di cristallo, / il terren fatto invetriato degno, / il naso cominciava per isdegno / in su lo extremo a congelar corallo»: Sonnet VII in *I sonetti faceti di A. C. secondo l'autografo ambrosiano*, ed. E. Pèrcopo, Napoli, 1908, p. 52. See too *Rime edite e inedite di A. C. detto il Pistoia*, ed. A. Cappelli, S. Ferrari, Livorno, 1884; *I sonetti del Pistoia giusta l'apografo trivulziano*, ed. R. Renier, Torino, 1888; D. DE ROBERTIS, «A. C.», in *DBI*, XVII, Roma, 1974, pp. 277-286.

[42] The Calco text in GRAEVIUS (n. 36), cols. 499-514. Cf. U. ROZZO, «La festa di nozze sforzesca del gennaio 1489 a Tortona», *Libri & documenti*, XIV, 1 (1989), pp. 9-23; R. ZAPPERI and D. RICCI ALBANI, «B. B.», *DBI*, XIII, Roma, 1971, pp. 362-364; and see below, chapter VII.

da Vinci for the same occasion (although the spectacle was postponed a year, to 1490, due to the untimely death of Ippolita Sforza d'Aragona, Isabella's mother). Both verse and scenery (as well as the music by Franchino Gaffurio) were created to impress the newlyweds with the adeptness of Ludovico in assuming for them the cares of government – a fact which may not have been lost on Isabella. [43] Bellincioni's poems, primarily written for occasions, were printed in Milan in 1493 and await a promised modern edition for re-evaluation.

Leonardo had occasion to stage at least one other vernacular play in Milan, this time a mythological entertainment, or *favola mitologica*, by the Alessandrian poet and ducal official, Baldassare Taccone (1461-1521[44]). The *favola* was performed, again with music, in the home of the Count of Caiazzo (Giovanni Francesco Sanseverino) on January 31, 1496. This is the tale of Danae, to whom Jove comes as a shower of gold, giving life to the hero Perseus. Here the tale is most likely based on Boccaccio's telling in his *Genealogia deorum gentilium* (II, 32-33), with the addition of one or two characters from classical comedy, and the Neoplatonic touch of Danae's rising as a blazing star to the «cielo» at the end of Act IV. The staging is documented in the stage notes and in Leonardo's drawings in the Metropolitan Museum of Art and the Biblioteca Ambrosiana. [45]

Vincenzo Colli, called Calmeta (ca. 1460-1508), secretary to Ludovico's wife Beatrice d'Este Sforza, and a vernacular poet and essayist in his own

---

[43] E. SOLMI, «La festa del Paradiso di L. da V. e B. B. (13 gennaio 1490)», *Archivio storico lombardo*, XXXI (1904), pp. 75-89; K. T. STEINITZ, «Les décors de théâtre de L. da V.», *Bibliothèque d'Humanisme et Renaissance*, XX (1958), pp. 257-265. On the music, C. A. VIANELLO, *Teatri, spettacoli, musiche a Milano nei secoli scorsi*, Milano, 1941, p. 22, but giving no source.

[44] His biography in chapter VI, below; cf. C. M. PYLE, *Politian's «Orfeo» and Other «Favole Mitologiche» in the Context of Late Quattrocento Northern Italy*, Ph.D. dissertation, Columbia University, New York, 1976, pp. 33-41; on the play, *ibid.*, pp. 181-187 and see chapter IX, below; on its language, P. BONGRANI, «Lingua e stile nella *Pasitea* e nel teatro cortigiano milanese», *Interpres*, V (1983-1984), pp. 163-241, esp. pp. 205-224 (reprinted in his *Lingua e letteratura a Milano nell'età sforzesca. Una raccolta di studi*, Parma, 1986 [Univ. di Parma, Istituto di Filologia Moderna, Testi e Studi: Studi, 1], pp. 85-158). The text is now available in *Teatro del Quattrocento. Le corti padane*, eds. A. Tissoni Benvenuti, M. P. Mussini Sacchi, Torino, 1983, pp. 293-334.

[45] See K. T. STEINITZ, «Le dessin de Léonard de Vinci pour la *Danae*», *Le lieu théâtral à la Renaissance*, ed. J. Jacquot, Paris, 1968, pp. 35-40; M. HERZFELD, «La rappresentazione della 'Danae' organizzata da Leonardo», *Raccolta vinciana*, XI (1920-1922), pp. 226-228; and the rich catalogue: *Leonardo e gli spettacoli del suo tempo*, ed. M. Mazzocchi Doglio, G. Tintori, M. Padovan, M. Tiella, Milano, 1983, and see below, chapter IX.

right, has left us in his *Vita del facondo poeta vulgare Serafino Aquilano* a sketch of the life at Ludovico's court in the 1490s.[46] The work is also, and primarily, valuable as a source on the life of Serafino Ciminelli (or Aquilano, after his birthplace: 1466-1500), a lightning-bug figure who darted from court to court, illuminating each with his music and verse, often improvised, and creating dramatic spectacles in the form of eclogues and allegorical skits.[47] Serafino followed his long-time patron, Cardinal Ascanio Sforza (Ludovico's brother), from Rome to Milan in 1490, there apparently learning the art of the *strambotto* from a Neapolitan's performances of poems written by Benedetto Gareth, il Cariteo, of Barcelona (in Naples from ca. 1467/68 to his death in 1514). From 1495 until Beatrice's death in January, 1497, Serafino sojourned at the Sforza court, participating in celebrations, games and theatrical events.

Another participant in theatrical activities, this time, like Leonardo, as set designer, was Donato Bramante of Urbino (1444-1514), who spent the years 1481-1499 in Milan, coinciding almost exactly with Leonardo's presence there, and who entered into enthusiastic exchanges with him. Both men wrote, though while Leonardo's written production, being of a technical and philosophical nature, remained in his private notebooks, Bramante entered the dialogue with other poets of the Sforza court, especially Pistoia and Gaspare Visconti, who was his patron for a time; he is mentioned in the latter's poem, *De Paulo e Daria amanti*.[48]

---

[46] V. CALMETA, *Prose e lettere edite e inedite*, ed. C. Grayson, Bologna, 1959, pp. 70-72. His poetic works are mostly lost, but for a new edition by R. Guberti of the *Triumphi*, see M. PIERI, «V. Colli», *DBI*, XXVII, Roma, 1982, pp. 49-52.

[47] See the first (and only) volume of *Le rime di S. de' C. dall'Aquila*, ed. M. Menghini, Bologna, 1894 (but 1896); C. GALLICO, *Un libro di poesie per musica dell'epoca di Isabella d'Este*, Mantova, 1961; B. BAUER-FORMICONI, *Die strambotti des S. dall'A*, München, 1967 (valuable also for its allusions to music); M. VIGILANTE, «S. C.», *DBI*, XXV, Roma, 1981, pp. 562-566; the recent study by A. ROSSI, *S. A. e la poesia cortigiana*, Brescia, 1980, including sketches of other poets of the time mentioned here, also P. VECCHI GALLI, «La poesia cortigiana tra XV e XVI secolo. Rassegna di testi e studi (1969-1981)», *Lettere italiane*, XXXIV (1982) pp. 95-141. On the dramatic works, V. R. GIUSTINIANI, «S. A. e il teatro del Quattrocento», *Rinascimento*, 2a. ser., vol. V (1965), pp. 101-117.

[48] L. BELTRAMI, *Bramante poeta. Colla Raccolta dei Sonetti in parte inediti*, Milano, 1884; see too A. BRUSCHI, «D. B.», *DBI*, XIII, Roma, 1971, pp. 712-725; Visconti's poem, printed by Filippo Mantegazza in 1495 (ROGLEDI MANNI [n. 20], no. 1112; HAIN, 16077), is discussed, and a resume given in R. RENIER, «Gaspare Visconti», (n. 39), pp. 777-792; on Visconti's patronage of Bramante, G. SIRONI, «Gli affreschi di Donato D'Angelo detto il Bramante alla Pinacoteca di Brera di Milano: chi ne fu il committente?», *Archivio storico lombardo*, ser. X, vol. IV (1978), pp. 199-207; and see chapters IV and XI below.

As we have seen, several humanists and printers weathered the storm of French occupation, and continued their activities into the 16th century. Earlier, a similar problem had faced those who, having been active and even committed politically to the earlier Sforza rulers, had now to make the transition to the protection of the usurper, Ludovico il Moro. One such poet, whom we have met as playwright, was Baldassare Taccone. Despite having composed the epitaph of the ill-fated ducal secretary, Cicco Simonetta, Taccone continued to move prominently in Ludovico's court and then moved on into the city under the French; another poet, Gaspare Visconti, was married to Simonetta's daughter, yet remained active under Ludovico. Also associated with Simonetta's household was Antonio Fileremo («lover of solitude») Campo Fregoso (ca. 1450-1530/40). He is named as one of the shining lights of the court by Calmeta, along with Niccolò da Correggio and Gaspare Visconti, upon whose death in 1499 he wrote a *capitolo* of mourning.[49] He too lived on, in seclusion, into the French dominion, continuing to write. His works include *Il riso di Democrito* and *Pianto di Eraclito*, two long series of *capitoli* (hence in *terza rima*, the rhyme scheme developed by Dante) containing carefully used echoes of Dante's and Petrarca's verses put to the expression of his balanced views on life, as well as other long pastoral meditations, often with borrowings and reworkings of the crystalline imagery of Poliziano.[50] Nor were such practices uncommon at the time; the imitation of one's predecessors, a sort of evocation of and vying with their prowess, was cultivated, lending a continuity to the work of poetry, in the vernacular as in Latin, and creating a familiar context within which new ideas or interesting variants on old ones could be expressed – a practice which continues in great works of art, music and poetry today.

Niccolò da Correggio (1450-1508) was count of Correggio, a dependency of Ferrara and thus of the Este family, to which he was closely related; but he spent much time in Milan, as did Galeotto del Carretto (pre-1455-1530), a nobleman from Casale in Piedmont, and Antonio Tebaldeo (1463-1537), the

---

[49] «Chi darà agli ochi mei d'acqua mai tanto, / ch'io possa lacrimar sì longamente, / che adequi al mio gran duol l'assiduo pianto?» in A. FILEREMO FREGOSO, *Opere*, ed. G. Dilemmi, Bologna, 1976, pp. 6-8; and see Dilemmi's introduction, pp. xxi-xxiii. Particularly valuable is the recent assessment of Campo Fregoso's work by G. FERRI PICCALUGA, «Gli affreschi», cit. (n. 1), *passim*; see also chapter XI, below.

[50] The woodcut reproduced on the cover of this volume is from the first edition of Fregoso's work (1506); on the iconography, see chapter XI, below. The texts are published in Dilemmi's edition (n. 49), pp. 13-85.

Ferrarese poet. These three contributed in great measure to the literary fabric of the Sforza court, providing poetic dialogue and possibly contributing to the theatrical events there, since Correggio and Carretto are known playwrights, the former being the author of plays including the Ovidian *Favola di Cefalo* performed in Ferrara in 1487, the latter of several plays offered to Isabella Gonzaga in the decade between 1494/5 and 1505, and at least one dedicated to Beatrice d'Este Sforza (hence prior to January, 1497).[51] Correggio's verses are mostly love poems of a Petrarchist vein, but, as with all these poets, he adds his own vision to the tradition, often with arresting meter or real concerns[52] which bring his works home to the reader, and pleased especially his favorite reader, Isabella d'Este Gonzaga, Beatrice's sister. Besides plays and sonnets, he composed a long poem on the Apuleian tale of Cupid and Psyche (later to be the basis of a play by Galeotto del Carretto) in octaves, the rhyme scheme of Ariosto's *Orlando Furioso*, but also – and first – that of the popularesque *cantari* sung in piazzas, conveying news, ancient or modern, and accompanied by the lute.

Correggio's close associate, the Milanese poet Gaspare Visconti (from a branch of the former ruling family: 1461-1499[53]), was also a playwright, composing at least one play, *Pasithea*, between 1493 and 1497, when Beatrice's death hung a pall over the festive court of Ludovico. The play, which was probably never performed, continued the trend of bringing into the vernacular theatrical forms and characters found in the Latin comedies of Terence

---

[51] See N. DA CORREGGIO, *Opere. Cefalo, Psiche, Silva, Rime*, ed. A. Tissoni Benvenuti, Bari, 1969; P. FARENGA, «N. da C.», *DBI*, XXIX, Roma, 1983, pp. 466-474; *Cefalo* is now edited in *Teatro delle corti padane* (n. 44, above), and was studied in my *Politian's «Orfeo»* (n. 44), pp. 169-180; biography: *Ibid.*, pp. 10-19; bibliography of MSS and printed editions: *Ibid.*, pp. 262-331. On G. del C., G. MANACORDA, «G. del C. poeta lirico e drammatico monferrino (14_-1530)», *Memorie della Reale Accademia delle Scienze di Torino*, Ser. 2, vol. XLIX (1900), pp. 47-125; R. RICCIARDI, «G. Del C.», *DBI*, XXXVI, Roma, 1988, pp. 415-419.

[52] E.g. sonnet 337: «S'io lego, scrivo, penso, parlo o ascolto, / s'io veggio, dormo, vado o fermo el passo, / se 'l mio voler raffreno o pur trapasso, / ognor mi trovo più ne i lacci involto»; or sonnet 347 on the prospects of ageing in a time of political decline: «Di male in peggio, e non a passo lento, / corron pur gli anni, e il tempo non ce aspetta, / e già mi par su l'arco la saetta / che tanto ha minacciato el cinquecento».

[53] Biography in RENIER, «G. V.», (n. 39), pp. 513-524, updated in chapter IV below; cf. my *Politian's «Orfeo»* (n. 44), pp. 19-33. For *Pasithea*: *Ibid*, pp. 187-197, and the first, diplomatic, edition at pp. 207-261; P. BONGRANI, «Lingua e stile» (n. 44), pp. 174-205; see also chapters VIII and IX, below. The play now appears in *Teatro delle corti padane*, pp. 337-396; a partial edition of his poetic works is G. VISCONTI, *I canzonieri per Beatrice d'Este e per Bianca Maria Sforza*, ed. P. Bongrani, Milano, 1979.

and Plautus, here conveying the Ovidian tale of Pyramus and Thisbe and adding the already nearly obligatory happy ending, through the auspices of the god Apollo.

In 1494 Visconti and Francesco Tanzi Corniger (a cleric and early editor of printed works in Milan) brought out an edition of the *Canzoniere* of Francesco Petrarca with Filelfo's Commentary at Scinzenzeler's press; it is considered more correct than most of the preceding editions.[54] Visconti's own Petrarchist verse betrays a turn of mind at times playful, at times pensive. His circle is responsible for a series of dialect poems (though the dialect is something of a synthesis of Bergamasque and Milanese), teasing in tone, on the favor gained at court by the Alessandrian poet, Taccone (whose poetry, by his own admission, leaves something to be desired, but is of historic value, for instance in his description of the ceremonies and trip surrounding the marriage of Bianca Maria Sforza, Galeazzo Maria's daughter, to the Emperor Maximilian in 1493[55]). One of the dialect poems was that already mentioned, written by Lancino Curti, the eccentric member of the circle who traded sonnets with Visconti, and who is remembered for his Latin verse, set in rhyme schemes natural to the Italian vernacular.

On the pensive side, Visconti is responsible for an epitome in Italian of Marsilio Ficino's *De amore* (a commentary on Plato's *Symposium*), which is distinct from Ficino's own translation of the same work.[56] This text provides us with concrete evidence of the diffusion of Florentine Neoplatonism to the North, a diffusion which had begun under Francesco Sforza and was undoubtedly given impetus by the arrival in Milan in the early 1480s of the Florentine poets.

## Leonardo, Pacioli and Bandello

Leonardo da Vinci, too, although his general bent has been seen as closer to a pragmatic Aristotelianism, had nevertheless been profoundly influenced

---

[54] J. G. T. GRAESSE, *Trésor des livres rares et précieux*, 7 vols. in 8, Genève, 1864, vol. V, p. 224.

[55] *Coronatione e sponsalitio de la serenissima Re / gina .M.Bianca.Ma.SF. Augusta al Illustrissimo .S.Lodovico.SF.uisconte Duca de Barri per Baldassare Taccone Alexandrino ca(n)celleri composta*, [Milano], L. Pachel, 1493 (HAIN, 15216); now edited by G. Biancardi in *Studi e fonti di storia lombarda. Quaderni milanesi*, 13 (1993), pp. 43-121.

[56] See chapter V, below; cf. M. FICIN, *Commentaire sur le Banquet de Platon*, ed. and transl. R. Marcel, Paris, 1978.

by the Platonism of Florence.[57] During his years in Milan (1482-1499, 1506-1513), where he was first invited largely on the basis of his engineering skills, Leonardo explored fully and rejected the idea of perpetual motion, and, especially in connection with his attempts to construct a man-powered flying machine, developed clear notions of the efficacy of certain sources of power, or prime movers, modifying Lombard water mills accordingly. He also worked on the physics of light and on the physiology of vision, studying the optic and cranial nerves, spinal cord and peripheral nerves. His studies of anatomy included those of the horse made for the famous equestrian statue of Francesco Sforza, which he executed in clay but was never to cast. The statue was celebrated in various writings of the time, including Taccone's *Coronatione e sponsalitio de la serenissima Regina M. Bianca Ma[ria] Sf[ortia] Augusta* of 1493. In Milan, where the Florentine vernacular was so prized, Leonardo gained confidence in his writing skills and set out to defend painting as a worthy sister to the literary arts vaunted by the humanists as more permanent records of fame. This resulted in the notes later assembled by his disciple Francesco Melzi to form the treatise *Della pittura* (published in Paris in 1651).

The arrival of Fra Luca Pacioli (ca. 1445-1517) in Milan in 1496 afforded Leonardo the intellectual companionship of a mathematician of a similarly practical bent. Pacioli, known today in the field of accounting for his invention of double-entry bookkeeping, brought Leonardo into contact with the rigor of mathematics in a Platonic context. Ludovico had commissioned Pacioli to write a treatise on Plato's five regular solids, which Pacioli entitled *De Divina Proportione* (1496-1497) and for which Leonardo, being instructed by «Messer Luca» in Euclidian geometry from the Latin translation of Euclid, supplied the illustrations (extant in two manuscripts).[58] At the fall of Ludovico il Moro, Leonardo and Pacioli were to seek refuge elsewhere, and

---

[57] A. MARINONI, «Introduzione» to L. DA VINCI, *Scritti letterari*, Milano, 1952, pp. 11-12. On his writings, also see *The Literary Works of L. da V.*, ed. J. P. Richter, Commentary by C. Pedretti, 2 vols., Berkeley and Los Angeles, 1977, and the article by C. DIONISOTTI, «L. uomo di lettere» (n. 39). His scientific achievements are discussed in the article by C. C. GILLISPIE, K. D. KEELE, L. RETI, M. CLAGETT, A. MARINONI, C. SCHNEER, in the *Dictionary of Scientific Biography*, VIII, New York, 1973, pp. 192-245. Most recently, see G. LOPEZ, «Leonardo a Milano», in *Storia illustrata di Milano* (n. 1), vol. 3, pp. 881-900.

[58] Biography of L. P. by S. A. JAYAWARDENE in *Dictionary of Scientific Biography*, vol. X, 1974, pp. 269-272; Bernardino BALDI'S *Vita* (1589) is edited in B. BONCOMPAGNI, «Intorno alle vite inedite di tre matematici ... scritte da B. B.», *Bullettino di bibliografia e di storia delle scienze matematiche e fisiche*, XII (1879), pp. 352-438 (at pp. 421-427). On his accounting, the literature is uneven, but see bibliography in R. G. BROWN, K. S. JOHNSTON, *Pacioli on Accounting*, New York, 1963.

to spend several years in Florence, after which Leonardo was once again brought back to Milan by the French governor, Charles d'Amboise. During the six years he then spent in Milan, under the patronage of d'Amboise, his studies of anatomy became increasingly sophisticated, benefitting from his application of the rules of geometry and mechanics he had developed over the years.[59] In 1512, when the French were expelled from Milan, Leonardo left for Rome, moving later to the manor house of Cloux in Amboise, given him by King François I, where he continued his studies and projects, even participating in the design of theatrical sets, until his death in 1519.

The effect of Leonardo's thought on the development of the fields he studied is extremely difficult to gauge, since his notes remained for the most part unpublished for centuries. However, one cannot discount the importance of oral transmission of knowledge, and his renown and direct contact with artists and intellectuals such as Pacioli or the anatomist Marcantonio Della Torre (1481-1511; briefly active in Pavia just before his death[60]) are likely to have diffused his often revolutionary ideas.

When Ludovico il Moro fled, the Milanese poets and humanists moved from the court into the city, to continue, like Baldassare Taccone, in government posts, albeit not centered around the ducal court, or to teach privately, some in schools being set up from the time of the bequest made in 1502 by Tommaso Piatti, Piattino's uncle. Others, like Campo Fregoso, retired to live and work in solitude or, like Niccolò da Correggio, centered their activities again on other courts. Despite the efforts of the French – to an extent successful – to foster cultural continuity, literary production was no longer centered on one figure or environment, and the political upheavals themselves could only contribute to a deep change in the patterns of thought. Even the University of Pavia was embattled, with whispers of Protestant ideas in evidence now and again.

---

On the treatise on proportion, P. L. ROSE, *The Italian Renaissance of Mathematics. Studies on Humanists and Mathematicians from Petrarch to Galileo*, Genève, 1975, pp. 56, 144, 148 n.; L. PACIOLI, *De divina proportione*, Milano, 1956 (Fontes Ambrosiani in lucem editi cura et studio Bibliothecae Ambrosianae, XXXI: a printing of the text and illustrations from MS & 170 sup.); also see the recent facsimile, L. PACIOLI, *De divina proportione*, Introduction by A. Marinoni, Milano, 1982 (Fontes Ambrosiani in lucem editi cura et studio Bibliothecae Ambrosianae, LXXII). The second manuscript is in the Bibliothèque Publique et Universitaire de Genève, MS Langues Etrangères 210.

[59] K. D. KEELE, «L. da V.'s Influence on Renaissance Anatomy», *Medical History*, 8 (1964), pp. 360-370.

[60] See M. T. GNUDI, «M. della T.», *Dictionary of Scientific Biography*, XIII, New York, 1976, pp. 430-431.

The Lombard *novellista* Matteo Bandello (1485-1561[61]), born in what is today Piedmont, received his education at the Convento delle Grazie, where Leonardo was working on the *Last Supper*. Although active as a Dominican priest in his younger years, Bandello was by no means insensible to the world around him, and his stories are built of the many strata of social situations which surrounded him in this turbulent period. Frequently based on historical events, even on histories unearthed by the humanists, they give us a rich view of life in Italy and especially in the city of Milan, as opposed to the glimpse of the Sforza court to be had from the letters and poems of those involved in that closed circle. For the intellectual life of Milan had indeed moved out into the city: schools like the *scuole piattine* were being set up, and nobles such as Cecilia Gallerana, the former mistress of Ludovico il Moro, herself a poet, or Ippolita Sforza Bentivoglio held *salotti* in their homes. The expulsion of the French and brief restoration (1512-15) of the young Massimiliano, Ludovico's son, afforded Bandello a respite under Sforza patronage, but he was forced to leave the city upon the return of the French, returning from 1522 to 1526 under Francesco II. Patronage also came from figures around the Gonzaga of Mantua like the *condottiere* Cesare Fregoso, whose widow Costanza he followed into exile in France in about 1541. His work on the *novelle* over the next twenty years in France, and the publication of the first three books there in 1554, help to explain their diffusion and popularity in that country, as well as their prompt diffusion (in some cases, such as in that of the tale of Romeo and Juliet, through their French translations) to England.

---

[61] N. SAPEGNO, «M. B.», *DBI*, V, Roma, 1963, pp. 667-673; C. GODI, «Per la biografia di M. B.», *Italia medioevale e umanistica*, XI (1968), pp. 257-292; A. C. FIORATO, *Bandello entre l'histoire et l'écriture. La vie, l'expérience sociale, l'évolution culturelle d'un conteur de la Renaissance*, Firenze, 1979. The standard edition is: *Tutte le opere di M.B.*, ed. F. Flora, 2 vols., Milano, 1952 (1934); the Latin works are now in Matthaei BANDELLI, *Opera Latina Inedita vel Rara*, ed. C. Godi, Padova, 1983 (with a long introduction); for a recent evaluation of Bandello's position as a Milanese writer, and the question of Milanese usage, see A. TISSONI BENVENUTI, «Milano sforzesca nei ricordi di Bandello: la corte e la città» in *Gli uomini, le città e i tempi di Matteo Bandello*, Secondo convegno internazionale di studi (Torino, Tortona, Alessandria, Castelnuovo Scrivia, 8-11 novembre, 1984), ed. U. Rozzo, Tortona, 1985, pp. 123-137 (cf. FIORATO, *op. cit.*, p. 1, on the question of Milanese vs. Lombard usage). On the Romeo and Juliet tale, *Giulietta e Romeo novella storica di Luigi da Porto di Vicenza*, ed. A. Torri, Pisa, 1831, R. PRUVOST, *M. B. and Elizabethan Fiction*, Paris, 1937; and most recently, D. PEROCCO, «Introduzione» and «Commento» to: M. BANDELLO, *Giulietta e Romeo*, Venezia, 1993, pp. 9-39, 95-122.

Thus, this time of political turbulence, leading to the dispersal of the great Visconti-Sforza library (much of it going to the Bibliothèque du Roy) and causing the spread from Lombardy of currents as disparate as the scientific and artistic ideas of Leonardo and the histories and sketches of life by Bandello, gave Milanese and Lombard culture and ideas a speedy, important and lasting effect on the culture of Europe as a whole.

# PART II
## Pier Candido Decembrio and Lombard Humanism

# CHAPTER II

## Pier Candido Decembrio and Rome:
## His Hand and the Vatican Manuscript of his Treatise
## on Natural History (MS Urb. lat. 276)

I have entitled this study «Pier Candido Decembrio *and* Rome» advi-
sedly. Those who have met Decembrio will recall that he did indeed spend
several years in the Curia, as *Magister Brevium* under Nicholas V, and this
fact alone may be said to justify his inclusion in the proceedings of a conference on humanism in Rome. But it is rather his handwriting and a Roman
puzzle which are the topics of my remarks. His hand is an elegant example of
a little-studied humanist script, in which Vatican manuscripts and archives of
the first half of the fifteenth century abound. The puzzle has to do with a
particular manuscript now in the Biblioteca Apostolica Vaticana among the
Urbino codices, a manuscript which contains Pier Candido's treatise on
natural history, *De animantium naturis*.

First, let me recapitulate the outline of Pier Candido's life, following, for
the most part, the monographic article of Mario Borsa.[1] I shall begin by

---

[1] For Decembrio's biography in general: M. BORSA «P.C.D. e l'Umanesimo in Lombardia»,
*Archivio storico lombardo*, XX (1893), 5-75, pp. 358-441; Idem, «Correspondence of
Humphrey, Duke of Gloucester, and P.C.D.», *English Historical Review*, XIX (1904), pp.
509-526; E. DITT, «P.C.D. Contributo alla storia dell'Umanesimo italiano», *Memorie del
R. Istituto Lombardo di Scienze e Lettere. Classe di Lettere, Scienze Morali e Storiche*, Vol.
XXIV (XV della Serie III), fasc. II, Milano, 1931. Additional information in: V. ZACCARIA,
«L'epistolario di P.C.D.», *Rinascimento*, III (1952), pp. 85-118; Idem, «Sulle opere di
P.C.D.», *Rinascimento*, VII (1956), pp. 13-74; Idem, «P.C.D. traduttore della *Repubblica*

digressing from Borsa, though not diverging from him, on the matter of Decembrio's birth date, which he fixes at 1399. The date of 1392 was proposed by Alberto Corbellini and accepted by Remigio Sabbadini, and, on their authority, by numerous subsequent scholars, up to this day. However, the earlier date can be seen to be erroneous, because Pier Candido himself states in a letter of 1444 to Humfrey Duke of Gloucester that he had not yet reached forty (*«quadragesimum nondum annum superavi»*) when he began translating Plato for the Duke, which occurred in 1437. Hence (trusting Decembrio's own words over distant sources), he could have been 38 in that year (as he would have been if born in 1399), was at the very oldest 39, and was certainly not 45 (as he would have been if born in 1392).[2] He was born in Pavia, and named by his father, the noted humanist Uberto Decembrio, after Pietro Filargo da Candia, the future Pope Alexander V (1409-1410).

In 1411, when his father Uberto was imprisoned by Facino Cane, Gian Maria Visconti's Captain, Pier Candido was sent to the D'Oria home in Genoa, where he had access to the library of the Doge Tommaso Fregoso. Later he would have access to that of the Visconti in Pavia, a library which included one of the most important manuscripts extant from Petrarch's own collection, Leonzio Pilato's translation of Homer, annotated by Petrarca at the

---

di Platone», *Italia medioevale e umanistica*, II (1959), pp. 179-206; R. WEISS, «New Light on Humanism in England During the Fifteenth Century», *Journal of the Warburg and Courtauld Institutes*, XIV (1951), esp. pp. 21-25; Idem, *Humanism in England During the Fifteenth Century*, Oxford, 1967³, *passim*; A. SAMMUT, *Unfredo Duca di Gloucester e gli umanisti italiani*, Padova, 1980; A.C. DE LA MARE, *Duke Humfrey's Library & the Divinity School 1488-1988,* Oxford, 1988. The date of Decembrio's birth has been given as 1392 rather than 1399 by: A. CORBELLINI, «Appunti sull'Umanesimo in Lombardia», *Bollettino della Società Pavese di Storia Patria*, XVII (1917), pp. 5-51; R. SABBADINI, *Enciclopedia Italiana*, XII, Milano, 1931, p. 457; P. O. KRISTELLER, «P.C.D. and His Unpublished Treatise on the Immortality of the Soul», *The Classical Tradition: Literary and Historical Studies in Honor of Harry Caplan*, Ithaca, New York, 1966, p. 538, reprinted in his *Studies in Renaissance Thought and Letters II*, Roma, 1985, pp. 282-283; *The Cambridge History of Renaissance Philosophy*, ed. C. B. Schmitt, Cambridge, 1988, p. 815.

[2] The letter was first published by BORSA, «Correspondence» (n. 1), pp. 520-522; for the date 1437: SAMMUT, *Unfredo* (n. 1), pp. 30, 181, and this letter at pp. 201-202; cf. ZACCARIA, «P.C.D. traduttore» (n. 1). Corbellini's arguments for 1392 include P.C.D.'s extreme youth upon being appointed to official positions, which we shall see in the case of Gaspare Visconti (chapter IV, below) and others, is not valid for this period. He also postulates a potential question of illegitimacy, due to the presence of P.C.D.'s father in Prague in 1399; but this, had it been so, would have made P.C.D. hesitate to indicate that period as the time of his birth, even if he had been inclined to remove a few years from an actual birthdate of 1392.

end of his life and bearing a note in Decembrio's hand as well. [3] Decembrio's entirely Northern parentage and upbringing will be of particular interest when we turn to the study of his hand.

In 1419 Pier Candido became ducal secretary to Filippo Maria Visconti, a post which he retained, filling diplomatic missions even outside of Italy, until Filippo Maria's death in 1447. Among the best known of his works is of course the biography of Filippo Maria. [4] It was during this time that his correspondence with Duke Humfrey of Gloucester, benefactor of the Oxford University Library, took place.

After the death of the Visconti ruler, Decembrio became active in the politics of the short-lived Repubblica Ambrosiana. But he soon found a situation more closely approaching that *otium* required for the pursuit of study, in the papal Curia as *Magister Brevium* to Nicholas V. He remained in Rome from 1450 until 1456, the year after Nicholas' death, when he went on to Naples as secretary to Alphonse of Aragon until this ruler's death in 1458. The new Pope Calixtus III, who had allowed him to remain in Rome a year beyond the death of Nicholas, also died in this period, and Decembrio was never to obtain the favor of Pope Pius II (Aeneas Sylvius Piccolomini).

While in Rome, Decembrio's contacts with humanists increased, and he was in rapport with Biondo Biondi, Poggio Bracciolini and Lorenzo Valla (all of whom he had known for some time), as well as with Giovanni Tortelli, Leon Battista Alberti, and of course his rival Francesco Filelfo.

The last eighteen years of Decembrio's life were spent in attempts to find a stable patron. But luck would not have it so, and we find him wandering from city to city, from court to court. He spent eight years in Ferrara, until March, 1476, when finally in his seventy-seventh year, he was received by

---

[3] Bibliothèque Nationale, Paris, MS Latin 7880 in two volumes. The MS was in Decembrio's hands from 1439-1446 according to the *Consignatio Librorum* of the Visconti Library, published by G. D'ADDA, *Indagini storiche, artistiche e bibliografiche sulla Libreria Visconteo-Sforzesca del Castello di Pavia compilate ed illustrate con documenti inediti...*, Milano, 1875, pp. 4 (no. 8), 16 (no. 163), 22 (no. 219). Cf. E. PELLEGRIN, *La bibliothèque des Visconti et des Sforza ducs de Milan, au XV<sup>e</sup> siècle*, Paris, 1955, pp. 76 (no. 8), 108 (no. 163), 123 (no. 219); Eadem, *La bibliothèque ...*, *Supplément*, Firenze and Paris, 1969, p. 22 and fig. 18; P. DE NOLHAC, *Pétrarque et l'Humanisme*, Paris, 1907 (rpt. 1965), II, p. 167; E. PELLEGRIN, *Manuscrits de Pétrarque dans les bibliothèques de France*, Padova, 1966, p. 285; A. PETRUCCI, *La scrittura di Francesco Petrarca*, Roma, 1967, p. 128, no. 50; KRISTELLER, «P.C.D.» (n. 1), n. 18.

[4] *Rerum Italicarum Scriptores*, XX, pars 1, Bologna, 1925-1935, eds. A. Butti, F. Fossati, G. Petraglione, pp. 3-438.

Galeazzo Maria Sforza in his adopted *patria* Milan, where he died a year and a half later, in November of 1477.

* * *

In the late 1450s, in Naples, as he states in his introduction, Pier Candido Decembrio composed a text, *De animantium naturis*, which he then dedicated to Marchese Ludovico Gonzaga of Mantua in 1460.[5] This text, based primarily on the medieval encyclopedia, De *natura rerum* of Thomas of Cantimpré, while indirectly citing those of somewhat earlier vintage, such as Aristotle and Pliny (though, to be fair, he also cites Isidore) treats of: four-footed animals, birds, marine monsters, fish, serpents and *«vermes»* (including amphibians and insects), and includes a geographical appendix which is distinct from his own *Cosmographia*.[6] The treatise exists today in four

---

[5] There exists a previous study of the manuscript by S. KILLERMANN: «Das Tierbuch des Petrus Candidus geschrieben 1460, gemalt im 16. Jahrhundert», *Zoologische Annalen*, VI (1914), pp. 113-221, with eight plates. Now see my *Das Tierbuch des Petrus Candidus. Codex Urbinas latinus 276. Eine Einführung*, Zürich, 1984 (Codices e Vaticanis Selecti, LX [with facsimile]), and «The Art and Science of Renaissance Natural History: Thomas of Cantimpré, Pier Candido Decembrio, Conrad Gessner and Teodoro Ghisi in Vatican MS Urb. lat. 276», *Viator*, 27 (1996), pp. 265-321. (On the spelling of Gessner's name, see n. 14, below). The MS is mentioned in: A. LUZIO and R. RENIER, «Il Filelfo e l'Umanesimo alla corte dei Gonzaga», *Giornale storico della letteratura italiana*, XVI (1889), pp. 147-148; F. CARTA, *Codici corali e libri a stampa miniati della Biblioteca Nazionale di Milano*, Roma, 1891, n. 2, pp. 158-9; S. BEISSEL, *Vaticanische Miniaturen – Miniatures choisies de la Bibliothèque du Vatican*, Freiburg im Breisgau, 1893, p. 29 and n. 1; A. MUÑOZ, «Due trattati de *natura animalium* del secolo XVI nella Biblioteca Vaticana», *L'Arte*, VII (1904), pp. 486-491; L. THORNDIKE, *A History of Magic and Experimental Science*, IV, New York, 1934, p. 397 and nn. 24, 25; B. DEGENHART, «Eine lombardische Kreuzigung», *Proporzioni*, III (1950): *Omaggio a Pietro Toesca*, pp. 65-68 and Plate XLIX; *Miniature del Rinascimento. Catalogo della mostra*, Città del Vaticano, 1950, p. 43 (no. 66); A. C. CROMBIE, *Medieval and Early Modern Science*, New York, 1959, vol. I, p. 160 and Plate XVIII; E. MARANI e C. PERINA, *Mantova. Le arti*, Mantova, 1961, II, p. 252; *Mantova. Le lettere*, ed. E. Faccioli, Mantova, 1962, II, p. 124, n. 7; *Mostra dei codici gonzagheschi. La biblioteca dei Gonzaga da Luigi I ad Isabella*, ed. U. Meroni, Mantova, 1966, p. 33 and n. 57, p. 58 and n. 53, and Tav. 101; D. A. FRANCHINI, R. MARGONARI, G. OLMI, R. SIGNORINI, A. ZANCA and C. TELLINI PERINA, *La scienza a corte. Collezionismo eclettico, natura e immagine a Mantova fra Rinascimento e Manierismo*, Roma, 1979.

[6] See my «The Art and Science» (n. 5), and KILLERMANN, «Das Tierbuch» (n. 5). For the *Cosmographia*, see K. KRETSCHMER, «Die Kosmographie des Petrus Candidus Decembrius», in *Festschrift Ferdinand Freiherrn von Richthofen zum sechzigsten Geburtstag … dargebracht*, Berlin, 1893, pp. 269-305, and see below, chapter XI, n. 34.

manuscripts, of which that in the Vatican Library is the most significant.[7]

The parchment manuscript measures 265 × 190 mm., and contains 234 folios (II, III, 1-232) in 29 quires (28 of 8 leaves and 1 of 10). It is bound in brown leather, visible at the hinges, with, appliquéed to the front and back boards and to the spine, reddish-brown smooth leather, marbled and tooled in gold. The spine bears the seal of the Lambertini Pope, Benedict XIV (1740-58), who devoted himself to the Library, and under whom the librarian, Cardinal Domenico Passionei, drew up a document on the state of the Library in 1750.[8]

The treatise, written in brown ink with red titles and rubrics, begins, «*CVM NEAPOLI otiosus degerem...*». Initials of chapters throughout the work are alternately red and blue Roman capitals. There are ten illuminated gilt initials (white vine with red, blue and green) at the beginning of large sections. Folio 1 (Fig. 4) bears the arms of Ludovico Gonzaga, in the «quarta maniera» (in use from September 22, 1433 to 1530)[9] and the letters *LV*, the first syllable of Ludovicus.[10] The miniature was first attributed to Cristoforo Moretti on stylistic grounds.[11]

The fact that the manuscript was indeed copied for Ludovico Gonzaga is corroborated (if corroboration were necessary) by a letter of 1460 addressed to Pier Candido by Ludovico, from which I quote:

> Havendo nui per il messo vostro insieme cum la vostra littera ricevuto il libro ne intitulati De natura animalium et Avium ne havemo preso grandissimo piacere parendone uno bellissimo dono per la materia se tracta quale è molto elegante e bella.... Et perché legendo nui ritroviamo pur alcune sorte de animali che quantunche vui tochati la qualità et natura sua tamen non possiamo de ponto comprendere la forma sua, haressemo ad caro che ne li faceste depinzere.... Faremo transcrivere il libro vostro et a ciaschuno capitulo depinzer lo

---

[7] The other three MSS are discussed in my *Das Tierbuch* (n. 5), chapter VI. The Vatican MS is also significant to natural history itself: see my «Some Late Sixteenth-Century Depictions of the Aurochs (*Bos primigenius* Bojanus, extinct 1627): New Evidence from Vatican MS Urb. lat. 276», *Archives of Natural History*, 21 (1994), pp. 275-288, and the update, *Ibid.*, 22 (1995), pp. 437-438.

[8] J. BIGNAMI ODIER, *La Bibliothèque Vaticane de Sixte IV à Pie XI*, Roma, 1973 (Studi e Testi, 272), p. 165. The author kindly informs me that the document is in MS Ottob. Lat. 3181, pars II, fols. 403-421.

[9] *Mostra dei codici gonzagheschi*, Tav. 33, facing p. 12.

[10] CARTA, *Codici corali* (n. 5), p. 158, n. 2.

[11] DEGENHART, «Eine lombardische Kreuzigung» (n. 5), pp. 66-67. The attribution is revised in chapter III, below.

animale suo de mano de bono maestro, sì per rispecto del scriptore como del pictore che serà una bella cosa et degna de la memoria vostra....[12]

In other words, Ludovico was looking at a draft of the text, and commissioned this copy to receive the desired illustrations. The Vatican manuscript is, in fact, dated 1460 at the end, in Arabic numerals which were added at a later date. But (and this was not mentioned by Stornajolo) it is also dated very faintly in red Roman numerals in the left margin by the author himself, who also wrote the majuscule subscription, identified at a glance by Augusto Campana (Fig. 2).

The illustrations were indeed added, though not, at least for the most part, when planned. And these illustrations lend to this manuscript still further significance, not only from an art historical point of view, but also from that of the development of descriptive method in the science of natural history. As Guy Beaujouan has pointed out,[13] real advances in the biological sciences could not take place until the hand could follow – or interpret – what the eye saw. This manuscript, whose text dates from the middle of the fifteenth century, was not illustrated until the late sixteenth century, but it was then taken in hand by masters of natural history illustration, often working from life, as well as from illustrations in the most reliable contemporary printed natural histories.[14] Thus we have, juxtaposed between two covers, examples of descriptive methods a full century apart. That in the text for the most part follows earlier authority, with some direct observation on the part of Decembrio; that in the illustrations clearly comes, whenever possible, from direct observation by the artists (excepting always the case of monsters and exotic beasts), and from up-to-date sources.

---

[12] A. LUZIO and R. RENIER, «Filelfo e l'Umanesimo alla corte dei Gonzaga», *Giornale storico della letteratura italiana*, XVI (1890), p. 148.

[13] In his essay, «Motives and Opportunities for Science in the Medieval Universities», *Scientific Change. Symposium on the History of Science (University of Oxford, 9-15 July, 1961)*, New York, 1963, p. 234.

[14] KILLERMANN, «Das Tierbuch» (n. 5), pp. 216-219, attributes the paintings to Conrad Gessner's artists, but this is unlikely, as is argued in my monograph, where they are attributed to Teodoro Ghisi; and see my «The Art and Science» (n. 5), pp. 288-313. On the spelling of Gessner's name, see H. WELLISCH, «Conrad Gessner: A Bio-Bibliography», *Journal of the Society for the Bibliography of Natural History*, 7 (1975), pp. 151-247, esp. pp. 152-153; revised edition, *Conrad Gessner: A Bio-Bibliography*, Zug, Switzerland, 1984, p. XIII, and H. FISCHER, G. PETIT, J. STAEDTKE, R. STEIGER, H. ZOLLER, *Conrad Gessner, 1516-1565. Universalgelehrter, Naturforscher, Arzt*, Zürich, 1967, p. 7.

\* \* \*

Let us turn now to the scripts that appear in the manuscript. I alluded a moment ago to the marginal date in a hand which appears on inspection to be that of Pier Candido Decembrio. This hand has been referred to often in the scholarly literature, [15] and it is known to those scholars who have worked on Pier Candido. But it has never been formally described. In the interest of further research, not only on the present manuscript, but also on a little-studied group of Northern Italian humanistic hands, and on the activities of Decembrio himself at the papal court in Rome and elsewhere, I think it of some interest to look more closely at that hand.

Signed examples of Pier Candido's minuscule and majuscule Latin scripts (and of his Greek script), dated 1437, have been published by Resta. [16] Close comparison with these examples proves another folio of the Ambrosiana *zibaldone* bearing the beginning of a draft of Decembrio's *De anima*, postu-

---

[15] References include: R. Biblioteca Estense, Modena, *Mostra di Codici autografici* [sic] *in onore di Girolamo Tiraboschi nel II centenario della nascita* (Prefazione di Domenico Fava), Modena, 1932, p. 49, no. 73; D. FAVA, «La mostra di codici autografi [sic] in onore di Girolamo Tiraboschi», *Accademie e biblioteche d'Italia*, VI (1932-1933), pp. 99-144, esp. 133, 135; G. RESTA, *Le epitomi di Plutarco nel Quattrocento*, Padova, 1962, pp. 48-57, pp. 103-108, and Tavole V, VI; J. J. G. ALEXANDER and A. C. DE LA MARE, *The Italian Manuscripts in the Library of Major J. R. Abbey*, London, 1969, p. XXXI; and M. FERRARI, «Dalle antiche biblioteche domenicane a Milano: codici superstiti nell'Ambrosiana», *Archivio ambrosiano*, XXXV (1979), pp. 170-197.

    Tentative identifications in: P. O. KRISTELLER, *art. cit.* (n. 1), p. 544; O. PÄCHT and J. J. G. ALEXANDER, *Illuminated Manuscripts in the Bodleian Library Oxford*, II (Italian School), Oxford, 1970, pp. vi, 73 (no. 697), 74 (no. 707). No. 697 is MS Duke Humfrey d. 1, the first folio of which is partially reproduced in the catalogue *Duke Humfrey and English Humanism in the Fifteenth Century*, Oxford, 1970, Item 12, Plate I. No. 707 is MS Canon. Class. Lat. 294, which contains a signed note in Pier Candido Decembrio's rather elegant Latin book hand (fol. 13ᵛ).

[16] From Biblioteca Apostolica Vaticana MS Barb. Lat. 112, and from Biblioteca Ambrosiana MS R. 88. sup. The latter is a partially autograph *zibaldone* of Decembrio's works and works copied by or for him, for example the list of works «QUE EX LATINIS SCRIPTO-RIBUS MAGIS NECESSARIA» (fols. 172ᵛ-173) possibly copied by his brother, Angelo (with a final addition, 'Eusebij de temporibus i[n] uno volumi[n]e', by P.C.D.). Compare the plates in P. SCARCIA PIACENTINI, «Angelo Decembrio e la sua scrittura», *Scrittura e civiltà*, 4 (1980), pp. 247-277. On this list, see M. FERRARI, «Per la fortuna di S. Ambrogio: appunti su umanisti e codici», *Archivio ambrosiano*, XXVII (1973/1974), p. 134, and for bibliography on the MS, Eadem, «Dalle antiche biblioteche», *cit.*, p. 183, n. 34.

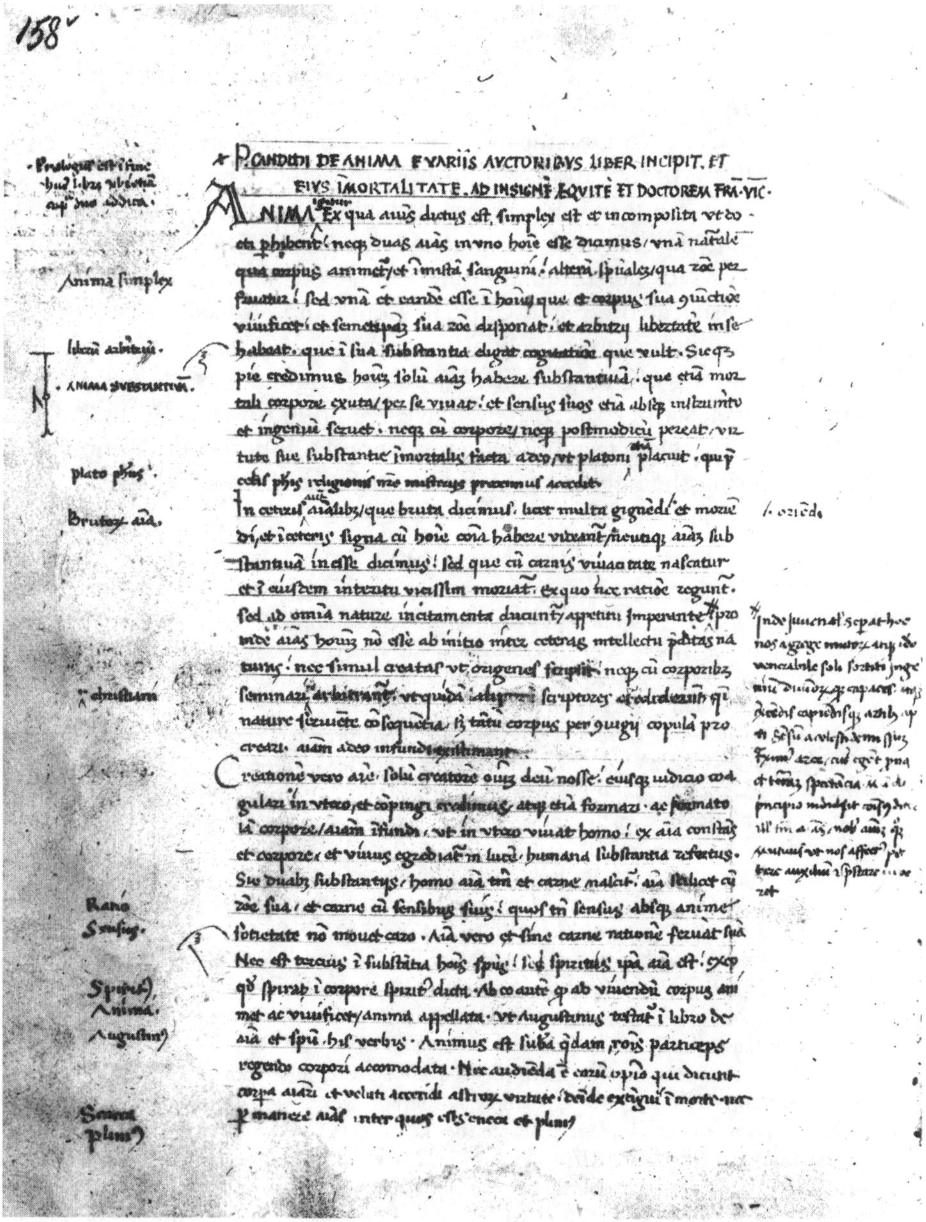

Fig. 1. The Hand of Pier Candido Decembrio: Draft of *De anima,* MS R 88 sup., fol. 158ᵛ.

lated as autograph by Kristeller, to be so (Fig. 1). The semi-cursive *ductus* and the form of the letters show this hand to belong to the Italian semigothic, in Cencetti's nomenclature,[17] which flourished among the humanists in Lombardy, Liguria and the Veneto and even extended down into Emilia Romagna at the end of the fourteenth and the beginning of the fifteenth centuries. It was in part modelled on Petrarch's hand, which was widely known and admired. It is not pre-humanistic, as some have thought, but coeval with developments in Florence with which we are familiar.[18] This is the type of script of the earliest copies of the Lodi Cicero discovered by Bishop Gerardo Landriani (an intimate friend of Decembrio's)[19] in 1421. Casamassima's hypothesis that Northern Italian humanists were looking at an earlier Carolingian model – ninth-century rather than eleventh – seems entirely plausible.[20]

To be noted in Pier Candido's version of this script are the fragmented composition of certain individual letters. For example, the *e, r, f, long s, v* are made up of discrete short, broad strokes, subtly shaded with a broad-nibbed pen, favored by the writer. Pier Candido's *g*, while not unique, is characteristic of some writers of this script (l. 17: *regunt[ur]*): note the long, oblique «wasp waist» and its sharp angle of juncture with the lower bowl. He retains a rounded *r*, and will begin a word, as he does in this case, with this 2-shaped *r*. Petrus Candidus will often end his Latin signature in a *long-s*, as

---

[17] G. CENCETTI, *Lineamenti di storia della scrittura latina*, Bologna, 1954, p. 264, and see SCARCIA PIACENTINI (n. 16), pp. 260-263.

[18] As described by B. L. ULLMAN, *The Origin and Development of Humanistic Script*, Roma, 1960. And see Gius. BILLANOVICH, «Alle origini della scrittura umanistica: Padova 1261 e Firenze 1397», *Miscellanea Augusto Campana*, Padova, 1981, pp. 125-140.

[19] BORSA, «P.C.D. e l'Umanesimo in Lombardia» (n. 1), p. 31; R. SABBADINI, *Storia e critica di testi latini*, ed. E. Billanovich and M. Billanovich, Padova, 1971, p. 84.

For the script in question, compare the 1422 copy of the now lost Lodi MS which contained Cicero's *Orator, De Oratore, Brutus*, MS Vat. Ottob. Lat. 2057, fol. 1 of which is reproduced in F. STEFFENS, *Lateinische Palaeographie*, Berlin and Leipzig, 1929, Plate 109b. I would now add a Cicero in the Bibliothèque Nationale, Paris, MS Latin 7704 to this paleographical group; see for example fol. 115, reproduced in E. CHATELAIN, *Paléographie des classiques latins*, I, Paris, 1884-1900, p. 6 and Plate XXb. Compare too the anonymous hand of Bodl. Laud. Lat. 70, of 1409, published by Ullman, *The Origin* (n. 18), Plate 42 (and p. 82); he does not discuss place of origin. Also see P. SCARCIA PIACENTINI, «La tradizione laudense di Cicerone ed un inesplorato manoscritto della Biblioteca Vaticana (Vat. Lat. 3237)», in *Revue d'histoire des textes*, XI (1981), pp. 123-146.

[20] E. CASAMASSIMA, «Literulae latinae. Nota paleografica», introduction to S. CAROTI and S. ZAMPONI, *Lo scrittoio di Bartolomeo Fonzio umanista fiorentino*, Milano, 1974, pp. XIV-XV.

he ends *creatas* and *origines* here (l. 20). Compare, in the same line, the first word, *naturas*, which ends in the sigmoid form. His minuscule *d* is often rounded in form, but can have a straight ascender (see both forms in lines 35, 36: *audie[n]da, dei[n]de*). Similarly, the *a* is now upright, now rounded, with both forms appearing in one word (*arbitrant[ur]*, l. 21). Ligatures occur between *g* and the following letter, and between *rounded d* and *e* (l. 6: *eande[m]*; l. 36: *dei[n]de*) and *rounded d* and *o* (ll. 3-4: *docti*).

The most characteristic abbreviation in Pier Candido Decembrio's script would appear to be that for *m/n*, which is usually very small (as is his script generally) and arched, with a slight downward tilt to the right (l. 6: *una[m]*, *eande[m]*, *i[n]*, etc.).

The display script and the majuscules throughout Pier Candido's script are, like the minuscules, usually of relatively small dimension and distinctive. The *A* rarely has a transverse (note the exception of the decorative initial, ll. 2-3). The lowest transverse of the *E* is usually shorter than the upper two, which are about equal. The *L* has a short transverse, and is the tallest of the capitals. Candido's *P* can be open at the top of the eye, but not at the bottom, and it extends slightly below the line. The upper loop of *R* meets the ascender one-half to two-thirds of the way down. The vertical measurements of the two eyes of the *B* are about equal, although the lower eye is wider than the upper. Capital *S* and *C* are both made with two strokes.

The marginal insertion marks most used by Decembrio are: /, //, ∴ . His «Nota» can be seen in the left margin of this folio, ll. 8-11, a vertically extended version of that used by Petrarch. Decembrio frequently uses a marginal «attende» or its abbreviated form. Two other indicator symbols occur: a vertical line with a three-scalloped rosette (similar to that used by Salutati) and a quickly sketched hand – more a symbol than a drawing, as can be seen opposite ll. 8 and 30 in the left margin.[21] He does not usually abbreviate *et*.

Pier Candido's margins are usually justified, even in a draft such as the one we see here. Almost invariably, he uses light brown ink, or light red for rubrics and titles.

* * *

If we now look back to our Vatican manuscript, we can see on certain folios marginal corrections and even textual insertions in the hand we have

---

[21] For precedents of these symbols in Petrarch, Boccaccio and Salutati, compare A. C. DE LA MARE, *The Handwriting of Italian Humanists*, I, fasc., 1, (Oxford, 1973): Plates II(b), III(c) and (f), VII(h); III(g); III(d) (cf. p. 8 and n. 3); VII(c), IX(f); I(b), III(e); VI(d) and (f); VII(c), IX(f).

just been studying. This fact thus renders the text of the Vatican manuscript what we might call «critical». One such example, an author's correction, indicates a close cooperation between author and copyist: «Crocodillus scribit(ur) et no(n) Cocodrillus», complains Pier Candido (fol. 2ᵛ), and the scribe corrects even further on a later folio by eliminating one *l*.

Although the manuscript was judged autograph by Killermann, comparison of Decembrio's hand with that of the copyist proves otherwise. Nevertheless, the scribe's hand (Fig. 3) calls to mind other similar scripts, not the least similar of which is one script of Pier Candido's brother, Angelo Camillo Decembrio, whose handwriting has been described in fine detail.[22] The *ductus* is extremely close, as are the forms of certain letters: *m*, *g*, *N*, *initial v*. But other letters are clearly distinct, for example the scribe's *r*, made with an open v-stroke, and the *a*, which in the scribe's hand is linked to the next letter by the upper trace of the loop, rather than by its tail, as in Angelo's. Another «spia» is the ampersand, which in the Vatican manuscript has a decided rightward slant, and whose transverse (technically speaking) actually extends below the line, as Angelo's does not.

The two hands are nonetheless of interest as examples of another manifestation of distinctive Northern Italian tendencies. This book script seems in fact to accompany the Semigothic already described, and, while closer to the Florentine tradition, is, I believe, still distinguishable from it. (Compare, if my visual memory serves me, certain traits, such as the flamboyant final *s*

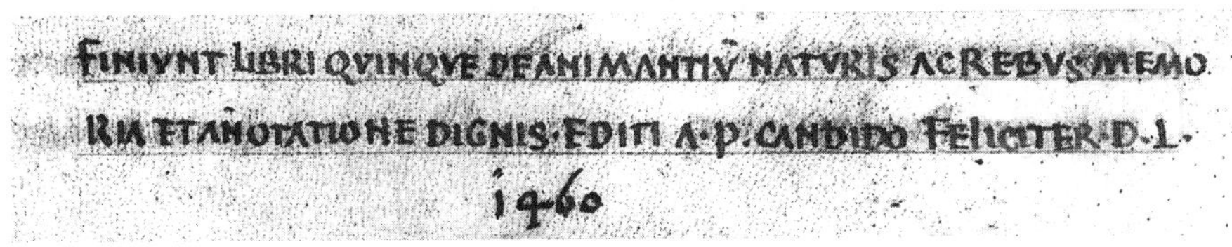

Fig. 2. Decembrio's Subscription, MS Urb. lat. 276, fol. 231ᵛ.

---

[22] P. SCARCIA PIACENTINI, «Angelo Decembrio e la sua scrittura» (n. 16). I am grateful to Prof. Giuseppe Billanovich for having brought this article to my attention and to the author for having provided me with an offprint. It should be noted that in reality the size of Angelo's hand tends to be small like his brother's. Thus the enlarged photographs in Plates Ib and IV of the article cited (the I of *Idem* in Pl. Ib is actually only 8 mm. high in the MS Ambros. Z. 184. sup, fol. 48ᵛ) exhibit a more striking similarity to the present copyist's hand than is actually the case.

in Basinio da Parma, [23] and the general appearance of the later hand of Sabadino degli Arienti[24]).

* * *

To return once again to the Roman context within which these remarks
are being made, how did this manuscript arrive in Rome? And when? And
from where?

We have already seen that it was copied for Ludovico Gonzaga of Mantua
in 1460, that is, after Decembrio himself had left Rome and was seeking patronage elsewhere in Italy. We know that it was illustrated, at least for the
most part, in the Sixteenth Century. And it is now housed among the Urbino
manuscripts in the Vatican Library.

Cosimo Stornajolo, in his catalogue of the Urbino manuscripts in the Vatican, gives an adequate description of the codex, then states: «*Codex non est
urbinas sed saec(ulo) septimo decimo inter urbinates adscitus, uti eruitur ex no-
tula in inventario vaticano* [he does not specify which inventory] *huic numero
adscripta: Sostituita nel luogo vuoto una Opera di P. C. Decembrio*».[25] In the
indices I have scanned to date, I have not come across the note cited.

However, I have seen three major seventeenth-century inventories of the
Urbino manuscripts, and in particular an alphabetical index compiled by
Alessandro Vanni in the year 1640 – that is, a full seventeen years before the
removal of the Ducal Library from Urbino to the Vatican by Alexander VII.

Le Grelle identifies Vanni as the last custodian of the Ducal library.[26]
Vanni's *Indice alfabetico della Libraria Manuscritta d'Urbino* was evidently a

---

[23] See the Plate which accompanies the Roma, 1966 edition of A. CAMPANA, *Basinio da Parma*
in the *collana* «Estratti del *Dizionario Biografico degli Italiani*», p. 9.

[24] Identified by Dr. Gino Corti in: *Art and Life at the Court of Ercole I d'Este: The 'De Triumphis religionis' of Giovanni Sabadino degli Arienti* ed. Werner Gundersheimer, Genève,
1972, Plate I. Compare the hand of the MS of Sabadino degli Arienti's *Hymeneo* which
appeared in sales catalogues of Laurence Witten (1978-1979) before being owned by H. P.
Kraus; comparison of the plates would indicate identity of the hands. I have not seen the
MSS. (I am informed by Antonia Tissoni Benvenuti that *Hymeneo* has been edited and
commented by I. Campori in a thesis at the University of Pavia, 1981). See P. STOPPELLI,
«Due manoscritti e un incunabolo sconosciuto di Giovanni Sabadino degli Arienti», *Studi e
problemi di critica testuale*, 25 (Oct. 1982), pp. 25-30.

[25] C. STORNAJOLO, *Codices Urbinates Latini*, I, Romae, 1902, pp. 252-253.

[26] In his Introduction to STORNAJOLO, vol. III, p. xii*. Since completing this article, I have
been able to see M. MORANTI and L. MORANTI, *Il trasferimento dei «Codices Urbinates»
alla Biblioteca Vaticana. Cronistoria, Documenti e Inventario*, Urbino, 1981, kindly brought

list of those manuscript books coming from Francesco Maria della Rovere's library at Castel Durante. The title folio bears a note, apparently in Vanni's hand and reading: «Con quelli anco che trovai nelle Casse, riportati da me / Alex(andro) Vanni Bibliotecario l'anno / 1640». In this same hand, we find the following entry in the index itself: «Publius Candidus [as he was called in several places] de Animaliu(m) naturis in 4° m.s., in p(er)gamena, legato / in cuoio rosso, cu(m) le borchie è nella 2ª scan(sia), all'ord(in)e 2° / n(umer)o 24».[27] Emendations visible in this entry (made in the same hand) refer to

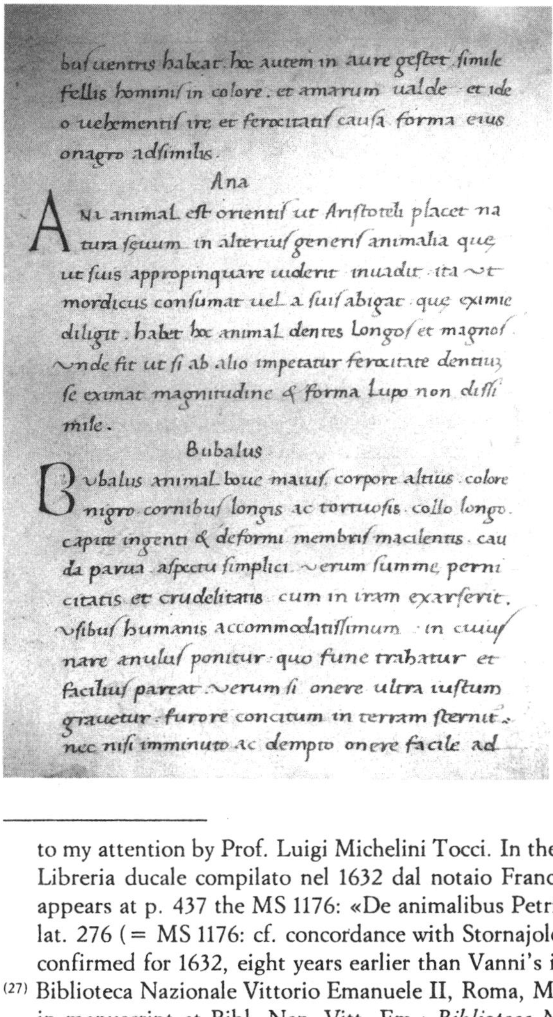
bus uentris habeat. hoc autem in aure gestet. simile
fellis hominis in colore. et amarum ualde. et ide
o uehementis ire et ferocitatis causa. forma eius
onagro adsimilis.
Ana
ANa animal est orientis ut Aristoteli placet na
tura seuum. in alterius generis animalia que
ut suis appropinquare uiderit inuadit. ita ut
mordicus consumat uel a suis abigat. que eximie
diligit. habet hoc animal dentes longos et magnos.
unde fit ut si ab alio impetatur ferocitate dentium
se eximat. magnitudine & forma lupo non dissi
mile.
Bubalus
Bubalus animal boue maius. corpore altius. colore
nigro. cornibus longis ac tortuosis. collo longo.
capite ingenti & deformi. membris macilentus. cau
da parua. aspectu simplici. uerum summe perni
citatis et crudelitatis. cum in iram exarserit.
usibus humanis accommodatissimum. in cuius
nare anulus ponitur. quo fune trahatur et
facilius pareat. uerum si onere ultra iustum
grauetur. furore concitum in terram sternit.
nec nisi imminuto ac dempto onere facile ad

Fig. 3. Copyist's Hand, Presentation Copy of *De animantium naturis,* MS Urb. lat. 276, fol. 10r.

to my attention by Prof. Luigi Michelini Tocci. In the transcription of the «Inventario della Libreria ducale compilato nel 1632 dal notaio Francesco Scudacchi» (pp. 369-451), there appears at p. 437 the MS 1176: «De animalibus Petri Candidi». The presence of MS Urb. lat. 276 (= MS 1176: cf. concordance with Stornajolo, p. 461) in the Ducal Library is thus confirmed for 1632, eight years earlier than Vanni's inventory.

(27) Biblioteca Nazionale Vittorio Emanuele II, Roma, MS Gesuitici 146, fol. 73. Cf. catalogue in manuscript at Bibl. Naz. Vitt. Em.: *Biblioteca Nazionale Centrale Vittorio Emanuele. Catalogo dei manoscritti Gesuitici*, I, fol. 28.

other shelf marks, and may be an indication that the location of the manuscript was changed within the collection before its arrival in Rome. Nonetheless, except for the *borchie* and the original red leather binding, both of
which could easily have disappeared in rebinding, the description fits the
manuscript now in the Vatican Library. The entry thus constitutes proof that
the manuscript was indeed part of the Urbino collection in 1640. (Converse-
ly, the absence of the manuscript from Veterani's 1521 inventory[28] does not
constitute proof of its absence from the collection at that time, though I do
cite the fact).

The manuscript is also present in the Index put together in 1657[29] and
annotated by Holstenius: «*Candidus de animalibus figurat*» (fol. 26$^v$). Again,
the script of the entry matches that of the surrounding entries, and thus the
manuscript was accounted for in the year of the move from Urbino to
Rome.

Later inventories of the Urbino collection, such as that of 1671[30] and that
of 1797[31] do show this manuscript, with its present shelf mark, as a later entry.
This could indicate a shifting of the manuscript within the Vatican Library
between the seventeenth and eighteenth centuries, a period during which there
was in fact a good deal of movement of codices within the Library.

We are left, then, with a little less of a puzzle than that with which we
began. The gap in our knowledge is narrowed to the period between the
manuscript's transcription in 1460 and its presence in Urbino in 1640 before
it passed on to Rome. While the manuscript is clearly not autograph, the
presence of the author's hand throughout the text, here demonstrated, adds
significance to a manuscript already valued for its remarkable illustrations.

---

[28] Published by C. GUASTI, *Giornale storico degli archivi toscani*, VI, (1862) pp. 127-147; VII
(1863) pp. 46-55, pp. 130-154.

[29] LE GRELLE, Introduction (n. 26), p. xv*; now MS Vat. Lat. 9475: INDEX BIBLIOTHECÆ
VRBINATIS, fol. 26$^v$ (cf. LE GRELLE, p. xlix). Cf. the catalogue in manuscript at the Biblio-
teca Apostolica Vaticana: *Inventarium Codicum Latinorum Bibliothecae Vaticanae*, Tomus
XIII. Opera et studio J. B. De Rossi ... Conlaborante Al. Vincenzi. An. 1872-1875, p. 92.

[30] MS Urb. Lat. 1771: CODICVM / MM.SS. / VRBINATIS BIBLIOTHECAE / INDEX /
QVEM / Sub Pontificatu Clementis X. / Pont. Max. / IVSSV / Reu$^{mi}$ P. Magistri Laurentij
Brancati à / Laurea primi Vaticanae Bibliothecae Custodis. / Composuit ac Scripsit ... //
Iacobus Vincentius Marchesius ... Anno 1671, fol. 108.

[31] MSS Urb. Lat. 1776, 1777, 1778 (Colophon in U.L. 1778, fol. 251$^v$: «Compilavit Maurus
Coster ... Anno Domini MDCCIIIC.»). Urb. Lat. 1776: BIBLIOTHECAE / VATICANO-
URBINATIS / CODICUM MANUSCRIPTORUM / INDEX / ALPHABETICO ORDINE
DISPOSITUS / TOMUS PRIMUS. / Litt. A. ad G.: fol. 212.

# CHAPTER III

## Harvard MS Richardson 23:
## A «Pendant» to Vatican MS Urb. lat. 276
## and a Significant Exemplar for P. C. Decembrio's
### *Opuscula Historica*

Pier Candido Decembrio was not a born politician. He served Filippo Maria Visconti as secretary faithfully and well, and his attachment to his de facto *patria*, Milan, led him to participate actively in the short-lived *Repubblica Ambrosiana* (1447-1450). But his undisguised awareness of Francesco Sforza's motive for coming to the aid of the Republic against the Venetians served him ill when the *condottiere*, who had partially legitimized himself by marrying Filippo Maria's daughter Bianca Maria, was named Duke of Milan. Sforza's disfavor was to have negative consequences for much of the remainder of Decembrio's long life (1399-1477).[1] For six years, from 1450 to 1456, he found welcome at the papal curia under Nicholas V and, briefly, Calixtus III. After the latter pope's death, Decembrio resided for two years

---

[1] He is termed a firm enemy of Francesco by 1448 in F. COGNASSO «La Repubblica Ambrosiana», *Storia di Milano*, ed. G. Treccani degli Alfieri, vol. VI, Milano, 1955, p. 425. For Decembrio's biography generally, M. BORSA, «P. C. D. e l'Umanesimo in Lombardia», *Archivio storico lombardo*, XX (1893), pp. 5-75, 358-441, here, esp. pp. 358-375. See too E. DITT, «P. C. D. Contributo alla storia dell'Umanesimo italiano», *Memorie del R. Istituto Lombardo di Scienze e Lettere*, vol. XXIV (XV della serie III), fasc. 2 (1931), pp. 21-108; P. ARGELATI, *Bibliotheca Scriptorum Mediolanensium*, Tomus Secundus, Pars Altera, Milano, 1745: *Scriptores Exteri*, XXVI, «Decembrius Petrus Candidus», cols. 2099-2105. On Decembrio's birthdate, see chapter II, above, paragraph 2.

at the court of Alphonse of Aragon in Naples. The years from Alphonse's death in 1458 until 1467, when he was finally taken in by Borso d'Este at Ferrara, were years of struggle and uncertainty for the venerable humanist, although he had returned to Milan.[2] It is then that we find him sending works to various princes of Italy in the hope of finding stable employment. Such works include his *De animantium naturis*, presented to Ludovico Gonzaga in 1460,[3] his biography of Francesco Sforza (1461),[4] his *De anima*, presented to Francesco Visconti (a supporter of Francesco Sforza) around the same time,[5] as well, in all likelihood, as the manuscript under study.

The Gonzaga copy of *De animantium naturis* is now Vatican manuscript Urb. lat. 276.[6] This parchment manuscript was commissioned from Decembrio by Ludovico, prepared and transcribed (by an unknown scribe), then corrected and dated opposite Decembrio's own subscription in the hand of the author. Gilt initials of Books and major subdivisions were decorated in the white-vine manner, with blue, green and red background. The first folio was further embellished with a miniature (Fig. 4) depicting two diaphanous singing angels in pale rose and pale yellow garments, with green and rose wings and gilded halos, lightly supporting the Gonzaga arms (*quarta maniera*) against a cerulean background. At the top, the gilt letters *L V*, for Ludovico, flank a red sun with a face, and the whole is surrounded by a rectangular gilt frame. The miniature measures 70 × 101 mm in a folio 265 × 190 mm.

This miniature was attributed by Bernhard Degenhart in 1950 to Cristoforo Moretti (fl. 1451-1485).[7] The attribution bears re-examination. The

---

[2] Borsa, «P.C.D. e l'Umanesimo» (n. 1), pp. 392-393, 397-398.

[3] Edited by me in a facsimile edition: *Das Tierbuch des Petrus Candidus. Codex Urbinas latinus 276*, 2 vols., Zürich, 1984 (Codices e Vaticanis Selecti, LX).

[4] *Annotatio Rerum Gestarum in Vita Illmi. Francisci Sfortie, Quarti Mediolanensium Ducis*, in L. A. Muratori, *Rerum Italicarum Scriptores ab Anno Aerae Christianae Quingentesimo ad Millesimumquingentesimum*, Tomus XX, Milano, 1731, cols. 1021-1046, and in *Rerum Italicarum Scriptores*, XX, 1, eds. A. Butti, F. Fossati, G. Petraglione, Bologna, 1925-1958, pp. 439-989.

[5] Edited by P. O. Kristeller in his *Studies in Renaissance Thought and Letters*, II, Roma, 1985, pp. 281-300, 567-584.

[6] On its composition and arrival at the Vatican through Urbino, see my *Das Tierbuch ... Eine Einführung* (n. 3), chapter V. More detailed findings in chapter II, above, and now see my «The Art and Science of Renaissance Natural History: Thomas of Cantimpré, Pier Candido Decembrio, Conrad Gessner, and Teodoro Ghisi in Vatican Library MS Urb. lat. 276» *Viator*, 27 (1996), pp. 265-321.

[7] B. Degenhart, «Eine lombardische Kreuzigung», *Proporzioni*, III, *Omaggio a Pietro Toe-*

miniature certainly belongs to the Lombard Gothic International tradition and even to the same circles as Moretti, including such Lombard artists as the Brothers Zavattari (fl. 1404-1479[8]) and Bonifacio Bembo (fl. 1446-1477[9]), who was engaged in miniature work in the tradition stemming from Michelino da Besozzo (fl. 1388-1442[10]) and including the Master of the *Vitae Imperatorum* (referring to the Italian translation of Suetonius copied in 1431 by Angelo Decembrio, Pier Candido's brother, Bibliothèque Nationale, MS ital. 131[11]). Michelino's own work may have been that praised by Uberto Decembrio, Pier Candido's humanist father, when he referred to a «Michele pavese», and by Pier Candido himself.[12]

*sca*, (1950) pp. 65-68, plates XLVII-LVII. On Moretti: F. MALAGUZZI VALERI, *Pittori lombardi del Quattrocento*, Milano, 1902, pp. 81-94; C. BARONI, S. SAMEK LUDOVICI, *Pittura lombarda del Quattrocento*, Messina-Firenze, 1952, pp. 73-78; P. TOESCA, *La pittura e la miniatura nella Lombardia. Dai più antichi monumenti alla metà del Quattrocento*, ed. E. Castelnuovo, Torino, 1966, pp. 227-228, pl. 494. I do not thus far find Moretti in the literature on documented miniaturists, though he was certainly associated generally with the circles discussed below. G. MONGERI, in a note to his edition of G. D'ADDA's «L'arte del minio nel ducato di Milano dal secolo XIII al XVI», *Archivio storico lombardo*, XII (1885), pp. 330-356, 528-557, 759-796, at p. 354 cites, without accepting, Bertini's opinion that the illumination of a Sforza MS now in the Bodleian (collection of Viscount Astor of Cliveden A. 6) might be by Moretti; cf. PELLEGRIN, *Supplément* (n. 11, below), pp. 56-57 and pl. 172. G. BOLOGNA, *Miniature lombarde della Biblioteca Trivulziana*, Milano, 1973, p. 69, tentatively assigns him the frontispiece of MS Triv. 514.

[8] BARONI, SAMEK LUDOVICI (n. 7), pp. 65-67. On the Zavattari, see *Il polittico degli Zavattari in Castel Sant'Angelo. Contributi per la pittura tardogotica lombarda*, ed. A. Ghidoli, Firenze, 1984 (bibliography, pp. 153-158, kindly supplied me before I could see the book by the reference librarians at Avery and Butler Libraries, Columbia University); I have been unable to see G. ALGERI, *Gli Zavattari. Una famiglia di pittori e la cultura tardogotica in Lombardia*, Roma, 1981.

[9] BARONI, SAMEK LUDOVICI (n. 7), pp. 107-116. For more recent bibliography, F. MAZZINI, «Bonifacio Bembo», *Dizionario Biografico degli Italiani*, VIII, Roma, 1966, pp. 109-111. Also see n. 13, below.

[10] Cf. TOESCA, *La pittura e la miniatura* (n. 7), pp. 185-186.

[11] E. PELLEGRIN, *La bibliothèque des Visconti et des Sforza, Ducs de Milan. Supplément.* Firenze, Paris, 1969, p. 34 and pl. 109, 110; cf. her *La bibliothèque des Visconti et des Sforza*, Paris, 1955, pp. 388-389. This master and his followers were first identified in 1912: see P. TOESCA, *La pittura e la miniatura* (n. 7), pp. 219-221, pl. 463-473.

[12] TOESCA, *La pittura e la miniatura* (n. 7), p. 185; C. EISLER, Introduction to *The Prayer Book of Michelino da Besozzo*, New York, 1981, p. 9, accepts this, citing a reference by Pier Candido. Decembrio's reference is in fact in his *Vita Philippi Mariae, Tertij Ligurum Ducis*, in *Rerum Italicarum Scriptores*, XX, 1 (above, n. 4), pp. 3-438, at chap. XL, p. 211: «Michelin[us] ... cuius fama inter ceteros etatis sue illustris fuit...». C. MAGENTA, who first points out these references in *La certosa di Pavia*, Milano, 1897, p. 32, n. 2, instead cites chapter

In the same tradition are several well-known miniatures, including the presentation of the *Liber iudiciorum* by Raffaello da Vimercato to Galeazzo Maria Sforza (MS Triv. 1329, from 1461), which Fernanda Wittgens attributes to the circle of the Bembo family.[13] According to Wittgens, one can speak of a school of miniaturists centered around Bonifacio Bembo and active from about 1440 to about 1480 (records of Bembo himself extend to 1477). Furthermore, Letizia Stefani sees in MS Ambrosiana G 40 sup. «una cultura segnata dall'arte di Bonifacio Bembo»,[14] and it is worthy of note that the white vine decoration of this manuscript seems, from her reproduction, to be drawn in a manner closely akin to that of the initials of MSS Urb. lat. 276 and Rich. 23, as described below (and see Figs. 4 and 5). Bembo himself appears as illustrator of three chivalric cycles in a manuscript now of the Biblioteca Nazionale Centrale, Florence,[15] and possibly as the creator of the Este portrait medallions in the manuscript which is now divided between Biblioteca Nazionale Vittorio Emanuele II, MS 293 and Biblioteca Estense, Modena, MS Alpha. L. 5, 16.[16] If these and other attributions made by Salmi are correct, Bembo was in close touch with the Este as well as the Sforza court. He may also have painted the Visconti-Sforza tarot cards, though there is still confusion about attributions to the Zavattari or the Bembo families.[17]

---

XXXIII; he takes Uberto's references from *De Republica*, MS Biblioteca Ambrosiana B 123 [sup.?] (no folio given): «Michaelem Papiensem nostri temporis Pictorem eximium». Cf. TOESCA, p. 185, n. 6.

[13] F. WITTGENS, «La miniatura del Rinascimento», in *Storia di Milano*, ed. G. Treccani degli Alfieri, vol. VII, Milano, 1956, p. 807 (the miniature at p. 808); cf. G. PORRO, *Catalogo dei codici manoscritti della Trivulziana*, Torino, 1884, pp. 455-456; *Biblioteca Trivulziana. Codici miniati del Rinascimento italiano*, ed. C. Santoro, Milano, 1952, pp. 23-24; *I codici medioevali della Biblioteca Trivulziana. Catalogo*, ed. C. Santoro, Milano, 1965, p. 288. On Bembo's work see also note 9, above, and the catalogue, *Arte lombarda dai Visconti agli Sforza. Palazzo Reale, Milano, Aprile-Giugno, 1958*, Milano, 1958 (not the commemorative volume by the same title of 1959), pp. 80-85 and pls. XC-XCIV. I am grateful to the librarians of Boston University's Mugar Memorial Library for allowing me access to this volume.

[14] L. STEFANI, «I codici miniati quattrocenteschi di S. Maria Incoronata», *Arte lombarda*, N.S. 61 (1982), p. 78, and fig. 14 at p. 75.

[15] N. RASMO, «Il codice palatino 556 e le sue illustrazioni», *Rivista d'arte*, XXI (1939), pp. 245-281.

[16] The attribution of the Vittorio Emanuele medallions was made by R. LONGHI, in *Proporzioni*, I, 11 (1950), p. 64 and pl. 24; cf. Bibliothèque Nationale, *Trésors des bibliothèques d'Italie. IVe – XVIe siècles*, Paris, 1950, no. 162 and pl. 13. M. SALMI attributed those of the Modena MS to Bonifacio and an anonymous artist, and considered the two manuscripts to be parts of the same codex in *Commentari*, 4 (1953), pp. 7-10 and figs. 1-7.

[17] See, for the attribution, M. SALMI, *La miniatura italiana*, Milano, 1955, p. 46; cf. G. MOAK-

Also in the Lombard tradition we are following are the coronation by a woman of the poet, Giov. Michele Carrara, in MS Triv. 763, entitled «*Armiranda» acta ludis Megalensibus*,[18] and the three dancers and a harpist of Bibliothèque Nationale MS ital. 973 (fol. 21ᵛ). The latter has been attributed to a follower of the Master of the *Vitae Imperatorum*, the Master of Ippolita [Sforza], who flourished from 1450 to 1465.[19]

I would here suggest that the miniature of Ludovico Gonzaga's arms flanked by angels in MS Urb. lat. 276 is also the work of the Master of Ippolita, who was probably at the height of his activity at the moment of that manuscript's composition in 1460.[20]

While we cannot exclude the possibility that there may have been two artists by the same name, the identification of the Master of Ippolita with Francesco Binasco[21] (who flourished under Ludovico il Moro and his sons Massimo and Francesco[22]) seems to be based on a misreading of Malaguzzi

---

LEY, *The Tarot Cards Painted by B. B. for the Visconti-Sforza Family. An Iconographic and Historical Study*, New York, 1966. On the confusion, M. DUMMETT, *The Visconti-Sforza Tarot Cards*, New York, 1986, pp. 12-13. There is now a facsimile edition of the 78 cards, *I tarocchi dei Visconti*, published by the Accademia Carrara, Bergamo, 1994, with a brief introduction by G. Mandel.

[18] F. MALAGUZZI VALERI, *La corte di Lodovico il Moro*, III, Milano, 1917, pp. 126-128 and fig. 126; cf. PORRO, *Catalogo... Trivulziana* (n. 13), p. 59; *Bib. Triv. Cod. min. del Rin.* (n. 13), p. 21; *I codici medioevali*, p. 186; color reproductions in G. BOLOGNA, *Miniature lombarde* (n. 7, above), p. 42 and C. SANTORO, *I tesori della Trivulziana. La storia del libro dal secolo VIII al secolo XVIII*, Milano, 1962, tav. XIII. Compare the fence in the *Liber iudiciorum* miniature (Triv. 1329) and the fence and two figures in Bib. Nat. MS ital. 561, reproduced in *Dix siècles d'enluminure italienne (VIᵉ - XVIᵉ siècles)*, Paris, Bib. Nat., 1984, no. 127, pp. 146-147, where a Ferrarese influence is alluded to.

[19] The attribution was made by R. CIPRIANI in the 1958 catalogue *Arte lombarda* (n. 13, above), p. 89, and see pp. 89-92, pls. CIV, CVI. Cf. E. PELLEGRIN, *Supplément* (n. 11, above), pp. 40-41, pl. 125; also pp. 44-46 and pls. 122b-124, 126-127, 142-143, 148-149. The dance miniature is also reproduced in the catalogue, *Dix siècles d'enluminure italienne* (n. 18), no. 135, at pp. 153-154; cf. nos. 127, 133-134, 136.

[20] I am grateful to Dr. Albinia de la Mare for urging me to propose this attribution, with which she concurs, and which I would not have otherwise felt able to make on the basis of reproductions and memory.

[21] Hypothesized by CIPRIANI, in *Arte lombarda* (n. 13), p. 89, and accepted, as a hypothesis, by PELLEGRIN, *Supplément* (n. 11), p. 40.

[22] P. WESCHER, «Francesco Binasco», *Dizionario Biografico degli Italiani*, X, Rome, 1968, pp. 487-489; cf. Idem, «F. B. Miniaturmaler der Sforza», *Jahrbuch der Berliner Museen* (=*Jb. der preuss. Kunstsamml. Neue Folge*), II (1960), pp. 75-91, and M. LEVI D'ANCONA, *The Wildenstein Collection of Illuminations. The Lombard School*, Firenze, 1970, pp. 97-105 (cf. review by F. O. BÜTTNER, *Scriptorium*, 28 [1974], pp. 175-177 [B. 309]).

Valeri or his own source, Paolo Morigia, who identified Francesco Binasco as
«favorito e salariato da Francesco Sforza *ultimo duca di Milano di detta
casa*».[23] Gerolamo D'Adda, discussing work done around 1461 for Bianca
Maria Visconti, Francesco I Sforza's wife, confused the issue by referring to
Binasco as «salariato da Francesco Sforza (*sic*) e miniatore ducale [che] fu
maestro di disegno, nella sua gioventù, a Galeazzo Maria Sforza» (citing no
reference for this information).[24] Until further work should disclose his name,
we must be content to refer to the artist as simply the Master of Ippolita.

A glance at the miniature at fol. 4 of the Harvard University MS Richardson 23[25] (Fig. 5) is enough to show this work's affinity to that of the Gonzaga manuscript. Clearly from the same atelier, as examination of the parchment folios confirms, this book was evidently another of Decembrio's of-
ferings in the attempt to secure patronage, this time from Borso d'Este, perhaps also about 1460, when Decembrio sent another text to Borso, though
possibly as late as 1465, when Decembrio was preparing to send a collection
of his works to Borso in a final (and successful) attempt to obtain patronage;[26] the manuscript is not dated externally. This miniature, while executed
more rapidly, is also by the Master of Ippolita or his atelier. Measuring 66 ×
84 mm. in a folio 257 × 168 mm., it is less finely painted than the Gonzaga
miniature. The garments of the two singing angels are shaded in blue-grey,
but the wings are of the same green (above) and rose (below), the halos and
frame are gilded, and the ground is the same cerulean blue. The initials *B O*
for Borso are here painted in white rather than gold (perhaps a reflection of
the Este white [guelf[27]] eagle?). The arms are intermediate between two pat-

---

[23] Italics mine. See P. MORIGIA, *La nobiltà di Milano*, Milano, 1595, p. 283; MALAGUZZI VA-
LERI, *La corte* (n. 18), III, p. 227 (n. 1 from p. 225).

[24] G. D'ADDA, «L'arte del minio» (n. 7 above), p. 552, n. 1.

[25] I thank James Hankins for calling my attention to the manuscript and the staff of Houghton
Library for making it available to me for study. It was pointed out and its contents are
analyzed by P. O. KRISTELLER, «Notes on Decembrio's writings», Appendix III (to ch. 17),
*Studies II* (n. 5, above), pp. 562 and 563. See below nn. 37 ff. See too S. DE RICCI and W. J.
WILSON, *Census of Medieval and Renaissance Manuscripts in the United States and Canada*,
New York, 1935, I, p. 961, and R. S. WIECK, *Late Medieval and Renaissance Illuminated
Manuscripts, 1350-1525, in the Houghton Library*, Cambridge, Mass., 1983, p. 115 and Fig.
56. There is now an ongoing catalogue by L. LIGHT, *Catalogue of Medieval and Renaissance
Manuscripts in the Houghton Library, Harvard University*, Binghamton, N.Y., 1995-.

[26] Cf. BORSA, «P.C.D.» (n. 1), pp. 401, 409.

[27] See A. SPAGGIARI and G. TRENTI, *Gli stemmi estensi ed austro-estensi. Profilo storico*, Modena, 1985, p. 26, n. 17. I am grateful to Lewis Lockwood for this reference, and for allowing me to consult his copy of the book.

terns revealed by an incomplete survey. These are: quartered, with three fleurs-de-lys (2 and 1) in 1 and 4, and white, single-headed Este eagles in 2 and 3 (this being the original sign of Marchese Rinaldo, ca. 1168);[28] or quartered, with black imperial two-headed eagles in 1 and 4, the three fleurs-de-lys in 2 and 3, and a shield with a white or silver single-headed eagle at the center.[29] The condition of the lower right quadrant of the coat of arms is poor, and the design (probably a white eagle) on the central shield has been obliterated.[30] Here and there in the whole, red and other underpainting shows through.

Also like those of the Gonzaga manuscript are this book's decorated initials: compare here the *C* in Urb. lat. 276 and the *A* in Rich. 23. The white vine twines in a similar pattern about the two gilt initials, and the blue, green and red ground extends outward in a foliate contour at the corners. A similarly decorated *V* (6 lines) occurs at fol. 22$^v$. The last two decorated letters, *S* (4 lines) at fol. 55 and *R* (5 lines) at fol. 83$^v$, are framed without these extensions, but otherwise the drawing (especially delicate in the white-vine tendrils) of all decorated initials in both manuscripts is the same.[31] Colored two-line majuscule letters, alternately red and blue and like those throughout MS Urb. lat. 276, begin chapters in the second and fourth works in the manuscript. There is even an indication of the *H*-like *M* found at some folios of Urb. lat. 276, but it is here corrected by erasure of the red cross-bar and addition of a *v* in brown ink (fol. 86$^v$).[32]

MS Rich. 23, like MS Urb. lat. 276, is a quarto manuscript written in a clear (though different) humanistic hand. It is composed of 98 very fine parchment folios, of which the first two are stitched separately, evidently (like fol. 98) having once been end-leaves, as is seen from the glue adhering to fols. 1$^r$ and 98$^v$. The third folio has been shorn of its first half and also stitched separately; the remaining 95 are sewn in eleven gatherings of eight folios and a twelfth of seven. Endleaves are now paper. The white vellum binding is identified as 18$^{th}$ century Italian in the sales catalogue entry pasted

[28] Cf. C. MANARESI, «Aquila araldica», *Enciclopedia Italiana*, III, 1929, p. 796.
[29] See SPAGGIARI and TRENTI, *Gli stemmi* (n. 27), pl. III, nos. 3 and 4.
[30] The heraldic inconsistencies, including the lack of the silver toothed edging around the fleurs-de-lys normally obligatory for non-members of the French royal house, are in keeping with Cipriani's characterization of the Master of Ippolita as «Maestro dell'araldica [che] si vale di tutti gli accorgimenti coloristici di Belbello senza intenderne il senso...»: *Arte lombarda* (n. 13, above), p. 89.
[31] Compare the frontispiece of MS Ambrosiana G 40 sup. mentioned above, and see n. 14.
[32] See my *Das Tierbuch* (n. 3), p. 67.

on the first end-paper.[33] All 98 parchment folios are numbered in pencil in a European hand in the lower right-hand corner. (Three folios, 23, 55 and 83, that is, those at or opposite the beginning of a work, are numbered in pencil in the upper right-hand corner, 20, 52 and 80, respectively, this count having been begun at the first folio of text, the present fol. 4). As in Urb. lat. 276, some signatures, also in the lower right-hand corners of folios, have not been cut off in binding. These are portions of signatures *a, b, c, d, e,* and *f.* Interestingly, the gatherings with consecutive signatures are not consecutively, but symmetrically, distributed in the manuscript. Signatures *a, b, c, d* appear in gatherings 3 through 6; signatures *e* and *f* in gatherings 11 and 12. Thus there are two quires without signatures, four with, four without and two with. This may indicate that these quires were prepared for use in another book, but instead supplemented with others for the preparation of the present codex, or there may be a more interesting codicological explanation. Signatures *a* and *e* begin with *aij* and *eij* respectively. *Punctoria* for ruling left and right margins are visible at the bottom of some folios, as in MS Urb. lat. 276. The margins thus prepared (ruled in silverpoint with two lines 5.5 mm. apart on the smooth side of the parchment) divide the folio (76), measured on its *recto*, thus: 27 + 5.5 + 83 + 5.5 + 48 mm. Thirty horizontal lines (29 written), also 5.5 mm. apart, are ruled on each folio in light red ink. (Urb. lat. 276, written in a larger script, has 25 lines [24 written] per folio, 7 mm. apart.). Top and bottom margins are 32 and 66 mm.

As in MS Urb. lat. 276, Decembrio has added final touches, marginally rubricating the first text (to fol. 19ᵛ), correcting the scribe throughout the manuscript in margins and occasionally in the text, adding one or two majuscule titles (fols. 55, 83) and the subscription (fol. 97ᵛ), and supplying two tables of contents (fol. 1ᵛ, in minuscule in his normal brown ink, and fol. 3ᵛ, with the title and dedication, in majuscule in red ink).[34] MS Rich. 23 thus becomes a valuable testimonial to his wishes for the texts at a fairly late date. His table of contents at fol. 3ᵛ reads:

OPVSCVLA .P. CANDIDI QVE IN HOC CODICE CONTI
NENTVR · ET ILLVSTRISSIMO PRINCIPI · DOMINO.
BORSIO · DVCI MVTINE INSCRIBVNTVR.

---

[33] This is an entry from Catalogue 16 of J. Martini, May, 1920, no. 10 at pp. 7-8. The manuscript was acquired from this dealer by W. K. Richardson, and bequeathed to Harvard University in 1951. WIECK, *Late Medieval and Renaissance* (n. 25), p. 115, terms the binding 17th century.

[34] A description of Pier Candido Decembrio's hand is in Chapter II, above and in my *Das Tierbuch* (n. 6), pp. 62-66.

DE LAVDIBVS VRBIS MEDIOLANENSIS
DE VITA PHILIPPI MARIE TERCII MEDIOLANEÑ · DVCIS
DE REBVS GESTIS A NICOLAO PICENINO.
DE HISTORIA ROMANA EPITOMA · AD REGEM.

Three of these four historical works are edited in the recent edition of *Rerum Italicarum Scriptores* and in Muratori's original compendium (though here two are in translation, one of these being a fragment).[35] The fourth, *De Historia Romana Epitoma* is a compilation and reworking of a text by Pier Candido's father, Uberto, as the younger humanist says early in the text: «Regum Consulum Imperatorum Romanorumque ducu(m) res gestas ac nomina, quibus populus Romanus per annos septingentos ab urbe condita usque ad Augustum Cesarem orbem subegit, hoc brevi opusculo *dei(n)ceps* [P.C.D. hand] scribere institui, ut labili admodum memorie exiguo compendio subveniri queat. Nam cum a patre meo minus polite q(uam) imperfecte huius modi historia confecta esset, sumpsi onus nove scriptionis». (MS Rich. 23, fol. 83ᵛ).[36] This text occurs only in manuscript.[37] All four texts predate

---

[35] *Rerum Italicarum Scriptores*, 1925 (n. 4, above), XX, 1: *Vita Philippi Mariae* is at pp. 3-438; *Panegyricus P. Candidi in Funere Illustris Nicolai Picenini ad Cives Mediolanenses* is at pp. 991-1009; *De Laudibus Mediolanensis Urbis Panegyricus* is at pp. 1013-1025. MURATORI (n. 4), XX, Milano, 1731: *Vita Philippi Mariae* is at cols. 985-1020; *Oratio...in Funere Nicolai Picinini* is at cols. 1051-1084 in the Italian translation of «Polismagna» (whom D. FAVA equates with Carlo di San Giorgio: *La Biblioteca Estense nel suo sviluppo storico. Con il catalogo della mostra permanente e 10 tavole*, Modena, 1925, p. 55); a fragment of *De Laudibus Mediolani* is at cols. 1085-1090 in Italian. *Vita Phil. Mar.* now appears in a modern Italian translation by E. Bartolini, based on the 1925 edition (though seemingly taking no account of the Este MS translation referred to below, n. 42): P. C. D., *Vita di Filippo Maria Visconti*, Milano, 1983, as well as that in German by P. Funk: P. C. D., *Leben des Filippo Maria Visconti und Taten des Franzesco Sforza*, Jena, 1913.

[36] V. ZACCARIA («Sulle opere di P. C. D.», *Rinascimento*, VII [1956], pp. 13-74; henceforth ZACCARIA) mentions an interesting marginal note in the Madrid codex containing this text (Bib. Univ. Cent., cod. 129, found by P. O. Kristeller): «Mentiris. Nam pater tuus hoc epitoma egregie conscripsit, nondum autem ediderat; tu vero postea tuum opus esse dixisti, nephandissime paterne glorie contaminator et latro». The hand of this note must be studied; Francesco Filelfo, Decembrio's rival and a likely candidate, is known to have made such comments in his works: cf. E. GARIN in *Storia di Milano*, VII (n. 13), p. 544, n. Zaccaria does not say opposite which passage the note appears, but it is likely to be opposite the opening sentences, quoted above.

[37] Six of the nine other manuscripts are listed by ZACCARIA (n. 36), p. 29: Ambros. G 98 sup., fols. 41-49; Ferrara, Bib. Com. II 66 N.A. 2, fols. 1-16ᵛ; Paris, B. N. [Latin] 9683, fols. 59-70; Stuttgart, Hist. 4to. 152, fols. 78-89; Florence, Riccard. 1206, fols. 53-60; Madrid, Bib. Univ. Cent. 129 (folios not given). KRISTELLER, «Notes» (n. 25, above), p. 563, adds (besides the Richardson MS): Munich, Clm 10296; New York, Pierpont Morgan Library, M

1460: *De Laudibus Urbis Mediolanensis* (fols. 4-22ᵛ in MS Rich. 23) is thought to be from 1435-1436;[38] *De Vita Philippi Mariae* (fols. 22ᵛ-55) is from 1447;[39] *De Rebus Gestis a Nicolao Picenino* (fols. 55-83) dates from 1444, the year of Piccinino's death,[40] and *De Historia Romana Epitoma* (fols 83-97ᵛ) is dedicated to King Alphonse of Aragon and dated about 1450 by Zaccaria.[41]

The same four texts are found in Italian translation in Modena, Biblioteca Estense, MS ital. 99 (alpha. P. 6,9).[42] The possibility thus arises that these translations were made from MS Rich. 23, especially since the trans-

---

425; Madrid, Biblioteca de Palacio, MS 94. The 1495 inventory of Ercole I's library lists an «Epitomatum petri candidi in latino coperto de brasilio stampato» (G. BERTONI, *La biblioteca estense e la coltura ferrarese ai tempi del duca Ercole I [1471-1505]*, Torino, 1903, Append. II², p. 240, no. 154). It is not clear to which known MS, if any, or even to which work this corresponds. P. O. Kristeller informs me that the University of Wisconsin Library MS 162 (formerly Phillipps 8074) contains at fols. 1-18ᵛ Decembrio's *Romanae historiae brevis epitoma* with a preface to Alphonsus.

[38] ZACCARIA (n. 36), pp. 21-22, 65, and Idem, «P. C. D. and Leonardo Bruni (Notizie dall'epistolario del Decembrio)», *Studi medievali*, ser. III, vol. VIII (1967), pp. 504-554, esp. pp. 520-527, accepts the dating of G. Petraglione, who edited the text with an introduction in *Archivio storico lombardo*, 34 (ser. IV, 8: 1907), pp. 5-45 (text at pp. 27-45; henceforth PETRAGLIONE). This edition is that printed, with minor changes, in 1958 in *Rerum Italicarum Scriptores*, XX, 1, pp. 1013-1025. Petraglione's edition is based on the only previously known manuscript, Milan, Ambr. Z 167 sup., which he dates tentatively, with Novati, at 1473 (p. 25). Muratori, on the other hand, dates the text itself at 1431 (cols. 1085-1086), giving no justification.

[39] ZACCARIA (n. 36), pp. 28, 66. The list of manuscripts precedes the text in *Rerum Italicarum Scriptores*, XX, 1 (n. 4, above), p. 2, and is given more fully by KRISTELLER, «Notes» (n. 25, above), pp. 562-563: MSS Maggi (present location unknown); Milan, Ambr., Trotti 418 and G S VI 4 (now Sussidio B 173); Trivulziana, 104 and 1273; Florence, Laur. Ashb. 1659; Rome, Bibl. Naz., Sessor. 413; Paris, Bib. Nat., Nouv. acq. lat. 846. Kristeller adds, besides the Richardson MS, Madrid, Bib. de la Universidad, 129.

[40] ZACCARIA (n. 36), pp. 27-28, 66. Zaccaria mentions Bologna, Bib. Univ., 12 II 7. Kristeller («Notes» [n. 25], p. 562) adds a second manuscript used in the 1958 edition: Paris, Bib. Ste. Geneviève, 2395, containing a preface to John II of Castille; and, again, the Richardson MS.

[41] ZACCARIA (n. 36), pp. 28-29, 66. This text had been attributed to Boccaccio, an attribution corrected by Hortis and Bertalot, as Zaccaria points out, p. 28, n. 5. On the manuscripts, see n. 35, above.

[42] KRISTELLER, «Notes» (n. 25), p. 563. FAVA, *La Biblioteca Estense* (n. 35, above), p. 55, lists only the *Vita di Filippo Maria* and *Gesti di Niccolò Piccinino*, translated, as in Muratori's original edition, by «Polismagna» (Carlo di San Giorgio: n. 35), whose hand Fava recognizes in the Modena manuscript. Fava states (pp. 177-178) that Muratori took the Italian *Vita di Niccolò Piccinino* (cols. 1050-1084) from the Modena manuscript.

lator, «Polismagna» (Carlo di San Giorgio), states in his preface to Borso d'Este (printed in Muratori, p. 1049) that he has worked «seguendo adunque l'opera per Candido a te mandata». However, there could have been an intermediary draft, now lost or not yet identified, as in the case of *De Animantium Naturis* as it was first sent to Ludovico Gonzaga for his approval. [43]

The relatively late date (1460-1465) we can assign to MS Rich. 23, based on codicological comparison with MS Urb. lat. 276 and on events in the life of Decembrio, coupled with the presence of the author's autograph corrections and additions to the codex at such a late date, render the Este manuscript a valuable witness for these four texts. Decembrio's corrected text, when studied, may give us, in effect, a mature version of texts written ten to thirty years earlier, and must now be collated with editions, where these exist, and with other manuscripts where they do not.

In the case of *De Laudibus Urbis Mediolanensis*, Decembrio's response to Leonardo Bruni's *Laudatio Urbis Florentiae*, MS Rich. 23 is even more significant. The only other manuscript of the Latin text is MS Ambr. Z 167 sup., which is thought to date from 1473 (as above, n. 38). It is on this manuscript that the modern edition is based. Here, Rich. 23 supplies us with an earlier version (though still intermediate if the dating of the text at 1435-1436 is correct) of Decembrio's Latin text, in which he attributes the exhortatory speech at the battle of Cremona near the end of the text (fols. 20-20$^v$) to Niccolò Piccinino, and not to Francesco Sforza. That the change had been made was known, for Polismagna's Italian translation also attributes the speech to Piccinino, but no copy of this Latin version was known. Decembrio changed the attribution to regain favor with Francesco's son, Galeazzo Maria, at a time of need. [44] Nor does Rich. 23 include the final sentence addressed to Galeazzo Maria and present in the 1473(?) Latin text (but not in Polismagna's Italian). [45] The title in Rich. 23 (Fig. 5) is not significantly different, and does not here echo Bruni's title as Petraglione conjectured it might have in the original version. [46]

MS Rich. 23 is furthermore valuable as clear evidence, taken with MS Urb. lat. 276, of the work of a mid-fifteenth century Milanese atelier active in producing (given the close similarity of the two miniatures, one is tempted to say «mass-producing») presentation copies of humanist texts. The atelier

---

[43] Cf. my *Das Tierbuch* (n. 6, above), pp. 57-58.
[44] PETRAGLIONE (n. 38, above), pp. 23, 25.
[45] Cf. PETRAGLIONE (n. 38), p. 23.
[46] PETRAGLIONE (n. 38), p. 25.

of the Master of the *Vitae Imperatorum* (thought to have been an Olivetan monk, fl. 1427-1447[47]) is known to have executed work for humanists including Pier Candido Decembrio.[48] It is not impossible that the Master of Ippolita was still working within this atelier or its continuation. Probably, however, the schools around the Bembo family and the Master of Ippolita were by this time distinct. Further codicological study of the production of these and similar manuscripts (types of *punctoria* and ruling, pigments, copyists employed) will help us to determine the distinguishing features and the extent of the different ateliers' production.

Fig. 4. Maestro d'Ippolita. The Arms of Ludovico Gonzaga, MS Urb. lat. 276, fol. 1.

Fig. 5. Workshop of the Maestro d'Ippolita. The Arms of Borso d'Este, MS Rich. 23, fol. 1.

---

[47] See CIPRIANI in *Arte lombarda dai Visconti agli Sforza* (n. 13, above), pp. 65-68 and tav. LXXVI-LXXIX. And see n. 11, above.

[48] PELLEGRIN, *Supplément* (n. 11, above), pp. 37-38. (It should be noted that the 1966 edition of TOESCA [n. 7], p. 220, n. 2 gives the shelf-mark of the Verona Bib. Capitolare Plutarch as CCXXIX, rather than CCXXXIX (200) as in PELLEGRIN and in P. O. KRISTELLER, *Iter Italicum*, II, London-Leiden, 1967, p. 296).

# PART III
*Court and Culture in Quattrocento Milan*

# CHAPTER IV

## Towards the Biography of Gaspar Ambrogio Visconti

Gaspar Ambrogio Visconti[1] (1461-1499) was a principal figure in the Italy of his time, especially in the Milanese court of Ludovico Sforza, il Moro. He is known to us as playwright and poet, and as something of an amateur philosopher.[2] He was respected and befriended by such men as Donato Bramante and Piattino Piatti,[3] and by fellow literati in Milan. Gaspare

---

[1] I find him referred to most often in manuscripts, documents and printed editions as *Gaspar* or *Guaspar*, with or without Ambrogio. In Latin too the form is usually *Gaspar*. The modern form of his name, *Gaspare*, was used by the 19th and early 20th century historians. The form *Gasparo* has recently been adopted by a number of critics and editors. This and *Gasparro* are substantiated by the edition of *De Paulo e Daria Amanti* (1495) cited below (n. 41), *sig.* a iiiʳ and a iiiᵛ, *sig.* m iʳ and m iᵛ. The remarkable collection of documents concerning the sculptor and architect Amadeo includes the transcription of an Italian version of document 1806; in this transcription the form *Gaspare* is used; I have not seen the document. See: *Giovanni Antonio Amadeo. Documents / I documenti*, eds. R. V. Schofield, J. Schell, G. Sironi, Milano, 1989, p. 414.

[2] A biographical and literary study was given us by R. RENIER: «Gaspare Visconti», *Archivio storico lombardo*, ser. 2, vol. XIII (1886), pp. 509-562, 777-824. See too: C. M. PYLE, *Politian's «Orfeo» and Other «Favole Mitologiche» in the Context of Late Quattrocento Northern Italy*, dissertation, Columbia University, New York, 1976, pp. 19-33, and chapters V, VIII and XI, below. On Visconti's language and poetry, P. BONGRANI, «La poesia lirica alla corte di Ludovico il Moro», in *Milano nell'età di Ludovico il Moro. Atti del convegno internazionale, 28 febbraio – 4 marzo 1983*, 2 vols., Milano, 1983, pp. 215-229 (reprinted in his *Lingua e letteratura a Milano nell'età sforzesca. Una raccolta di studi*, Parma, 1986, pp. 37-65).

[3] P. MALAGUZZI VALERI, *La corte di Lodovico il Moro*, 4 vols., Milano, 1913-1923, II, pp. 136,

was a favorite of Beatrice d'Este Sforza, Ludovico's wife from 1491 to 1497, dedicating his poems to her in a manuscript recently published.[4] But his biography has been rendered extremely difficult by the fact that in Northern Italy there were eight Gaspari Visconti contemporary with him, and five others near enough or known enough to be easily confused with him. (See Appendix I, below). This essay aims to clarify some biographical points and to publish a modern edition of an overlooked letter to him from another member of the same circle, Giovanni II Tolentino (Appendix II, below).[5]

Gaspare Visconti was descended from a distinguished branch of the former ruling family of Milan. The members of his line were Counts of Arona, Breme and Groppello, *Signori* of Cassano Magnago in Seprio and Visano in the Bresciano, and several were *Podestà* and *Commissari* of Bergamo, Cremona, Brescia and Monza at various times in the course of the fourteenth and fifteenth centuries. His line, with its numerous Gaspari, can be reconstructed from the several sources available (Fig. 6).[6]

The poet's line was of an extraordinary resilience politically. His great-grandfather (see below, Appendix I, no. 9), the Ghibelline statesman, diplomat, and Knight of the Garter Gaspare Visconti (mid-14th century – ca. 1434), lived a long and politically active life under no fewer than five Visconti rulers of Milan: the brothers Galeazzo and Bernabò, the first duke, Giangaleazzo, Duke Giovanni Maria, and Duke Filippo Maria. He was ambassador to the Council of Constance in 1415, to Savona in 1422, to Monferrato in 1428 and to the Emperor Sigismund in 1431. His last will dates from 1434.

---

231-236. Cf. A. BRUSCHI, «Donato Bramante», *Dizionario Biografico degli Italiani*, 13, Roma, 1971, pp. 712-725; G. SIRONI, «Gli affreschi di Donato D'Angelo detto il Bramante alla Pinacoteca di Brera di Milano: chi ne fu il committente?» *Archivio storico lombardo*, ser. X, vol. IV (1978), pp. 199-207; and on Piatti, A. SIMIONI, «Un umanista milanese, Piattino Piatti», *Archivio storico lombardo*, ser. 4, vol. II (1904), pp. 21, 277, 284, 289.

[4] G. VISCONTI, *I canzonieri per Beatrice d'Este e per Bianca Maria Sforza*, ed. P. Bongrani, Milano, 1979.

[5] The letter is edited from IOANNIS TOLLENTI- / NATIS.II.EQVI- / TIS:EPISTO- / LARVM / LIBRI / .III. Milano, 1512, extant in a copy (one of only two know to me) at the British Library. On Giovanni II Tolentino: Carlo MARCORA, «I Commentarii di Giovanni II Tolentino», *Archivio storico lombardo*, XC (1963), 330-339, and chapters VI and VII, below.

[6] The principal source is P. LITTA, *Famiglie celebri italiane* (and variants on this title), Milano, 1819-1902, Vol. I, Fascicolo 9, s.v. «Visconti di Milano», Tables II, X, XI, XIII. The fascicles are variously bound. Other sources are those mentioned throughout this article. The poet's daughter Faustina, evidently twin to the son Paolo, is added from a note on fol. I of MS Triv. 1093.

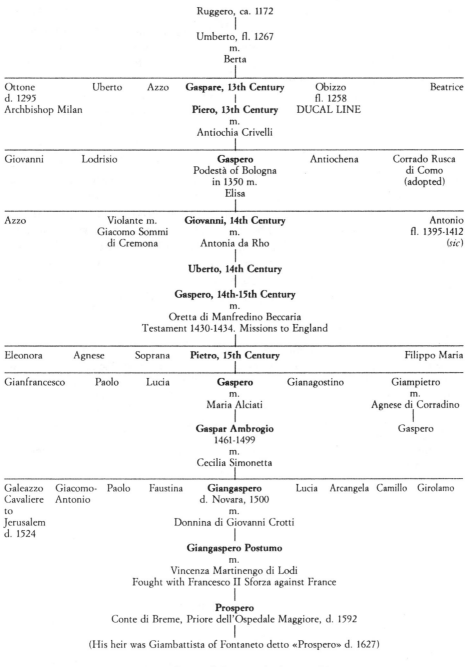

Ruggero, ca. 1172
|
Umberto, fl. 1267
m.
Berta
|

| Ottone | Uberto | Azzo | **Gaspare, 13th Century** | Obizzo | Beatrice |
| d. 1295 | | | **Piero, 13th Century** | fl. 1258 | |
| Archbishop Milan | | | m. | DUCAL LINE | |
| | | | Antiochia Crivelli | | |

| Giovanni | Lodrisio | **Gaspero** | Antiochena | Corrado Rusca |
| | | Podestà of Bologna | | di Como |
| | | in 1350 m. | | (adopted) |
| | | Elisa | | |

| Azzo | Violante m. | **Giovanni, 14th Century** | Antonio |
| | Giacomo Sommi | m. | fl. 1395-1412 |
| | di Cremona | Antonia da Rho | (*sic*) |

**Uberto, 14th Century**

**Gaspero, 14th-15th Century**
m.
Oretta di Manfredino Beccaria
Testament 1430-1434. Missions to England

| Eleonora | Agnese | Soprana | **Pietro, 15th Century** | Filippo Maria |

| Gianfrancesco | Paolo | Lucia | **Gaspero** | Gianagostino | Giampietro |
| | | | m. | | m. |
| | | | Maria Alciati | | Agnese di Corradino |
| | | | | | |
| | | | **Gaspar Ambrogio** | | Gaspero |
| | | | 1461-1499 | | |
| | | | m. | | |
| | | | Cecilia Simonetta | | |

| Galeazzo | Giacomo- | Paolo | Faustina | **Giangaspero** | Lucia | Arcangela | Camillo | Girolamo |
| Cavaliere | Antonio | | | d. Novara, 1500 | | | | |
| to | | | | m. | | | | |
| Jerusalem | | | | Donnina di Giovanni Crotti | | | | |
| d. 1524 | | | | | | | | |

**Giangaspero Postumo**
m.
Vincenza Martinengo di Lodi
Fought with Francesco II Sforza against France

**Prospero**
Conte di Breme, Priore dell'Ospedale Maggiore, d. 1592

(His heir was Giambattista of Fontaneto detto «Prospero» d. 1627)

Fig. 6. Genealogy of Gaspar Ambrogio Visconti.

He is buried in Sant'Eustorgio. [7] This man's son, Pietro (d. 1461), was invested with Gropello (Pavia), Breme (Lomellina) and Visano (Brescia) by Filippo Maria Visconti. After serving in the short-lived Republican government of Milan (1447-1450), Pietro joined forces with the Sforza at the opportune moment and was selected to place the ducal cap upon Francesco Sforza's head in 1450. He was invested by Francesco with Cassano Magnago (Seprio) sometime before his death in 1461. [8]

On the day in which Francesco Sforza took possession of Milan in 1450, he created Pietro's son, Gaspare, *cavaliere*. With this title, the elder Gaspare, our poet's father (Appendix I, no. 1), became *siniscalco*, a high functionary in the service of Francesco's son, Galeazzo Maria Sforza. This Gaspare was among the knights who went to Ferrara in 1452 to honor the Emperor Frederick III – the very occasion on which Frederick created the infant Niccolò da Correggio *cavaliere*. The poet and courtier Niccolò was to become one of our poet's closest associates, the dedicatee of his printed poetic works, and a favorite of Isabella d'Este Gonzaga, Beatrice d'Este Sforza's sister. [9] Gaspare Senior eventually also became *consigliere ducale*, and he was invested in 1470 with Breme in the Lomellina (West of Pavia). [10]

---

[7] The monument is depicted in Litta between «Visconti», Tavv. XII and XIII or, depending on the binding, after Tav. XIII; it is described in detail and a brief biography given in M. CAFFI, *Della chiesa di Sant'Eustorgio in Milano*, Milano, 1841, pp. 38-40.

[8] LITTA, «Visconti», Tav. XIII. C. SANTORO, *Gli offici del comune di Milano e del Dominio Visconteo-sforzesco (1216-1515)*, Milano, 1968 (hereafter: SANTORO, 1968) confirms Litta's mention of his position as *Commissario ducale* in Cremona in 1440, in an entry on p. 324. The appointment runs from December 30, 1439 to May 24, 1440; thus the appointment of a Pietro Visconti as *Commissario* of Brescia beginning on May 24, 1440 (her p. 287) refers in all probability to the same man, who is here described as: «Camerario e affine del Duca». Santoro's source is of general interest here: G. VITTANI, «Gli atti cancellereschi viscontei» in *Inventari e regesti del Regio Archivio di Stato in Milano*, II, part 1, Milano, 1920 (documents 460 and 620). Santoro also lists a Petrus Vicecomes as Capitano of the Citadella Alessandria as of May 19, 1450: C. SANTORO, *Gli uffici del dominio sforzesco (1450-1500)*, Milano, 1948 (hereafter: SANTORO, 1948), p. 673. This could argue for a relationship between the Visconti and Taccone families prior to the poets' friendship (cf. chapter VI, below).

[9] For the life and works of Niccolò da Correggio: A. ARATA, *Niccolò da Correggio*, Bologna, 1934; N. DA CORREGGIO, *Opere*, ed. A. Tissoni Benvenuti, Bari, 1969 (Scrittori d'Italia, No. 244); PYLE, *Politian's 'Orfeo'* (n. 2), pp. 10-19, cf. pp. 262-328.

[10] LITTA, «Visconti», Tav. XIII. This is disputed by Ettore Verga who reports the testament of the father, Gaspare di Pietro, as extant in the Archivio del Duomo in Milan (he gives no location), and states that he died in 1462, «lasciando il nostro ancor bambino sotto la tutela della madre Margherita Alzati, o quando questa non volesse o non potesse accettare, sotto quella del proprio fratello Giampietro...»: E. VERGA, «Per la storia degli schiavi orientali in Milano», *Archivio storico lombardo*, ser. 4, vol. IV (1905), pp. 188-195, p. 193. LITTA, «Vi-

The poet Gaspar Ambrogio was born to Gaspare Visconti and Margherita Alzati or Alciati in the year of his grandfather Pietro's death, 1461. [11] At his birth he bore the relatively distinctive, and for a Milanese appropriate, name Ambrogio. We have Duke Francesco Sforza to thank for the tremendous difficulty in defining his biography, for it was by ducal order that he was renamed Gaspar Ambrogio – and to our distress more often than not called simply Gaspar. [12] Thus it is that our poet has retained so large a measure of privacy from historians working in successive centuries.

---

sconti», Tav. XIII, reports the poet's father alive in 1470. If Verga were right, the poet Gaspare would be the one invested with Breme in that year. Perhaps 1462 was the year of Gaspare Senior's testament, rather than his demise. Renier («Gaspare Visconti», p. 522 n. 1) believed a document of 1478 conferring on a Gaspare Visconti the «divisione caligarum albi et morelli coloris» (the ducal device) referred to the father of the poet, but he was writing before Verga, who claimed proof that Giampietro, the elder Gaspare's brother, was Gaspar Ambrogio's guardian at least from 1472 (pp. 193-194 and see below and Appendix I).

[11] G. A. SASSI, *Historia Literario-Tipographica Mediolanensis ab anno MCDLXV ad annum MD* in *Philippi Argelati ... Bibliotheca Scriptorum Mediolanensium*, 2 vols. in 4 parts, Milano, 1745, vol. I, part 1, col. CCCLXI, says: «anno MCCCCIC. tumulo datus», and Argelati himself (*Bibliotheca*, II, 1, col. 1604) gives the date of his death as March 8, 1499, at the age of 38. From this we must work backwards to find the year of his birth, although we have no positive confirmation of the date. E. MOTTA, «Morti in Milano dal 1452 al 1552. (Spogli del necrologio milanese)». *Archivio storico lombardo*, XVIII (1891), pp. 241-290, notes the lacuna in the *necrologio* for the year 1499, pp. 271-272. LITTA, «Visconti», Tav. XIII, writing in the 19th century, says: «Morì di 38 anni nel 1499, ed un *Castiglioni* domenicano recitò in S. Eustorgio la sua orazione funebre». However, P. O. Kristeller has pointed out to me that the Dominican of the Castiglioni family is Gioacchino Castiglioni Marcanova, who died around the year 1472 (see L. GARGAN, *Lo studio teologico e la biblioteca dei domenicani a Padova nel Tre e Quattrocento*, Padova, 1971 [Contributi alla storia dell'Università di Padova, no. 6], pp. 76-83). This man wrote numerous funeral sermons; an article by T. VERANI («Notizie del P.M. Giovacchino Castiglioni Milanese dell'ordine de' PP. Predicatori tratte da due Codici del Secolo XV», *Nuovo Giornale de' letterati d'Italia*, 43 [Modena, 1790], pp. 71-176), referred to by Gargan, p. 76, n. 2, lists funeral orations given by Castiglioni between 1454 and 1465. Verani's number 8 (p. 93) is in fact «In funeris G.V.» It is difficult to sort out the error: the poet's great-grandfather Gaspare made his testament at an old age in 1434 (CAFFI, n. 7 above) and probably died soon after; the poet's grandfather did die in 1461, but his name was Pietro; as we have seen, the poet's father Gaspare is said by Litta to have been invested with Breme in 1470, and his brother is first noted as the poet's guardian in 1472, so the father probably did die about 1470. Unfortunately, Litta does not give specific sources for each point, but offers a critical bibliography in Tav. I and occasional references *passim*.

[12] P. MORIGIA, *Historia dell'antichità di Milano*, Venezia, 1592 (reprint, Bologna, 1967), p. 592, and Idem, *La Nobiltà di Milano Descritta dal R. P. F. Paolo Morigi De' Gesuati di San Girolamo ...*, Milano, Gio. Battista Bidelli, 1619, pp. 269-270.

Gaspar Ambrogio, then, was educated by Guidotto de' Prestinari of Bergamo, under whom he studied Greek, Latin and possibly Hebrew, [13] while at the same time devoting himself to music and vernacular poetry:

> Egli è la verità che mi diletto,
> per che mi spiace de marcir nel ozio,
> d'alontanarmi da ogni vil negozio,
> e sòno e leggo e fo qualche sonetto. [14]

There are several notices usually assigned to the poet's early years which probably refer to his father. For example, Litta places the poet among the deputies in 1470 at a «giuramento di fedeltà», presumably to Duke Galeazzo Maria Sforza (1466-1476), when the poet was nine years old (calculating from Argelati's statement of his death at 38). [15] If Gaspar Ambrogio's father was already dead, the boy's participation as representative of his branch of the family would seem appropriate; if not, the question is moot, and the reference is to his father. Rodolfo Renier disputed this notice on the sole basis that at nine the boy would have been too young to participate in such a ceremony. However, regardless of whether or not the father is referred to, the argument on the basis of age cannot be upheld, judging from the youth of the participants in state functions, including marriage, at that time.

Paolo Morigia describes the poet as «Cavaliere Consigliere di Galeazzo Sforza quinto duca di Milano», that is, counsellor to Duke Galeazzo Maria. [16] This would certainly put him at an unusually young age for a counsellor (between 1466 and 1476, when Galeazzo Maria was assassinated, Gaspar Ambrogio was between 5 and 15 years old), and the notice is not supported by Caterina Santoro's more recent research. [17] The notice of a Gaspare *consigliere* at any time before 1478 when the poet turned seventeen and was in fact named *consigliere ducale*, if it were substantiated in documents, would indeed cast doubt on the death of the father even as early as 1470. As it is, however, this must be a confusion on the part of Morigia between the poet and an older nearly contemporary Gaspare, or even a mistake in identi-

---

[13] (MICHAUD), *Biographie universelle ancienne et moderne*, nouvelle édition, Leipzig, s.a., Vol. XLIII, pp. 624-625, *s.v.* «Gaspard Visconti».

[14] RENIER «G.V.», p. 516 n. 1, quotes from F. ZANOTTO, *Lirici del secolo primo, secondo e terzo cioè dal 1190 al 1500*, Venezia, 1846. This is vol. 11 of the 12-vol. *Parnaso italiano* edited by Zanotto, Venezia, G. Antonelli, 1833-51. I have not seen the volume.

[15] LITTA, «Visconti», Tav. XIII.

[16] MORIGIA, *Historia* (n. 12), p. 592 and Idem, *Nobiltà* (n. 12), pp. 269-270.

[17] SANTORO 1948 (n. 8).

fying the current regime. Renier believed that Morigia had confused Galeazzo Maria with Giangaleazzo, *sixth* duke of Milan. [18]

In April, 1472 Giampietro Visconti, who assumed the responsibility of his nephew Gaspar Ambrogio's affairs after the death of the latter's father, drew up a document with Cicco Simonetta and his wife Elisabetta Visconti; this was the promise of their daughter Cecilia to the young Ambrogio as soon as the two should reach «l'età legittima». And the two were married, probably at a fairly young age. [19] This action on the part of Giampietro is a strong argument for the death of the father before 1472, but not necessarily earlier than 1470. At seventeen the poet was indeed created *consigliere ducale* on the day in 1478 in which the ducal vestments were conferred upon Giangaleazzo Sforza, Sixth Duke of Milan, whose rule was to be usurped by his uncle Ludovico il Moro. In this year too, the division of properties in Gaspar Ambrogio's family brought him the *Signoria* of Cassano Magnago in Seprio, a town still visible on the map to the north of Milan. [20]

In 1483 «Senator» Gaspar Ambrogio (as members of the *Consigli* could

---

[18] RENIER, «G.V.», p. 515. However, the fact that the words «Galeazzo Sforza quinto Duca di Milano» occur twice, and in two repetitious but very distinct works by the sixteenth century historian Morigia does not support a theory of confusion in naming the ruler of the time. It must be mentioned nevertheless that the error of calling Giangaleazzo «Galeazzo Maria» is not unheard of elsewhere; it is even committed by Renier himself at p. 522, n. 1, when he states that Galeazzo Maria (who was assassinated in 1476) bestowed the ducal insignia on Gaspare in 1478. G. GIULINI, *Memorie spettanti alla storia, al governo ed alla descrizione della città e campagna di Milano ne' secoli bassi raccolte ed esaminate dal conte G. G.*, 7 vols., Milano, Colombo, 1854-1857, begins his account of the wedding of Gian Galeazzo Sforza and Isabella d'Aragona with the sentence: «Il duca di Milano Galeazzo Maria Sforza era nel 1488 in minore età sotto la tutela di suo zio Lodovico Maria Sforza», obviously referring to Giangaleazzo. (This whole «Illustrazione» [GIULINI, VI, pp. 649-655] is used in its entirety – although another error, calling Bianca Maria mother of the duke instead of his sister [p. 652] is corrected – by the editors of B. CORIO, *Storia di Milano* of 1502, ed. E. De Magri *et. al.*, 3 vols., also published in Milan by Colombo, 1855-1857: Vol. III, Chap. 5, note 7 beginning on page 447 [cf. my chapter VII, below, nn. 16 and 17]. The same error is not found in Corio's text itself).

[19] VERGA, «Per la storia» (n. 10) pp. 193-194, cites an «instrumento» of 10 April 1472 in the Archivio del Duomo. Cf. LITTA, «Visconti», Tav. XIII; RENIER, «G.V.», p. 520, n. 1. At fol. I of Gaspar Ambrogio's *zibaldone*, MS Triv. 1093, appear the notices of two births, of Paolo and Faustina, in 1477, with astrological specifications, so the couple may have wed as early as 1476.

[20] RENIER, «G.V.», p. 517, doubts that Visconti would have been named *Consigliere ducale* at the age of 17. Again the doubt appears unfounded given the customs of the times. For the properties, LITTA, «Visconti», Tav. XIII. Many of the holdings of this branch of the family

be called) drew up his testament.[21] And at the death of his uncle and guardian, Giampietro, in about 1486, he inherited outright his own patrimony, which had been badly managed by Giampietro, as well as the property of his uncle. At this point the poet, apparently taking advantage of his new-found status, purchased for fourteen ducats on October 2nd a very young Ethiopian slave, Dionisio (who had been bought by the dealer in Tunis), signing an unusually detailed document on account of the age of the slave (four years) and the uncommonness of slavery in Milan.[22] In that same month, Gaspar Ambrogio sold his house in San Giovanni sul Muro and purchased two houses and land from the heirs of Giovanni de Varisio, in the parish of S. Pietro in Caminadella.[23]

It is after this date that Grazioso Sironi would place the commission by Gaspar Ambrogio of the fresco by Bramante depicting Heracleitus weeping and Democritus laughing, extant in the Brera Pinacoteca. Bramante was possibly a member of Visconti's household for several years from at least 1487.[24] The theme of the two frescoes, a topos in 15th century Italy which may have begun with a fresco commissioned by Ficino, now lost,[25] certainly

---

are not locatable on present-day maps or even on historical maps of fifteenth century Lombardy, and are not listed in such works as C. MARANELLI, *Dizionario geografico dell'Alto Adige, del Trentino, della Venezia Giulia, e della Dalmazia*, Bari, 1915, or the *Enciclopedia Italiana*.

[21] J. DE SITONIS DE SCOTIA, *Theatrum Equestris Nobilitatis Secundae Romae...*, Mediolani, MDCCVI, p. 10, under «Mediolani Senatores ab Horatio Lando praetermissi» (p. 6), no. 176: «Gaspar Ambrosius Vicecomes V. 1483. Instrum. Testam. an 1483. 4 septembr. per Nicol Casatum Med. Not.» (On Sitoni, see C. GODI, «Notai e famiglie milanesi nel MS. Braidense AG.X.26 di Giovanni Sitoni di Scozia», *Aevum*, LXIII (1989), pp. 531-545). SANTORO, 1968 (n. 8), p. 203, gives information which clarifies the title: «... il Consiglio Segreto e il Consiglio di Giustizia o *Senati*, come vennero anche detti sulla fine del secolo XV». (Italics mine).

[22] E. VERGA, «Per la storia» (n. 10) pp. 194-195 and 195, n. 1. See too the document of purchase there appended, pp. 196-199.

[23] SIRONI, «Gli affreschi» (n. 3 above), pp. 201, 204. This property was adjacent to the site chosen in March 1508 for the construction of Santa Maria alla Fontana di Milano, on the design of Amadeo: document 1806, pp. 411-414 in *Giovanni Antonio Amadeo* (n. 1).

[24] SIRONI, «Gli affreschi» (n. 3), pp. 199-201, 204; cf. chapter XI, n. 42, below. Further documentation of the period of Bramante's residence is expected from Richard Schofield; cf. B. MARTINELLI, «La biblioteca (e i beni) di un petrarchista: Gasparo Visconti», *Veronica Gambara e la poesia del suo tempo nell'Italia settentrionale*. Atti del Convegno (Brescia – Correggio, 17-19 ottobre 1985), eds. C. Bozzetti, P. Gibellini, E. Sandal, Firenze, 1989, pp. 213-261, p. 215.

[25] P. O. KRISTELLER, *Marsilio Ficino and his Work after Five Hundred Years*, Firenze, 1987, p.

reflects the interests of our poet, who in the 1490s was paraphrasing Ficino and writing brief philosophical essays of his own. The commission of a fresco of Heracleitus weeping (presumably in frustration over man's inability to learn the discourse of nature through himself) and Democritus laughing (as he was known perhaps from his essay on cheerfulness) might be thought to be mere affectation were it not for what we know of the poetry and thought of Gaspare Visconti.[26] So too, it does not seem to me that the scientific works described as situated in the study off his bedchamber were necessarily there for the sole benefit of his house guest.[27] Duties of state and court may have kept Gaspare Visconti occupied, but his bent for intellectual pursuits was real. It seems also to fit in with currents in the Milan of his day.

Beclouding this period when he was coming into his own at the age of 25, Gaspare's rights to the inheritance of Giampietro's estate were contested by his two cousins, Giovanni and Filippo, also nephews of Giampietro. The contests occurred over the period 1487-1489 before a Judge Battista Visconti, and were not finally settled until Innocent VIII intervened in 1492 on behalf of Gaspar Ambrogio.[28]

In 1488-1489 the poet and/or another Gaspare, possibly his first cousin, took part in the embassy to Naples to escort Isabella d'Aragona to Milan as the bride of the young duke Giangaleazzo Sforza.[29] This is the occasion on which Giovanni II Tolentino addressed one of a number of extant descriptions of the festivities to Baldassare Taccone.[30]

---

11 and pl. 22. On the fresco (Frontispiece to this volume) and its theme, and their relation to the woodcut on the cover of the present volume as well as to various themes touched on *passim* here, see chapter XI, below.

[26] See chapter V, below. For possible sources and later uses of the theme, Creighton Gilbert refers us to A. PIGLER, *Barockthemen*, 2 vols., Budapest, 1974, II, p. 312.

[27] MARTINELLI, «La biblioteca» (n. 24), p. 216.

[28] VERGA, «Per la storia» (n. 10), pp. 194-195 and 195 n. 1.

[29] Litta, giving no source, states that both the poet and his first cousin of the same name took part in this voyage, while CORIO, *Storia di Milano*, 1502, lists only one Gaspare Visconti and does not specify which: «Vitaliano Borromeo, Gasparo Visconti, Ambrogio del Maino degnissimi cavalieri, e molti altri nobilissimi milanesi». GIULINI, *Memorie* (above, n. 18), followed by the editors of Corio (Milano, 1855-1857, III, pp. 447-453), gives another list, with no source, in which G.V. directly follows a Battista Visconti – who might be the judge of the local arbitrations of 1487-1489. This is undoubtedly the Battista discussed in LITTA, «Visconti», Tav. XVI, son of Francesco and Elisabetta di Francesco Conte di Carmagnola. He served as *consigliere ducale* from 1489, and was taken prisoner by the French in 1500. (See below). The list of participants in CORIO, *Storia*, III, pp. 447-448, corresponds, except orthographically, to that in Paris, Bibliothèque Nationale, MS italien 1592 (*Archivio Sforzesco*, X), fol. 209ʳ.

[30] See below, chapter VII, and chapter VI, *Appendice*, no. 3.

The letter of six months later from Tolentino to Gaspare Visconti, written when Tolentino, ten years the poet's junior, was eighteen, and appended here (Appendix II), is indicative not so much of details of Visconti's life as of the friendship between the two. Gaspare Visconti, like Baldassare Taccone his exact contemporary, must have been a mentor to the young nobleman, and Tolentino's letters to them both show great affection and good will, if a more imitative than original intellect. [31] In this letter he bemoans, in the very words of Plautus' Alcesimarchus in *Cistellaria*, II, i, 4 and 5-15, his love-lorn state. [32] The comic source of his words, and the exaggerated anguish they express, lend a lightness to the letter which cannot have escaped its addressee. Nonetheless, Giovanni must have been in love, for he envies Gaspare for being able to detach himself from such cares and immerse himself in literary pursuits. He encloses with his letter the tetrastich written to his beloved. Later (among letters from 1493, the year when Gaspare's *Rithmi* were published), he writes an epigram to Visconti, also appended here.

Caterina Santoro cites a document naming «D. Gaspar Vicecomes ad beneplacitum» to the *Consiglio Segreto* on July 4, 1493. [33] This is probably a reappointment of Gaspar Ambrogio, this time under Ludovico, who had

---

[31] See his letters to Taccone appended to chapter VI, below. For an analysis of one of them, see R. SCHOFIELD, «Giovanni da Tolentino Goes to Rome: A Description of the Antiquities of Rome in 1490», *Journal of the Warburg and Courtauld Institutes*, XLIII (1980), pp. 246-256.

[32] The imitated passages are italicized in the letter. This *canticum* portion of Plautus' text, for comparison, reads (in a compromise between Lindsay's text, Oxford, 1904, and the Loeb edition, Cambridge, Mass. and London, 1917):

> iactor, crucior, agitor, stimulor, versor
> in amoris rota, miser exanimor,
> feror, differor, distrahor, diripior,
> ita nubilam mentem animi habeo.
> ubi sum, ibi non sum, ubi non sum, ibi est animus,
> ita mi omnia sunt ingenia;
> quod lubet, non lubet iam id continuo,
> ita me Amor lassum animi ludificat,
> fugat, agit, appetit, raptat, retinet,
> lactat, largitur; quod dat non dat; deludit:
> modo quod suasit, id dissuadet,
> quod dissuasit, id ostentat.
> maritumis moribus mecum experitur,
> ita meum frangit amantem animum;
> ...

[33] Archivio di Stato di Milano, *Registro ducale* 92, c. 132ᵛ. Cf. SANTORO, 1948 (n. 8 above), p. 23.

been officially but secretly invested by the Emperor Maximilian just days earlier on June 24. [34]

The poet Gaspare was definitely a member of the company conducting Bianca Maria Sforza to Austria in December 1493 when she went to meet her husband the Emperor Maximilian (married by proxy in November in Milan), for we have the testimony of his friend and fellow courtier, Baldassare Taccone, to confirm that:

> ...
> Ma tu che legi qui ben creder poi
> che'l Moro un pezo seco se n'è gito,
> con cortesani e con la turba magna
> a Barlassina e Como l'acompagna.
>
> Mandò in là seco molti ambasciatori,
> con ornamenti e veste in excellenza.
> Del stato e de Melan trasse i migliori:
> quel da Sipion con gran magnificenza,
> misser Iason: se farà milli honori
> con l'oration composta in tanta scienza;
> e per adietro el conte da Gaiazzo
> ha havuto in questa impresa e stento e impazo.
>
> *E'l mio patron, misser Guaspar Visconte,*
> e gli altri che per orden non vi nomo,
> ...
> vi vanno ancor... .
>
> Per tanti laghi, neve et alpe vanno,
> e in Alamagna, non molto discosto
> el Re Maximïan vi trovaranno,
> el quale aspetta molto ben disposto.
> Madonna Bianca al re consignaranno
> e la più parte in dietro torna tosto;
> con la regina resterà in sua corte
> quelli che 'l Signor Mor gli dà per sorte.

(*Coronatione e sponsalitio,* LXXVII,5-LXXX,8) [35]

---

[34] C. SANTORO, *Gli Sforza,* Varese, 1968, p. 295.

[35] B. TACCONE, *Coronatione e sponsalitio de la serenissima Regina M. Bianca Ma. Sf. Augusta al Illustrissimo S. Lodovico Sf. visconte Duca de Barri per Baldassare Taccone Alexandrino*

The historian Tristano Calco also mentions «antiquae stirpis Vicecomites Baptista et Gaspar, ex Senatu lecti opulenti Equites» among the company conducting Bianca Maria to Austria. [36]

From the year 1493 we have the publication of the first collection of Gaspare Visconti's vernacular poems, published as *Rithmi* by Francesco Tanzio Corniger in Milan on «IV. Cal. Martias» (February 26) «quamquam invito Domino», but nonetheless dedicated to Niccolò da Correggio. [37] These must be the poems referred to five years earlier, when they must have been being composed, in a letter from Giovanni II Tolentino to Baldassare Taccone: «Admonebis Gasparem Vicecomitem, grande Musarum decus, ut cum in nostrum suburbanum venerit, sua rithmice scripta elegantissima secum ferat. Ipsum miro desiderio ad venationes iamdudum expecto. Vale, et me (ut soles) ama. Belreguardi ... [October 14, 1488]». [38] Gaspare's poems in general are mines of information on customs and objects of the time: he is often cited for his reference in one of the *Rithmi* to «certi Orologii piccioli, e portativi...» – the first, and very precious, pocket watches. [39]

---

ca[n]celleri composta, Milano, 1493. Italics mine. «Misser Iason» is the jurist Giasone del Maino; the «Conte da Gaiazzo» is Gian Francesco Sanseverino, patron of Taccone's *Danae*. I have corrected the text in accordance with the recent edition by G. BIANCARDI, «La *Coronatione* di Bianca Maria Sforza. Un poemetto in ottave di B. T.», in *Studi e fonti di storia lombarda. Quaderni milanesi*, n.s., Anno 13, Num. 33-34 (1993), pp. 43-121, esp. pp. 86, 114-115.

[36] In his *Nuptiae Augustae: hoc est, Maximiliani Imperatoris cum Blanca, Ioannis Galeacii Mediolanensium Ducis sorore* (printed with *Tristani Calchi Mediolanensis Historiographi Residua*, Mediolani, MDCXLIV), p. 103; G.V. is again mentioned at p. 112. The text is more accessible in J. G. GRAEVIUS, *Thesaurus Antiquitatum et Historiarum Italiae*, vol. II, pt. 1, Lugduni Batavorum (Leiden), 1704, cols. 525-536 (G.V. at cols. 526, 532).

[37] Fol. a: AD ILLVSTREM DOMINVM NICOLAVM / VICECOMITEM ET COREGIAM. GASPAR / VICECOMES. Fol. a iii: RHITHIMI (*sic*) DEL MAGNIFICO MESERE GASPAR / VESCONTE. *Coloph.*, fol. k 4: ... HOS RHI / THMOS MAGNIFICI AC SPLENDI / DISSIMI EQVITIS GASPARIS VI / CECOMITIS LINGVA VFRNA / CVLA (*sic*) COMPOSITOS: q̄ q̄ IN / VITO DOMINO: IN MILLE / EXEMPLA IMPRIMI IVS / SIT MEDIOLANI: AN / NO A SALVTIFERO / VIRGINIS: PARTV / M.CCCC.LXXXXIII. / QVARTO CALEN / DAS MARTIAS. / FINIS. (HAIN 16078; IGI 10338; BMC, VI, 723). Cf. SASSI, *Historia Literario-Typographica Mediolanensis*, (note 11 above) cols. CCCLVII-CCCLXI and pages DV-DVI. ARGELATI, *Bibliotheca*, T. II, pars 1, cols. 1604-1605. I retain the spelling of the colophon, and believe the title «RHITHIMI» at fol. a iii to be a printing error. Inc. c.188 of the Biblioteca Trivulziana, fol. a iii, in fact reads: RIME DEL MAGNIFICO MESERE GARPAR (*sic*) / VESCONTE, thus representing a revised printing.

[38] Edited in chapter VI, below, *Appendice*, no. 1.

[39] SASSI, *Historia*, cols. CCCLX-CCCLXI; MALAGUZZI VALERI, *La corte* (n. 3), IV, 72. In this

Fourteen ninety-four brought a new edition of the Italian poetic works of Petrarca, printed by Scinzenzeler in Milan, and containing a letter by Francesco Tanzio Corniger crediting himself and Gaspare Visconti with the correction and editing of the works, and with rescuing them from the state into which they had fallen:

> ...tanto scorretti, che quasi più erano li versi depravati, che quelli che stesseno bene; curandosi il prefato Maestro Henrico [Scinzenzeler] ... che quasi si vede questo nostro poeta essere restituto [*sic*] alla pristina sanitate, et questo, parte per la mia laboriosa solicitudine et diligentia circa lo emendare de dicta depravatione, sì maximamente per la solerte industria et subtilissimo ingegno del Magnifico cavaglier Messer Gaspar Vesconte, il quale aciò che meglio et più commodamente io il potesse fare, me ha concesso uno suo Petrarcha, quale lui con molti exemplari et con grandissima diligentia havea corretto, perochè senza questo opportuno adiuto non haveria ragionevolmente potuto acceptare questa tanta et tale impresa, né del exemplare de qualunque altro me saria tanto fidato. [40]

period of great literary activity, Lancino Curti addressed his satiric poems about Taccone to G. V.: F. MARRI, «Lancino Curti a Gaspare Visconti», in *Studi filologici letterari e storici in memoria di Guido Favati*, 2 vols., Padova, 1977, vol. II, pp. 397-423; cf. D. ISELLA, «Lo sperimentalismo dialettale di L. C. e compagni», in *In ricordo di Cesare Angelini. Studi di letteratura e filologia*, Milano, 1979, pp. 146-159; R. MARCHI, «Rime volgari di L.C.», in *Studi di letteratura italiana offerti a Dante Isella*, Napoli, 1983, pp. 33-52. Curti also addressed two of his Latin *Sylvae* to Visconti; see *Lancini Curtii Sylvarum Libri Decem. / M.D.XXXIX. Coloph.*: Mediolani Apud Rochum & Ambrosium Fratres de Valle / Impressores Philippus Foyot Faciebat M.D.XXXIX, fols. 125ᵛ, 177-179.

[40] Fol. 102 (=101, *sig.* N iii), 2ⁿᵈ vol. of F. PETRARCA, *Trionfi, Sonetti*, two volumes in one, separate colophons: [I], Fol. 128, *sig.* q iiii: ... Mediolani an(n)o d(omi)ni .1494.die.10. Februarii; [II], Fol. 102ᵛ, *sig.* N iiiᵛ: Finisse gli sonetti di Misser Francesco Petrarca Impressi in Milano per Magistro Vlderico Scinzenzeler / Nel anno del signore .M.CCCC.LXXXXIIII. A di .xxvi. de marzo. I have modernized the punctuation. I have seen the copy at Houghton Library, Harvard University, which bears the notice at 102ᵛ: «Iste petrarcta (*sic*) est Lucretiae Imperialis», and inside the front cover, the *ex libris* of P. Brunet. Cf. my *Politian's «Orfeo»* (n. 2 above), p. 31; SASSI, col. CCCLXI; ARGELATI, II, 1, col. 1605; HAIN-COPINGER-REICHLING, 12775; BRUNET, IV, p. 542; J. E. WALSH, *A Catalogue of the Fifteenth-Century Printed Books in the Harvard University Library*, III, Binghamton, N.Y., 1994, p. 137, no. 3128, and cf. no. 3129. POLAIN cites G. V.'s role in *Catalogue des livres imprimés au quinzième siècle des Bibliothèques de Belgique*, III, Bruxelles, 1932, no. 3068. J. G. T. GRAESSE, *Trésor de livres rares et précieux*, vol. V, Genève, London, Paris, 1864, p. 224, also mentions Visconti's role, but evaluates the edition: «Quoique plus correcte que la plupart des édd. précédentes et soignée d'après plusieurs mss ... [elle] renferme plusieurs corrections très arbitraires». Also see MARTINELLI (n. 24 above), pp. 239-40, who cites this

In 1495, Filippo Mantegazzo published Visconti's poem in *ottava rima*, *De Paolo e Daria Amanti*, centered on the topos of the «false death» of the young *innamorata* in a tale akin to that of Romeo and Juliet.[41] This work has long been known to art historians by virtue of the illuminated manuscript copy now in the Kupferstichkabinett, Berlin.[42] The poem begins, like the *cantari* of the time, with an invocation to God. Before even lauding Ludovico il Moro, the author shifts to praise of Bramante's learning (more vast than stars in the sky, than fish in the sea, than saints in heaven: fol. a iiii). Visconti then turns to praise of his patron Duke Ludovico Sforza (publicly named Duke of Milan on February 4, 1495, just two months before the printing of this poem). Near the end of the text, Visconti refers to himself as having had «le stelle nel suo male immote / Di gran persecution de pocha stima» before the benign intervention of il Moro (fol. m iᵛ). From the facts we have, these words must refer to his orphaned youth, perhaps including some years of his life in Giampietro's household. His life under the protection of il Moro seems to have been singularly fortunate.[43]

---

passage as well. A. PETRUCCI, *La scrittura di Francesco Petrarca*, Città del Vaticano, 1967, pp. 90-91, credits Pietro Bembo, no doubt correctly, with the first significant edition, printed by Aldus in 1501. The Visconti-Tanzi edition is however worthy of notice as a predecessor in the enterprise.

[41] Fol. [a i]: .DE PAVLO E DARIA AMANTI. *Coloph.*, fol. o iiii: Impresso per magistro Philippo Mantega / tio dicto el Cassano in la Excelle(n)tissima / Citade de Milano nel Anno. Mcccclxxx / xy. a di primo de Aprile. (HAIN, 16077; IGI, 10337; BMC, VI, 787). Cf. SASSI, col. CCCLXI; ARGELATI, II, 1, col. 1604; MALAGUZZI VALERI, I, pp. 92, 192-193. And see H. HAUVETTE, «La légende de la 'Morte vivante'. Etude de littérature comparée», *Revue des cours et conférences*, 33²-34² (July, 1932 – April, 1933), 33²: pp. 577-589, 673-687; 34¹: pp. 44-55, 157-170, 237-245, 338-348, 443-457, 536-551, 663-672, 709-726; 34²: pp. 84-92; esp. 34¹: pp. 50-53; also published separately as *La «Morte vivante». Etude de littérature comparée*, Paris, 1933. The poem is not incomplete as Hauvette says, but Visconti interrupts the tale by the fiction of a lacuna in its source; the outcome of the two lovers' deaths is nonetheless clear.

[42] On the MS, Kupferstichkabinett 78.C.27 (*olim* Hamilton 681), cf. L. BIADENE, «I manoscritti italiani della collezione Hamilton nel R. Museo e nella R. Biblioteca di Berlino», *Giornale storico della letteratura italiana*, X (1887), pp. 321-322; E. PELLEGRIN, *La Bibliothèque des Visconti et des Sforza ducs de Milan, au XVᵉ siècle*, Paris, 1955, pp. 356-357; H. BOESE, *Die lateinischen Handschriften der Sammlung Hamilton zu Berlin*, Wiesbaden, 1966, p. 328. I thank Professor P. O. Kristeller for references to the Berlin catalogues.

[43] G. FERRI PICCALUGA, «Gli affreschi di casa Panigarola e la cultura milanese fra Quattro e Cinquecento», *Arte lombarda*, n.s., 86-87 (1988), pp. 14-25, esp. p. 16 and nn. 31, 32, notes G.V.'s reference, at fols. k ii, ff. to a trip to the Middle East with a group of humanists. She also notes his title, «Miles auratus» (indicating his rank as a *Cavaliere del Santo Sepolcro*) in MS Triv. 182, a collection of *carmina* by Pietro Lazzaroni dedicated to G.V.

Around this time, between the years 1493 and January, 1497, when Beatrice d'Este Sforza died, and probably close to the composition of *De Paolo e Daria*, so similar in theme, Gaspare Visconti wrote his play *Pasithea*.[44] This is perhaps the most remarkable of the *favole mitologiche*, the earliest preserved secular dramatic works in the Italian vernacular. Based on the tale of Pyramus and Thisbe (another version of the double suicide theme), the play incorporates the classical characters of the carefree, spendthrift son, the miserly father, the crafty servant. But following the more recent norms of humanistic comedy, the young woman assumes a spoken part – even speaking against the misogynistic tradition.[45] The play is situated in both a city scene and a pastoral or satyric scene, and in the end, the two lovers are revived by Apollo who takes pity on Pasithea's beauty. Many strains of thought and theatrical tradition are brought together in this play, for which there is no record of performance.

In about 1495, Gaspare Visconti composed a fragmentary treatise on love, paraphrasing and rearranging portions of Marsilio Ficino's *De amore* of 1469 (published in 1484). At roughly the same time, he dedicated his *canzoniere* to Beatrice d'Este Sforza, with a letter again dwelling on Neoplatonic ideas on love.[46] The Neoplatonic allusions to beauty in *Pasithea* were thus not casual, but rather the result of absorption of and thought about intellectual currents of the time.

We now have valuable information on Visconti's library, unearthed by Grazioso Sironi and published by Bortolo Martinelli.[47] The evidence is in an inventory made by a notary a year and a half after the poet's death. The inventory is not a proper catalogue, and some works are clearly out of order, others certainly missing, but it gives us, in its record of some 137 works, an idea of the substantial holdings and the interests of this poet of fortunate circumstances. Although Ficino is not present in the list, his presence is clear

---

[44] See my *Politian's «Orfeo»* (n. 2), pp. 187-197 (a diplomatic edition of *Pasithea* at pp. 207-261); and chapter VIII, below. *Pasithea* now appears in *Teatro del Quattrocento. Le corti padane,* eds. A. Tissoni Benvenuti and M. P. Mussini Sacchi, Torino, 1983, pp. 337-396. Cf. P. BONGRANI, «Lingua e stile nella *Pasitea* e nel teatro cortigiano milanese», *Interpres*, V (1983-1984), pp. 163-241 (reprinted in his *Lingua e letteratura a Milano* [n. 2] pp. 85-158).

[45] See chapters VIII and X, below.

[46] See my edition of the fragment in chapter V, below; *De amore* was first published in *Platonis opera omnia*, 2 vols., Firenze, [1484] (HAIN *13062); the *canzoniere* and letter are published by Bongrani in VISCONTI, *I canzonieri* (n. 4 above), pp. 4-150.

[47] SIRONI, «Gli affreschi» (n. 3), pp. 204-205; MARTINELLI, «La biblioteca» (n. 24 above).

in the poet's work, as is that of Apuleius, who is listed.[48] Poliziano is represented by the 1489 edition of his *Miscellanea*; his *Cose vulgare* (*sic*, 1494) would have been one of the first works to be dispersed, but the vernacular Poliziano's influence on Visconti is direct.[49] Besides the expected large number of works by Petrarca (including certainly the edition in which he participated), Visconti's library even contains a high proportion of silver age poets, and the *Suda Lexicon*, all of which were used extensively by Poliziano. The library is assumed by present scholars to have been dispersed soon after the death of the poet and his son, in short, after this inventory was made; however it should be noted that Paolo Morigia, writing at the end of the 16th century of the poet's great-grandson Prospero Visconti (or the Giambattista of the Fontaneto line, «detto Prospero» due to being Prospero's heir), speaks explicitly of his

> degna libraria e copiosissima, nella quale si trovano libri di tutte le scienze, e professioni, fra li quali se ne vedevano alcuni in lingua Longobarda scritti in scorza d'arbori, o sia di Tiglia. Questo si compiaceva oltra modo di nobilissima anticaglie, onde haveva una lunga serie di Medaglie antiche, e di molta stima appresso de gl'intelligenti.[50]

Gaspar Ambrogio's own antiquarian interests are represented in the inventory of 1500 by the entry «Epitaphia antiquorum», and his library's eclectic nature is also clear. It is not impossible that the poet's library remained the core of this later library.

The author of the letter appended here, Giovanni II Tolentino, makes a tantalizing allusion to our poet in his *Commentarii*: «Millesimo quadringentesimo Nonagesimo octavo undecimo Kal. Decembres. Gaspar vicecomes musarum alumnus...». The citation is cut off by the loss of the subsequent quire in the Ambrosiana manuscript, S. P. II 254,[51] but it nonetheless offers

---

[48] Martinelli refers to the 1500 edition of Apuleius commented by Beroaldo, which of course Gaspare Visconti could not have owned, but editions of Apuleius' *Opera*, all prominently including *Metamorphoseos sive de asino aureo*, were printed from 1469 on (Sweynheym and Pannartz, Roma, GW 2301; also GW 2302-2304, of which 2304 [IGI 772] is Milano, Leonhard Pachel, 1497, an edition G.V. could easily have owned).

[49] Chapters VIII and X, below; BONGRANI, *Lingua e letteratura* (n. 2 above), *passim*.

[50] MORIGIA, *La Nobiltà* (n. 12), p. 269. (Giambattista of the Fontaneto line was great-great-great-grandson of the Knight of the Garter Gaspare, through his son Filippo Maria. See LITTA, «Visconti», Tavv. XIII, XI).

[51] MARCORA, «I commentari» (n. 5), p. 337; folio 8ᵛ of the MS itself bears the word *alumnus* as key word to the next quire. A facsimile of the first folio is published between pp. 332 and 333.

a further indication of the esteem in which Gaspare was held as a poet above all. The retrieval of the next quire could be of considerable significance to our understanding of the end of the poet's life.

We owe to the work of Grazioso Sironi confirmation of the date of the poet's death or at least of a *terminus ante quem*. In discovering the patron of the above-mentioned frescoes by Bramante to be Gaspar Ambrogio Visconti, he also found, in the *fondo notarile* of the Archivio di Stato di Milano, a document dating from May 6, 1499, referring to Gaspar Ambrogio as deceased.[52] Thus the March 8th date given by Argelati and others and the year, on which doubt had been cast by the lack of documents in the *necrologio* for 1499,[53] are lent plausibility. The notice in the multi-volume *Storia di Milano* of recent years of a Gaspare Visconti marching out to meet Louis XII at Binasco to escort the French king in triumph to Milan on October 5, 1499 should thus refer to Gian Gaspare, the poet's son (Appendix I, no. 8).[54] This is again the result of the confusion wrought by the many Gaspari.

Many of the documents brought to light by Léon-Gabriel Pélissier in 1896 which seemed to refer to the poet, must now be recognized as referring either to his son, Gian Gaspare, or to one of his cousins Gaspare (nos. 2, 3 or 4 in Appendix I). Pélissier documents Ludovico's assignment of the command of troops at Ghiara d'Adda to a Gaspare Visconti on August 26, 1499, and both a Gaspare Visconti and Ambrosio del Mayno as part of a solemn embassy on September 4, 1499.[55] Just after the defeat and capture of Ludovico on April 10, 1500, a number of Ghibellines including a Gaspare and a Battista Visconti fled toward Venice. They were under surveillance at Bergamo on April 11. By about the 20th of April, Niccolò da Correggio's wife and one of Cajazzo's sons are recorded in Venice. But on the same date, Battista and Gaspare Visconti and Ambrosio del Mayno are recorded as imprisoned in the «Rocha» of Bergamo.[56]

---

[52] SIRONI, «Gli affreschi» (n. 3), p. 204. Notaio Nicola Omodeo, filza 5419.

[53] MOTTA, «Morti in Milano», (n. 11, above), pp. 271-272.

[54] *Storia di Milano*, VIII, Milano, 1966, p. 30. The *Storia*'s source, L.-G. PÉLISSIER, *Louis XII et Ludovic Sforza (8 avril 1498 – 23 juillet 1500)*, 2 vols., Paris, 1896, refers to «J. Gaspar»: II, pp. 234 ff., esp. p. 237.

[55] On Ghiara d'Adda: PÉLISSIER, *Louis XII*, II, p. 33; on the embassy of Sept. 4: ibid., II, p. 217. On the Battle of Novara: N. VALERI, *L'Italia nell'età dei principati, dal 1343 al 1516*, Verona, 1969, p. 568.

[56] PÉLISSIER, *Louis XII*, II, pp. 297, 299.

Other documents of Pélissier record that a Gaspare was taken prisoner by the French after the Battle of Novara in April 1500, when Ludovico il Moro was defeated. This was true of the poet's son, and may also have been true of one of his cousins, and they may have been imprisoned in different places; or all documents may refer to the son (though this is less likely because his compound name seems to be respected). A Gaspare seems even to have been destined for imprisonment in France along with his fellow Ghibelline cousin Battista Visconti; these two names figure on a list prepared by Gian Giacomo Trivulzio for a convoy of hostages destined for France. [57] Battista was imprisoned, tortured and sent to France, from where he was ransomed, according to Litta («Visconti», Tav. XVI). The Gaspare with Battista must have been subjected to similar treatment. Sironi publishes a document of December 5, 1500 showing the poet's son Gian Gaspare to have died in captivity in Novara at the age of about 18. [58] His son, Gian Gaspare Ambrogio (Appendix I, no. 11), born posthumously to his wife Donnina di Giovanni Crotti, carried on the name.

## Appendix I

In the interest of future work on the subject, it may be of use to list the other contemporary and near contemporary namesakes here, to facilitate distinguishing them from the poet. The eight contemporaries were:

(1) Gaspare Visconti, the poet's father. Created *cavaliere* in 1450; became *siniscalco* to Galeazzo Maria Sforza. Married Margherita Alciati. In Ferrara in 1452 to honor the Emperor Frederick III. According to Ettore Verga (n. 10), this man died in 1462. However, Litta (n. 6: «Visconti», XIII) describes him as eventually becoming *consigliere ducale* and being invested with Breme in the Lomellina in 1470. Verga states (pp. 193-194) that this Gaspare's brother Giampietro acted as the young poet's guardian in 1472 to arrange his

---

[57] PÉLISSIER, *Louis XII*, II, p. 247.
[58] SIRONI, «Gli affreschi» (n. 3), pp. 204-205. This, along with the knowledge of Battista's torture, gives a fuller picture than Morigia's statement that he died at Novara «gloriosamente combattendo»: MORIGIA, *Historia*, 1592, p. 592; and see below, Appendix I, no. 8.

marriage to Cicco Simonetta's daughter; if this document is correctly reported, the poet's father was dead by then.

(2) G.V., Castellano of Lecco, 1494; son of Giacomo and Orsina di Luigi Cusani; grandson of Gianfilippo; great-grandson of Pietro, also Castellano of Lecco: Litta (n. 6), «Visconti», Tav. XIV. Cf. Santoro, 1948 (n. 8), p. 606: *nominato nel 1478. Istruzioni da Lodovico il Moro del 1495* (MS Trivulziano 1396, fol. 25). Possibly the subject of the entry in Santoro, 1968 (n. 8), p. 370: Castellano ponte di Lecco, 11 marzo, 1500, with Giovanni Giacomo, Luigi Visconti (the name of this Gaspare's son, the end of his line).

(3) G.V., first cousin of the poet, son of Giampietro and Agnese di Corradino Beccaria; married Giovanna di Franchino Rusca. This may have been the man who went to Naples in the party which then conducted Isabella d'Aragona, bride of Giangaleazzo Sforza, to Milan in 1489, as did the poet, according to Litta (n. 6), «Visconti», XIII. However, his position on the Litta tree is called into question by E. Verga (n. 10: p. 194, n. 2). Verga recon-structs the tree of Renier (n. 2: p. 522, n. 1), which shows this Gaspare as son of the poet's uncle, Giampietro. Verga says that documents seen by him in the Archivio del Duomo indicate that Giampietro had no legitimate children. It is not impossible that Gaspar Ambrogio, being the ward of Giampietro, was considered by some to be his son. However, since the present Gaspare is reported to have married Giovanna Rusca and seems to have been active in the Battle of Novara after the poet's death, he clearly existed independently. Verga's documents should be consulted further to clarify this and other questions.

(4) G.V., son of Azzone, Podestà of Como; grandson of an early 15th century Gaspero; great-grandson of a 14th-early 15th century Pietro. Litta (n. 6), «Visconti», Tav. XI: «Milite, morto prima del 1506»; married Orsina di Giacomo Lampugnani. Santoro, 1948 (n. 8), p. 26: «Spect[abilis] vir» G.V., Consigliere segreto *ad beneplacitum*, 29 July, 1495.

(5) G.V., Castellano of Pavia; imprisoned by the French in 1500; died June 11, 1533, Milan. Litta (n. 6), «Visconti», Tav. XII: «Signori di Fontaneto». This man would be considered second cousin to the poet today; he too is a great-grandson of the Gaspare no. 9, below.

(6) Gasparinus V., son of a Filippo Maria of Novara (another of the line «Signori di Fontaneto») and of Giovanna del Marchese Rolando Pallavicino. Litta (n. 6) however says: «Legittimato nel 1456 da Antonio Porro, conte Palatino» («Visconti», Tav. XI). This may well be the Gasparinus in Santoro, 1948 (n. 8), p. 306: Potestà Vallis Sicide (like Fontaneto, west of Milan and Novara), «pro annis 2, videlicet 1478 et 1479», nominated 12 November, 1477, Milan. Argelati (n. 11), Tom. II, pars 1, col. 1604, states, probably

erroneously, that the poet Gaspare «Gasparinus quoque vocabatur», apparently (as Renier [n. 2] notes, «G.V.», p. 516) referring to a letter of 1463 by Francesco Fllelfo which he cites in col. 1605. Renier also suggests that this Gasparinus may be the son of Filippo Maria of Novara.

(7) G.V., «Viceduca di Bari» in 1497, mentioned (Litta [n. 6], «Visconti», Tav. XII) in connection with Giovanni Maria, brother of the above Gasperino (Litta, «Visconti», Tav. XI-XII). (Giammaria apparently made pacts with the *Viceduca* «per asciugare la palude Brebbia di 12 m. pertiche ne' territori di Biandronno, Besnate ed altri». Giammaria is the father of the Castellano di Pavia, G.V. number 5, above, and grandson of Gaspare, no. 9, below).

(8) Giangaspero, son of the poet: «Cameriere ducale. Uomo colto nelle lingue orientali e di molta dottrina faceva sperare di superare i meriti del padre, ma ... fu ucciso nel 1500 contro i francesi alla battaglia di Novara ...». This man married Donnina di Giovanni Crotti (Litta [n. 6], «Visconti», Tav. XIII), who bore him a son, Giangaspero Ambrogio, posthumously. P. Morigia, *La nobiltà* (n. 12), pp. 269-270 (who may well have been one of Litta's sources, or even his only source here) says of him: «il qual di dottrina non fu inferiore al Padre, perché anch'esso possedeva tutte le quattro lingue, et era nella poesia molto versato, e morse a Novara gloriosamente combattendo ...».

The five nearly contemporary Gaspari Visconti were:

(9) Gaspero, great-grandfather of the poet, born mid-fourteenth century. (Litta [n. 6], «Visconti», Tav. XI.) He was an interesting figure who served closely the ruling house of the Visconti, beginning with Galeazzo (1354-1378) and Bernabò (1354-1385). He was on intimate terms with Duke Giangaleazzo (1378-1402) and continued to serve under Dukes Giovanni Maria (1402-1412) and Filippo Maria (1412-1447). It was he who was sent in 1367 to England to seal the agreement for the brief marriage between Violante Visconti, Galeazzo's daughter, and Lionel Plantagenet Duke of Clarence and son of King Edward III of England. Lionel died in Alba just months after the wedding, at which Petrarca had been a guest of honor in June, 1368. After this and other similar missions to England, Gaspare Visconti was created Knight of the Garter. In 1415 he was ambassador to the Council of Constance. In 1431 it was he who «fece un trattato coll'imperatore Sigismondo, onde indurlo a muovere gli Ungheri contro i Veneziani». (Litta, «Visconti», Tav. XI; Caffi [n. 7], p. 38). He died, presumably in about 1434, when he made his last testament, at a venerable age. Litta reproduces the monument described by Caffi and designed by Visconti in 1427 for the Cappella di S. Giovanni

Evangelista in Sant'Eustorgio, Milan, between his Tav. XIII and Tav. XIV or bound before Tav. XIII.

(**10**) Gaspero, fl. 1430s, son of a Pietro Podestà of Bergamo, grandson of Azzo (Signore di Ierago in Gallarate, Contado di Seprio). Litta (n. 6), «Visconti», Tav. X, conjectures that he was in the company who paid honor to the Emperor Sigismondo in 1431; he probably died just before 1434, when his wife appears as *tutrice*. Their daughter Elisabetta married Cicco Simonetta.

(**11**) Giangaspero Ambrogio, grandson of the poet, posthumous son of the above Giangaspero (number 8), and thus born sometime after the Battle of Novara of April, 1500. According to Litta (n. 6: «Visconti», Tav. XIII) this man, «Capitano di 500 fanti[,] militò nelle guerre che Francesco II Sforza ebbe a sostenere contro i francesi». He married in 1548 Vincenza Martinengo di Lodi. (His son Prospero, «legittimato col fratello Paolo nel 1548» [*loc. cit.*] was Counselor and «Gentiluomo di Camera» to William, Duke of Bavaria, and at the court of the Emperor Maximilian II. He possessed a rich and famous library which, having no direct heirs, he left in 1592 to Giambattista [«detto Prospero»] di Fontaneto [Litta, «Visconti», Tav. XI] who died in 1627. The library was at some point later dispersed).

(**12**) Gaspero Visconti, Archbishop of Milan, 1584-1595, successor to Carlo Borromeo. (Morigia, *Historia* [n. 12], pp. 319, 322). He was son of Giambattista of the Fontaneto line, and thus great-great-grandson of the above Gaspare, number 9. (Litta [n. 6], «Visconti», Tav. XI).

(**13**) There is also, it is to be hoped lastly, a Gaspero, «Parroco di Castelleto» (South of Lago Maggiore) in 1517. (Litta [n. 6], «Visconti», Tav. XX).


Appendix II


Letter and Epigram by Giovanni da Tolentino
addressed to
Gaspare Visconti


*From*: IOANNIS TOLLENTI- / NATIS.II.EQVI- / TIS:EPISTO- / LARVM / LIBRI / .III. Milano, 1512. (Brit. Lib. 10905.d.22.) I have normalized punc-

tuation, *s* and *u*. The passages quoted (and in part paraphrased) from Plautus, *Cistellaria*, II, i, 4-15 are quoted above in n. 32; they are italicized
below.

[a viii]                    Ioannes Tollentinas: Gaspari
                            Vicecomiti Equiti ornatissimo.
                            Salutem.

EGO vero Vicecomes Generosissime neque te desidia accusabo, neque si igna-
viam meam purgare contendam, non vereor (dum veniam quaero) maius
mihi crimen imputari. Sed si (ut scribis) amas, et durae legi colla subdidisti,
poteris et huic inter capedini nostrae non modo ignoscere, sed et sortem
meam miserari, quia prae omnibus *iactor, crucior, agitor, stimulor, versor in*
// [a viiiʳ] *amoris rota miser.* Angit me praeterea tui desiderium, quo nemo
dulcior frater, nemo gratior amicus, nemo iucundior sodalis, quicum meas
solicitudines fabulari possem. Ad id enim nostra devenit rabies, ut neque
ocii, neque amicorum, neque mei ipsius reminiscar, ocium vero tuum et lau-
do et vehementer admiror, quod in flammis etiam Minervam invenias, et
quidem antelucanam, quo maxime tempore fervet ignis. Faelix nempe qui
tempus ita disponis, et tam facilem sortitus sis amicam, abs qua quottidie
saluteris. Sed posteaquam ex litteris tuis quid agas cognovi, existimo et ipse
licentiore uti epistola ut tu statum meum intelligas. Ego enim quod superest
ocii ex domesticis negociis, non Minervae et Marti (ut solebam) non Camae-
nis, quas colui, non musicae quae me plurimum oblectabat, sed totum tum
in exquirenda amica, tum in percontandis nuntiis, tum in effingendis arche-
typis dedico. Ita vagus omnem penitus abieci decorem. Subinde venit mollis
illa, et suavis recordatio oblectamentorum, animusque cogitationibus pasci-
tur. *Exanimor, feror, diferor, distrahor, dirripior, nul-*// [b] *lamque mentem
animi habeo. Ubi sum, ibi non sum; ubi non sum, ibi est animus. Quod libet,
non libet, iam id continuo. Ita mei amor lassi animum ludificat, fugat, agit,
appetit, raptat, retinet. Quod dat, non dat; deludit modo. Quod suasit, dissua-
det; quod dissuasit, id ostentat. Videas mecum maritimis modis experiri.* Praeterea si nescio quid mellis acquiro, id omne fomentum ignis efficitur. Pote-
ram sane faelix amare. Sed quoniam in amore nostro fortuna parat insidias,
et me privare illa enititur, hoc est quod me cruciat angitque. In tanta vero
rabie in qua nullum offendi solatium, tentavi si forte huius possem oblivisci.
Sed actum est superioribus diebus in hanc ferme materiam erupi in quoddam

tetrasticon, quod ideo ad te mitto, ne nuda proficiscatur epistola et ut tar-
ditas cum fenore compensetur. Vale, et nos (ut soles) ama. Papiae nonis
Iuniis. M.cccc.lxxxviiii.

Io. Tol. Ad Cinthyam puellam Amicam.

Si clarium movisse potest paeneia Daphne,
    Cinthya tu poteris solicitare Iovem.
[b<sup>v</sup>]    Si potes ergo Iovem, tanto magis uror in illis
    Ignibus. Heu fati iam venit hora mei.

[c ii<sup>v</sup>]    De calamis Gaspari Vicecomiti dono datis.

Haec mihi dona dedit Veneris lasciva propago.
    Si scribes, Dominam flectere posse puta.

# CHAPTER V

## Neoplatonic Currents and Gaspare Visconti's *Fragmentum* (MS Triv. 1093)

In 1968 Paul Oskar Kristeller published an article in which he explicitly recognized the importance of currents other than Florentine Neoplatonism in the growth and spread of Renaissance thought and culture.[1] This balanced view is clearly the one to be adopted. But it remains the case, as studies since 1970 on philosophy and literature, as on the arts, have continued to indicate, and as my own work on the Italian mythological plays of the late fifteenth century has begun to reveal, that the importance of the Neoplatonic currents emanating from Florence cannot be minimized.

The diffusion of these currents, and especially of Neoplatonic love theory, was of prime importance in the development of Renaissance artistic theory and iconography, as is well known, and repercussions were felt in literature and in music, both in Italy and in the rest of Europe as the sixteenth century progressed.[2] However, it is also interesting to note the promptness

---

[1] P. O. KRISTELLER, «The European Significance of Florentine Platonism», in *Medieval and Renaissance Studies*, Proceedings of the Southeastern Institute of Medieval and Renaissance Studies, Summer 1967, ed. J. M. Headley, Chapel Hill, 1968, pp. 206-229; cf. Idem, «La diffusione europea del platonismo fiorentino», in *Il pensiero italiano del Rinascimento e il tempo nostro. Atti del V Convegno Internazionale del Centro di Studi Umanistici*, Montepulciano, 8-13 agosto 1968, ed. G. Tarugi, Firenze, 1970, pp. 23-41.

[2] To mention a few key works: A. CHASTEL, *Marsile Ficin et l'art*, Genève, 1954; repr. 1975; Idem, *Art et humanisme au temps de Laurent le Magnifique*, Paris, 1961; 3rd ed. 1981; E. H.

of this diffusion within Italy, but outside of Florence, and among those not
normally associated with the Platonic revival. I refer specifically to the poets
of the Northern courts of fifteenth-century Italy.

In response to Kristeller's call in the above-mentioned article for documentation of the diffusion of these ideas, I offer the text at hand, which illus-
trates both early Italian diffusion of Florentine Neoplatonism, and the special interest held for poets by Ficino's *Commentarium in Convivium de
amore*.

The text is a *Fragmentum* found in MS Trivulziano 1093, a *zibaldone*, or
collection of writings, of the Milanese poet, statesman and courtier, Gaspare
Visconti (1461-1499).[3] The manuscript, of III + 185 paper folios, can be
dated to the years around 1496, a date which appears in a contemporary hand
upside-down at the bottom of the verso of the unnumbered front flyleaf.[4]
The composition of the bulk of the manuscript (excluding posthumous additions) can be situated with certainty only between 1493 and 1499. The former

---

GOMBRICH, «Botticelli's Mythologies, A Study in the Neoplatonic Symbolism of his
Circle», *Journal of the Warburg and Courtauld Institutes*, 8 (1945), pp. 7-60; E. PANOFSKY,
*Studies in Iconology. Humanistic Themes in the Art of the Renaissance*, New York, 1962;
Idem, *Idea. A Concept in Art Theory*, tr. J. J. S. Peake, New York, 1968; E. WIND, *Pagan
Mysteries in the Renaissance*, New York, 1968; A. BUCK, *Der Platonismus in den Dichtungen
Lorenzo de' Medicis*, Berlin, 1936; Idem, *Der Einfluss des Platonismus auf die volksssprach-
liche Literatur im Florentiner Quattrocento*, Krefeld, 1965; J. FESTUGIÈRE, *La philosophie de
l'amour de Marsile Ficin et son influence sur la littérature française au XVIe siècle*, Paris,
1941; D. P. WALKER, «Ficino's 'Spiritus' and Music», *Annales musicologiques*, 1 (1935), pp.
131-150; Idem, «The Harmony of the Spheres», in *Studies in Musical Science in the Late
Renaissance*, London and Leiden, 1978, pp. 1-13. And see J. C. NELSON, *Renaissance Theory
of Love*, New York and London, 1963; B. GUTHMÜLLER, «Mythos und dramatisches Festspiel an den oberitalienischen Höfen des Quattrocento», in his *Studien zur antiken Mythologie in der italienischen Renaissance*, Weinheim, 1986, pp. 65-77, 172-176; and chapter IX,
below.

[3] Descriptions of the manuscript are in G. PORRO, *Catalogo dei codici manoscritti della Trivulziana*, Torino, 1884, pp. 463-464, and G. VISCONTI, *I canzonieri per Beatrice d'Este e per
Bianca Maria Sforza*, ed. P. Bongrani, Milano, 1979, pp. xix-xxiii. Even if the body of poetic
texts published from this manuscript by Bongrani must be termed a finished collection,
additions and insertions throughout the manuscript by the author (and posthumously by
others), as well as the inclusion of a play, *Pasithea* (ff. 75v-100r), seem to me to require the
use of the term *zibaldone*. The play and Visconti's biography are presented in chapters IV
and VIII of this volume.

[4] This folio bears on its recto in pencil the number 264, which also appears on the label of the
Biblioteca Belgioiosa inside the front cover. It continues around the inside of the spine of
the book, gathering the sixteen quires, and is pierced by the stitches which join the quires to
a sheepskin cover, now backed with blue-grey cardboard.

date is that of the publication of Visconti's *Rithmi*, only one of whose poems appears in the present manuscript;[5] the latter is the year of the poet's death. The collection of poems on ff. 2$^v$-42$^r$ is dedicated at f. 1$^r$ to Beatrice d'Este Sforza, Duchess of Milan. Her death in January 1497 is thus the *terminus ad quem* for this portion of the manuscript, and probably for the play *Pasithea* (ff. 75$^v$-100$^r$) as well.[6] Visconti made use of this *canzoniere* twice, dedicating it once to Beatrice (the presentation copy is Triv. 2157 on purple parchment[7]), and once, with additions from ff. 44$^r$-134$^r$, to Bianca Maria Sforza, wife of the Hapsburg Emperor Maximilian I (this presentation copy is Vienna, Österreichische Nationalbibliothek, MS Series nova 2621 on parchment[8]). MS Triv. 1093 is clearly the working draft for the collections. It is written by scribes, probably in Visconti's employ, and corrected by the author.[9]

Bongrani discerns seven hands in the manuscript,[10] including that of the author (A$_t$), which he identifies by means of comparison with the hand of a signed letter in the Archivio di Stato, Mantua, which I have seen.[11] The hand A$_5$ he treats, correctly I believe, as operating after Visconti's death to insert in blank spaces various compositions presumably found among the poet's papers. I do not see this work as that of an undiscriminating and uninterested scribe hastily completing a sorry task, as does Bongrani.[12] Rather, it

---

[5] PORRO, *Catalogo* (n. 3), pp. 463-464. The colophon of the printed volume reads in part: ... F. TANCIVS GORNIGER (*sic*) / POETA MEDIOLANENSIS HOS RHI/THMOS MAGNIFICI AC SPLENDI/DISSIMI EQVITIS GASPARIS VI/CECOMITIS LINGVA VFRNA/CVLA (*sic*) COMPOSITOS ... IN MILLE / EXEMPLA IMPRIMI IVS/SIT MEDIOLANI: AN/NO A SALVTIFERO / VIRGINIS : PARTV. / M.CCCC.LXXXXIII. / QVARTO CALEN/DAS MARTIAS. / FINIS. My transcription here, from the copy I have seen in the Biblioteca Nazionale Centrale Vittorio Emanuele II, Rome, does not agree with that in HAIN at number 16078.

[6] Chapter VIII, below; cf. my *Politian's «Orfeo» and other «Favole Mitologiche» in the Context of Late Quattrocento Italy*, Ph.D. Dissertation, Columbia University, New York, 1976, pp. 187-190.

[7] Cf. PORRO, *Catalogo* (n. 3), pp. 462-463; VISCONTI, *I canzonieri* (n. 3), pp. xxiii-xxiv.

[8] O. MAZAL and F. UNTERKIRCHER, *Katalog der abendländischen Handschriften der Österreichischen Nationalbibliothek. «Series Nova»*, Teil 2.1, Wien, 1963, pp. 286-287; cf. VISCONTI, *I canzonieri* (n. 3), pp. xxiv-xxv.

[9] BONGRANI, in VISCONTI, *I canzonieri* (n. 3), pp. xx, xxxv-xxxix; cf. my *Politian's «Orfeo»* (n. 6), pp. 188-190.

[10] BONGRANI, in VISCONTI, *I canzonieri* (n. 3), pp. xix-xxiii.

[11] Gonzaga Busta 1614: segn. E. XLIX. 2, published by Bongrani in VISCONTI, *I canzonieri* (n. 3), Tavola I.

[12] BONGRANI, in VISCONTI, *I canzonieri* (n. 3), p. xxxii.

appears to me a work of devotion, albeit one perhaps completed in haste. The hand of A₅ does indeed seem to be a fast-moving hand, but speed is not always to be attributed to lack of interest or intellectual nonchalance (witness the hand of Angelo Poliziano), although it can sometimes, and in the case of A₅ does, result in errors. In support of the scribe's involvement in his task is the density of the compositions gathered, and his own avowed interest in copying the text we are here considering, evident in his closing words: *Hactenus inventum summa cura exscripsim(us)* (f. 132ʳ⁽¹³⁾).

This text, then, probably inserted by A₅ after the poet's death in the spring of 1499, bears the title at f. 131ʳ: *Fragmentum*, and is there said to be by *Magnificus Dominus Gasparus Vicecomes*. It is in Italian prose with a Northern patina, and inspection proves it to be composed of portions of the early Orations of Ficino's *De amore*, with minor additions by the *Fragmentum*'s author.[14] Ficino's Latin commentary had been composed at least by July of

---

[13] Cf. Bongrani: in VISCONTI, *I canzonieri* (n. 3), p. xxxii.

[14] See the collation with Ficino's *De amore* below. I cannot begin to give a complete bibliography on this work here. I cite the basic or classic works on the subject, and those recent works to which the reader may turn for further references. The text appears in the second volume of M. FICINO, *Opera omnia*, Basel, 1576; repr. Torino, 1959, pp. 1320-1363; and, edited from Vatican MS Vat. lat. 7705, in M. FICIN, *Commentaire sur le Banquet de Platon*, ed. and tr. R. Marcel, Paris, 1956; repr. 1978. On this edition, see P. O. KRISTELLER, «Some Original Letters and Autograph Manuscripts of Marsilio Ficino», in *Studi di bibliografia e di storia in onore di Tammaro De Marinis*, 3, Verona, 1964, pp. 17-18. See too, *Marsilio Ficino's Commentary on Plato's Symposium*, ed. and tr. S. R. Jayne, Columbia, Missouri, 1944, 2nd ed., Dallas, 1985; J. A. DEVEREUX, «The Textual History of Ficino's *De amore*», *Renaissance Quarterly*, 28 (1975), pp. 173-182; S. GENTILE, «Per la storia del testo del 'Commentarium in Convivium' di Marsilio Ficino», *Rinascimento*, ser. 2, 21 (1981), pp. 3-27 (it should perhaps be stated that the note in MS Vat. lat. 7705 at f. Iʳ is in the hand of Gaetano Marini [1740-1815], according to Prof. A. Campana [personal communication]; cf. GENTILE, p. 15, n. 1 and Marcel's introduction to FICIN, *Commentaire*, p. 40); indispensable is the catalogue, *Marsilio Ficino e il ritorno di Platone. Mostra di manoscritti, stampe e documenti*, 17 maggio-16 giugno 1984, eds. S. Gentile, S. Niccoli, P. Viti, Firenze, 1984, esp. pp. 60-69.
The manuscripts of the Latin version of *De amore* are listed in Marcel's edition (pp. 39-45), in Devereux's article with additions (pp. 174-175) and in Gentile's article (p. 20, n. 1). Compare the list of Ficino manuscripts in KRISTELLER, *Supplementum ficinianum*, 2 vols., Firenze, 1937, I, pp. v-lv and II, pp. 368-369. Devereux's list includes two others found by Kristeller: Morgan Library MS M. 918 (cf. P. O. KRISTELLER, «Marsilio Ficino as a Beginning Student of Plato», *Scriptorium*, 20 [1966], p. 48, n. 23) and MS Scale VII (olim XXXIII) in the Biblioteca del Vittoriale, Gardone (cf. DEVEREUX, pp. 179-180; GENTILE, p. 20, n. 1).
Printed editions, beginning with *Platonis opera omnia*, 2 vols., Firenze, [1484] (Hain *13062); and 1 vol., Venezia, 1491 (Hain *13063), which contain Ficino's *De amore* are referred to in the above-mentioned works, and cf. KRISTELLER, *Supplementum*, I, pp. lvii-lxxv.

1469,[15] and was printed with Ficino's translations of Plato at Florence in 1484 and Venice in 1491, both editions available during the lifetime of Gaspare Visconti, and in particular during the years of composition of MS Triv. 1093.

Comparison of our text with corresponding sentences of Ficino's own vernacular translation of his *De amore* (*Sopra lo amore*), completed by 1474 but not printed until 1544 (and then, seemingly, in response to a translation by Ercole Barbarasa of the same year[16]), shows the Trivulziana text's borrowings to have been translated and paraphrased independently. Accepting the attribution of the text to Visconti made by the hand A₅, we are thus in the presence of an extract of portions of Ficino's Latin text noted down and reworked in Italian translation by Gaspare Visconti.

Most of this Italian text can be related to specific points in the first and third Orations of Ficino's *Commentary*. I give the collation by sentence (referring to Marcel's easily available edition), in lieu of a second apparatus:

| Triv. 1093 | Ficino, *De amore* (Marcel) |
|---|---|
| 1 | I.2. par. 2.1-3 |
| 2 | I.2. par. 2.4 |
| 3 | I.2. par. 3.1 |
| 4 | I.2. par. 3.12 |
| 5 | I.3. par. 1.3 |
| 6 | I.3. par. 1.2,1 |
| 7, 8 | I.3. par. 1.1 |
| | (cf. par. 4) |

---

[15] FICIN, *Commentaire* (n. 14), p. 45; GENTILE, «Per la storia» (n. 14), pp. 9-19; *Marsilio Ficino e il ritorno di Platone* (n. 14), pp. 60-61

[16] P. O. KRISTELLER, «Marsilio Ficino as a Man of Letters and the Glosses Attributed to Him in the Caetani Codex of Dante», *Renaissance Quarterly*, 36 (1983), p. 24. The editions are: M. FICINO, *Sopra lo Amore o ver' Convito di Platone*, Firenze, Neri Dortelata, November, 1544; *Il comento di Marsilio Ficino sopra il Convito di Platone, & esso Convito, tradotti in lingua toscana per Hercole Barbarasa da Terni*, Roma, Francesco Priscianese Fiorentino, 1544, before April 19: cf. *Marsilio Ficino e il ritorno di Platone* [n. 14], p. 69. Marcel prints the dedicatory letter to the Barbarasa translation at FICIN, *Commentaire* (n. 14), p. 269. The Italian version was edited, on the basis of the Florentine edition and with a preface dated 1914, by Giuseppe Rensi in the series, Cultura dell'Anima (Lanciano, Carabba Editore). On this edition have been based subsequent printings, such as those of Milano, 1973 (preface by G. Ottaviano) and a more recent printing by Atanor in Rome. Now see the critical edition by S. Niccoli: M. FICINO, *El libro dell'amore*, Firenze, 1987; cf. *Marsilio Ficino e il ritorno di Platone* (n. 14), p. 65 (and see pp. 65-69).

| | |
|---|---|
| 9 | (cf. I.3. par. 4) |
| 10, 11 | I.2. par. 3.2-7 |
| 12 | I.2. par. 3.8-9 |
| 13 | (cf. I.4. par. 2.1) |
| 14 | I.2. par. 3.10 |
| 15 | I.2. par. 3.11 |
| 16 | (cf. I.4. par. 1.2) |
| 17 | III.2. par. 1.1. |
| | (cf. III.1. par. 1.4) |
| 18 | III.2. par. 1.2-7 |
| 19 | ? |
| 20 | III.2. par. 1.7-8 |
| 21 | III.2. par. 1.9 (with addition by Visconti) |
| | (cf. VI.3. par. 4 and VI.4. par. 1) |
| 22-25 | III.2. par. 1.10-13 |
| 26 | III.2. par. 2.1 |
| 27 | III.2. par. 2.2 |
| 28 | III.2. par. 2.3-4 |
| 29 | III.2. par. 2.5 (with addition by Visconti) |
| 30 | (Addition by Visconti) |
| 31 | III.2. par. 2.10-11 |
| 32 | III.2. par. 2.12 |
| 33 | III.2. par. 2.13 |
| 34 | III.2. par. 3.1 |
| 35 | III.2. par. 3.2 (with addition by Visconti) |
| 36 | III.2. par. 3.3 |
| 37 | III.2. par. 3.4 |
| 38 | III.2. par. 3.5 (with addition by Visconti) |
| 39 | III.2. par. 3.6 |
| 40 | V.8. par. 4.2 |
| | (cf. III.3. par. 1.1 and par. 2.1) |
| 41 | Summary by Visconti |
| | (cf. above, 1 and 2) |

The extracts are arranged to form a coherent whole, beginning and ending with the three points of love's nobility as found in its antiquity (set forth in sentences 1 and 2, and elaborated in sentences 3-9), its greatness as perceived in its present manifestations (sentences 10-15), and its utility as seen in the consequences of its activity (sentences 16-19). The text then launches into a further discussion of the consequences of love (sentences 20-25) and its unifying function and power (sentences 26-40). Sentence 41 is a recapitulation of sentences 1 and 2.

At one or two points in the text, Visconti seems to rephrase or extend Ficino's ideas a trifle (sentences 19?, 21, 29, 30, 35, 38, 41), exhibiting the philosophical bent evident in his poetic and dramatic works. Interestingly, and perhaps worth further consideration, his text includes none of the mentions in Ficino's *Oratio* III, *cap.* ii of the cosmic order (spheric arrangement, concentricity, and so forth). [17]

Visconti's interest in Ficino's commentary does not stop with the text here reproduced. In the dedicatory letter of his *canzoniere* for his patroness, and apparently kindred soul, Beatrice d'Este Sforza, [18] Visconti's study of Ficino also shows itself. Here he is defending the lessons of love against the opinions of theologians, false philosophers, and those of small intelligence who say love is ignobly born. Again we find a clear and systematic treatment of the questions and, near the beginning, clear echoes of Ficino's *De amore*, in particular those parts of it found in the text from MS Triv. 1093. For example, Visconti states in his dedicatory letter that true philosophers term Love the most eminent among the eminent gods. [19] He goes on to refer to Plato's *Phaedrus* and *Alcibiades* (accepted by Ficino and included in his edition of 1484 [20]). Finally, he argues against those who say Love is not noble and ancient, using the argument that the Creator kept Love (Charity) close to himself, and through Love divided the Chaos into harmonious elements. [21]

These examples serve to suggest that the reworking of Ficino's *De amore* in MS Triv. 1093 is not distant in time from the dedicatory letter to Beatrice. Bongrani dates the presentation manuscript for Beatrice (MS Triv. 2157) at 1495-1496. [22] Thus the present text, probably earlier than the letter to Beatrice in which Visconti makes his own use of the concepts found in Ficino's *De amore*, would date from about 1495.

---

[17] These omissions, like the arrangement of the text, are most likely a sign of Gaspare Visconti's own thinking, rather than an indication of another version of the text by Ficino: cf. DEVEREUX, «The Textual History» (n. 14), p. 173.

[18] MS Triv. 1093, ff. 1r-2r; VISCONTI, *I canzonieri* (n. 3), pp. 4-7.

[19] VISCONTI, *I canzonieri* (n. 3), p. 5; cf. *Fragmentum* (Appendix), sent. 3-4.

[20] Cf. KRISTELLER, «Marsilio Ficino as a Beginning Student» (n. 14), pp. 44-45. The *Phaedrus* commentary is edited and translated by M. J. B. Allen as *Marsilio Ficino and the Phaedran Charioteer*, Berkeley, Los Angeles, London, 1981; cf. Idem, *The Platonism of Marsilio Ficino. A Study of his Phaedrus Commentary*, Berkeley, Los Angeles, London, 1984.

[21] VISCONTI, *I canzonieri* (n. 3), p. 5; cf. *Fragmentum* (Appendix), sent. 6-9.

[22] BONGRANI, in VISCONTI, *I canzonieri* (n. 3), p. xxxiv, n. 3; cf. p. xxiii, n. 2.

## Appendix

### Gaspare Visconti's *Fragmentum*

The following text is taken from Milan, Bibl. Trivulziana, MS 1093, ff. 131[r]-132[r]. For bibliography see note 3 above. In the margin the scribe added the following *notabilia*: sent. 4, «Plato»; sent. 6, «Hesiodus, Parmenides, Acusileus, Orpheus, Mercurius»; sent. 20, «Dio Areopagita»; sent. 37, «Empedocles»; sent. 40, «Eriximachus».

In editing Visconti's *Fragmentum*, I have adopted modern conventions of punctuation and paragraphing. I retain the orthography and linguistic patina of Northern fifteenth-century Italy, although when necessary for comprehension I have divided words and joined them according to modern usage. Accents are also in keeping with modern usage. In one or two places, I have chosen to expand abbreviations in keeping with the dominant usage in the text (e.g. p[raese]nte, in sentence 2). I have normalized capitalization, for instance of the word Chaos (e.g. sentence 5), and eliminated majuscules where they do not enhance understanding. The text is accompanied by an apparatus giving the manuscript's readings. I have numbered the sentences for the purposes of the above discussion.

*Fragmentum Magnifici Domini Gasparis Vicecomitis.*

**(fol. 131[r])**

1. Se[(a)] nui vogliamo laudare alchuna cosa è neccessario laudarla da cose antecedente, et etiam da praesente et conseguente. 2. Le cose antecedente mostrano la nobilità, le praesente la magnitudine, le conseguente la utilità.

3. Lo amore adoncha per le cose antecedente se dice essere stato praecipuo et antiquissimo. 4. Così Phaedro disputa apresso a Platone in el quale la nobilità apertissimamente è dimonstrata, affirmando lui l'amore esser antiquissimo de tutti li dèi. 5. A Platone similmente è aparso quando lui scrive el Chaos nel Thimeo, perché in quello li colloca et constituisse l'amore. 6. De questa medesma sententia esser stato Hesiodo legiamo ne la Theogonia, et in

_____

[(a)] mu (*sic*) *del.*

libro de la natura [di] Parmenide pithagorico et Acusileo poeta et Orpheo et Mercurio: essendo manifesto che'l chaos era avante el mondo, et essendo l'amor collocato in quello, precesse Saturno, Jove et tutti gli altri dèi. 7. Per tanto Orpheo domanda l'amore essere antiquissimo et perfecto in sé medesmo, et etiam consultissimo.[b] 8. Et credo in questo seguir la sententia di Mercurio Trismegisto che sente tal cosa. 9. Et questo che è proximo al vero, imo verissimo, non è da negare perché, se l'amore de la divina virtù non havesse precesso quel Chaos, che da sua natura già molto tempo era rude, impolito, confuso et indigesto, per niuno modo havria desiderato questa forma, la qual nui vediamo, del mondo.

10. Oltra di questo, quanta sia la magnitudine de l'amore si può compraehendere per questo: se li mortali e li dèi fanno li comandamenti de l'amore, et spesse volte domati et incatenati senteno li colpi de quello ne la mente et ne l'animo suo, chi è quello che dubitarà apellarlo grande? 11. Et de questa openione fu Orpheo et Hesiodo. 12. Admirabile etiam l'amore predica Phedro, et rende questa causa apressa a Platone perché ciaschuno chi se vede illaqueato et irretito de la pulchritudine de alchuna cosa la suole admirare. 13. Et veramente non è altro amore se non desiderio de perfruer dela pulchritudine. 14. Et se dice etiam fare li dèi (o[c] vero cum alchun altro vocabulo vogli apellar gli angeli): admirando mai se satiano de contemplare la divina bellezza, et li mortali la spetia et la forma de li corpi eleganti. 15. Et tal grandeza et admirabilità de amore se monstra ne le cose presente.

16. Possiamo anchor laudar l'amor da cose consequente. 17. Per la qual cosa non mediocre utilità se monstra de quello, el quale certamente se sforza de far deffender et conservar ogni cosa. 18. Veramente a quello è per sua natura innata et ingenita **(f. 131ᵛ)** una certa cupidità de propagare, manifestare et generare una absoluta et consummata perfectione, quale in niuna altra cosa possiamo vedere, salvo che in Dio, il che la divina intelligentia, studiosissimamente havendo contemplato in sé dicta perfectione, la voluntà subito de epsa intelligentia desidera de edure et manifestare in luce tutte le cose. 19. Et questo è che ha in sé de generare el flagrantissimo amore.

20. Non immeritamente Dionisio nostro Areopagita dice che'l divino amore non è potuto lassar el Re de tutte le cose star senza foecundità de procreatione et germinatione, essendo etiam el transito de lo infinito de tal amore, dedito a propagatione et germinatione, transfuso dal summo auctore Idio in tutte le altre cose. 21. Per questo amore gli sancti spirti de Idio mo-

---

[b] consulissimo, ti *supra scr.*
[c] e MS.

veno i celi et ciaschuni danno li suoi doni uno a l'altro et l'altro a l'altro secondo che segueno per ordine. 22. Per questo le stelle diffondano el lume suo neli elementi. 23. Per questo el fuocho col suo calore move lo aere, lo aere l'aqua, l'aqua la terra; et vice versa [la] terra tira a sé l'aqua et questa tira lo aere, et lo aere el focho. 24. Le herbe simelmente et gli arbori per amor desiderose de propagare la sua semenza generano cose simile a sé. 25. Li animali etiam bruti et li huomeni grandissimamente son rapiti et inflammati da queste illecebre cupidità et esce de amore a procreare sobole.

26. Il che, se lo amore è certo fare ogni cosa, perché non comprobaremo[d] tutte le cose esser conservate da quello? 27. Lo officio de epso è sempre di conservare et fare. 28. Certamente le cose simili par consistano per cose de una medesma et simel natura, et l'amore tira la cosa simile ad una cosa a sé simile. 29. Ciaschune parte de la terra per uno amore mutuo ingenito et naturale copulante se conferissano a le altre parte simile de sé; ita ché una parte aiuta l'altra, et l'altra l'altra, et mai non se disiungano per amore, et così se conserva el tutto. 30. In tal modo tutti gli altri elementi procedeno. 31. Platone nel libro del regno[e] dice che'l celo[f] se move per uno innato et naturale amore et l'anima del ciel è tutta insema in ciaschuni puncti del celo. 32. El celo adunque, desideroso de perfruir de la (f. 132r) sua anima, per tal causa corre aciò possa perfruire de tutta l'anima da ogni canto per tutte le sue parte. 33. Et vola celerrimamente aciò che quanto sia possibile, lui sia tutto insieme de ogni canto dove da ogni canto l'anima è tutta insieme. 34. La qual cosa, se così non se facesse, essendo abandonata in qualche parte, in tal unitate nasceria una discordia che dissolveria tal cosa. 35. Qual unità un mutuo amore de dicte parte se la fa et conserva, et per niuno modo la lassa perire. 36. La qual cosa è licito a vederla ne li humori deli nostri corpi et neli elementi del mondo. 37. Per la concordia de li quali, sì come dice Empedocle pithagoreo, el[g] mondo[h] et etiam el corpo nostro consiste; per la discordia se destrue la concordia de tal pace. 38. Et amore ce presta una certa vicissitudine, ché si uno piglia[i] de l'altro, quello li rende. 39. Per tanto Orpheo dice, «Tu, amore, rege le habene de tutte le cose». 40. Eriximaco comme-

---

[d] tt *del.*
[e] el *del.*
[f] cilo *MS*
[g] del *del.*; el *supra scr.*
[h] per la concordia de li quali *del.*
[i] dal *del.*; del *supra scr.*

mora apresso a Platone esser niuna arte che lo amore non trova et governa et non sia maestro de quella.

41. Sì che l'amore, per l'antiquità, è nobilissimo; poi, per esser subiecta ogni cosa a quello, è grande et admirabile; tercio, perché da lui procede tutti li beni et è causa et fomento de ogni cosa, si como havemo demonstrato, ha inenarrabile utilità in sé. [j]

---

[j] Hactenus inventum summa cura exscripsim(us) *subscr.*

# CHAPTER VI

## Per la biografia di Baldassare Taccone

Il nome dell'autore della favola mitologica *Danae*[1] è forse più conosciuto dagli storici dell'arte, a causa degli schizzi fatti da Leonardo da Vinci per la rappresentazione del 1496,[2] che non dagli storici e critici letterari. Eppure, alla sua epoca, l'alessandrino Baldassare Taccone occupava un posto im-

[1] Il testo venne pubblicato per la prima volta da A. G. SPINELLI, *Per le nozze Mazzacorati-Gaetani dell'Aquila d'Aragona*, Bologna, 1888; ora è anche nel *Teatro del Quattrocento. Le corti padane*, a cura di A. Tissoni Benvenuti e M. P. Mussini Sacchi, Torino, 1983, pp. 293-334. Un'analisi dettagliata si trova nel mio *Politian's 'Orfeo' and Other 'Favole Mitologiche' in the Context of Late Quattrocento Northern Italy*, tesi di Ph.D., Columbia University, New York, 1976, pp. 181-187 (e per una versione preliminare di questa biografia, pp. 33-41). Vedi pure l'analisi linguistica di P. BONGRANI, in «Lingua e stile nella 'Pasitea' e nel teatro cortigiano milanese», *Interpres*, V (1983-84), pp. 205-224 (ristampato nel suo *Lingua e letteratura a Milano nell'età Sforzesca. Una raccolta di studi*, Parma 1986, pp. 85-185) e l'analisi interpretativa nel capitolo IX qui sotto; cfr. anche il mio, «Per un'iconologia dello spettacolo: dalle nozze sforzesche del 1489 alle favole mitologiche», *Arte lombarda*, 105-107 (1993): Atti del Convegno, «Metodologia della ricerca. Orientamenti attuali. Congresso Internazionale in onore di Eugenio Battisti» (Milano, 27-31 maggio 1991), pp. 84-87. Il titolo originale dell'opera, che figura sul fol. 488ᵛ del MS Sessor. 413 della Biblioteca Nazionale Centrale Vittorio Emanuele, Roma, e stampato (con varianti minori e con l'aggiunta della parola «Danae») dallo Spinelli, ci indica qualche particolare della rappresentazione: *Danae / Comedia recitata in casa del Signore Conte di Cajazzo / allo Illustrissimo / Signore Duca e populo de Milano adi ultimo de genaro / MCCCCLXXXXVJ*.

[2] I disegni si trovano ora al Metropolitan Museum of Art di New York e alla Pinacoteca Ambrosiana di Milano. Cfr. principalmente M. HERZFELD, «La rappresentazione della 'Da-

portante nella corte di Ludovico il Moro. Egli si trattenne inoltre a Milano almeno tre anni dopo la caduta di quest'ultimo, tornandovi col governo di Massimiliano Sforza, o forse prima, per rimanervi poi sotto il secondo dominio dei francesi, fino alla morte. Della sua posizione non secondaria sono testimonianza viva alcuni epigrammi e lettere indirizzatigli dal nobile Giovanni II Tolentino (1471-1517),[3] nipote del genero di Francesco Sforza, contenuti in un volume, ora rarissimo, delle sue lettere.[4] Fra gli altri epigrammi e lettere nello stesso volume figurano nomi come Matteo Bandello, Jacopo Antiquario, e Piattino Piatti (a cui sono indirizzati una decina delle lettere e

---

nae' organizzata da Leonardo», *Raccolta vinciana*, XI, 1920-22, pp. 226-228; K. STEINITZ, «Le dessin de Léonard de Vinci pour la *Danae*», in *Le lieu théâtral à la Renaissance*, a cura di J. Jacquot, Paris, 1968, pp. 35-40; Eadem, «Leonardo architetto teatrale e organizzatore di feste», in *Leonardo da Vinci letto e commentato ... Letture vinciane I-XII (1960-1972)* (IX, 15 aprile 1969), Firenze, 1974, pp. 249-274 (soprattutto le pp. 257-261 e figg. 5-10).

[3] Su cui, si veda C. MARCORA, «I Commentarii di Giovanni II Tolentino», *Archivio storico lombardo*, XC (1963), pp. 330-339; Ph. ARGELATI, *Bibliotheca Scriptorum Mediolanensium*, 2 voll. in 4 parti, Milano, 1745, vol. II, pars 1, coll. 1495-1496; cfr. II, 2, 2109 E, 2110 C (su Dulcinus); 2177 B - 2178 B (su Taccone). Il nonno, legittimato egli stesso nel 1434, sposò Isotta Sforza, figlia naturale dello Sforza; fu nominato consigliere onorario al Consiglio Segreto nel 1450; morì nel 1470. Cfr. C. SANTORO, *Gli uffici del dominio sforzesco (1450-1500)*, Milano, 1948, p. 4, n. 5 e p. 7, n. 5; P. LITTA, *Famiglie celebri d'Italia*, Milano, 1819-1893, vol. VI, s.v. Mauruzi di Tolentino, Tav. III (Ramo di Milano); F. SANSOVINO, *Della origine et de' fatti delle famiglie illustri d'Italia*, Libro Primo, Venezia, Altobello Salicato, 1582, cc. 279ᵛ-285: «Signori Maurutij o Tolentini» (questo ramo alla c. 281ʳ⁻ᵛ). Altri accenni biografici si trovano nel capitolo VIII di questo volume.

[4] *IOANNIS TOLLENTI- / NATIS.II.EQVI- / TIS:EPISTO- / LARVM / LIBRI / .III.*, il cui colophon, alla carta *e iiii*, legge: *Impressum Mediolani per Ioannem Ca- / stilioneum Anno Salutis nostrae. / M.cccc.xii. Sexto Idus Apri- / lis: Ludovico .xii. Galloru(m) / Rege: & Mediolani Du- / ce Invictissimo.* Cfr. *Editori e tipografi a Milano nel Cinquecento*, a cura di E. Sandal, 3 voll., Baden-Baden, 1977, 1978, 1981 (Bibliotheca Bibliographica Aureliana, LXVIII, LXXII, LXXXIII), vol. 3, p. 56, num. 525. Non corrisponde all'edizione citata da Marcora, p. 334, n. 7 (Sandal, vol. II, p. 35, numero 195). Ho letto le lettere nella copia segnata 10905.d.22 della British Library [ora vedi il capitolo VII, qui sotto, n. 2]. Tutte le lettere indirizzate a Taccone e quegli epigrammi che lo riguardono si ripubblicano qui in appendice. Due delle lettere, l'una del 9 giugno 1491, scritta dal porto di Bereguardo sul Ticino (e non sul Po come volle lo Spinelli) dove era la flottiglia ducale, l'altra da Milano il 7 maggio 1493 (i numeri 9 e 10, in appendice), sono citate da ARGELATI, *Bibliotheca* (n. 3), vol. II, pars 2, col. 2177 come «extant cum aliis ipsius Tolentini editis *Mediol. 1511.* (sic) *in* 4». Ci si può chiedere se lo Spinelli (*Introduzione* alla *Danae* [n. 1], p. 8), citando lettere «del Taccone», senza ubicarle, non abbia letto in fretta le parole dell'Argelati: «Scripsit: ... *Epistolae plures ad Joannem Tolentinum*, *uti eruitur a binis Taccono nostro scriptis ab eodem Tolentino*,...» (corsivo mio).

qualche epigramma, e che fornisce l'epigramma iniziale). Ma il nome che appare più di ogni altro e a cui sono indirizzate le lettere più lunghe, di grande interesse storico (come le altre contenute in questo volume), è quello di «Balthasarus Tachonus». Le lettere in questione, che portano date dal 1488 fino al 1512, sono ricche di dettagli sulla vita di un certo ceto letterario e intellettuale attorno alla corte sforzesca. Spiccano soprattutto una descrizione dell'entrata in Milano e delle nozze di Giangaleazzo Sforza con Isabella d'Aragona nel febbraio del 1489 (n. 3 in appendice);[5] e un *itinerarium*, inclusa una *descriptio urbis* di Roma, del 1490 (parzialmente pubblicato altrove, ed incluso qui nella sua interezza, n. 7 in appendice[6]).

Taccone (o Tacconi) nacque ad Alessandria in Piemonte nel 1461, come si desume dalla notizia della morte all'età di sessant'anni tratta dal Necrologio milanese dal Motta.[7] La famiglia apparteneva alla nuova nobiltà (i «nobili del popolo») creata ad Alessandria da Filippo Maria Visconti nel 1417 e che avrebbe dovuto in cambio servire come una specie di polizia viscontea per risolvere, fra l'altro, le lotte guelfo-ghibelline di quella città.[8] Un Giacomo Taccone, che sarebbe il padre del poeta (come viene confermato nella lettera n. 9, qui sotto in appendice), viene menzionato negli *Annali di Alessandria* di Girolamo Ghilini, come uno dei quattro «gentiluomini» del quartiere di Marengo presenti alla cerimonia della piantagione di alberi per l'inaugurazione dell'abbellimento della città nel 1466.[9]

---

[5] Su queste nozze: PYLE, «Per un'iconologia» (n. 1), p. 84 e il capitolo VII del presente volume.

[6] R. SCHOFIELD, «Giovanni da Tolentino Goes to Rome: A Description of the Antiquities of Rome in 1490», *Journal of the Warburg and Courtauld Institutes*, XLIII (1980), pp. 246-256; mi dispiace un poco in quest'articolo, prezioso per la sua erudizione, vedere Giovanni trattato da umanista, e perciò criticato per mancanza di accuratezza nelle sue descrizioni (è chiamato infatti «unrepentant charlatan»: p. 248), mentre non fu altro che uomo di armi, giocondo, aristocratico con gusti permeati dall'Umanesimo. Cfr. anche P. P. BOBER, R. RUBINSTEIN, *Renaissance Artists and Antique Sculpture. A Handbook of Sources*, London e Oxford, 1986, pp. 77, 109.

[7] E. MOTTA, «Morti in Milano dal 1452 al 1552 (spogli del necrologio milanese)», *Archivio storico lombardo*, ser. II, VIII (1891), p. 271 e n. 3: «dom. *Baldesar de Thaconibus* an. LX ex diaria epatica post febrem sine pestis suspicione judicio Mag.ri Jo. Ant. Dugnani decessit». I documenti per l'anno 1521 ora mancano dal necrologio.

[8] C. A-VALLE, *Storia di Alessandria dall'origine ai nostri giorni*, Torino, 4 voll., 1853-1855, vol. IV: Sezione biografie, p. 108 e vol. III, pp. 76-80.

[9] G. GHILINI, *Annali di Alessandria overo le cose accadute in essa città nel suo, e circonvicino territorio dall'anno dell'origine sua [1168] sino al MDCLIX...con due tavole...*, Milano, 1666, p. 104: Anno 1466, num. 6.

La prima notizia che possediamo (se è lecito prestar fede ad una notizia non documentata) data dalla rivalutazione della memoria di Cicco Simonetta nell'anno 1487.[10] Secondo lo Spinelli, Taccone, che aveva allora 26 anni, compose l'epitaffio per la tomba del Simonetta a Pavia. Nell'epitaffio, riportato dall'Argelati, si legge:

PRINCIPIS INSVBRVM FIDVS QVIA SCEPTRA TVEBAR
ACEPHALON TVMVLO GENS INIMICA DEDIT.
ME CECVM DICVNT VIDI QVI MVLTA SVPERSTES
CREDE MICHI SINE ME PATRIA CECA MANES.

DVM FIDVS SERVARE VOLO PATRIAMQVE DVCEMQVE
MVLTORVM INSIDIIS PRODITVS INTERII.
ILLE SED IMMENSA CELEBRARI LAVDE MERETVR
QVI MAVVLT VITA QVAM CARVISSE FIDE.[11]

L'anno 1488 porta Taccone fuori Milano, benché in circostanze non troppo disagevoli, come risulta dalla lettera n. 2, in appendice. Inoltre sembra aver preso parte ai festeggiamenti organizzati da Bergonzio Botta a Tortona in occasione delle nozze di Gian Galeazzo Sforza ed Isabella d'Aragona.[12] Nel 1489 avrebbe raccontato al Tolentino di aver visto l'emblema tolentinate nelle mani di una statua di donna in un tempio dedicato ad Ercole, mentre stava «apud Moeneum saxum» per distribuire gli stipendi ai soldati (v. la lettera n. 4 dell'aprile 1489; si tratta di una fortificazione non identificata); Tolentino si riferisce nella stessa lettera ad una prossima visita da parte del Taccone, che dovrà spedire in anticipo spine di cardi e fave (simboli di fertilità, ma anche, i primi, pianta e piatto indigeni in Piemonte, luogo di nascita del nostro e sito delle feste nuziali già accennate) per annunciare l'arrivo suo. Certamente le assenze di Taccone da Milano non furono ininterrotte. Se si

---

[10] A. SPINELLI, *Introduzione* alla sua edizione (n. 1), p. 8. L'editore promise qui e in un suo articolo sull'*Archivio storico lombardo*, XIV (1887), «Di un codice milanese», p. 809, di pubblicare «tutto ciò che del Tacconi in vari anni di ricerche ho trovato». Purtroppo lo studio promesso non sembra che sia mai stato compiuto, e non ci rimangono che i due scritti citati, che parlano di avvenimenti della vita del Taccone, ma senza guidarci verso le fonti adoperate. Le nostre ricerche negli archivi di Milano e di Alessandria sono riuscite solo parzialmente, e ne riportiamo qui i risultati con la speranza che ulteriori indagini li possano completare, forse cercando fra le carte dello stesso Spinelli.

[11] ARGELATI, *Bibliotheca* (n. 3), II, 2, *Scriptores Exteri*, coll. 2165-2166.

[12] Giudicando dall'attribuzione, attendibile, al Taccone della serie di testi scritti per quell'occasione proposta da U. ROZZO: «L'*Ordine de le imbandisone* per le nozze di Gian Galeazzo Sforza con Isabella d'Aragona», *Libri & documenti*, Anno XIV, n. 2 (1989), pp. 1-14.

tratti o no di soste molto prolungate fuori città, l'ultima delle quali attorno a questa epoca in Liguria (v. la lettera n. 6, dell'ottobre 1490), è difficile dire.

Nel settembre 1492 ritroviamo il Taccone insieme con il suo collega Niccolò da Correggio, e forse anche col poeta Gaspare Visconti, diretto verso Roma per rendere omaggio al nuovo Papa, Alessandro VI.[13] La sua presenza in questa compagnia e il favore allora concessogli dal Moro trovano conferma in alcune poesie sue, latine ed italiane, nel codice milanese, ora Sessoriano 413, della Biblioteca Nazionale Centrale Vittorio Emanuele di Roma, e soprattutto nella composizione seguente:

De Urbe Roma
Est haec Roma? Fuit. Quid nunc? Est maxima quaedam
 Colluvies orbis, congeriesque virum.
En quo cessit honos, tantarum & gloria rerum!
 Quo decus & pietas, quo sine fine pudor!
In ventos abiere procul, perit illa vetusta
 Roma, triumphantis quae caput orbis erat.
Luminis antiqui tantum duo lumina vivunt:
 Ascanius Romae, Maurus in Italia.[14]

Questi versi fanno parte di una serie di poesie indirizzate «Ad Illustrem et inclytum dominum Nicolaum Vicecomitem & Coregium, in officio legationis ad summum pont(ificem): Balthasaris Taconi Alexandrini canzellarij». Dunque il nostro era già cancelliere, pienamente integrato nella corte di Ludovico il Moro («Maurus», fratello del cardinale Ascanio Sforza) nel 1492,[15] e in

---

[13] SPINELLI, *Introduzione* alla *Danae* (n. 1), p. 8. Per la partecipazione del Correggio, G. TIRABOSCHI, *Biblioteca modenese*, Modena, 1782, vol. II, p. 117. B. Corio ed i suoi editori elencano un «Gasparo/e Visconti» senza specificare di quale degli otto Gaspari contemporanei si tratta: *Storia di Milano*, Milano, 1855-1857, III, pp. 427, 447-448. Sugli omonimi del Visconti, cfr. Appendice I del capitolo IV, qui sopra.

[14] Cod. Sess. 413, c. 74. Questo segue un altro epigramma, anch'esso diretto (giudicando da elementi interni) dal Taccone al Correggio, e scritto a Firenze, probabilmente sulla via per Roma.

[15] ARGELATI, *Bibliotheca* (n. 3), II, 2, col. 2178, dice invece che il Taccone «in hac Insubriae Metropoli Ducalis Cancellarius florere coepit anno MCCCCXCIII», cfr. anche la fine della lettera num. 10, in appendice. È naturalmente possibile che il titolo generale sia stato aggiunto nel copiare i versi dell'anno 1492 sul manoscritto, la cui provenienza milanese Spinelli identifica dalla carta («Di un codice milanese» *cit.* [n. 10], p. 808). Caterina Santoro ci dà notizia di un *Alexander Taconus* che sembra portare il titolo di «Cancelliere al Consiglio Segreto» dal novembre del 1495; però la data manca dall'atto stesso (*Registro Ducale* 189, c. 38), apparendo solo sulla lettera di nomina: SANTORO, *Gli uffici* (n. 3), p. 34. Se possiamo

contatti stretti coll'autore del *Cefalo* (1487), favola mitologica che precede di quasi un decennio la sua *Danae*[16]).

L'anno seguente, 1493, il Taccone si definisce cancelliere anche nel titolo del suo poema commemorante il matrimonio di Bianca Maria Sforza con l'Imperatore Massimiliano: *Coronatione e sponsalitio de la serenissima Re/gina. M. Bianca. Ma. SF. Augusta al Illustris/simo .S. Ludouico. SF. uisconte Duca de Bar/ri per Baldassarre Taccone Alexandrino ca(n)cel/leri composta,* [17] nel quale allude, fra l'altro, al suo «patron misser Guaspar Visconte» (stanza 79), a indicazione delle relazioni strette – testimoniate anche dalle lettere tolentiniane numeri 1 e 4 (1488-1489) in appendice – col terzo poeta e drammaturgo di corte, autore della *Pasithea* negli anni 1493-1497. [18]

Ludovico il Moro gli conferisce la cittadinanza di Milano il 25 febbraio 1497 in quanto «scrib(am) nostr(um) dilect(um)». [19] Questa menzione e questo favore così vicini alla recentissima morte, il 2 gennaio, della sposa del Moro, Beatrice d'Este, ci indicano un rapporto piuttosto intimo con il duca e forse anche il riconoscimento di un aiuto spirituale da parte del poeta, noto anche per il suo animo gentile, cosa che spingeva i colleghi perfino a prenderlo in giro, come nei sonetti in dialetto artefatto conosciuti in manoscritto e

---

o no vedere in questo una notizia tardiva della nomina non è molto chiaro. L'identificazione possibile di questo *Alexander* con Baldassare è sostenuta dal fatto che pure altrove, benché più recentemente, ci si riferisce al Taccone col nome «Alessandro», probabilmente da una confusione con la città natale: cfr. F. MALAGUZZI VALERI, *La corte di Lodovico il Moro*, 4 voll., Milano, 1913-1923, vol. IV, p. 171.

[16] Sul *Cefalo*, e per il testo e la bibliografia, si veda *Teatro del Quattrocento* (n. 1), pp. 201-255; cfr. N. da CORREGGIO, *Opere. Cefalo, Psiche, Silva, Rime*, a cura di A. Tissoni Benvenuti, Bari, 1969; N. PIRROTTA, E. POVOLEDO, *Li due Orfei*, Torino, 1975 (pp. 45-46, 50, 361, 369-370); PYLE, *Politian's 'Orfeo'* (n. 1), pp. 10-19, 169-180, 262-331 e cfr. il capitolo IX, qui sotto.

[17] Colophon: Imp(re)ssit Leonardu(s) pachel. M. cccc. lxxxxiii. Cito dalla copia nella Biblioteca Braidense, Incunab. AM. IX. 35. (HAIN-REICHLING 15216; IGI 9254; cfr. T. ROGLEDI MANNI, *La tipografia a Milano nel XV secolo*, Firenze, 1980, p. 198, num. 949). Il testo è stato di recente curato da G. Biancardi in *Studi e fonti di storia lombarda. Quaderni milanesi*, 13 (1993), pp. 43-121; ringrazio Paolo Bongrani di questa indicazione bibliografica.

[18] Sulla *Pasithea* si vedano il mio *Politian's 'Orfeo'*, pp. 187-197 e i capitoli VIII, IX e X qui sotto; inoltre: BONGRANI, «Lingua e stile» (n. 1); e il testo in *Teatro del Quattrocento* (n. 1), pp. 337-396.

[19] Biblioteca Trivulziana, Archivio Storico Civico, Registro numero 7 (*Litterarum ducalium* 1497-1502): Atto n. 12. Cfr. *I registri delle lettere ducali del periodo sforzesco*, a cura di C. Santoro, Milano, 1961, p. 281. Taccone si nomina «scriba» quando, nello stesso periodo, dedica certi «Monosyllabi» a Niccolò da Correggio, come vedremo più avanti (alla n. 27).

recentemente pubblicati. [20] È significativo notare a questo riguardo, che egli non si faceva illusioni sul valore dei propri versi. Alla fine di un epigramma indirizzato a Niccolò da Correggio, a dimostrazione del fatto di non prender- si troppo sul serio, volgeva l'ironia nei suoi stessi riguardi: «Rem veram fa- teor: poeta no(n) sum». [21]

Fu durante il periodo relativamente stabile e fiorente della corte del Mo- ro, prima della morte di Beatrice, che vennero composte le poche opere lette- rarie in volgare per cui conosciamo Baldassare Taccone. L'allegoria politica di 73 versi, in cui consiste l'*Atteone*, ci è pervenuta nei codici della Biblioteca Nazionale Centrale di Firenze, II ii 75, e della Bibliothèque Nationale di Parigi, Ital. 1543. Venne stampata nel 1884 da Felice Bariola, che la datava tra il 1480 e 1494 (anno della morte di Gian Galeazzo Sforza, a cui s'indirizza nominalmente la rappresentazione) e con maggior probabilità prima del 1489 (dato il silenzio del testo a proposito della moglie di lui, Isabella d'Aragona, che sposò nell'89). [22] L'ambiguità del significato del tema del cacciatore che, vedendo la dea Diana al bagno, venne trasformato in cervo e straziato dai propri cani, non è di facile risoluzione. O lo sfortunato rappresenta – come si pensa subito – il giovane duca Gian Galeazzo Sforza, vittima dello zio Ludo- vico (e allora il capitolo finale in lode del Moro sarebbe un prudente, e anzi, obbligato gesto politico), [23] o, come ipotizzava Bariola, allude al regno san-

---

[20] Cfr. F. MARRI, «Lancino Curti a Gaspare Visconti», in *Studi filologici letterari e storici in memoria di Guido Favati*, 2 voll., a cura di G. Varanini e P. Pinagli, Padova, 1977, (Medioe- vo e Umanesimo, 28-29), vol. II, pp. 397-423; i sonetti sono curati in Idem, «Lingua e dialetto nella poesia giocosa ai tempi del Moro», in *Milano nell'età di Ludovico il moro*, 2 voll., Milano, 1983, I, pp. 255-270; cfr. D. ISELLA, «Lo sperimentalismo dialettale di Lan- cino Curzio e compagni», in *In ricordo di Cesare Angelini. Studi di letteratura e filologia*, Milano, 1979, pp. 146-159; R. MARCHI, «Un nuovo sonetto contro Baldassare Taccone», *Diverse lingue*, I (1986), pp. 71-78.

[21] Cod. Sessor. 413, c. 490: «Nostris carminibus nihil vocamur, / Nam quicquid patimur mali, fatemur / Fortunam, Nicolae, non amicam. / Expertus doleo, nec ut poeta / Scripsi ridicula procacitate. / Rem veram fateor: poeta non sum».

[22] *L'Atteone (Favola) e le rime di Baldassare Taccone. Per le nozze Bellotti-Bariola*, settembre 1884, a cura di F. Bariola, s.l., 1884. A. TISSONI BENVENUTI segue D. ISELLA («Lo speri- mentalismo dialettale», [n. 20]) nella datazione dopo il 1493: *Teatro del Quattrocento* (n. 1), p. 293, n. 1. In questo caso, la datazione è del 1493-94, anno della morte del duca; cfr. ROZZO, «L'*Ordine de le imbandisone*» (n. 12), pp. 2, 8.

[23] In questo caso, come in tante altre occasioni, la politica del Moro, quella di intimidire il giovane e influenzabile duca, riempiendogli l'animo di apprensione davanti alle grandi diffi- coltà del governo, si rappresenterebbe palesemente nell'orribile fine del giovane cacciatore ardente (qui un principe) davanti alla visione di bellezza della perfida dea, che lo fa attaccare dai propri cani, fino a quel punto fedeli e amati.

guinoso di Giovanni Maria Visconti all'inizio del secolo. Ma le due ipotesi
sono insoddisfacenti, rappresentando la prima un'allusione imprudente, la
seconda un'allusione remota dallo spirito del popolo. Il testo ci fornisce, però, ancora una prova (se ne avessimo bisogno) di quale ramo della famiglia
sforzesca il poeta onorasse e servisse: la rappresentazione, offerta per il Carnevale Ambrosiano sulla Piazza del Duomo dal signor Francesco Fontana,
finisce infatti col capitolo encomiastico di 33 versi, recitato da Mercurio «al
S.re Duca di Milano in commendatione del Moro». Eccone un brano, rife-
rentesi a Ludovico e indirizzato al duca Gian Galeazzo:

> In lui clementia et pietà s'afferra;
>   Italia in lui si posa; in lui s'annida
>   Terror, soccorso, aiuto, pace et guerra.
> Felice te! felice fin ch'e' guida;
>   Et felice sarai di passo in passo,
>   Et fie felice ognun ch'in lui si fida.
>
> (*Atteone,* vv. 24-29)

L'opera poetica del Taccone trova una sua giustificazione (come, d'al-
tronde, quella dei suoi colleghi più versatili artisticamente, Niccolò da Correggio e Gaspare Visconti) come testimonianza storico-sociale dell'epoca sua.
Sparse nei codici più conosciuti dell'ambiente sono varie poesie latine ed italiane del Taccone. Alcune sono senza indicazione di data, ma, come abbiamo
già visto, chiaramente attribuibili al viaggio romano del 1492, di cui ci offro-
no dati sociali e di costume idonei (e no) ad una tale occasione.

Così pure nel già ricordato poema in ottave, che celebra le nozze nel 1493
di Bianca Maria Sforza, nipote di Ludovico il Moro, con Massimiliano I
d'Austria, imperatore, troviamo un accenno alla statua colossale in gesso
(mai fuso in bronzo) di Francesco Sforza eseguita da Leonardo da Vinci. Lo-
dando il Moro, il poeta scrive:

> Vedi che in corte fa far di metallo
>   per memoria dil padre un gran colosso:
>   i' credo fermamente e senza fallo,
>   che Gretia e Roma mai vide el più grosso.
>   Guarde pur come è bello quel cavallo!
>   Leonardo Vinci a farlo sol s'è mosso:
>   statuar, bon pictore e bon geometra,
>   un tanto ingegno rar dal ciel s'impetra.
>
> E se più presto non s'è principiato,
>   la voglia del Signor fu semper pronta.
>   Non era un Lionardo ancor trovato,

qual di presente tanto ben l'inpronta
che qualunche che'l vede sta amirato,
e se con lui al parangon s'afrunta
Fidia, Mirone, Scoppa e Praxitello,
diran ch'al mondo mai fusse el più bello.

(*Coronatione*, 102-103[24])

Nei brani qui citati, si allude, fra l'altro, alla massa di metallo richiesta da Leonardo e accumulata da Ludovico, per essere adoperata, alla fine, nella costruzione di armi. Inoltre si sottolinea l'abilità geometrica dell'artista: un talento apprezzato in quell'epoca, che aveva grande considerazione per le arti pratiche (si pensi, ad esempio, ai lavori teorico-pratici dell'Alberti, o al *Panepistemon* del Poliziano) e per le loro applicazioni.

In questo poema, di valore soprattutto per il dettaglio con il quale descrive lo sposalizio imperiale, il poeta corrobora la relazione fatta dallo storico ufficiale dello stesso avvenimento, Tristano Calco, e la lettera, stampata da Luzio e Renier, di Beatrice d'Este Sforza alla sorella Isabella d'Este Gonzaga. [25]

All'età di 33 anni, Taccone partecipò con Leonardo alla festa in casa del Conte di Cajazzo (Gian Francesco Sanseverino) cui, come si accenna all'inizio, è legata la sua notorietà. [26] Scrisse una 'favola' sulla base del mito di Danae, il cui padre Acrisio, conoscendo la profezia secondo cui sarebbe stato ucciso dal figlio di sua figlia, rinchiude l'infelice in una torre. Giove ne sente la notizia, e si manifesta alla sfortunata in guisa di pioggia d'oro. Da questa visita nasce Perseo. Dagli appunti di Leonardo sugli schizzi fatti per la rappresentazione, sappiamo che fu l'autore stesso ad assumere il ruolo del guar-

---

[24] La punteggiatura della prima edizione (n. 17) è stata da me aggiornata a confronto con quella dell'ediz. di G. Biancardi (n. 17), p. 92. Altra testimonianza, più esplicita, al cavallo sta nell'epigramma del Tolentino, *Epistolarum Libri III*, fol. c ii *verso*: «In Divi Francisci Sf. Statua equestri. // Inclyta pax Latii fueram, tum fulgur in armis / Et mea scipiadum gloria maior erat. / Hunc mihi magne nepos et tu Lodovice colossum / Ponitis, ut vivat nomen in orbe meum».

[25] T. CALCO, *Nuptiae Augustae: hoc est, Maximiliani Imperatoris cum Blanca, Ioannis Galeacij Mediolanensium Ducis sorore*, stampate con i suoi *Residua, hoc est, Historiae Patriae Liber XXI & XXII*, Mediolani MDCXLIV, anche nel *Thesaurus Antiquitatum et Historiarum Italiae, Mari Linguistico & Alpibus Vicinae*, a cura di J.G. Graevius, t. II, pars 1, Lugduni Batavorum, MDCCIV, coll. 525-536; cfr. A. LUZIO e R. RENIER, «Delle relazioni di Isabella d'Este Gonzaga con Ludovico e Beatrice Sforza», *Archivio storico lombardo*, XVII (1890), pp. 383-388.

[26] Si veda la nota 2, e, sulla favola mitologica, il capitolo IX, qui sotto.

diano, Siro, che resiste ai tentativi di Giove, ma a cui tocca poi di portare il messaggio della gravidanza di Danae ad Acrisio, per il quale servizio viene messo in catene, fino al quinto atto, che si risolve in un lieto fine.

L'ultima opera poetica del maggior periodo sforzesco che porta il nome di Taccone sono i «monosillaba nonnulla ad Nic(olaum) Cor(rigium)» ricordati dall'Argelati e risalenti all'edizione milanese di Sidonio Apollinare del 1498:[27]

Balthasaris tachoni ducalis scribae ad Nico/laum Corrigium virum illustrem.
Monosyllabi.

| | |
|---|---|
| Iste Pius, latia lingua doctissimus, in | quo |
| Non minor eloquii pellucet Meonii | vis, |
| Ut iam doctorum dici queat & pater & | lux, |
| Defossas qui querit opes ac sollicitat | res, |
| Emicat ingenio, quam fulget vel radiis | Sol, |
| Repperit ingentes thesauros, divitias | & |
| Sidonium sidus, mel sudans, ambrosiam, | lac; |
| Utque legant omnes, nunc nobis & studiis | dat. |
| Tu Nicolae, decus Musarum, quique hominum | rex |
| Diceris, exulta: illa ferox non Sidonium | Mors |
| Abstulit a nobis. Letetur Pegasidum | grex, |
| Atque Pium titulis ornemus perpetuis | nos. |

Baldassare Taccone dimostrò una certa abilità politica; nonostante la sua lealtà a Ludovico il Moro – simile a quella esibita da altri artisti, umanisti e uomini politici del tempo – riuscì in qualche modo a sopravvivere, almeno per qualche anno, all'occupazione francese della città di Milano, forse grazie alla politica illuminata del governatore Charles d'Amboise, iniziata nel 1499. Le lettere indirizzate dal Tolentino al nostro s'interrompono, nell'edizione

---

[27] ARGELATI, *Bibliotheca* (n. 3), Tom. II, pars 2, col. 2177: «Extant in libro 'Sydonii Apollinaris poëma', Mediolani, apud Scinzenzeler, 1498, fol.» Cioè: *Sidonii apollina/ris poema Au/reum eius/demque / episto/le.* Colophon: *Impressum Mediolanni* (sic) *per magistrum Uldericum scinzenzeler. Impensis vene/rabilium dominorum Presbyteri Hyeronimi de Asula necnon Ioannis de abba/tibus placentini. Sub Anno domini. M.cccc.Lxxxxviii. Quarto Nonas maias.* [4 v 1498]. HAIN-COPINGER *1287; IGI 8967; BMC, VI, 773; ROGLEDI MANNI, p. 194, numero 916. È un'edizione commentata da «Joannesbaptista Pius bononiensis» (fol. A ii). Ho consultato la copia della Biblioteca Nazionale Centrale Vittorio Emanuele II, colloc. 70.6.G.22.1. Cfr. J. A. SASSI, *Historia Literario-typographica Mediolanensis,* in Argelati, *Bibliotheca* (n. 3), Tom. I, pars 1, p. DCIII, e la nota *k,* dove sono pubblicati questi versi. Ho collazionato le due edizioni. La *n* di «sudans» (v. 7) è emendata da una *u.* Cfr. l'*Introduzione* di Spinelli alla *Danae* (n. 1), pp. 8-9.

del 1512, tra gli anni 1493 e 1511, per riprendere poi con tutta l'intimità di prima, e senza alcun segno di contatti interrotti tra i due amici.

Troviamo, però, nell'Archivio di Stato di Milano, un *Instrumentum procuratorie* per l'anno 1502 nel quale il Taccone appare come il venditore di una proprietà a Johannes Petrus de Gambaloytis. [28] Per il primo periodo dell'occupazione francese (dal 1500 al 1513), non troviamo altro documento della sua presenza a Milano, a parte il chiaro riferimento nella lettera n. 12, in appendice, ad una visita prossima presso Giovanni da Tolentino nei dintorni di Milano nel 1511; infatti, sembra chiaro dalla lettera numero 13 che egli si trovi a Roma nel 1512. Dunque un'assenza più o meno lunga da Milano fin dal 1502 è probabile, e i luoghi di soggiorno si situerebbero o ad Alessandria o, eventualmente, ad Innsbruck in Austria, presso la corte imperiale, dove si rifugiarono i due figli sforzeschi, o anche, e forse con maggior probabilità come si vedrà, a Roma. Lo ritroviamo invece come «cancelliere del senato» nel governo brevemente restaurato da Massimiliano Sforza (1513-1515). [29]

Successivi documenti biografici ci rivelano le sue attività ufficiali nel secondo decennio del Cinquecento. Il 28 gennaio 1517 un «Balthasar Tachonus Nobilis [e, più avanti nello stesso documento, 'Notarius'] et Cancellarius in Capitaneatu Justitiae Mediolani» stende un atto che vieta l'uso delle armi dentro la città di Milano. L'atto è al nome di «Odet de Foys, Breton», cioè Odet de Foix Vicomte de Lautrec, Maréchal de France (1485-1528), governatore di Milano in quell'epoca. [30] Il nostro continuò dunque ad esercitare l'ufficio di cancelliere anche sotto i francesi nel 1517 (anno della morte dell'amico Giovanni da Tolentino).

L'occupazione francese aveva col tempo nuociuto al morale della città, e, collo stimolo anarchico fornito dalle attività di Gerolamo Morone (lo stesso Morone che sarà nominato «Gran Cancelliere» dall'ultimo duca sforzesco Francesco II), il portare le armi era diventata cosa comune, come illustra un passo dei *Commentarii di M. Galeazzo Capella delle cose fatte per la restituzione di Francesco Sforza Secondo Duca di Milano*: «Tanto era finalmente

---

[28] Archivio di Stato di Milano, *Indice Lombardo. Notai.*, vol. 207, e Filza 6249, protocollo 51. Ringrazio il Dott. Gino Corti dell'aiuto nella lettura di questa mano notarile, e dei documenti citati alla nota 33, più avanti. Per i Gambaloita: ARGELATI, *Bibliotheca* (n. 3), I, 2, col. 666, Num. DCCCXXXII (Gambaloita, Jo. Philippus).

[29] SANTORO, *Gli offici del comune di Milano e del Dominio Visconteo-sforzesco (1216-1515)*, Milano, 1968, p. 392 (dall'Archivio di Stato di Milano, *Reg. Duc.* 64, fol. 108ᵛ).

[30] Il documento è trascritto da M. FORMENTINI, *Il ducato di Milano*, Milano, 1877, pp. 399-403, cfr. anche la p. 732.

l'odio contra Franzesi, che 'l Morone haveva in molti con diversi artificii ge-
nerato, che in tutti i sestieri et parrocchie della città si facevano bandiere, et
si eleggevano capitani, i quali da tutti quelli, che per l'età potevano portare
armi, et quando bisognasse, pigliando forma di soldati, fussero seguitati.
Erano ancora ogni dì confortati a questo dalle predicazioni di Frate Andrea
da Ferrara dell'ordine di S. Agostino ... ».[31] Per lo stesso anno 1517, lo Spinelli allude a «due lettere importanti a lui [Taccone] dirette da Girolamo
Morone», che purtroppo non sembrano più reperibili.[32]

Dell'anno 1518 abbiamo nell'Archivio di Stato di Milano due documenti
di compravendita dai quali veniamo a conoscenza dell'acquisto di terra da
parte di Taccone da certi «fratelli Bovati», un segno del probabile ritorno in
permanenza a Milano, e sicuramente segno del favore presso i potenti del
momento.[33] Sembra piuttosto probabile, date le sue alleanze abituali, che il
Taccone, mentre serviva il governo francese allora dominante, lavorasse anche per un'ulteriore restaurazione degli Sforza, il che sarebbe accaduto solo
dopo la sua morte, brevemente nel 1522 e ancora dal 1530 al 1535.

Baldassare Taccone morì, come abbiamo detto, all'età di sessant'anni, di
una malattia «sine pestis suspictione», e le esequie furono celebrate il 1 dicembre 1521 nella parrocchia di Sant'Eufemia.[34] Ignoriamo se fu inumato lo
stesso anno nella Basilica di Sant'Ambrogio, sotto il dominio francese, o se le
spoglie vennero trasferite in quel luogo tranquillo e prestigioso dopo il ritorno del duca sforzesco, l'anno seguente. Comunque sia, la memoria sua si
commemora non solo con una, ma due lapidi oggi inserite nel muro sud-est
della canonica bramantesca. Possiamo capire che fu il Taccone stesso a comporre i due epitaffi, sia dai testi (e.g., le parole «V < ivus > F < ecit >» nel
primo), sia dalla lettera numero 12 (in appendice), con cui Tolentino gli ricon-
segna un epitaffio, nonché dal fatto che la data chiaramente leggibile sulle due
lapidi (senza segni d'erosione di una I) è il 1520, invece del 1521, la data

[31] *Op. cit.*, trad. Francesco Philipopoli Fiorentino, Venetiis, Apud Giolitum de Ferrariis
MDXXXIX, fol. XIII$^v$.

[32] SPINELLI, *Introduzione* alla *Danae* (n. 1), p. 9. Per il Morone, cfr. *Ricordi inediti di Gerolamo Morone Gran Cancelliere dell'ultimo duca di Milano sul decennio dal 1520 al 1530*, pubblicati dal C. Tullio Dandolo, Milano, 1855 (è chiamato anche «Supremo Cancelliere» alla
p. 106).

[33] *Indice Lombardo. Notai.*, Filza 8087, protocolli 673 e 691. Cfr. n. 28.

[34] MOTTA, «Morti in Milano» (n. 7), p. 271: «Poi...Baldassare Tacconi che cantò gli sponsali
di Bianca Maria Sforza coll'imperatore Massimiliano: morto...a S. Eufemia, al 1° di dicembre 1521».

verificata, secondo il Motta, sul necrologio milanese. Sulla più grande lapide, rettangolare, si legge: VBI POST MVLTAS / ERVMNAS TEMPORV̄ /
VARIETATE ET VITAE / TEDIA BALTHASAR / TACHO MVSARVM /
CVLTOR POST DEVM / AC PRINCIPV̄ MEDIO / LANEN'. CANCELL.
/ CONQVIESCAT / ·V.·F.· / NE SE POSTERITATI / CREDERET /
M·D·XX. Quella piccola, che corrispondeva, con tutta probabilità, al sito
del sepolcro stesso, è in forma di cuscino con una nappa a ciascuno dei quat-
tro angoli, e con una chiara impronta concava, come lasciata da una testa che
vi si fosse fino a poco prima appoggiata o per accomodare la testa di una
statua funeraria. Porta l'iscrizione: SOLVS HVMARI / VOLVIT BALTHA-
SAR / TACHO ALEX. POETA / SVI HERENT LATERI / NEMO VNVS
INFERATVR / SECVM. MDXX. [35]

Benché lo Spinelli trovi nella presenza di un epigramma del Taccone nella
*Coryciana* (il libro di poesie radunate da B. Palladius in onore di Janus Cory-
cius, o Johann Goritz) [36] del 1524 un'indicazione che il Taccone era ancora in
vita, siamo più inclini a credere alla notizia riportata dal Motta dal necrologio milanese, anche se i documenti che includevano l'anno 1521 ora mancano
dall'Archivio di Stato. La *Coryciana* celebra, fra l'altro, la scultura della Ma-
donna col Bambino e Sant'Anna di Andrea Sansovino, commissionata da Co-
rycius e datata 1512, [37] ed è quest'opera precisamente che loda l'epigramma
del Taccone:

---

[35] L'iscrizione della lapide maggiore è riportata correttamente da V. FORCELLA, *Iscrizioni delle
chiese e degli altri edifici di Milano dal secolo VIII ai giorni nostri*, Milano, 1890, pp. 248-
249, num. 314; ARGELATI, *Bibliotheca* (n. 3), T. II, pars 2, coll. 2177-2178, fa qualche
alterazione nel testo. Anche l'iscrizione sulla «cuscina» si legge correttamente nel FORCEL-
LA, p. 248, num. 313.

[36] Ho consultato la copia a stampa della Biblioteca Nazionale Centrale Vittorio Emanuele II di
Roma, colloc. 69.5.D.2. Il colophon è al fol [268]ᵛ: *Impressum Rome apud Ludouicum Vi-
centinum / Et Lautitium Perusinum. Mense Iulio / MDXXIIII.* Cfr. G. W. PANZER, *Annales
Typographici ab Anno MDI ad Annum MDXXXVI Continuati*, vol. VIII, Norimbergae,
1800, p. 268, numero 207; J. G. T. GRAESSE, *Trésor de livres rares et précieux ou Nouveau
dictionnaire bibliographique*, V, Dresden, 1864, p. 109. I manoscritti sono: Biblioteca del-
l'Accademia dei Lincei (Corsiniana), MS Niccolò Rossi 207 (45 D 4) (non visto; cfr. P. O.
KRISTELLER, *Iter Italicum*, II, Leiden, 1967, p. 114); Biblioteca Apostolica Vaticana, MS
Vat. lat. 2754 (*Iter*, II, p. 352; l'epigramma alla c. 37ᵛ). Cfr. P. P. BOBER, «The *Coryciana*
and the Nymph Corycia», *Journal of the Warburg and Courtauld Institutes*, XL (1977), pp.
223-239.

[37] G. H. HUNTLEY, *Andrea Sansovino Sculptor and Architect of the Italian Renaissance*, Cambridge, Mass., 1935, pp. 65-67, 130 n., figg. 47 (per la data), 48; Cfr. BOBER, «The *Coryciana*» (n. 36), p. 228, n. 27.

Sansovij, sed non Phidiae, sumus inclyta proles,
   Anna, puer Mariae Christus, et alma parens.
Corycij pietas Divos in marmora duxit;
   Ædítui clamant: parcite luminibus![38]

Evidentemente, l'epigramma sarà stato scritto anni prima della pubblicazione del libro, e cioè durante il periodo di maggior attività del circolo attivo attorno al Goritz. Pare che il Goritz non si sia persuaso facilmente a rendere la collezione pubblica.[39] La presenza del nostro fra i partecipanti al volume celebrativo, in sé stessa significativa di una certa importanza nella vita culturale, non solo milanese, ma anche romana, ci dà pure un'indicazione per ricerche ulteriori da proseguire nelle biblioteche e negli archivi romani per il primo periodo di dominio francese di Milano. (Cfr. anche la lettera n. 13, del 1512, in appendice).

Fra i suoi discendenti che compaiono nei documenti notarili milanesi, il primo che si noti (tra il 1526 e il 1529) è un «Orfeo, < filius > q(uondam) Baldassare».[40] Possiamo concludere anche dal nome scelto per il figlio, come dal proprio epitaffio, che Baldassare Taccone, pure non essendo stato il più abile, fu almeno un fedele seguace delle Muse.

---

[38] *Coryciana* (1524: n. 36), p. M [= 77].

[39] BOBER, «The *Coryciana*» (n. 36), p. 228, e, per l'attività del circolo, comunicazione personale.

[40] Archivio di Stato di Milano, *Archivio Notarile. Notai in ordine alfabetico*, Cartella 56. Fasc. «Tacconi Orfeo q(uondam) Baldassare», contenente 22 documenti. Si può notare che l'*Indice Lombardo*, vol. 207, Filza 8396, numero 845, indica una compravendita di un Girolamo q(uondam) Orfeo che data al 15 luglio 1532.

Appendice

Lettere di Giovanni II Tolentino
a Baldassare Taccone,
con qualche epigramma
(edizione del 1512)

**Brit. Lib. 10905.d.22.** Edizione per la maggior parte diplomatica. Abbreviature sciolte (salvo nei titoli e nei saluti per mantenere la patina dell'edizione); *s-lunga* normalizzata in *s*; *u* e *y* normalizzate in *v*; *V* mantenuta; ortografia mantenuta; punteggiatura ed uso di maiuscole aggiornati. Da notare: l'iniziale maiuscola di ciascuna lettera è alta tre righe (cfr. Fig. 9); mani indicatrici al fol. **d** accanto all'epigramma a proposito di B. Taccone e di Tommaso Corio. In **neretto** le segnature e le poche correzioni di errori di stampa; fra < > le interpolazioni; fra [] le espunzioni proposte. La lettera n. 3 è riprodotta nelle Figure 9 e 10; e si vedano le Figure 7 e 8.

**[a i]**      IOANNIS TOLLENTI-
NATIS.II.EQVI-
TIS:EPISTO-
LARVM
LIBRI
.III.

Platinus Platus ad lectorem.
Mel geminum: tersam dulci cum carmine prosam
In Tollentino codice, lector, habes.

**1. [a iiii^v]**      Ioannes Tollentinas Balthasari Tacho.
suo.S.P.

MAgno afficior dolore quod tu Mediolano, ut ex tuis litteris et nuntii verbis cognovi, propediem discessurus sis. Hei mihi, nunc veluti fera in silvis errare possum. Neminem nunc cui scribam video. Nulla litterarum solatia, nulle voluptates, nulla denique curarum levamina nobis accedent. O dulces nostrae lucubrationes! O litterarum fructus affatim exhaustus! O, inquam, morum et vitae praecepta, et disciplinae argumenta, quo nunc gressum vestrum dirrigetis (*sic*)? Nonne sicuti extorto gubernaculo navis fluctibus hinc et inde agitabimini, et obruemini? Et quibus causis? Levibus atque ridiculis? Maximae graeculo senatori gratiae erunt reddendae, maiores gorgoneo capiti ultione gaudenti. Anne ego tantum scelus impune diu laturus sum? Minime quidem; sed lupum auribus teneo. In scopulo moramur, quo se aura vertat.

Admonebis Gasparem Vicecomitem, grande Musarum decus, ut cum in nostrum suburbanum // **[a v]** venerit, sua rithmice scripta elegantissima secum ferat. Ipsum miro desiderio ad venationes iamdudum expecto. Vale, et me (ut soles) ama. Belreguardi pridie idus octobris. M.cccc.lxxxviii. [14 × 1488]

**2.**                          Ioannes Tollentinas Balthasari tachono
                                         Salutem. P.

AD octavum Kal. novembris ex venatione domum redeunti mihi redditae fuerunt litterae tuae perornatae atque copiosae, quae maximam voluptatem attulerunt. Nam iam diu ab ste aliquid litterarum accipere exoptabam, ut quomodo te haberes, et quibus terris insideres, ex eis cognoscerem. Nunc autem tuis litteris plane perspexi tibi bene esse, et in delitiis versari, et me non solum abste diligi, sed etiam vehementer amari. Tibi, Balthasar, pro exilio, Agros Elisios incolere datum esse arbitror. Haec praestitere qui oderunt. Sed nihil ad rem. Tu velim quicquid ibi agatur, et quid acturum te putes, et de omnibus rebus quae in dies acciderint, me diligentissime facias cer-// **[a vᵛ]** tiorem. Hoc enim erit mihi gratius nihil. Praeterea principes nudius tertius Mediolanum reversi sunt, qui Genuensium legatos adiurandam fidelitatem expectant, et Parthenopen paucos post dies maximo apparatu transmittentur. Vale. Mediolani quinto Kal. Novembres. M.cccc.lxxxviii. [28 × 1488]

**3.**                          Ioannes Tollentinas Balthasari Tachono
                                         Salutem.

SI quando, Balthasar, his precipue superioribus diebus te Mediolani fuisse exoptavi; nam si haec audieris, tibi puto idem fore. Quam iucundus, hylaris, gloriosus, triumphalis dies ille, quo principis nostri uxor foelicissima urbem adventavit! Non mihi linguae oraque centum sufficerent. Nempe non Mario Caesarique, fusis devictisque Gallis Cimbrisque, maiorem urbem ingredientibus triumphum extitisse crediderim. Tota urbis facies, parietes ipsi gestire et laetitiam prae s[a]e ferre videbantur, qui multis circumquaque supraque tapetibus, auleisque insignibus instructi ab Iovis arce // [a vi] ad aedem maiorem usque tendebant. Hec Kal. Februariis acta sunt. Quo die sponsa Abiate Mediolanum profectura erat. Quinque naves mira arte mirabilique ornatu pridie eius diei Ludovicus, singularis animi Princeps, construxerat. Ex his, tres – cum principis matre, sororibus, ac non nullis nobilium puellis mirifice exornatis – eam ad excipiendam miserat. Ipse autem, eius adventu nunciato reliquas solvens, magna procerum atque ex primoribus viris caterva comitante ad Divi Christofori templum usque subsecutus est. Illustrissimus vero sponsus splendidissima equitum et optimatum turba ac omnibus magistratibus (quod quidem spectaculum admirabile, tanto auro, argento, serico, torquibusque fulgentibus viris videbatur) eius ad viridarii navalia obviam processerat.

Perpulchrum erat advenientem classem tot tantisque viris insignibus, mulieribus puellisque repletam intueri, hinc principem nostrum tantis nobilibus viris stipatum. Sonis tormentorum scorpionumque strepitu ac tubarum clangoribus omnia resonabant. Arcem demum ingredientes plerique principem ipsum consalutaverunt. // [a vi<sup>v</sup>] Arx autem variis coloribus, frondibus ducalibus, signis omniumque eiusdem oppidorum, vicorum ac caeterarum principatus arcium, praesertim curia decorabatur. Aulea tapetes insignes ubique iacebant.

Postero vero die, qui cerimonias nuptiasque ad peragendas in aedem maiorem constituebatur, sacerdotes ecclesiasticique omnes cum omnium sanctorum reliquiis, medici ac iurisconsulti infulati sub umbella, eam ex arcis porta excepere – quos omnes principes, dehinc senatorii ordinis quisque, ac caetera nobilium societas, catervatim sequebantur. Hos ypotoxotae omnes ac caeteri levis armaturae equites cum suis ductoribus praecesserant.

Extabat in ingressu fori arcus triumphalis, insignes Francisci Sforciae victorias – et praecipue Venetorum apud Caravagium profligationem – superbe continens. Ante aedis vestibulum spectabatur tugurium quoddam eminens et splendidum, in quo ornatissimae Mediolanenses matronae sponsam excipientes in templum concomitatae sunt, a cuius porta ad aram usque mirabilis porticus extendebatur. Solium princeps et sponsa multo auro decoratum tenebant. Sedes pro // [a vii] dignitate cuique dabantur. Nuptialem orationem Episcopus Sanseverinas disertissimam habuit.

Post celebratam missam, duo a principe auro donati sunt: legatus Florentinorum et Bartholomeus Chalcus, ducalis secretarius, quos vestibus attalicis
condonatos dimisit. Lateronum munus Ioannes Bonromeus Comes et Ioannes Franciscus Palavicinus sponsae subierunt. Peractis tandem de more sacrificiis, inclinato iam sole, duces ad regium cubiculum usque consequuti sumus.

Haec ex tempore, ut de his omnibus amicos nostros, tum maxime Conradolum Stangam, virum omni ex parte integerrimum, certiorem facias, qui
tantis voluptatibus interesse non potuit. Vale. Mediolani Quinto idus Februarii. M.cccc.lxxxviiii. [9 ii 1489]

**4.**                     Ioannes Tollentinas: Balthasari Tachono
                                        Salutem.P.

Vides quam laboriosus ad tibi scribendum efficior, nullum namque temporis
spacium praetermitto quin aliqua vel le-// [a vii^v] viuscula acciderint meis te
litteris plane admoneam. Ego sane munus hoc libentissime suscepi, ut de
omnibus rebus que hic gerantur te in dies certiorem faciam, et ut dignum
posteris aliquid memoratu relinquam, ex quo florentem aetatem nostram ho-
nestis artibus liberalibusque studiis imbuisse comperiatur nec (quod plurimis
contigit) vitae rationem apud deum immortalem et apud censores reddere
cogamur. Quod in litteris quas proxime accepi scribis – te, apud Moeneum
saxum dum stipendia militibus impenderes, in Herculis aede femineam statuam conspexisse, Tollentinatum signa in manibus tenentem aurata – haud
mirum est. Sed paucis accipe, que a patre puer admodum audivi, nam proa-
vum meum narravit, post adeptam victoriam adversus Pannoniae regis fi-
lium, cuius haec erant signa, magnam classem Ligustici maris littore parasse,
et dum a Florentinis stipendio conduceretur, et eorum dux eligeretur, apud
Moeneum suis copiis nonnullos dies consedisse, atque huius rei memoriam
reliquisse, propterea nos quoque in signis crines aureos faemi-// [a viii] ne
fingimus.

Quod de Vicecomitte nostro scribis, ipse litteris suis exponet, quas ad te
tabellarius regius deferet. Sed ego tanti uiri sortem miseror et doleo, qui
puellae delitiis iamdudum tenetur et torquetur. Ad nos cum veneris, quam
primum mittas obviam et carduos spinas et fabas octogeniculares, ut certior

tuus adventus sit et optatior et felicior. Vale. Mediolani pridie idus aprilis. M.cccc.lxxxviiii. [12 iv 1489]

5.                    Io. Tollentinas: Balthasari Tachono. S.

MAximo litterae tuae metu nos sublevarunt. Verebar enim ne in nostrorum inimicorum manus devenirent, quod sane non minus damnum quam dedecus attulisset, nam quantum ipsi nobis quottidie adversantur, haud facile existimare posses. Sed audi parumper, Balthasar, quae illa Medusa, sive potius erinnis, nudius tertius egit, dum ego aucupio intenderem. Nam litteras tuas interceptas viro cuidam doctissimo perlegendas tradidit, utpote quae thesaurum grandem tum sibi conflasse arbitrabatur. Sed ubi nihil ad se pertinere animadvertit, mihi redeunti inscioque ipsas reddidit. Legi coram et demum subrisi; ipsa, indignata, reticuit.

Sed ut ad nos redeamus, princeps heri ad hasticos ludos, quos paucos post dies editurus est, inter urbis nostrae primores me elegit, praemia attalicas vestes posuit. Ad haec fortissimos equos phaleris insignes paravi, munusque strenue obire haud vereor aetate iam pubescente. De omnibus rebus // [b ii] quae acciderint te meis litteris certiorem faciam. Vale. Deosque rogabis, ut nobis pulchram navare operam permittant. Papiae Kal. Iuliis. M.cccc.lxxxviiii. [1 vii 1489]

6.                    Io Tollen. Balthasari Tachono. S.P.

GAudeo et quidem vehementer pristinam te incolumitatem recuperasse; summo namque me timore affecerat tua ipsa aegritudo, quam gravissimam fuisse tuae litterae declararunt. Agendae igitur deo gratiae sunt immortali ipsaeque arae magnis muneribus replendae. Nos quoque ipsi thura dabimus, quod incolumem, et te voti compotem reddiderit. Te vero, Balthasar, moneo hortorque, ut valitudinem optimam diligentissime cures, ne id tibi quandoque aegrotanti, quod Atheniensi cuidam (ut meminit Valerius) viro eruditissimo accidat, qui, cum lapidis ictum capite excepisset, omnia praeter litteras tenacissima memoria retinuit. Hoc Ligures afferrent puellae, quibus te avide inservire audio, earumque delitiis implicari. Cavebis ergo, ut non modo decus arcamque, sed ne vitam propriam (quod plerumque solent) suis illecebris exhauriant. Vale. Belreguardi idibus octobribus. M.cccc.lxxxx. [15 × 1490]

**[b iiᵛ]**          IOANNIS TOLLENTINATIS. II.
                    EQVITIS EPISTOLARVM.
                         LIBER. II.


7.                    Io. Tol. Balthasari Tachono. S. P.


Rogasti saepius Balthasar, ut lauretanum iter iampridem a me confectum aliqua ad te epistola describerem. Cuius lectione, et si mihi comes non affueris,
quaecumque tamen memoratu digna ipse viderim, singillatim tu quoque
possis intelligere, facturum me id quidem pollicitus fui. Ecquid tale non li-
benter facerem, te presertim exigente, quem gloriae meae adeo cupidum co-
gnosco, ut nihil aeque cures, quam ad studia et immortalitatem me semper
excitare? Fortasse dices: «Vnde haec tam longa cunctatio? Desuntne tibi in
scribendo verba? An obtorpuit animus?». Nempe nihil horum accidit, sed
variae calamitates, que mihi his temporibus cum plaerisque comunes fuere,
tum domesticae fraudes et iniuriae ita me exagitarunt, ut quandoque despe-
randum censuissem, nisi haec humanitatis studia labantem animum
confirmassent.// **[b iii]** Sed de his alias coram. Tu excusationem accipies.
Quamquam ea apud Balthasarem minime opus esse arbitror. In itinere igitur
declarando, opere pretium facturus mihi videor si urbes et flumina breviter
atque in transcursu, Romanas postremo ruinas propensiori stilo perscripsero,
quae omnia si non eleganter, quam accurate tamen et verissime (ut potero)
exponam.
        Quinto idus Martias iter ingressi Laude, Cremona, Regio, mox per Fla-
miniam Mutina, Bononia, Forocornelii, Faventia, Forolivii, Bertanorio, Ce-
senna transivimus – quibus urbibus, quamvis vetustissimis, nihil tamen me-
morabile vidi, praeter Mutinae, Bruti et Cassii conditoria ac cuiusdam Clo-
diae Plotinae quam Catonis libertam fuisse tradunt. Traiecto Rubicone, Ari-
minum, Pisaurum, Fanumque Fortunae venimus. Arimini marmoreum pon-
tem a Iulio Caesare constructum transivi. In medio civitatis foro fons oritur,
amplo cratere exceptus. Ibi arcum triumphalem conspexi. Alium Fani Fortunae sublimiorem aliquantulum, quem cives in deae honorem erexerunt. Passus inde mille Methaurus transitur, // **[b iiiᵛ]** apud quem memorabilis illa
Carthaginensium strages fuit, duce eorum Asdrubale interempto. Aspexi arcem, quam Romani in facti memoriam condidere, Scapizanum hodie nuncu-
patur. Accessimus et Senogaliam, Anconitanumque portum, quo mirabilior
alter nullus haeret littoribus. In eo turris adhuc stat ab Antonino Pio extructa

cuius vestibulum vasta saxi mole cingitur. Auximum postea nos recepit urbs vetustissima opulentissimaque, et marmoreis undique parietibus conspicua, in quibus graece et latinae litterae eleganter incisae passim fere leguntur. Plurimae ibi Romanorum statuae plurimaque delubra iacent. Ad Sacratissimam Virginem Lauretanam tandem pervenimus. Horrenda sane res, cum eius sacellum nullis se contingi aedificiis patiatur. Reliquum templi arcis instar, praecelsis turribus latissimisque muris munitum est. Miraculorum, quae Sanctissima Virgo et dei mater alma mortalium casus miserata praestitit, tanta est multitudo, ut ea si mihi linguae centum totidemque ora essent percurrere // [b iiii] minime possem.

Ad Tollentinates inde nostros me contuli, opulentum sane et peramoenum oppidum, a Chiento flumine irrigatur, domus cultae, regiones, strate, delubra magna, spaciosum forum et ornatissimum in quo Senatus habetur palatium. Optima ibi viget reipublicae forma, Senatus gravis, perhumanus populus. Quatuor binis mensibus creantur, quos principes vocant: hi ceu Consules olim Romae rempublicam administrant. Magistratus huius incredibilis est maiestas; ulli enim hominum, etiam si regum maximus in senatum proficisceretur, assurgere illis haud licet. Quanta vero in me ornando omnium studia fuerint, haud facile dictu est. Quippe ubi me adventantem sensere, totus illico populus omnisque Senatus effusus est; dii boni quam imperitum me, quam parum merentem mille fere passus ab oppido progressi, omnes tubarum clangore et cornicinum concentu excepere. In Senatum eunti principes praeter morem obvii facti, sex quibus illic fui diebus lustrium [ed. *lusticium*] indictum, spectacula aedita // [b iiiiᵛ] et convivia sumptuosissime facta fuere. Haec profecto Balthasar nunquam sine magno rubore mihi veniunt in mentem. Dum vero singula perlustro foemineam statuam ex alabastrite in foro animadverti magni ab omnibus pretii estimatam. Mercari eam voluerunt Vrbini Comes et Cardinalis quidam magna repromitentes. Recusavere Tollentinates, utpote non ignari quantum decoris signum illud patriae afferat. Tabula est etiam marmorea graecis et latinis litteris exculpta quam Pomponius legatus vir consularis posuit. Tria deinde mihi sanctorum corpora ostenderunt incorrupta adhuc, necnon Nicolai proavi mei ispidum cor. Inter Auximum et Tollentinum dirrutae urbis vestigia videntur: Muros Regini accolae appellant. Ego nusquam loci huius memoriam reperio, nisi Ricinensium oppidum fuerit. Tu quando plura annotasti de hoc aliquid ad me scribas velim. Per Umbriam proficiscens Spoletum cum applicuissem, vetustissimum delubrum ingressus, Giganteum Bellum in basse marmorea vidi. Miratus sum diu Olimpum // [b v] montem Pelio atque Ossae subiectum, Iovis dexteram fulmine armatam. In alia basse Iovem in Ida educatum, amadriades pueri vagitum tintinabulis et choreis cohibentes. In sepulcro vero quodam hominum cum leonibus pugnas. Damnatorum poenam fuisse arbitror qui in harena feris obiecti spectaculo Romanis erant. In Interamnae autem urbis foro tabula posita est marmorea in qua latine sic legitur: Providentia Tiberii Caesaris Augusti ad aeternitatem ipsius et Romani nominis dedit. Quaedam etiam sunt notae, quas interpretari nunquam potui.

Vrbem hanc Nar fluvius influit. Deinde per Narniensem et Otriculanum agrum, per Veientanos, Ortanos, Fabianos, Regnanosque Romam venimus. Quam ubi in eius conspectu fuimus, ita me allocutum scias: «Salve terrarum Caput numine deum ellecta, quae eferatas molires nationes, indomitos contunderes populos et longinqua tuae ditioni subigeres imperia, quo una in toto terrarum orbe Deorum atque hominum patria fieres. Salve faecunda tellus quae caelum ipsum alumnis clarius reddi-// [b vᵛ] disti, et quo tandem eloquio tuae recenseri laudes possent, in qua tot praestantissimi duces, consumatissimi philosophi, clarissimi rethores et iurisconsulti, omnium denique bonarum artium principes floruere. Salve quam totiens imaginatus sum, nunc te intueor, iam iam perlustrabo, et singula quaeram diverticula».

His dictis, urbem haud sine reverentia ingressus, ad Divi Angeli arcem primum tetendi: altitudine murorum, lapide praeduro, et Tyberi latus preterlabente fere inexpugnabilem. Hadriani molem fuisse plurimi asserunt, quod ut credam faciunt nomina Imperatorum, quae in arcis latere incisa sunt: Hadriani, S. (*sic*) Antonini et Commodi. In culmine turris angelus dextera gladium tenet, quod miraculum tunc deus omnipotens ostendit, quum subito sternutamento mortui homines concidebant. Ab eadem arce ad Divi Petri templum usque concamerata tendit via. Extant Romuli et Remi (ut aiunt) piramides. Inveni Capitolium, Tarpeium Saxum, Valeriique Publicolae domus vestigia, locum in quo septa fuerunt. At a sinistro Capitolii latere // [b vi] lupam pueros geminos lactantem, Neronis et Agrippinae monumenta. In atrio, quod Senatoris vocant, Herculem auratum Clava Leonem mactantem, Iovem tonantem, Venerem pariter et Cupidinem nudos, Castorem et Pollucem, Apolinem ex alabastrite, et Claudium, aereum Commodi defractum Colossum. In triclinio, nudus homo spinam e pede eruens columna sedet, opus adeo mirabile, ut propius accesserim visurus an marmorea loqueretur imago. Nullum sane marmor aesve mollius illo exculptum nostris invenitur temporibus. Fui in circo maximo, in Vespasiani Amphitheatro, quod Colliseum appellant: mira aequidem loci magnitudo, in qua totus populus Romanus ludos olim spectavit. Mirabilior vero parietum structura, marmoreis porticibus insculpta sunt Herculis gesta praeclara; exolevit nunc omne aurum quo lita quondam fuere. Vidi et marmoreas Traiani Antoninique columnas, in quibus eorum victoriae ita mirabiliter celatae sunt, ut mirantium expleri nunquam possit animus. Domitiani item

// **[b vi<sup>v</sup>]** Naumachiam et Claudii aquarum ductus, quos qui diligentius consideraverit, nil magis in toto orbe mirandum censebit, quippe a .xl. lapide ad eam excelsitatem influxere fontes, ut in omnes urbis montes levarentur. Ibi est aerea Marci Antonii equestris statua, inter ceteras porro praestantissima atque non parum omni ex parte collaudata. Ea est enim effigies, ea membrorum compactio, ut nihil addi posse videatur.

Inde in Carinas redeuntibus vicus scaeleratus aspicitur, ubi Tulia carpentum per patris corpus egit. A quo haud longe fuit quondam Pompeiana domus, de qua mentionem facit Suetonius in Tiberio. In arcus tris triumphales oculos converti, quibus Titi Augusti, Septimii Commodi fratris, et Constantini magnificae res gestae comprehenduntur. Prope ibi est Forum Boarium, Traiani et Antonini aedium ruinae, Templum Pacis a Vespasiano constitutum, in quo ex basalte lapide columnae maximi olim praetii prostratae iacent. In vestibulo cupa grandis ex porphirit[a]e. Alia est in Neronis hortis, ubi Aurea Domus sita fuerat. Obeliscos (ut Plinius refert) tres // **[b vii]** inveni. Primum ad Divi Petri templum, quem Augustus pro gnomone habuit. Apici pila aurea inheret, quam Manlius mathematicus addidit. In medio litterae iste sunt: Divo Augusto Iulii Caesaris filio sacrum. Secundus est apud Minervam aegiptiis litteris inscriptam continens rerum naturae interpretationem. Tertius in Vaticano Caii et Neronis principum circo, ex omnibus unus in molitione effractus.

Iter deinde ad Dioclitiani Thermas direximus: tantae sublimitatis aedificia, ut humanum visum haebetent. Ibi magnum est baptisterium, hyemales aestivalesque zetae, privata et publica balnea, sublimes ex solido lapide columnae, ingens ex porphirite crater, in quo fons scaturiebat. Nec vero praeterire possum Pantheon ab Agrippa constitutum. Syracusana sunt in eo columnarum capita ex ophite et porphirite. Porta aerea valde emicans, cinctum triplici columnarum ordine vestibulum, e quibus nonnullae sunt striatae. Ad Praxitelica etiam Phidiacaque opera visenda properavi. Equi duo aerei absque sessore stant, quibus subiecta sunt artificum nomina; soloque sedent to-// **[b vii<sup>v</sup>]** tidem marmorei gigantes, cornua copiae tenentes, quae omnia divina manu fabricata iudicans, maxima cum ammiratione discessi. Tum civis quidam Romanus: «Quid si in privatorum quoque aedibus non inferiora fortasse his quae publice vidisti offenderes? Ego Hercle pauca habeo quae iam videbimus». Domum igitur intrantes satiris duobus auro coruscantibus occurrimus. Plurimas deinceps virorum et mulierum statuas sumus conspicati. Inter quas Marcum Antonium et Faustinam cognovimus. In tabula marmorea calendarum cursusque solaris ratio continetur. In medio areae Neptunus extat, tridente aequora quassans, contra quem Appollo cythara modulans carmen, Arion delphino sedens, Castor

Poluxque, Baccanalia, munus gladiatorum, Nero Aenobarbus, venationes-
que nonnullae, variaeque animalium species in collibus errantium.

O quotiens, cum omnia oculis perlegere non possem, te, Balthasar, exoptavi. Quid de Quinti Flaminii Circo referam, qui nunc pro foro habetur?
Quid de Pompeii Theatro? Quid de Foro Magno? Quid de ripa Tiberis, in
qua continue merces exponuntur? // [b viii] Profecto si litteris omnia tradere
vellem, non epistola sed hystoria opus esset.

Quatriduo Romae acto, per Ætruscos reditus fuit. Vrbem vetustate
exesam Sutrium accessimus. Viterbii fontes plurimi sypunculis ornatissi-
mis aquam emittentes iucundissimum efficiunt murmur. Primo ab urbe
lapide celeberrima illa Balnea inveniuntur, quod vulgo Bulicamen appel-
lamus. Illinc recto itinere via est ad Faliscos, quos Camillus obsedit. Ibi
nonnulli adhuc cuniculi apparent. Senas mox petivimus, qua urbe Camillus capta, regionem suo nomine appellavit, quae etiam num Camillana
dicitur. Relictis a dextra Fesulis, a sinistra Pisis Pistorioque Fluentiam
applicui. Superato Appennini iugo Transpadanaque ora peragrata, in pa-
triam redivimus.

Habes ergo, Balthasar, omnem itineris nostri rationem, quam si incomp-
tius forte quam expectabas enarratam accepisti, nolim te tamen in oratianum
illud errumpere: «Parturient montes; nascetur ridiculus mus». [*De arte poetica*, 139]. Nosti enim curas nostras; conscius es miseriarum adversaeque fortunae, quae potius ad querimoniam quam ad talia scribenda me impellit.
Vale. Mediolani.xii.Kal.Decem. M.cccc.lxxxx. [20 xi 1490].

8. [b viii\^v]                Io. Tollentinas ad Balthasarem Taco-
                              num de itinere lauretano.

                    Lauretum vidi, mox inclita moenia Romae.
                    Perfectis votis, in patriam redii.

9.                       Io. Tollen. Balthasari Tachono .S.P.

Balthasar salve. Non possum satis explicare quantum honoris et amplitudinis
nobis attulerit illa Aquensis profectio. Summae mihi profecto fuisset leticiae,

si te una nobiscum esse fortuna permisisset, ut illum apparatum vidisses quem nobis Quargentini (*sic*) decrevere. Nam adventu nostro nuntiato, cum passus mille circiter ab oppido abessem, centum iuvenes loricati nobis pedites obviam progressi sunt, quos deinde subsequuta est cohors praetoria. Ipseque pretor, eques cum sacerdotibus infulatis et ducali quodam praefecto, veluti sub umbella nos excepturus processit. Dignum sane spectaculum, cum oppidum illud ingredientibus pueri immaturaeque puellae nobis peana uno ore canerent, quod olim Imperatoribus // **[c]** triumphantibus de victo hoste dari solebat. Biduo ibi moratus Alexandriam petii, nec parvo quidem honore ab amita exceptus. Concomitabatur Iacobus pater tuus, qui mihi de te multa narravit. Sed illa Polixena cuius amore flagrabas nusquam oculis nostris se obtulit. A nonnullis tamen accepi ipsam omnibus puellis Alexandrinis et forma et venustate praestare. Haec nuper ad te scripsi quae tibi pariter legenti quam mihi scribenti iucunda esse non ignoro. Mediolani vero quo propediem rediturus sum, maiora intelliges. Tu Balthasar etiam atque etiam vale. Belreguardi Quinto Idus Iunias. M.cccc.lxxxxi. [9 vi 1491]

**10. [cᵛ]**     Io. Tollentinas Balthasari Tachono .S.

Existimo te fortassis admiraturum, quod tamdiu de his quae apud nos Mediolani geruntur (ut pollicitus sum) ad te non scripserim. Quare ne hoc in amiciciae nostrae veterisque consuetudinis suspitionem quandoque te traheret nonnulla ennarrabo. Primum quod in Gallias Hispaniasque et ad divi Iacobi Galeci Templum usque vota solvendi gratia pro-// **[c ii]** fecturus sum, cui rarissimae profectioni iampridem accingor. Deinde Zenobiam sororem Nicolao Georgio, equiti ornatissimo, diebus exactis desponsavimus, et variis curis solicitudinibusque vexati fuimus, quibus parum abfuit quin in gravissimam aegritudinem inciderem; nunc tamen omnipotentis auxilio satis belle valeo.

Postremo non parvo afficiebar dolore ex iniquissimis malivolorum tuorum accusationibus; sed haec omnia in aliud tempus differre censeo, ut ad te veniam. Laetor summopere tui maximi commodi causa. Potest enim tibi provincia non beatissima contingere? In qua futurum sit, ut quam saepissime cum tanto viro loqui, et publica negotia tractare oporteat. Quae consuetudo potior vel optari potest. Ex qua non minorem fructum ex otio privato quam ex administratione publica percepturus esse videaris. Haec dum scriberem calamo nondum recondito redditae mihi fuerunt litterae tuae. Provocati ergo non scribimus. Vale. Mediolani nonis Maii. M.cccc.lxxxxiii. [7 v 1493]

[c vi]                      IOANNIS TOLLENTINATIS
                            .II. EQVITIS EPISTOLA-
                            RVM LIBER .III.

**11. [d]**              De Balthasare Tachono et Thoma Corio.

                 Prosequitur tanto Corius quid amore Taconem?
                 Nempe quod ex corio nascitur iste taco.

**12. [d viii]**           Io. Tollentinas Eques Balthasari
                           Tachono Salutem.

Quae paulo ante scripsi, in sententia manent, nam amanuensis noster harum rerum imperitus, et colombanus architriclinus aliis negotiis implicitus hanc provintiam penitus respuunt. Quamobrem virum fac repperias peritissi-mum, cui munus illud tuto committere queam. Hoc ut quamprimum facias te vehementer rogo. In diebus genialibus te ad prandium expecto, non in Appolline nostro, sed in ludo pro more apollineo, ut deinde personati ami-cam in urbe una conveniamus, quam etiam plerumque ardemus. Veri nam-que amantis est nunquam torpescere. Epitaphium et versiculos tuos remitto. Vale Mediolani. xii.Calen.Martias. M.ccccc.xi. [1 iii 1511]

**13. [e]**          Io. Tollen. Balthasari Tachono. S.

Nudius secundus Ephimeridas (*sic*) et Annales nostros ad te misi, ut ante-
quam edantur tuam sententiam proferas. Eo autem die tuum Dialogum legi,
qui mihi undique perplacuit. Velim // [e$^v$] etiam mittas concilia quae nuper
Roma Mediolanum allata sunt, et Sanseverinatis orationem apud Pontifi-
cem, et ea quae memoratu digna traduntur. Alterum libellum meum expecto, in quo si aliquid inconcinne vel parum latine dictum invenies, non mihi,
sed adolescentiae olim meae et iniquae tempestati attribues. Vale Mediolani.
xii. Cal. Februarias.

M.ccccc.xii. [21 i 1512]

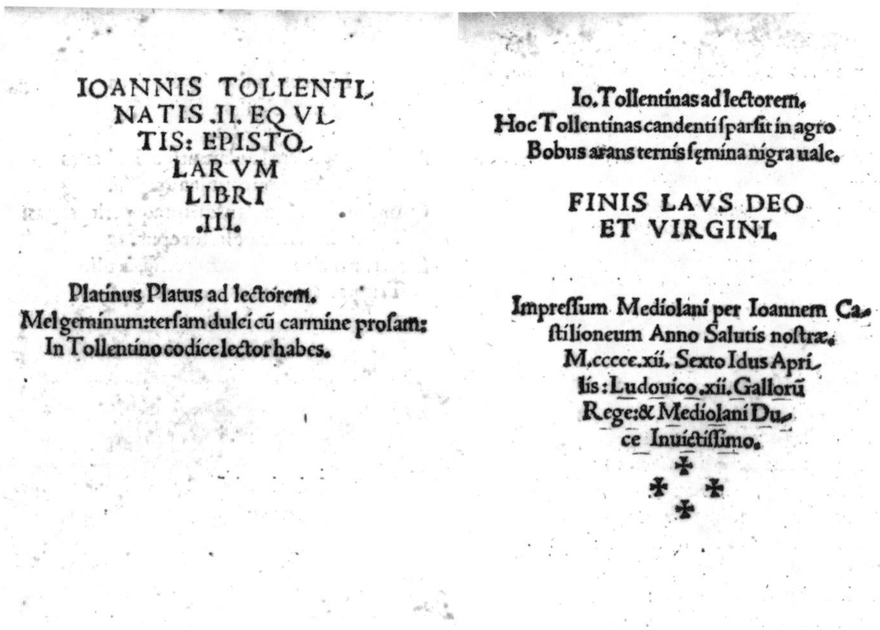

IOANNIS TOLLENTI.
NATIS .II. EQVI.
TIS: EPISTO.
LARVM
LIBRI
.III.

Platinus Platus ad lectorem.
Mel geminum:tersam dulci cū carmine profam:
In Tollentino codice lector habes.

Io. Tollentinas ad lectorem.
Hoc Tollentinas candenti sparsit in agro
Bobus arans ternis femina nigra uale.

FINIS LAVS DEO
ET VIRGINI.

Impressum Mediolani per Ioannem Ca-
stilioneum Anno Salutis nostræ.
M.cccce.xii. Sexto Idus Aprilis: Ludouico .xii. Gallorū
Rege:& Mediolani Du-
ce Inuictissimo.

✠ ✠
✠

Fig. 7. IOANNIS TOLLENTINATIS. II. EQVITIS: EPISTOLARVM LIBRI. III.,
Milano, Giovanni da Castiglione, 1512, fols. a i and e iiii: Title and Colophon.

## IOANNIS TOLLENTINATIS .II. EQVITIS EPISTOLARVM LIBER PRIMVS.

Oannes Tollétinas Eques. Alberto Ferrufino faluté. Q uod tibi Mediolano difcedens pollicitus fum : me ad te fepius de his. S. quæ hic geruntur rebus perfcripturum : data opera paraui. Non enim uercor & fi rufticæ habitationi alienum fore uideatur : quin in fcribendo plurimú te expleam. Scias igitur nos in maximis uariifq; uoluptatibus quottidie uerfari: neruorum uocûq; cantibus: uenatiõibus: follículofq; noftro faluberrimo : ac deniq; cæteris rebus quibus adolefcétes maxime oblectantur incumbere. Verum hæc omnia mihi mométanea uidétur : cum prefertim cogito meam unicá fpem: meum folatium: ac illam: quam nó fecus acuitâ propriam caram habeo: urbi reliquiffe. De qua quoniam iampridem ame nihil eft auditum : pro tuo

**a iii**

Fig. 8. IOANNIS TOLLENTINATIS. II. EQVITIS: EPISTOLARVM LIBRI. III., Milano, Giovanni da Castiglione, 1512, fol. a iii: First Initial «I».

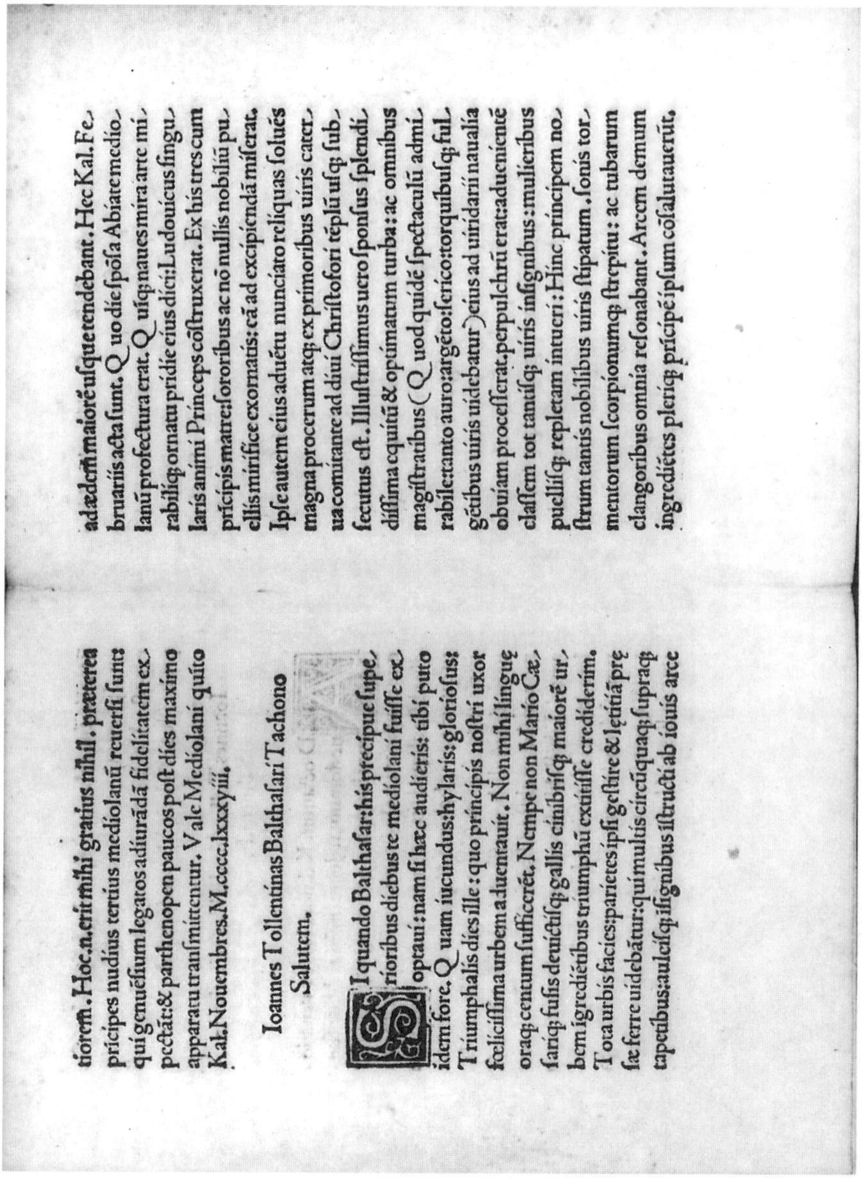

...tiorem. Hoc.n.crit mihi gratius nihil. praeterea
pricipes nudius tertius mediolani reuersi sunt
qui genuessium legatos adiurada fideliratem ex-
pcctat:& parthenopen paucos post dies maximo
apparatu transmittentur. Vale Mediolani quito
Kal.Nouembres.M.cccc.lxxxviii.

Ioannes Tollentinas Balthafari Tachono
Salutem,

I quando Balthasar:his precipue superioribus diebus te mediolani fuisse ex-
optaui:nam si haec audieris:tibi puto
idem fore. Q uam iucundus:hylaris:gloriosus:
Triumphalis dies ille:quo principis nostri uxor
felicissima urbem aduenauit. Non mihi linguae
oraque centum sufficeret, Nempe non Mario Ca-
fariq: fulsis deuictisq: gallis cinibrisq: maiore urbem ingredietibus triumphu extitisse crediderim.
Tota urbis facies:parietes ipsi gestire & leriria pre
se ferre uidebatur:qui multis circuquaq: supraq:
tapeibus:auleisq:issignibus istructiab ionis arce

ad ed.cim maiore usque tendebant. Hec Kal.Fe-
bruariis acta sunt. Q uo die sposa Abiatemedio-
lanu profectura erat. Q uisq naues mira arte mi-
rabiliq ornatu pridie eius dici.Ludouicus singularis animi Princeps costruxerat. Ex his tres cum
pricipis matre:sororibus ac no nullis nobiliu puellis mirifice exornatis:ea ad excipienda miserat.
Ipse autem eius aduetu nunciato reliquas solues
magna proccrum atq ex primoribus uiris caer-
ua comitante ad diui Christofori templu usq: subsecutus est. Illustrissimus uero sponsus splendidissima equitu & optimatum turba:ac omnibus
magistratibus (Q uod quide spectaculi admi-
rabile:tanto auro:argeto:serico:torquibusq:ful-
gctibus uiris uidebatur )eius ad uiridarii naualia
obuiam processerat:perpulchru erat:aduenicnte
classem tot tanus: uiris insignibus:mulieribus
puellisq: repleram intueri:Hinc principem nostrum tantis nobilibus uiris stipatum ,sonis tormentorum scorpionumq: strepitu: ac tubarum
clangoribus omnia resonabant. Arcem demum
ingredictes pleriq: pricipe ipsum cosalutauerut.

Fig. 9. IOANNIS TOLLENTINATIS. II. EQVITIS: EPISTOLARVM LIBRI. III.,
Milano, Giovanni da Castiglione, 1512, fols. a vᵛ - a vi: Letter of 9 February, 1489.

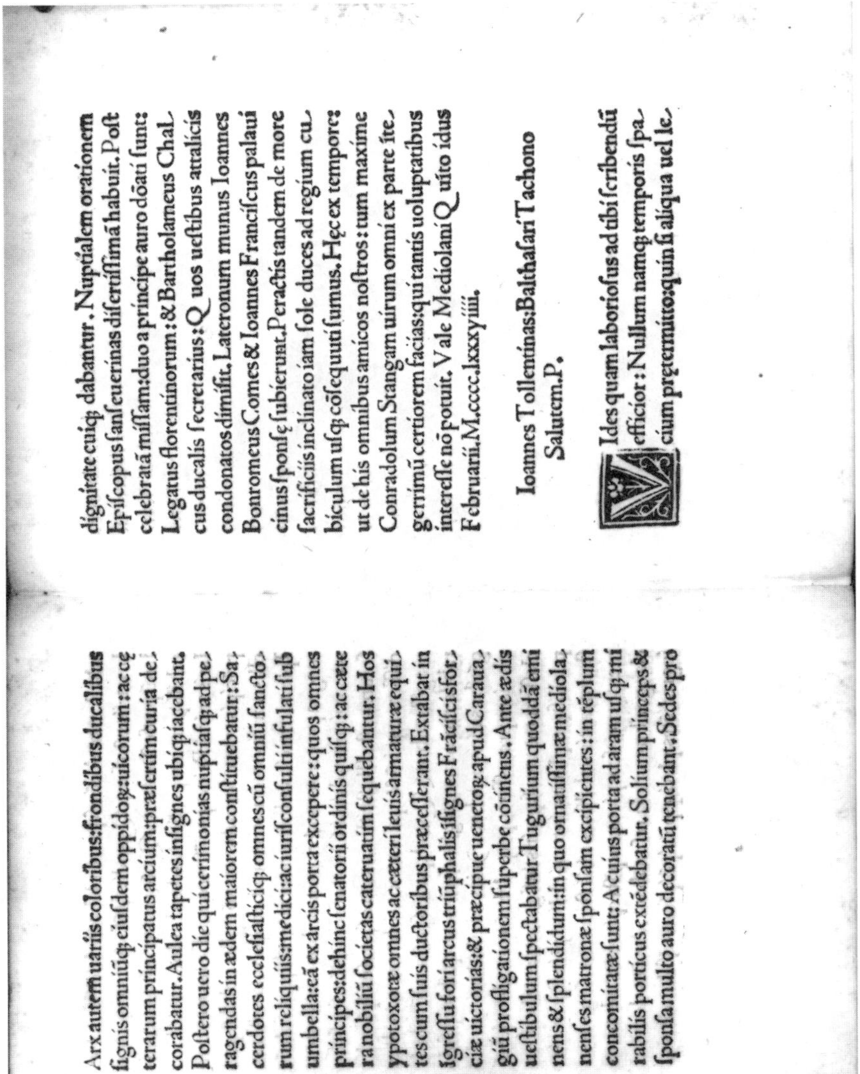

Arx autem uariis coloribus: frondibus ducalibus signis omniufq; eiufdem oppidos; uicorum: accç terarum principatus arcium: praefertim curia decorabatur. Aulea tapetes infignes ubiq; iacebant. Poftero uero dic quicerimonias nuptiafq; ad peragendas in aedem maiorem conftituebatur: Sacerdotes ecclefiafticiq; omnes cú omniú sanctorum reliquiis: medici: ac iurifconfulti infulati fub umbella: ea ex arcis porta excepere: quos omnes principes: dehinc senatorii ordinis quifq; ac caetera nobilisì societas cateruatim fequebatur. Hos Yporoxore omnes ac caeteri leuis amaturae equites cum fuis ductoribus praecesserant. Exftabar in igreffu foriarcus triúphalis: figens Frácifcisforciae uictorias: & praecipue uenetog; apud Carauagium profligationem fuperbe cóuinens. Ante aedis ueftibulum fpectabatur Tuguriú quoddá eminens & fplendidum: in quo ornatifsimae mediolanenfes matronae fponfam excipientes: in réplum concomitatae funt; Ac uius porta ad aram ufq; mirabilis porticus excedebatur. Solium princeps & fponfa multo auro decoratú tenebant. Sedes pro

dignitate cuiq; dabantur. Nuptialem orationem Epifcopus sanseuerinas diseriffimá habuit. Poft celebratá miffam; duo a principe auro dóati funt: Legatus florentinorum: & Bartholomeus Chalcus ducalis secretarius: Quos ueftibus attalicis condonatos dimifit. Lateronum munus Ioannes Bonromeus Comes & Ioannes Francifcus palaui cinus sponfae subicruat. Peractis tandem de more sacrificiis inclinato iam sole duces ad regium cubiculum ufq; cófequuti fumus. Hęc ex tempore: ut de his omnibus amicos noftros: tum maxime Conradolum Stangam uirum omni ex parte ftegerrimú certiorem faciasq; tantis uoluptatibus intereffe nó potuit. Vale Mediolani Q uito idus Februarii. M.cccc.lxxxviiii.

Ioannes Tollentinas: Balthafari Tachono
Salutem. P.

Ides quam laboriofus ad tibi fcribendú efficior: Nullum namq; temporis fpacium prętermitto: quin fi aliqua uel le

Fig. 10. IOANNIS TOLLENTINATIS. II. EQVITIS: EPISTOLARVM LIBRI. III., Milano, Giovanni da Castiglione, 1512, fols. a ivᵛ - a vii: Letter of 9 February, 1489.

# CHAPTER VII

## Una relazione sconosciuta delle nozze di Isabella d'Aragona con Giangaleazzo Sforza nel febbraio 1489: Giovanni II Tolentino a Baldassare Taccone

Un'edizione cinquecentina di non poco interesse per la storia milanese dell'epoca sforzesca e francese contiene lettere ed epigrammi di Giovanni II Tolentino (1471-1517),[1] nipote del Consigliere Ducale Giovanni Tolentino che era sposato con Isotta, figlia naturale di Francesco Sforza. Si tratta dell'edizione: IOANNIS TOLLENTI-/NATIS .II. EQVI-/TIS: EPISTO-/ LARVM / LIBRI / .III., stampata a Milano da Giovanni da Castiglione durante la vita dell'autore, nel 1512[2] (Fig. 7).

---

[1] Per la biografia, oltre a C. MARCORA, «I commentarii di Giovanni II Tolentino», *Archivio storico lombardo*, XC (1963), pp. 330-339, si veda la n. 3 al capitolo VI, sopra, e A. C. FIORATO, *Bandello entre l'histoire et l'écriture. La vie, l'expérience sociale, l'évolution culturelle d'un conteur de la Renaissance*, Firenze, 1979, pp. 180-182; M. BANDELLO, *Opera latina inedita vel rara*, a cura di C. Godi, Padova, 1983, pp. 61, 66-70.

[2] Si veda il capitolo VI, n. 4 e *Appendice*. Il gentile professor Carlo Pedretti mi comunica che possiede un'altra copia dell'edizione; cfr. anche: L. FUSCO e G. CORTI, «Lorenzo de' Medici on the Sforza Monument», *Achademia Leonardi Vinci*, V (1992), pp. 11-32. Gli autori credevano unica la copia in possesso del Pedretti (p. 32), come io la copia della British Library. L'epigramma alla c. c iiᵛ dell'edizione si trova anche alla c. 104ᵛ del MS Italien 1543 della Bibliothèque Nationale di Parigi: cfr. *Documenti e memorie riguardanti Leonardo da Vinci a Bologna e in Emilia*, a cura di C. Pedretti, Bologna, 1953, pp. 152-153; G. UZIELLI, *Ricerche intorno a L. da V.*, Ser. I, Vol. I, Torino, 1896², pp. 162-163; R. CASTAGNOLA, «Milano ai tempi di Ludovico il Moro. Cultura lombarda nel codice italiano 1543 della Nazionale di Parigi», *Schifanoia*, 5 (1988), pp. 101-185.

Possibilissima un'ignoranza totale del nome dell'autore; impossibile invece ignorare l'identità dei destinatari e di coloro a cui è dovuta la cura del volume. L'epigramma iniziale è opera dell'umanista milanese Piattino Piatti;[3] la lettera introduttiva è della penna di Matteo Bandello;[4] la cura dei testi è stata eseguita da Antonio Sabino da Imola[5] che fornisce pure la lettera di conclusione; diverse lettere sono indirizzate al Piatti, altre a Battista Spagnuoli Mantovano,[6] altre ancora a Baldassare Taccone (autore della *Danae*, favola mitologica messa in scena da Leonardo da Vinci[7]), al poeta Gaspare Visconti;[8] ci sono pure epigrammi, uno indirizzato a Jacopo Antiquario,[9] e altri a proposito di Tommaso Corio,[10] di Baldassare Taccone, di Gaspare Visconti; lettere ed epigrammi alla moglie Taddea Landi, figlia del conte Pompeo Landi; epigrammi a diversi (incluse le amiche «Cinzia», menzionata anche nella sua cronaca, *I Commentari*, «Laura», e «M»).

Siamo dunque di fronte ad un personaggio di un certo rilievo nell'ambiente letterario umanistico dell'epoca. Le sue lettere fanno prova di un interesse per lo studio, di una certa eloquenza e soprattutto di raffinatezza di gusti e di vita. Abita uno dei palazzi dei Tolentini a Milano, ma sta spesso nella villa di Bereguardo sul Ticino. È uomo di armi come il nonno e il padre; giostratore famoso da giovane (secondo le parole del Litta[11]), viene armato

---

[3] Oltre A. SIMIONI, «Un umanista milanese, P. P.», *Archivio storico lombardo*, XXXI (1904), pp. 5-50, 227-301, si veda il recente articolo di A. MONTANARI, «Le Elegie ed Epigrammi di Piattino Piatti: contributo al censimento dei testimoni», *Libri & documenti*, XIV, 2 (1988), pp. 56-82.

[4] Si vedano N. SAPEGNO, «M. B.», *Dizionario Biografico degli Italiani* (*DBI*), V, Roma, 1963, pp. 667-673; M. E. COSENZA, *Biographical and Bibliographical Dictionary of the Italian Humanists and of the World of Classical Scholarship in Italy 1300-1800*, 6 voll., Boston, 1962-1967, I, pp. 381-382 e V, *Synopsis and Bibliography*, p. 184; la n. 1, sopra, e la n. 61 al capitolo I.

[5] Corrispondente di Battista Mantovano: COSENZA (n. 4), vol. IV, p. 3130.

[6] Carmelitano e famoso poeta, tradotto in lingua francese ed inglese verso la metà del '500, e conosciuto a poeti quali lo Shakespeare (cfr. *Love's Labour's Lost*, IV, 2, 96-103). Cfr. COSENZA (n. 4), III, pp. 2127-2133.

[7] Si vedano i capitoli VI e IX in questo volume.

[8] Si vedano soprattutto i capitoli IV, V e VIII di questo volume.

[9] E. BIGI, «I. A.», *DBI*, III, Roma, 1961, pp. 470-472. Bandello (III, 26) lo descrive così: «Era l'Antiquario uomo di buonissime lettere e di vita integerrima e appo tutti per i castigatissimi costumi in grandissima stimazione».

[10] Non ne trovo notizia in ARGELATI, *Bibliotheca Scriptorum Mediolanensium*, 1745, in COSENZA (n. 4, sopra), né nel *DBI*.

[11] I fatti della vita sono desunti da P. LITTA, *Famiglie celebri d'Italia*, Milano, 1819-1893, vol. VI, «Maruzzi di Tolentino», Tav. III; dai *Commentari*, editi da Marcora (n. 1), che s'inter-

cavaliere nel 1486 all'età di 15 anni, e vince all'età di vent'anni una giostra col conte Gian Francesco della Mirandola, che ha due anni di piú. [12] Nello stesso anno, 1491, sembrano diventare ancora più aperte le intenzioni di Ludovico il Moro di soppiantare il duca Giangaleazzo Sforza, e Ludovico toglie a Giovanni e ai suoi fratelli – «ingiustamente», come scrive Giovanni – lo stipendio ricevuto dal nonno e dal padre. Non trovo, però, segno fra i *Commentari* di un esilio di cinque anni menzionato dal Litta, benché Giovanni faccia nel 1493 un viaggio di sei mesi fuori d'Italia, in Francia e in Spagna, fino a raggiungere l'oceano Atlantico. Nel 1495 sposa Taddea, figlia del Conte Pompeo Landi, è nominato consigliere ducale, [13] e gli vengono affidati il governo di Pavia e la difesa del passaggio del Ticino. Nel 1499, secondo il Litta, non sembra offrire gran resistenza ai francesi, che entrano poi in Milano. Sembra anzi che faccia un giuramento entusiasta al nuovo duca, il re di Francia, che alloggia diverse volte presso i Tolentini a Bereguardo e altrove. Come ha saputo fare pure Baldassare Taccone, Giovanni II Tolentino si dimostra capace di adattarsi e di rendersi accettabile anche nel momento del nuovo cambio del governo nel 1513, a favore degli Sforza. Quando muore nel 1517, all'età di 46 anni, Milano è di nuovo sotto i francesi.

Nei momenti di pace, Giovanni II Tolentino svolge il suo ruolo nella corte ducale, ma altrimenti sembra libero di condurre una vita da gentiluomo, forse anche da mecenate – però di una tale attività non abbiamo finora prove, benché ciò sarebbe logico e spiegherebbe le relazioni attestate dal volume di lettere in questione. Ha 17 anni nell'ottobre 1488 quando scrive al Taccone (che ne ha dieci di più) rammentando l'ozio letterario, e il *solatium* provato nello studiare e discutere insieme. [14] Quattro mesi piú tardi gli manda la descrizione delle nozze del giovane duca Giangaleazzo Sforza con Isabella d'Aragona, che ci interessa qui. Un'altra sua lettera indirizzata al Taccone descrive un suo viaggio del 1490 a Roma (ma in termini forse piú retorici che accurati [15]), durante il quale passò per l'antica sede familiare, Tolentino nelle Mar-

---

rompono però tra gli anni 1498 e 1510, e dalle lettere nel volume in questione, che datano dagli anni 1488 fino al 1512.

[12] *Commentari*, fol. 5: MARCORA (n. 1), p. 335.

[13] La nomina non risulta dai documenti pubblicati da C. SANTORO, *Gli uffici del dominio sforzesco (1450-1500)*, Milano, 1948; però è probabile, date le nomine del padre Niccolò (p. 15) e del nonno Giovanni (pp. 4, 7). (Non tutte le nomine elencate dalla Santoro si basano sui Regesti Ducali, bensì su lettere e missive, la cui conservazione è più casuale).

[14] Lettera n. 1, in appendice al capitolo VI del presente volume.

[15] Secondo R. Schofield che l'ha curata con ampie e dotte note: «Giovanni da Tolentino Goes to Rome: A Description of the Antiquities of Rome in 1490», *Journal of the Warburg and*

che. Altre lettere del volume trattano di consigli di lettura ricevuti da Battista Mantovano, di figli nati, allegra notizia che si comunica a Piattino Piatti, e di vicende arcane della «piccola politica» a cui partecipano i cortigiani milanesi. Dei vari epigrammi uno, in lode delle virtù del vino, è indirizzato al Piatti, un altro, che cita Catone il vecchio come ispirazione per il ritorno ai campi, si rivolge a Jacopo Antiquario.

Una ricca fonte, dunque, queste lettere, forse più per una ricostruzione dell'ambiente intellettuale e sociale della cerchia di uomini di lettere attorno alla corte milanese, che non per il materiale reale in esse contenuto. Ciò risulta altrettanto vero anche per quanto riguarda la lettera qui sotto esame, quella che descrive al Taccone gli avvenimenti della giornata delle nozze di Giangaleazzo Sforza con Isabella d'Aragona – giornata già conosciuta in ricco dettaglio dalle cronache di Tristano Calco e (soprattutto) di Stefano Dolcino.[16]

Siamo a conoscenza – dal Calco e da documenti non identificati riassunti da Michele Daverio nel primo Ottocento[17] – della compagnia di nobili scesi

---

*Courtauld Institutes*, XLIII (1980), pp. 246-256. È stampata per intero in appendice al capitolo VI di questo volume, num. 7.

[16] S. DOLCINO, *Nuptiae Illustrissimi Ducis Mediolani P. Stephanus Scalae Canonicus Nicolao Lucaro Rhetori Cremonensi S.* Coloph.: *Opera & impensa Spectabilis Viri .D. Io Antonii Coruini de Arretio: uir i(n) hac arte ingeniosissimus. Antonius Zarotus Parmensis i(m)pressit Mediolani .M.cccc lxxxviiii. Idibus Aprilibus.* Di cc. 14 (Hain 6414; GW 9064; IGI 3586; BMC VI, 721); è discussa ampiamente da R. SCHOFIELD, «A Humanist Description of the Architecture for the Wedding of Gian Galeazzo Sforza and Isabella D'Aragona (1489)», *Papers of the British School at Rome*, LVI (1988), pp. 213-240 e Tavv. XX-XXII. Cfr. T. CALCO, *Nuptiae Mediolanensium Ducum sive Joannis Galeacii cum Isabella Aragona Ferdinandi Neapolitanorum Regis nepte*, nei suoi *Residua*, Mediolani, MDCXLIV, pp. 63-85; anche nel *Thesaurus Antiquitatum et Historiarum Italiae, Mari Ligustico & Alpibus Vicinae ... Collectus Cura & Studio Joannis Georgii Graevii*, T. II, pars 1, Lugduni Batavorum, MDCCIV, coll. 499-514, soprattutto le coll. 510-514. Si vedano pure le nn. 24 e 25. Lo Schofield pubblica, alle pp. 238-240 dell'art. cit., estratti da due altre descrizioni: l'anonima *Descriptione de l'ordine et feste celebrate in le noze delo illustrissimo Zoanne Galeaz Duca de Milano*, MS Italien 1592 della Bibliothèque Nationale di Parigi, cc. 209-217; e G. A. BOSSI, *Epithalamium de Io. Galeazio sexto Mediolanensium Duce et Elisabella uxore*, MS N 133 sup. della Biblioteca Ambrosiana di Milano, cc. 139-143 (che non ho potuto vedere).

[17] In G. GIULINI, *Memorie spettanti alla storia, al governo ed alla descrizione della città e campagna di Milano ne' secoli bassi*, VI, Milano, 1857, pp. 649-655; il riassunto venne ristampato, senza identificarne la fonte, nello stesso anno e dalla stessa casa editrice Colombo, come nota all'edizione ottocentesca di B. CORIO, *Storia di Milano*, a cura di E. de Magri *et al.*, 3 voll., Milano, 1855-1857, III, pp. 447-453, n. 7, cfr. p. 427. La prima delle due pubblicazioni, quasi identiche, erra nel chiamare la madre del duca «Bianca Maria» anziché Bona (Giulini, p. 652); gli editori del Corio correggono in «sorella», p. 450. Ci manca una conva-

a Napoli per incontrare e accompagnare a Milano la sposa, di recente resa orfana dalla morte di Ippolita Sforza sua madre, la quale aveva fatto il viaggio in senso opposto ventiquattro anni prima.[18] Abbiamo dal Calco la descrizione del matrimonio per surrogato a Napoli prima della partenza del corteo per Genova. Il viaggio invernale per mare durò dal 30 dicembre 1488 fino al 18 gennaio 1489, con grande disagio della sposa, malgrado le soste a Gaeta, a Civitavecchia, a Livorno, e altrove. Dopo sei giorni di ricupero festivo a Genova,[19] il corteo passò a Tortona dove ebbero luogo le famose feste preparate da Bergonzio Botta, nobile di stirpe tortonese, nato a Pavia.[20] Lì ci troviamo di fronte ad un banchetto mitologico del tutto simile a quelli offerti ad Eleonora d'Aragona a Roma nel 1473, durante il viaggio matrimoniale per Ferrara, e a Costanzo Sforza e Camilla d'Aragona a Pesaro nel 1475;[21] ban-

---

lida della fonte primaria da documenti identificabili. Si tratterà, o di altre lettere di un inviato come Jacopo Trotti (come mi ha suggerito plausibilmente il sig. Guido Lopez), o di una versione in volgare della relazione del Dolcino (con cui sembrano esserci in comune molti dettagli) o di altro cronista. Mi sembra più probabile quest'ultima ipotesi, dato il fatto che lettere di inviati si troverebbero più facilmente negli archivi delle potenze destinatarie che non in quello ducale o di San Fedele, dove localizza questi documenti il Giulini (p. 649). Le lettere del Trotti sono custodite nell'Archivio di Stato di Modena.

[18] F. A. GALLO, «La danza negli spettacoli conviviali del secondo Quattrocento», *Spettacoli conviviali dall'antichità classica alle corti italiane del Quattrocento. Atti del VII Convegno di Studio* (Centro di Studi sul Teatro Medioevale e Rinascimentale), Viterbo, 1983, pp. 261-267, soprattutto le pp. 262-263; C. FALLETTI, «Le feste per Eleonora d'Aragona da Napoli a Ferrara (1473)», *Ibid.*, pp. 269-289, a p. 281.

[19] G. Lopez, tenendo conto di lettere inedite del Trotti (cfr. n. 17), calcola cinque giorni e mezzo (comunicazione personale): cfr. il suo articolo, «Una Signoria fra due epoche», in *Gli Sforza a Milano*, Milano, 1978, e U. ROZZO, «La festa di nozze sforzesca del gennaio 1489 a Tortona», *Libri & documenti*, XIV, 1 (1989), pp. 9-23, alla n. 17.

[20] Cfr. CALCO, *Nuptiae Mediolanensium Ducum*, nel *Thesaurus* (n. 16), coll. 508-510. Ora si veda pure E. CASINI ROPA, «Il banchetto di Bergonzio Botta per le nozze di Isabella d'Aragona e Gian Galeazzo Sforza nel 1489: quando la storiografia si sostituisce alla storia», *Spettacoli conviviali* (n. 18). Sul Botta, si vedano G. TANI, «B. B.», *Enciclopedia dello spettacolo*, II, Roma, 1954, pp. 889-890; R. ZAPPERI e D. RICCI ALBANI in *DBI*, 13, Roma, 1971, pp. 362-364.

[21] Cito qui solo le fonti principali. 1473: L. OLIVI, «Delle nozze di Ercole I d'Este con Eleonora d'Aragona», *Memorie della Regia Accademia di Scienze, Lettere ed Arti in Modena*, ser. II, vol. V (1887) pp. 15-68; C. CORVISIERI, «Il trionfo romano di Eleonora d'Aragona nel giugno del 1473», *Archivio della Società Romana di Storia Patria*, I (1878), pp. 475-491; X (1887), pp. 629-687; C. FALLETTI, «Le feste» (n. 18). 1475: *Le nozze di Costanzo Sforza e Camilla d'Aragona celebrate a Pesaro nel maggio 1475. Narrazione anonima, accompagnata da 32 miniature di artista contemporaneo pubblicata a cura di Tammaro de Marinis...*, Firenze, 1946. Cfr. il mio «Per un'iconologia dello spettacolo: dalle nozze sforzesche del 1489 alle favole mitologiche», in *Arte lombarda*, 105-107 (1993): Atti del Convegno, «Metodologia

chetti che hanno tutti e due stretti rapporti col teatro, come hanno sottlinea-
to anni fa Nino Pirrotta ed Elena Povoledo. [22]

La lettera del Tolentino, datata 9 febbraio 1489 (Figg. 9 e 10), [23] serve
da complemento alle relazioni più estese come quelle del Dolcino e del Calco, oltreché ad una del «Servitor Stephanus» indirizzata a Lorenzo de' Medici[24] e ad un'altra di Jacopo Trotti indirizzata ad Ercole d'Este. [25] Il Tolentino ci fornisce una descrizione personale, piena di entusiasmo, scritta
all'amico affinché ne faccia parte agli altri amici assenti anch'essi dai festeggiamenti. Scrive quanto avrebbe voluto condividere la giornata con
l'amico. Con lo svolazzo abituale della sua retorica, prosegue a dire che
cento lingue e cento bocche non gli basterebbero per comunicare la delizia,
la gioia, la gloria del giorno trionfale, giorno che rivaleggia perfino con
quello del ritorno di Mario e di Cesare dopo la vittoria sui Cimbri. (Purtroppo, la gioia comunicata si legge oggi – e si sarebbe letta anche al momento della pubblicazione delle lettere del Tolentino – con un'ironia che
nasce dalla conoscenza dei fatti ulteriori).

La descrizione del Tolentino dell'entrata di Isabella nella città di Milano
il primo febbraio, a somiglianza con quelle degli altri cronisti, dà conto delle
tappezzerie e degli arazzi che pendevano da tutti i muri, dal castello fino alla
cattedrale. Racconta come Ludovico, che occupa una posizione di notevole
rilievo in tutte le relazioni, aveva fatto raggruppare il giorno prima cinque
navi ornatissime (i bucintori), di cui tre vengono mandate per ricevere la spo-

---

della ricerca. Orientamenti attuali. Congresso Internazionale in onore di Eugenio Battisti»
(Milano, 27-31 maggio 1991), pp. 84-87.

[22] Li due Orfei, Torino, ERI, 1969 pp. 17-21, 49-50 e Einaudi, 1975 pp. 9-12, 37-39, e ancora
prima: N. PIRROTTA, «Intermedium», in Die Musik in Geschichte und Gegenwart, Basel-
London, 1957, vol. 6, coll. 1310-1326.

[23] La lettera del Tolentino è la n. 3, in appendice al capitolo VI di questo volume.

[24] Pubblicata prima in A. FABRONIO, Laurentii Medicis Magnifici Vita, 2 voll., Pisa, 1784, vol.
II: Adnotationes et Monumenta ad Laurentii Medicis Magnifici Vitam Pertinentia, p. 295, n.
171 (che si riferisce alla p. 168 del primo volume); fu ripresa da W. ROSCOE, The Life of
Lorenzo de' Medici, called The Magnificent, 2 voll., London, 1825[6], II, pp. 430-432, e (tra-
scritta con varianti) nella traduzione italiana di G. Mecherini, Pisa, 1816[2], III, LXXXIX-
XCII. Si tratta senz'altro di un inviato di Lorenzo e non di Stefano Dolcino, come voleva K.
T. STEINITZ, «The Voyage of Isabella d'Aragon from Naples to Milan, January 1489», Bibliothèque d'Humanisme et Renaissance, XXIII (1961), pp. 17-33, soprattutto la p. 30.

[25] Pubblicata in facsimile da G. LOPEZ, «Le prodezze di Ferdinando. Un enfant terrible alla
corte di Ludovico il Moro», Etruria oggi, 23 (dicembre 1989), pp. 72-74.

sa: una porta la madre dello sposo, Bona di Savoia, un'altra le sorelle, e la terza varie figlie di nobili, ornatissime anch'esse. Ludovico segue con una folla di gentiluomini sulle altre due navi. Tutti proseguono fino alla chiesa di San Cristoforo sul Naviglio Grande. Intanto, lo sposo procede con una turba di cavalieri e nobili e con i magistrati, tutti vestiti in seta, oro e argento, con splendide ghirlande, verso gli approdi situati nel suo parco.

Abbiamo una percezione personale della flottiglia, bellissima da vedere, che, avanzando verso l'autore che sta nel corteo dello sposo, si mostra piena di gente insigne. Tutto risuona al rombo delle macchine da guerra, al fragore dei proiettili, e al clangore delle trombe. Arrivati al castello, coloro che entrano salutano il duca. Il castello stesso è ornato con arazzi e tappezzerie straordinari, di colori variatissimi, con ghirlande ducali e con gli stendardi di tutte le città, i villaggi e gli altri castelli del ducato.

Il giorno seguente, che è quello delle cerimonie nuziali in duomo (il 2 febbraio), la sposa viene scortata fin dalla porta del castello da una compagnia di preti ed ecclesiastici con le reliquie di tutti i santi, e con medici e avvocati, protetti da un baldacchino, seguiti da tutti i principi e da tutti gli uomini di ceto senatoriale, e infine dalle compagnie dei nobili restanti. Poi seguono tutti gli arcieri a cavallo, e gli altri cavalieri vestiti di armatura leggera.

Tolentino descrive l'arco trionfale all'entrata del «foro», ornato da un fregio raffigurante le vittorie importanti di Francesco Sforza, soprattutto quella sopra i Veneziani a Caravaggio (il 14 settembre 1448, una battaglia che diede allo Sforza un vantaggio decisivo nei rapporti con la Repubblica Ambrosiana).[26] Davanti alla chiesa, vediamo un «tugurium» (descritto da Stefano Dolcino come una volta posata su otto colonne quasi triangolari, alte e graziose, con una figura di metallo in cima che rende la costruzione alta quasi come la vecchia chiesa [di S. Maria Maggiore][27]). Attraverso questa struttura passano le nobili donne milanesi che seguono la sposa dentro alla chiesa, dove un meraviglioso portico si stende fino all'altare. Il duca e la sua sposa occupano un trono dorato; agli altri è dato un posto adeguato alla dignità di ciascuno. Il vescovo Sanseverino pronuncia l'orazione nuziale con eloquenza.

---

[26] N. VALERI, *L'Italia nell'età dei principati*, Verona, 1969, p. 412.

[27] DULCINUS, *Nuptiae Illustrissimi Ducis Mediolani* (n. 16), cc. a4 verso – a5; cfr. anche SCHOFIELD, «A Humanist Description» (n. 16), pp. 215, 236.

Dopo che si è celebrata la messa, il legato fiorentino (cioè Pietro Alemanno[28]) e Bartolomeo Calco, segretario ducale, ricevono in dono abiti tessuti in oro. Gli agenti della tesoreria («lateronum munus»), il conte Giovanni Borromeo e Gian Francesco Pallavicino, s'inginocchiano davanti alla sposa. Terminate le funzioni, il sole essendo già tramontato, Giovanni e gli altri seguono la coppia ducale fino alla camera regia.

Alla fine, Giovanni saluta l'amico Taccone, dicendo che la lettera è stata scritta d'impulso e chiedendogli di informare degli avvenimenti soprattutto Corrado Stanga (futuro ambasciatore alla corte di Napoli[29]), uomo di perfetta integrità, che non aveva potuto parteciparvi. (Stanga risulta inviato a Genova nel 1488, il che suggerirebbe la sua presenza in quella città, o forse sempre a Tortona, dov'è forse rimasto anche il Taccone dopo il banchettospettacolo del Botta, che recentemente gli è stato attribuito[30]).

Questa lettera è di un tono diverso da quello di tutte le altre relazioni conosciute. Scritta in uno stile ricercato, con in mente la posterità, è anche una lettera scritta ad un amico intimo, anziché una cronaca di storico come quelle del Calco o del Dolcino, o anziché un resoconto di ambasciatore come le lettere scritte a Lorenzo ed a Ercole. Il tono qui è di un'eleganza intima, e l'entusiasmo viene espresso e filtrato tramite l'eloquenza, precisamente come si vorrebbe in una lettera scritta da un cortigiano educato ai precetti dell'umanesimo. Siamo pure messi al corrente dei fatti da un punto di vista nuovo, da partecipanti a lato del giovane duca. Osserviamo con Giovanni dal giardino del duca l'approdo della flottiglia di bucintori; sentiamo avvicinarsi il momento bramato dell'arrivo della sposa. La relazione è breve, non ci offre i dettagli di quelle dei cronisti, ma ci offre la visione personale, *engagée*, di un familiare della corte ducale, e conferma le altre relazioni della medesima occasione.

Il libro di epistole di Giovanni II Tolentino è tutto così. Le lettere vengono descritte dal Bandello, nella lettera introduttiva, come «copiosae, ... ele-

---

[28] Lettera di «Servitor Stefanus» (n. 24); documenti pubblicati da Daverio (n. 17).

[29] L. CERIONI, *La diplomazia sforzesca nella seconda metà del Quattrocento e i suoi cifrari segreti*, 2 voll., Roma, 1970 (Fonti e Studi del *Corpus Membranorum Italicarum*, VII), I, pp. 236-237. Posso aggiungere: L. G. PÉLISSIER, «Ludovic Sforza et le contingent napolitain (juillet-août 1499). Lettres de l'ambassadeur milanais Conradolo Stanga au duc de Milan», estratto dalla *Revue d'histoire diplomatique*, Paris, 1896 (Notes Italiennes d'Histoire de France, XIX).

[30] U. ROZZO, «L'*Ordine de le imbandisone* per le nozze di Gian Galeazzo Sforza con Isabella d'Aragona», *Libri & documenti*, XIV, 2 (1989), pp. 1-14, a p. 2.

gantes, et ... perfaciles». L'epigramma del Piatti le definisce «mel geminum, tersam dulci cum carmine prosam». Ed è vero: sono le lettere di un gentiluomo, non di uno studioso, non di un umanista, ma di un uomo di lettere di una certa sensibilità, che rende la testimonianza alquanto intima, e perciò valida per una comprensione dell'ambiente dell'epoca sua.

# PART IV
*Theater as Mirror in Northern Italian Culture*

# CHAPTER VIII

## The Birth of Vernacular Comedy: Gaspare Visconti's *Pasithea*

Theatrical history affords us valuable subject matter for the reconstruction of an epoch, for to create a full picture of the theater, one must take into account the education and social and political context of the authors, the ideas behind the themes of the works and the literary devices used to express these themes, as well as the techniques employed in the presentation of the plays: music, staging and, where possible, dance. Only thus can one hope to formulate a balanced, living image of a living phenomenon expressive of its age and culture.

In an attempt to approach in this way the development of vernacular theater in the Italian Renaissance, and taking into account recent work in the fields of musicology and art history as well as other work on Renaissance currents, I have made a study of seven extant *favole mitologiche* of the late Quattrocento in the Northern courts of Italy, from Poliziano's *Orfeo* on through the play which I have edited from its one manuscript source, and with which I will deal here: Gaspare Visconti's *Pasithea*.[1] These plays were

---

[1] The five other plays are: *Orphei Tragoedia, La favola di Orfeo e Aristeo* and the *Rappresentazione di Febo e Fetonte (Pitone), o di Dafne*, all three anonymous, Niccolò da Correggio's *Favola di Cefalo* and Baldassare Taccone's *Danae*. The more complete study is my *Politian's «Orfeo» and Other «Favole Mitologiche» in the Context of Late Quattrocento Northern Italy*, Ph.D. Dissertation, Columbia University, 1976; a diplomatic edition of *Pasithea* appears at pp. 207-261. Cf. *Teatro del Quattrocento. Le corti padane*, eds. A. Tissoni Benvenuti and M. P. Mussini Sacchi, Torino, 1983, pp. 335-396; A. Tissoni Benvenuti, *L'Orfeo del Polizia-*

strictly court entertainments, directed to an aristocratic, educated public. Their language is largely normalized to Tuscan; they have pastoral-mythological themes and settings; they employ the same poetic meters – primarily *ottava rima* and *terza rima* – and in all of them the presence of music, and specifically of sung passages including the occasional *frottola*, can be assumed. Nino Pirrotta has of course worked extensively on this last aspect in his book, *Li due Orfei*,[2] and other musicologists have also interested themselves in the matter, in part because of the direct connection between these plays and the earliest operas, whose themes, it should be noted, correspond almost exactly to those of the Quattrocento *favole* (Orpheus and Eurydice, Cephalus and Procris, Apollo and Daphne).

The phenomenon of these little vernacular pastoral-mythological plays was largely a Northern one. It is possible, though not proven, that the one Tuscan author, Angelo Ambrogini, il Poliziano, was at the court of Mantua when he composed (or revised) his *Orfeo*, and he would then have been subject to the tastes of that area. Cardinal Francesco Gonzaga, to whom the Latin ode in *Orfeo* is addressed, is known to have favored such spectacles as Cardinal-legate to Bologna, and to have decorated his villa in Rome with themes from classical mythology and adorned it with *orti conclusi*.[3] He was in fact Cardinal-legate to Bologna when the earliest dated of these mythological spectacles, only fragmentarily preserved, but based on the Cephalus and Procris tale as related in Ovid's *Metamorphoses*, was performed there.[4]

Perhaps largely because their most famous author, as well as their linguistic patina, was Tuscan, this Emilian-Lombard character of the plays has not been emphasized.[5] Certainly, however, it is also true that the impetus for

---

*no. Con il testo critico dell'originale e delle successive forme teatrali*, Padova, 1986; and chapters IX and X, below.

[2] N. PIRROTTA, *Li due Orfei. Da Poliziano a Monteverdi*. Con un saggio critico sulla scenografia di Elena Povoledo, Torino, ERI, 1969; Torino, Einaudi, 1975; revised English translation: *Music and Theatre from Poliziano to Monteverdi*, Cambridge, 1982. References are to the later Italian and the English editions.

[3] PIRROTTA, *Li due Orfei* (n. 2), p. 9; Eng. ed., pp. 7-8. The date of the original play is now considered to be earlier; cf. chapter IX, n. 16, below (also for the locus).

[4] PIRROTTA, *Li due Orfei* (n. 2), pp. 11-12, Eng. ed., pp. 10-11; and see F. CAVICCHI, «Rappresentazioni bolognesi nel 1475», in *Atti e memorie della R. Deputazione di Storia Patria per le Provincie di Romagna*, Ser. III, XXVII (1908-1909), pp. 71-85, and *Teatro del Quattrocento* (n. 1), pp. 33-44, for the extant fragments of the text.

[5] Cf. V. BRANCA, «Suggestioni veneziane nell'*Orfeo* del Poliziano», in *Il teatro italiano del Rinascimento*, ed. M. de Panizza Lorch, Milano, 1980, pp. 467-482; but cf. also chapter IX, n. 16, below.

the virtual rash of these plays in the North at the end of the fifteenth century came from Tuscany, in the sense of receiving its cue from the famed Florentine's *Orfeo*, itself close in spirit to the *feste* offered his city by Lorenzo de' Medici.[6] In all of the successive vernacular *favole* I have considered, there appear stylistic borrowings, and even whole passages, from *Orfeo*, even though its form – a combination of eclogue, carnival *festa, sacra rappresentazione* and classical comedy, though undivided by acts or scenes[7] – was not strictly held to. This point too is worthy of emphasis. While the character of these *favole* is very similar, one cannot easily group them simply on the basis of form. Five of the seven, including *Pasithea*, are divided into five acts; Poliziano's *Orfeo* and the closely imitative *Dafne* have no divisions of scene or act.

Among the seven plays, *Pasithea*, written probably between 1493 and 1497[8] and thus coming, I believe, at or near the end of the series of *favole mitologiche*, moves in a new direction. While based in large part on the Babylonian legend of Pyramus and Thisbe, and while containing a scene which refers directly to the myth of Apollo and Daphne,[9] Gaspare Visconti's *Pasithea* consists primarily of elements, characters and situations taken from classical Roman comedy. It is the epitome of what Vittorio Rossi called a *dramma mescidato*.[10] And to an extent that Rossi may never have dreamed of, it leads us directly to the vernacular *commedie erudite* (or are they better styled, with Nino Pirrotta, *commedie classicheggianti?*) of Mantovano, Ariosto, Bibbiena and others.

The name Gaspare Visconti is likely to ring a bell, not only for those who know the author of this play and his poems – or *Rithmi*, to use the name under which some were published in 1493[11] – but because in the poet's day

---

[6] For a fuller discussion of this, see my «Il tema di Orfeo, la musica e le favole mitologiche del tardo Quattrocento», in *Interrogativi dell'Umanesimo, IV. Atti del XIII Convegno Internazionale di Studi Umanistici* (Montepulciano, 25-31 July, 1976), Firenze, 1981, pp. 121-139, and chapter IX, below.

[7] I have discussed this form in relation to the content of the play in *Politian's «Orfeo»* (n. 1), pp. 114-132.

[8] *Ibidem*, pp. 187-190.

[9] Cf. OVID, *Metamorphoses*, IV, 51-166 (Pyramus and Thisbe); I, 452-567 (Apollo and Daphne).

[10] V. ROSSI, *Il Quattrocento*, Milano, 1938, pp. 531-532.

[11] HAIN 16078. The work was dedicated to Niccolò da Correggio, author of *Cefalo*; the other poems appear in manuscripts at the Biblioteca Trivulziana, Milan, and in Vienna (see above, chapters IV, n. 37 and V, nn. 5, 7 and 8), as well as in G. VISCONTI, *I Canzonieri per Beatrice d'Este e per Bianca Maria Sforza*, ed. P. Bongrani, Milano, 1979.

and around his time, there were no fewer than thirteen Gaspari Visconti, including of course the Archbishop of Milan (1584-1595), successor to San Carlo Borromeo. [12]

To recapitulate briefly, our poet Gaspare Visconti was born in 1461 and originally baptised, appropriately enough for a Milanese, with the name Ambrogio. By order of Francesco Sforza, and to our distress, however, he was renamed Gaspar Ambrogio, and more often than not simply called Gaspare. He was a learned man, and like many noble courtiers of the time, completed diplomatic missions as well as artistic ones for the court of the Sforza in Milan. He became «Senator» before 1483, and possibly took part in the embassy of 1488-1489 to Naples to escort Isabella d'Aragona to Milan as the bride of the young Duke Giangaleazzo Sforza. He was also a member of the escort conducting Bianca Maria Sforza to Austria in 1493 when she wed the Emperor Maximilian. In 1494 Visconti and F. Tantius Corniger edited Petrarca's *Canzoniere*, [13] and in 1495 Visconti's own poem, *De Paolo e Daria Amanti*, was published in Milan. [14] Gaspar Ambrogio Visconti died in the spring of 1499, several months before the downfall of Lodovico il Moro, his patron.

Gaspare Visconti's *Pasithea* was written in Milan, probably, as I have said, between 1493 and January 1497 when Beatrice d'Este Sforza, Ludovico il Moro's wife, died. After that, the court was in mourning, and the author himself died only two years later.

The name of one of the two principal characters, and hence the title of the play, *Pasithea*, may have been suggested to Visconti by the lines from Poliziano's *Stanze per la giostra*, [15] where Venus sends Pasitea with a dream to Iulio:

> Pasitea fe' chiamar, del Sonno sposa,
> Pasitea, delle Grazie una sorella,

---

[12] For a biographical sketch of the poet, see chapter IV, above, and its Appendix I for the other contemporary Gaspari. (Cf. my *Politian's «Orfeo»* [n. 1], pp. 19-33, and n. 58, on pp. 23-25).

[13] HAIN-COPINGER-REICHLING 12775. A more complete description is in L. POLAIN, *Catalogue des livres imprimés au quinzième siècle des Bibliothèques de Belgique*, III, Bruxelles, 1932, no. 3068.

[14] G. A. SASSI, *Historia Literario-Typographica Mediolanensis ab anno MCDLXV. ad annum MD.*, in *Philippi Argelati... Bibliotheca Scriptorum Mediolanensium*, Milano, 1745: Sassi, col. CCCLXI; Argelati, II, 1, 1604. For a more detailed discussion of these early printed works, see chapter IV, above.

[15] A. POLIZIANO, *Stanze cominciate per la giostra di Giuliano de' Medici*, edizione critica a cura di V. Pernicone, Torino, 1954.

Pasitea che dell'altre è più amorosa,
quella che sovra a tutte è la più bella...

*(Stanze*, II, 22, 1-4)

While the name Pasithea appears as early as Hesiod, in the *Theogony* (l. 246)
Pasithea is a Nereid, rather than one of the Graces. She occurs as a Grace and
wife-to-be of Hypnos in the *Iliad* (XIV, 269, 276) which of course Poliziano
knew intimately. In the *Stanze*, Poliziano specifies not only that she is one of
the Graces, but that she is the most beautiful one, a point which is taken up
by Visconti in the fifth act of his play, where a shepherd describes her as «più
bella che Venere dea», and states that if it is she who has died, «Beltate è
morta seco, e leggiadria».[16]

Visconti's play appears in a partially autograph *zibaldone* of the poet's
works at the Trivulziana Library in Milan.[17] The folios bearing the text of
*Pasithea* were probably written by a copyist in the service of the poet.
However, a few corrections appear in a hand which seems to correspond to
Visconti's (e.g. fols. 83$^v$, 96$^r$), thus rendering the text authoritative.

*Pasithea* begins with a Prologue, recited by a player in the character of the
playwright Caecilius Statius of the second century B.C. Caecilius relates his
life in the afterworld, describing a scene reminiscent of Dante's Limbo and
later imitations by Boccaccio and Petrarca.[18] Here, Caecilius tells of whiling
away pleasant hours in the company of Terence and Plautus; he lauds his
«patria» Milano which has never seen better days than it now enjoys «sotto
un moro all'ombra» (l. 23, with obvious reference to Ludovico il Moro); and
he recites the «Argumento» of the play. This last is a plot summary written in
the spirit of the 12-line *argumenta* added to Terence's plays in the second
century A.D. by Gaius Sulpicius Apollinaris of Carthage,[19] the teacher of

---

[16] *Pasithea*, V, ii, 66 and 72. The citations throughout will follow the numeration of *Teatro del Quattrocento*, but I have in most cases preferred my transcription (cf. *Politian's «Orfeo»* [n. 1], pp. 207-261).

[17] MS 1093, fols. 75$^v$ - 100$^r$. G. PORRO, *Catalogo dei codici manoscritti della Trivulziana*, Torino, 1884, pp. 463-464, terms the MS autograph. P. BONGRANI discusses the hands appearing in the MS, and publishes an autograph letter in «Le rime di Gaspare Visconti», in *Studi di filologia e di letteratura italiana offerti a Carlo Dionisotti*, Milano-Napoli, 1973, pp. 137-208 (tav. I now in his introduction to the edition cited in n. 11, above).

[18] DANTE, *Inferno*, IV, 67-151; BOCCACCIO, *Amorosa Visione*, IV, 31 – VI, 42; PETRARCA, *Trionfi*, *passim*.

[19] The same can be said for Mercurio's prologue to Poliziano's *Orfeo*; for a discussion of this, see my *Politian's «Orfeo»* (n. 1), pp. 116-118.

Aulus Gellius who is himself cited for his opinion on Caecilius in a separate preface to the play.

Act I opens in a street (as with all the *favole mitologiche* except Baldassare Taccone's *Danae*, staged by Leonardo da Vinci, the sets must be inferred from the text) before the house of Chrysalo, the stingy father of a spendthrift son, Dioneo. (This name is clearly taken from the *Decameron*, and the author is doubtless aware of its connection with *lussuria*). Chrysalo is despairing of his ruin, to the point of having thoughts of suicide, but his servant – none other than Pseudolo – dissuades him. Pseudolo is sent to ask Promo, Chrysalo's «spenditore», to speak to Dioneo about his lavish spending; left alone, however, Pseudolo soliloquizes on the miserliness of his master before going to see Promo.

Seeing Chrysalo, at the start of Act II, Promo understands his desperate state, and decides to speak to Dioneo, whom he considers a reasonable individual. Our first view of Dioneo is as he speaks with a neighbor who has acted as intermediary between him and his beloved, Pasithea. Why has she missed their rendez-vous twice running? he asks, and learns that her mother is ill and has required nursing. Promo and Pseudolo confront Dioneo with their news of his father, but he sends them back to deal with Chrysalo themselves.

The third act opens with what may be one of the musical passages of the play, a soliloquy by Dioneo in the form of a *capitolo* in *terza rima*, beginning with a sort of litany in honor of his love:

> Benedecto sia il dì nel qual mi gionse
> Amor, col suo splendente aurato strale,
> Che dolcemente il cuore e il spirto ponse.
> Benedecto sii tu, dì triomphale,
> Da me signando cum la biancha pietra,
> Anzi cum una perla orïentale.
> Benedecto sia l'archo e la pharetra,
> E benedecta sia l'ardente face,
> Che sin ne le medolle me penetra.
> Consumo et ardo, e il foco che mi sface
> Mi porta tal dolcezza dentro a l'alma,
> Che a mala pena quasi n'è capace.
>
> (III, i, 1-12)

Suddenly, he realizes that he is late for his rendez-vous with Pasithea. In one of those abrupt shifts of scene for which Poliziano's *Orfeo* has been criticized, but which is surely due to the type of set used – possibly the *luoghi deputati* discussed by E. Povoledo and by L. Stegagno Picchio[20] – we see Pasithea with the go-between Mastropa, apparently in or beside a house. Mastropa urges Pasithea to keep her rendez-vous with Dioneo, then leaves her to soliloquize – in *terza rima* as did Dioneo – on the forces of love and honor causing her torment:

> Hei me che non fu mai nel mar galea
> Sì combattuta da contrari venti,
> Come è il dolente cuor di Pasithea.
> Milli desiri più che fiamma ardenti
> Me assaltano il penser cum tanta forza,
> Che stretta son cerchar farli contenti.
>
> (III, iii, 81-86)

At last, we see the two lovers together, and Pasithea's conflict is resolved by Dioneo's request for her hand in marriage. She accedes, and the lovers plan to meet at the first cock's crow in the wood beyond the city gate.

Pasithea is alone at the opening of Act IV, stealing through the town by night, «come uno homo d'arme» (l. 9), and it is she who arrives first at their trysting place. She spies a beast coming toward her, and flees into a cave, dropping her veil. But Scene ii takes us back to the town – reinforcing the hypothesis of *luoghi deputati* – and we find the «faithful» servant Pseudolo awakening his master, not at the first cock's crow, but at the sixth, disguising his mistake in true comic servant fashion. Dioneo goes to the wood – and by now the closeness kept to the legend of Pyramus and Thisbe will have been noted – sees the beast's footprints and the torn veil, and resolves to kill himself. As in Poliziano's *Orfeo*, however, and true to Horatian tenet, the death is not shown but narrated by two shepherds (this too in *terza rima*, the meter of eclogues) within earshot of Pasithea, who then resolves to join her beloved in death.

But it is the fifth act which brings us back to the world of the *favola mitologica*, with the appearance of Apollo, at the end of his amorous pursuit of Daphne, addressing his own beloved, «alhora alhora conversa in lauro». He bewails her metamorphosis, and vows to make her tree sacred to his name, and first among trees, «exceptuato solamente il moro» (l., 18) with double reference to the mulberry tree of the Pyramus and Thisbe legend and to Vi-

---

[20] E. POVOLEDO, in PIRROTTA, *Li due Orfei* (n. 2), pp. 337-460, *passim*, Eng. ed., pp. 283-383, *passim*; L. STEGAGNO PICCHIO, «Luoghi deputati», in *Enciclopedia dello Spettacolo*, VI, Roma, 1959, cols. 1739-1741.

sconti's patron. In the next scene, having heard the tale of the two lovers'
deaths from a shepherd's lips, Apollo uses the same image to refer flat-
teringly to Ludovico's compassion:

> Onde se'l moro è sempre inamorato,
>   Haver non se ne die' gran maraviglia,
> Che'l sangue de gli amanti non pur fuore
>   Ma tinto l'ha per sino in mezzo al cuore.
>
> (V, ii, 61-64)

However, on hearing from the same shepherd of Pasithea's great beauty,
Apollo goes off to revive her for his own pleasure. In the two scenes immediately following, Chrysalo is told, first of his son's death by his own hand, and
then of his son's miraculous revival, for Apollo has after all taken pity on the
young couple and revived them both. Apollo joins Chrysalo and Pseudolo,
and commands Chrysalo to allow his son to wed Pasithea. Chrysalo, a new
man, acquiesces, and Pseudolo ends the play with the words:

> Intramo in loco a dar lo anel più idonio,
>   Ché senza intrar non vale il matrimonio!
>
> (V, v, 215-216)

Clearly, this is the most classical of the *favole mitologiche* we know from
the late fifteenth century. Stock characters from Latin comedy abound: a
miserly father, a spendthrift son, the neighbor acting as intermediary, the
servant Pseudolo («pieno de inganni», as he is described in the cast of characters in the manuscript), not to mention the stock ending of the party en-
tering the house for a wedding, as well as the *argumentum* from the manuscript tradition of the classics already mentioned and of course the conven-
tional division into five acts.

And yet, we cannot overlook the other elements in the play. The Pyramus
and Thisbe legend itself may have come into the Italian literary tradition in
part directly from Ovid, but probably also receiving impetus from the French
medieval tradition.[21] References to the tale appear in Dante (*Purgatorio*,

---

(21) V. BRANCA, *Il cantare trecentesco e il Boccaccio del Filostrato e del Teseida*, Firenze, 1936, p.
1; F. A. UGOLINI, *I cantari d'argomento classico*, Genève-Firenze 1933, p. 101. On the legend
itself, see Georg HART, *Ursprung und Verbreitung der Pyramus- und Thisbe-Sage*, Teil
einer, Münchner Inaugural-Dissertation, Passau, 1889; Idem, *Die Pyramus- und Thisbe-
Sage in Holland, England, Italien und Spanien*, Zweiter Teil, Passau, 1891; F. SCHMITT-VON
MÜHLENFELS, *Pyramus und Thisbe. Rezeptionstypen eines Ovidischen Stoffes in Literatur,
Kunst und Musik*, Heidelberg, 1972.

XXVII, 37-42), Petrarca (*Trionfo d'Amore*, II, 20) and Boccaccio (*Amorosa visione*, XX, 43-88; *De claris mulieribus*, XII). In the more popular tradition, it occurs in the *novelle* of Giovanni Sercambi and of Giovanni Sabadino degli Arienti, and, significantly for the history of theater, as a *cantare* in octaves which has more than a few passages corresponding to passages in Visconti's *Pasithea*.[22] Medieval and novellistic appear to be the emphasis in Visconti's play on Pasithea's honor and the joke of the servant awakening his master at the sixth rather than the first cock's crow. There is also the inevitable admixture of the pastoral in the roles of the two shepherds, though their eclogue takes a curiously morbid twist as they recite, not tales of love, but the tale of a double suicide. And the mythical makes its appearance as well, with the arrival of Apollo, and indirectly through the naming of Pasithea after one of the three Graces.

Here, then, is the most «mescidato» of the plays we know from the end of the fifteenth century. Yet its essential flavor is so classical that we are forced to contradict Rossi's own judgment that «nel secolo quindicesimo nessuno ebbe ardire o ingegno da trattare le schiette forme terenziane e plautine in un'opera originale».[23] Gaspare Visconti did just this, albeit with many echoes of Poliziano's *Orfeo*, of *Petrarchismo*, of *Stilnovismo*. His new «comedia», as it is called in the preface, is almost a comedy in form. He even follows a classical norm for comedy which Poliziano had pointed out in his preface to the *Andria* of Terence[24] (though Poliziano may not be his source), that is, the form of recitation being divided into *diverbia*, in which two, three, and rarely four, persons converse, and *cantica*, in which one person recites. Even in the last scene, where one might reasonably expect more people on stage rejoicing, there are only three named: Chrysalo, Apollo and Pseudolo.

Visconti holds to the *cantica* portions as well, in the soliloquies of Dioneo and Pasithea. Perhaps he even took the word *cantica*, which he certainly

---

[22] G. SERCAMBI, *Novelle*, ed. G. Sinicropi, «Scrittori d'Italia», 250-251, Bari, 1972, II, pp. 586-589, Novella CXXXI. Sabadino's version is edited in E. LOMMATZSCH, *La hystoria di Piramo et Tisbe von Giovanni Sabadino degli Arienti um 1470 ...* Im Anhang: *La historia di Pirramo e Tisbe, Florentiner Druck von 1567*, in *Behrens-Festschrift. Supplementheft der Zeitschrift für französische Sprache und Literatur*, Jena and Leipzig, 1929, pp. 230-274. For exact correspondences, see below, Appendix.

[23] ROSSI, *Il Quattrocento* (n. 10), p. 532.

[24] A. POLIZIANO, *La commedia antica e l'«Andria» di Terenzio*, ed. R. Lattanzi Roselli, Firenze, 1973, p. 13.

knew from Livy (VII, 2: 9-10), literally, for these are two of the few passages in the play which are obvious candidates for musical setting. (We know from the sung *capitoli* of the time, and from such passages in other *favole mitologiche* that the form was set to music). Otherwise, the change from octaves to *terza rima* is difficult to understand, unless there was a manner of recital specific to this form of which we are ignorant.

The staging of the play, which, in the absence of stagenotes, we must infer from the text, had to be a *scena molteplice*, especially to accomodate Acts IV and V, partly in the city, partly in the woods outside the city gates. Even within the city, Chrysalo appears in his house, Promo in his, and Pasithea in hers (and, in her first meeting with Dioneo, probably at a window of her house). The shepherds, in the city in Act V after Dioneo's death, discuss Chrysalo's laments «che fuor escono / De la serrata casa» (ll. 97-98), and which even the audience has been able to hear («Hei me, misero me, qual fia la morte / Che fuor mi caverà de questa sorte?», ll. 95-96). Houses, then, and windows and doors (for Pseudolo knocks on Promo's door in Act I and is admitted), though the doors may or may not face directly onstage. And woods, with a cave, the interior of which is visible to the spectators, though not to all those onstage, for in it Pasithea, hiding from the wild beast, laments Dioneo's tardiness in a gratifying response to Poliziano's fourteenth *Stanza* (Book I):

> Quanto è meschina donna che se fida
>   In homo e creda a un simulato riso.
> Peroché benché in vista talhor rida,
>   Altro ha nel cuor che quel che monstra in viso.
> Manda uno amante sì pietose strida
>   Spesso, che par ch'el cuor li sia diviso,
> E par che avampi d'uno inmenso foco,
>   Et poi non ama et altri piglia in gioco.
>
>                             (IV, iii, 105-112)[25]

Then, on hearing shepherds approach, she changes hiding places and listens from a bush as they converse, yet is not seen by them. There are no engines, for Apollo makes no miraculous descents or ascents as he does in Taccone's *Danae*.[26] But there is a laurel tree, Apollo's Daphne, just now transformed, and whose loss paves the way for the resuscitation of Visconti's two lovers.

---

[25] On this soliloquy, see chapter X, below.
[26] See my *Politian's «Orfeo»* (n. 1), pp. 182-183, 186, and chapter IX, below.

Thus it is that we can enter even today the world of the *favole mitolo-giche*, and can visualize, at least partially, the performances of these little plays at gala occasions offered to the members of a court, or in some cases to the people of a city. Their composition and production were distractions for the poets, scholars and men of politics who composed them and arranged for their presentation. They were pastimes. Yet however light and entertaining these *favole* may have been, they could not be cut off from the humanist currents of the time. In exhibiting so many elements of classical comedy, and so few from the medieval religious tradition to which Poliziano's *Orfeo* has, I think to an exaggerated extent, been linked, Gaspare Visconti's *Pasithea* leads us away from its own little genre and directs us towards the *commedia erudita* or *classicheggiante* of the high Renaissance in Italy.

## Appendix

### Comparison of Visconti's *Pasithea* with the *Cantare di Pirramo e Tisbe*

As I have discussed elsewhere, following the lead of Carducci, within Italy the *cantari* are a likely vehicle for transmission of the subject matter used in the *favole mitologiche* and carried on into the earliest *melodrammi* (cf. G. CARDUCCI, «Delle poesie toscane di Messer Angelo Poliziano. Discorso», in his *Le Stanze, l'Orfeo e le Rime di Messer A.P.,* Firenze, 1863, pp. LXIX-LXXVI; *Politian's «Orfeo»* [n. 1], pp. 203-204; *Il tema di Orfeo* [n. 6], pp. 138-139). One finds, for example, passages common to the *cantare, La historia di Pirramo e Tisbe,* and that portion of *Pasithea* based directly on the Babylonian tale.

The *cantare* version in octaves was published by E. Lommatzsch, in appendix to his «La hystoria» [n. 22], at pp. 268-274; the text also appears in a critical edition by F. A. UGOLINI, «I cantari di Piramo e Tisbe», *Studi Romanzi,* 24 (1934), pp. 19-201: version «B».

Comparing the play with the *cantare* in octaves, one finds correspondence between the following passages:

| *Pasithea* | *Pirramo e Tisbe* |
|---|---|
| III, iv, 209-210 (*inc.*: «Fuor de la porta...») | XXVI, 6 - XXVII, 2 (*inc.*: «fuor della porta...») |

IV, i, 9

IV, i, 25

IV, ii, 71-80

IV, v, 181-186 («Qual sorte adversa, o caso acerbo tanto, / O dolcissimo sposo, me t'ha tolto? /.../ Pria vo' lavar le piaghe tue di pianto, / Et milli baci dare al freddo volto...»)

IV, v, 191

IV, v, 192-196

XXXIII, 7

XXXV, 2

XL, 1-2, XLI, 1-8, XLV, 3-8

LI, 1-8 («E piangendo baciavagli il suo bel volto / e la ferita col pianto sì lavava, / dicendo: "Oh, amor mio, chi mi t'ha tolto, / qual caso averso o qual fortuna prava?"»).

LIV, 7-8

LVI, 5-6

LXIV, 1-4

# CHAPTER IX

## Il neoplatonismo e le favole mitologiche del tardo Quattrocento settentrionale: per un'iconologia del teatro

Le favole mitologiche del tardo Quattrocento in Italia, rappresentazioni contenenti una proporzione elevata di brani musicati, create principalmente per le corti e per le case nobili dell'Italia settentrionale, si possono trattare come medaglioni, fusi non in bronzo ma in parole, in musica, in scenografia e in gesti.[1] In quanto sono opere letterarie, e nello stesso tempo in parte visive, si possono studiare da un punto di vista che mi piace chiamare «iconologico». Scelgo appositamente il termine *iconologico*, anziché *iconografico*,[2]

---

[1] Le favole di cui si tratta qui sono: *La fabula de Cefalo e Procris*, forse di Tommaso Beccadelli, (Bologna, 1475); *La fabula di Orfeo*, di Angelo Poliziano (circa 1475: si veda la n. 16); *La Representazione di Febo e Feton, o di Dafne*, di Gian Pietro della Viola (Mantova, 1486?); *La fabula de Cefalo*, di Niccolò da Correggio (Ferrara, 1487); *Pasithea*, di Gaspare Visconti (Milano, 1493-97); *Danae*, di Baldassare Taccone (Milano, 1496); *Le noze* (sic) *di Psiche e Cupidine*, di Galeotto del Carretto (1499-1502?). L'*Orfeo* del Poliziano è stato curato in un'edizione critica da A. TISSONI BENVENUTI: *L'Orfeo del Poliziano. Con il testo critico dell'originale e delle successive forme teatrali*, Padova, 1986; le altre rappresentazioni si trovano nel volume, *Teatro del Quattrocento. Le corti padane*, a cura di A. Tissoni Benvenuti e M. P. Mussini Sacchi, Torino, 1983 (d'ora in poi, *Teatro*). Tranne la *Dafne* e *Le noze*, le opere citate vengono discusse ed analizzate in C. M. PYLE, *Politian's «Orfeo» and Other «Favole Mitologiche» in the Context of Late Quattrocento Northern Italy*, tesi di Ph. D., Columbia University, New York, 1976. Cfr. anche B. GUTHMÜLLER, «Mythos und dramatisches Festspiel an den oberitalienischen Höfen des Quattrocento», nei suoi *Studien zur antiken Mythologie in der italienischen Renaissance*, Weinheim, 1986, pp. 65-77; 172-176; e l'ultimo libro di F. STERNFELD, *The Birth of Opera*, Oxford, 1993, che collega l'*Orfeo* polizianesco alla tradizione che conduce all'opera musicale oltre un secolo più tardi.

[2] Il termine «iconografia del teatro» – forse suggerito per primo da H. KINDERMANN, «Wir brauchen theatergeschichtliche Ikonographien!», *Maske und Kothurn*, 3 (1957), pp. 289-293 – viene discusso in modo penetrante da M. I. ALIVERTI, «Per una iconografia della comme-

secondo una distinzione implicita nei lavori di Warburg, di Panofsky e di Wind, e chiaramente codificata da Bialostocki nell'*Enciclopedia universale dell'arte*, dove vengono messi in luce i legami tra un'immagine e la sua tradizione ed il suo contesto storico-culturale ed intellettuale.[3] L'iconografia cerca di descrivere analiticamente, di capire e di codificare un'immagine, mentre l'iconologia mira, partendo dall'analisi del contenuto di un'opera d'arte, a studiare sinteticamente la stessa opera come un fenomeno completo, in tutta la sua complessità, e nel suo contesto storico. L'iconologia cerca di definire, ad esempio, perché un'immagine viene impiegata in un certo momento storico, e, inoltre, ciò che l'immagine esprime di quel momento. È così, secondo le parole di Bialostocki, un «metodo di interpretazione integrale dell'opera d'arte nel suo completo contesto storico, muovendo dall'analisi del contenuto». La divisione tra i due termini è stata finora fluida. Coloro che studiano l'iconografia s'interessano spesso del contesto culturale, intellettuale e anche sociale. Credo, però, che la definizione dell'iconologia (almeno nel significato operativo che intendo dare al termine) consenta di andare oltre la lettura dell'opera (sia che si tratti di immagine, sia di testo) nel suo contesto storico, e permetta di utilizzare l'opera anche come *strumento* per una lettura di questo stesso contesto, prendendo alla lettera l'idea del teatro come specchio.[4]

---

dia dell'arte. A proposito di alcuni recenti studi», *Teatro e Storia*, IV (1989), pp. 71-88. L'iconografia teatrale è ormai diventata un campo di studio a sé, occupandosi di documenti iconografici (pitture, intagli, ecc.) da cui si possono desumere informazioni sul comportamento degli attori (sia nei loro ruoli teatrali sia nella società) o sulle stesse rappresentazioni teatrali.

[3] A. WARBURG, *La rinascita del paganesimo antico. Contributi alla storia della cultura* (1893-1920), Firenze, 1980; E. PANOFSKY, *Studies in Iconology. Humanistic Themes in the Art of the Renaissance* (1939), New York, 1967, soprattutto la p. 8 (ed. ital., *Studi di iconologia*, Torino, 1975, pp. 8-9); E. WIND, *Pagan Mysteries in the Renaissance*, New York, 1968 (ed. ital., *Misteri pagani nel Rinascimento*, Milano, 1971); J. BIALOSTOCKI, «Iconografia e iconologia», nell'*Enciclopedia universale dell'arte*, Vol. VII, Venezia e Roma, 1958, coll. 163-177, soprattutto col. 170. Cfr. A. CHASTEL, *Art et Humanisme à Florence au temps de Laurent le Magnifique*, Paris, 1961 (ed. ital., *Arte e umanesimo a Firenze al tempo di Lorenzo il Magnifico*, Torino, 1964); E. H. GOMBRICH, *Symbolic Images. Studies in the Art of the Renaissance*, II, Chicago, 1972, 1985³, pp. 5-7 (ed. ital., *Immagini simboliche*, Torino, 1978, pp. 9-12; Gombrich limita la sua definizione alla scoperta del programma di un'opera d'arte); C. GILBERT, «On Subject and Non-subject in Italian Renaissance Pictures», *The Art Bulletin*, XXXIV (1952), pp. 202-217; E. BATTISTI, «Iconologia», nel *Dizionario enciclopedico di architettura e urbanistica*, Roma, 1969, pp. 134-135 (dove l'autore sembra accettare una sinonimia fra i due termini).

[4] Cfr. P. VENTRONE, «Riflessioni teoriche sul teatro nella Firenze dei primi Medici», *Inter-*

L'applicazione di un'interpretazione iconologica ai soli testi teatrali (non essendoci documenti «iconografici», nel senso stretto della parola, riguardanti la scenografia per le favole mitologiche quattrocentesche) riceve sostegno dal fatto che la prima edizione dell'*Iconologia* di Cesare Ripa (1593) conteneva solo il testo, fornendo così al lettore delle immagini mentali. [5] Il significato di tali immagini mentali nel contesto culturale ed intellettuale dell'epoca è tuttavia sintomatico, e ci aiuta a capire la mentalità del tardo Cinquecento, così come una lettura dei testi teatrali qui studiati io credo ci aiuti a comprendere il tardo Quattrocento. [6]

---

*pres*, XII (1992), pp. 150-196, a p. 167, n. 46. Però qui intendo parlare del teatro come specchio, non solo della vita umana e divina, bensì della cultura coeva, e perfino degli effetti delle culture antecedenti, classica e medievale. Questa idea è diversa anche da quella del «theatrum orbis» esplorata da F. A. YATES nel suo *Theatre of the World*, London, 1969: si vedano soprattutto le pp. 162-168; cfr. J. JACQUOT, «*Le théâtre du monde* de Shakespeare à Calderón», *Revue de littérature comparée*, 31 (1957), pp. 341-372.

[5] Thomas Heck, nella sua relazione presso il Theatre Iconography Symposium al Netherlands Institute for Advanced Study (Wassenaar) nel giugno 1995, ha accennato alla mancanza di immagini nella prima edizione di C. RIPA, *Iconologia overo descrittione dell'imagini universali cavate dall'antichita et da altri luoghi*, Roma, Heredi di Gio. Gigliotti, 1593. (Cfr. F. ASCARELLI, *Le cinquecentine romane. «Censimento delle edizioni romane del XVI secolo possedute dalle biblioteche di Roma»*, Milano, 1972, p. 246).

[6] La scelta del termine «iconologia del teatro» si è imposta, per l'approccio che ho sempre cercato di attuare, mentre mi preparavo a partecipare al convegno in onore di Eugenio Battisti nel 1991. Fu senza dubbio Aby WARBURG ad adoperare per primo un approccio che chiamerei addirittura «iconologico» al teatro, nello studio «I costumi teatrali per gli intermezzi del 1589. I disegni di Bernardo Buontalenti e il *Libro di conti* di Emilio de' Cavalieri»» (1895), nella sua *Rinascita* (n. 3), dove richiede alle sue fonti teatrali una spiegazione profonda di questioni culturali o intellettuali (ad esempio alle pp. 66, 84, 100). Anche il lavoro di Battisti può suggerire un approccio simile, nel senso che egli fu sempre cosciente del contesto sociale e storico: si veda la p. 101 di E. BATTISTI, «La visualizzazione della scena classica nella commedia umanistica» nel suo *Rinascimento e barocco*, Torino, 1960. C. MOLINARI, *Le nozze degli dèi. Un saggio sul grande spettacolo italiano nel Seicento*, Roma, 1968, sottolinea i rapporti fra correnti umanistico-filosofiche e gli spettacoli del Cinque e Seicento (cfr. soprattutto le pp. 34, 189, e *passim*). I preziosi lavori di Jean Jacquot e di D. P. Walker sulle feste (n. 58) hanno preso in considerazione il contesto politico ed intellettuale, per non parlare di quelli di Frances A. YATES (nn. 4, 94). M. L. DOGLIO ha fatto allusione anni fa all'iconografia in un suo articolo, «Mito, metamorfosi, emblema dalla *Favola di Orfeo* del Poliziano alla *Festa de lauro*», *Lettere italiane*, XXIX (1977), pp. 148-170, dove ha tentato di collegare l'*Orfeo* allo stato d'animo del Poliziano (a una data però non più accettata). Il recente lavoro di Antonia Tissoni Benvenuti sull'*Orfeo* del Poliziano (n. 1) prende in considerazione il contesto intellettuale e culturale dell'opera. Si veda anche il catalogo della mostra: *Le tems revient. 'L tempo si rinuova. Feste e spettacoli nella Firenze di Lorenzo il Magnifico*, a cura di P. Ventrone, s.l., Silvana Ed., 1992.

I testi teatrali pongono notevoli sfide a un tale approccio. Contrariamente alle arti visive, che occupano lo spazio tridimensionale, permettendo così un'impostazione anche simbolica degli oggetti rappresentati, i testi si svolgono linearmente nel tempo. Così il testo, l'evoluzione drammatica, e, quando c'è, la musica, forniscono una dimensione temporale. Però il fatto che questi particolari testi vengono scritti per essere rappresentati sulla scena ci obbliga a visualizzarli (precisamente come le *icones* del Ripa) anche nello spazio. [7] Nel quindicesimo secolo in Italia le scenografie facevano muovere l'occhio dello spettatore da un livello all'altro dei vari luoghi deputati, costruiti su un palco o su carri per una rappresentazione all'aperto, o su uno o più palchi in una sala grande. Perciò, per studiare le rappresentazioni teatrali iconologicamente, le dobbiamo considerare sia con la lente tematica, sia con quella scenografica; riservando un'analisi testuale dettagliata ad un'altra sede, affronterò qui a larghe pennellate gli aspetti tematici e scenografici.

Le rappresentazioni che qui si considerano, così come le prime opere musicali (chiamate, infatti, da Romain Rolland «l'opéra avant l'opéra»[8]), si basarono soprattutto sulle favole d'amore prese dalle *Metamorfosi* di Ovidio. [9] I loro autori, a cominciare dall'umanista fiorentino Angelo Poliziano (1454-1494), hanno scelto le favole di Orfeo ed Euridice, di Apollo e Dafne, di Cefalo e Procri, di Callisto (la rappresentazione è ora perduta), di Piramo e Tisbe – tutti motivi che saranno ripresi anche dalle primissime opere in musica scritte oltre un secolo più tardi. Sono state utilizzate anche le favole di

---

[7] Una simile quadridimensionalità, pur senza il testo, caratterizza la danza. Due validi studi recenti sul ballo di questo periodo sono B. SPARTI, *Introduction* a: GUGLIELMO EBREO OF PESARO, *De Pratica seu Arte Tripudii. On the Practice or Art of Dancing*, Oxford, 1993, pp. 3-72 e P. LA ROCCA e A. PONTREMOLI, *Il ballare lombardo. Teoria e prassi coreutica nella festa di corte del XV secolo*, Milano, 1987.

[8] R. ROLLAND, *Musiciens d'autrefois*, Paris, 1914⁴, pp. 19-54; è interessante leggere nel presente contesto le parole di Rolland a proposito della musica nella storia (p. 3): «... L'histoire de l'Opéra éclaire l'histoire des moeurs et de la vie mondaine. Toute forme de musique est liée à une forme de la société, et la fait mieux comprendre».

[9] F. W. STERNFELD, «The Birth of Opera: Ovid, Poliziano, and the *Lieto Fine*», *Analecta Musicologica*, 19 (1979), pp. 30-51, a p. 31, sottolinea, riferendosi ai *Tristia*, V, 7, vv. 25-26, che i versi ovidiani si prestano bene ad una traduzione scenica. L'edizione Loeb più recente glossa questo passo come un probabile riferimento alle *Heroides*, che lo Sternfeld ritiene siano state scritte per essere rappresentate. Il passo dei *Tristia* (vv. 25-28) non è specifico rispetto al testo in questione: «Carmina quod pleno saltari nostra theatro, / versibus et plaudi scribis, amice, meis, / nil equidem feci – tu scis hoc ipse – theatris, / Musa nec in plausus ambitiosa mea est»; OVIDIUS, *Tristia. Ex Ponto*, tr. A. L. Wheeler, rev. ed. G. P. Goold, Cambridge, Mass. e London, 1988, p. 236.

Danae, questa probabilmente presa dal Boccaccio, e di Psiche e Cupidine, dalle *Metamorfosi* del filosofo platonico Apuleio di Madaura.

Per quanto riguarda la scenografia, queste favole mitologiche presentavano delle sfide che venivano affrontate con entusiasmo, anche nell'Italia del Quattrocento, utilizzando la meccanica adoperata per le sacre rappresentazioni e perfino per le commedie umanistiche:[10] si crearono delle macchine ingegnose che permettevano, ad esempio, l'apertura di una porta dell'Ade incastrata in una montagna; i personaggi si trasformavano in stelle che salivano in cielo; o gli dèi scendevano per realizzare un lieto fine anti-ovidiano.[11] Questo «lieto fine» è subito diventato *de rigueur* nel contesto delle rappresentazioni del quindicesimo secolo, malgrado un'aderenza testuale abbastanza stretta alle fonti classiche, aderenza almeno tematica, se non proprio alla lettera o stilistica.[12]

Anche la musica ha avuto un ruolo importante nella rappresentazione delle favole mitologiche. I brani di un certo rilievo normalmente si cantavano, così come quelli di particolare bellezza lirica. Questi brani cantati servirono a mettere in rilievo la struttura dell'azione in un modo simile a ciò che fanno le arie nell'opera moderna. Il resto del testo si poteva declamare in uno

---

[10] N. PIRROTTA e E. POVOLEDO, *Music and Theatre from Poliziano to Monteverdi*, Cambridge, 1982²; qui, Part II: E. POVOLEDO, *Origins and Aspects of Italian Scenography (from the End of the Fifteenth Century to the Florentine* Intermedi *of 1589)* (citerò principalmente dall'edizione più recente, quella riveduta in inglese e, tra parentesi, da quella italiana del 1975: *Li due Orfei. Da Poliziano a Monteverdi*, Torino, 1975); E. BATTISTI, «La visualizzazione» (n. 6), p. 108.

[11] STERNFELD, «The Birth» (n. 9), attribuisce l'esistenza di tali lieti fini a spunti socio-politici, che, a mio parere, operarono sicuramente, ma insieme con le correnti intellettuali che si discuteranno più avanti.

[12] Le parole e anche lo stile furono imitati, con risultati brillanti, ad esempio per la scena di fuga («Non mi fuggir, donzella, / ch'i' ti son tanto amico / e che più t'amo che la vita e 'l core...».: *Fabula di Orfeo*, 128-130), che già il Boccaccio aveva tratto da Ovidio, e che apparve nella più influente delle favole, l'*Orfeo* polizianesco, per essere poi apertamente adoperata o imitata in tutte le favole susseguenti. Si veda G. BOCCACCIO, *Il ninfale fiesolano*, ed. A. Balduino, in *Tutte le opere di Giovanni Boccaccio*, ed. V. Branca, III, Milano, 1974: stanze 99-108. Cfr. OVIDIUS, *Metamorphoses*, cura e trad. di F. J. Miller, 2 voll., Cambridge, Mass. e London, 1966-1968, I, pp. 500-525; A. WARBURG, «La *Nascita di Venere* e la *Primavera* di Sandro Botticelli. Ricerche sull'immagine dell'antichità nel primo Rinascimento italiano» (1893), nella sua *Rinascita* (n. 3), pp. 33-38. Ho analizzato ed interpretato questo motivo del lieto fine nella sua evoluzione dall'epoca classica fino al Medioevo e al Rinascimento, con particolare riferimento alla *Rappresentazione di Dafne*, davanti all'Equipe d'Histoire du Théâtre, Groupe de Recherches Théâtrales et Musicologiques, Centre National de la Recherche Scientifique, a Parigi il 27 maggio e il 10 giugno 1977.

stile «tra quello della parola parlata e quello del canto» (secondo un'interpretazione delle parole del Poliziano stesso), in uno stile, cioè, analogo – ma
non identico – al recitativo dell'opera moderna. [13]

Noi oggi, riguardando sia le prime opere in musica che queste favole
rappresentate in teatro, accettiamo come cosa ovvia i temi selezionati, vedendo in essi un *corpus* che riappare pure nell'arte visiva coeva; però ci
possiamo chiedere, come ci chiederemmo per l'arte visiva, perché vennero
scelti questi particolari miti invece di altri disponibili nelle fonti letterarie.
Cercando di dare una risposta a questa domanda, potremo già constatare
un crescente interesse per le relazioni tra cielo e terra, tra divinità e mortali,
e potremo esplorare la questione se quel fenomeno sia o no in rapporto,
anche superficialmente, con alcune delle idee contemporanee – in particolare le idee neoplatoniche – che circolavano nell'Italia del tardo Quattrocento. Potremo, inoltre, esplorare la questione se tale interesse sia o no in
rapporto con il lieto fine che viene apposto, in queste rappresentazioni teatrali, alle favole così ben conosciute. Potremo infine chiederci se l'aggiunta
della musica non si basi su queste stesse idee e sui coevi fatti socio-politici
già menzionati. Nell'esplorare tutti questi punti, vedremo emergere delle
strutture-modello.

*   *   *

La tradizione ovidiana medievale ha moralizzato le favole del poeta latino
nell'*Ovide moralisé*, nell'*Ovidius moralizatus*, [14] ed altrove. Arrivati al quindicesimo secolo in Italia, però, troviamo queste ed altre narrazioni medievali
(come, ad esempio, le enciclopedie medievali) sfrondate in modo consistente
delle loro moralizzazioni (benché non siano totalmente prive di *exempla*, come testimonia il servo incorruttibile nella *Danae* di Baldassare Taccone, e
anche lo stesso personaggio di Danae, come vedremo più avanti). Solo una
favola teatrale frammentaria basata sul mito di Cefalo e Procri, rappresentata
in occasione di nozze nel 1475 a Bologna, sembra avere un intento puramente

---

[13] N. PIRROTTA, *Studies in the Music of Renaissance Theatre*, in *Music and Theatre* (n. 10),
Part I, p. 36, dove si citano le parole del Poliziano (ediz. ital., pp. 35-36); cfr. A. POLIZIA-
NO, *Opera*, Basel, 1553, pp. 165-166, nel vol. I della riedizione curata da I. Maïer, Torino,
1971.

[14] «*Ovide moralisé*», *poème du commencement du quatorzième siècle publié d'après tous les manuscrits connus*, a cura di C. de Boer, Amsterdam, 1915; *Ovidius Moralizatus* nel 2° vol. di:
P. BERCHORIUS, *Reductorium morale, Liber XV*, a cura di J. Engels, Utrecht, 1960-1966.

didattico, in questo caso una lezione severa diretta alla sposa sulla fiducia verso il marito; e per ciò che si può vedere, non è stato apposto nessun lieto fine. Così troviamo in genere, come ci si aspetta nell'età dell'Umanesimo, un ritorno verso le fonti classiche (con l'eccezione notevole del lieto fine), ed una tendenza ad allontanarsi dalle fonti preminentemente cristiane del Medioevo europeo.

Come al solito, però, la separazione tra le due epoche non è netta. Il Medioevo ci offre una forte tradizione di poesia d'amore profano, e sia le favole mitologiche sia, più tardi, i melodrammi, si basano tutti sulle favole d'amore. Incominciando da Dante e dal Dolce Stil Nuovo, che prende le mosse dai *troubadours* e dai *trouvères*, oltre che dalla Scuola Siciliana, per proseguire con la poesia del Petrarca e del Poliziano, la poesia lirica italiana è spesso una poesia d'amore; e di poesia lirica, come fioriva nella lingua italiana dal Petrarca in poi, si compongono i testi sia delle favole mitologiche quattrocentesche sia dei libretti delle prime opere intorno all'inizio del Seicento.

La poesia «lirica» ci rammenta inoltre che la musica godeva di un'importanza capitale all'epoca di queste rappresentazioni. Gli studiosi di musicologia non hanno trascurato di indagare intorno alle favole mitologiche, e di collegarle strettamente con lo sviluppo degli intermezzi del Cinquecento e dell'inizio dell'opera alla fine di quel secolo. Fin dall'*Ars nova* nel secolo del Petrarca, i cambiamenti nel modo di comporre e di presentare la musica sono stati notevoli. Questi cambiamenti, accentuati verso la fine del Quattrocento, implicano una nuova concentrazione sul canto e sui modi di produrlo, che influisce pure sulla esecuzione della parola in teatro, e di conseguenza su queste rappresentazioni. Però non possiamo neppure trascurare le altre funzioni quattrocentesche della musica, come quelle magico-medicinali del Ficino e dei suoi seguaci.[15]

---

[15] Si vedano i lavori già citati del Pirrotta e dello Sternfeld, e inoltre D. P. WALKER, *The Ancient Theology*, London, 1972; Idem, *Music, Spirit and Language in the Renaissance*, a cura di P. Gouk, London, 1985; H. M. BROWN, *Music in the Renaissance*, Englewood Cliffs, 1976; B. HANNING, *Of Poetry and Music's Power: Humanism and the Creation of Opera*, Ann Arbor, 1980; N. PIRROTTA, *Musica tra Medioevo e Rinascimento*, Torino, 1984, che non corrisponde precisamente al più esteso *Music and Culture in Italy from the Middle Ages to the Baroque*, Cambridge, Mass., 1984; C. PALISCA, *Humanism in Italian Renaissance Musical Thought*, New Haven e London, 1985; J. HAAR, *Essays on Italian Poetry and Music in the Renaissance, 1350-1600*, Berkeley, 1986, e G. TOMLINSON, *Music in Renaissance Magic. Toward a Historiography of Others*, Chicago e London, 1993.

Il tema d'amore, unito all'importanza della musica, sembra offrirci ragioni sufficienti per la scelta di queste particolari favole come temi teatrali. Però
il tempo e il luogo delle loro prime comparse ci inducono ad indagare più
profondamente la questione. Il Poliziano, autore della prima favola mitologica che possediamo nella sua interezza,[16] trascorse gli anni della sua formazione nella Firenze di Lorenzo de' Medici, e frequentò lo Studio fiorentino
fin dall'età di 15 anni.[17] Malgrado la giovane età, il suo genio lo fa uno dei
compagni intellettuali più stretti di Marsilio Ficino. La sua è una di quelle
menti straordinariamente vaste che spiccano fra le altre di un secolo; la sua
abilità filologica lo renderà famoso e, al momento della sua morte prematura
all'età di 40 anni nel 1494, uno dei più remunerati fra gli umanisti nello Studio Fiorentino;[18] le sue limpide immagini poetiche trasmettono al volgare
l'aspetto visuale della poesia vergiliana, che imita nei suoi versi latini.[19] Negli ultimi quindici anni della sua vita il Poliziano si orienterà più verso una
visione aristotelica del mondo[20] – l'analisi e la logica supereranno l'ideale

---

[16] Accetto l'ipotesi recente che propone una datazione dell'*Orfeo* del Poliziano nello stesso
periodo (1475-1478, o, direi, forse ancora prima) delle *Stanze per la giostra*: si veda TISSONI
BENVENUTI, *L'Orfeo* (n. 1), cap. III, soprattutto le pp. 65-70. Quest'ipotesi valida, in particolare se accostata agli argomenti che porterò più avanti a proposito delle correnti neoplatoniche nella favola, sembra mettere in questione l'idea, per altro molto interessante, di
Vittore BRANCA («Momarie veneziane e *fabula di Orfeo*», nel suo *Poliziano e l'umanesimo
della parola*, Torino, 1983, pp. 55-72, a p. 58; anche in *Umanesimo e Rinascimento. Studi
offerti a Paul Oskar Kristeller*, Firenze, 1980, pp. 57-73, a p. 62 e cfr. n. 5 al capitolo VIII,
sopra) per cui la favola sarebbe stata ispirata alle momarie, o spettacoli acquatici, rappresentati nella laguna di Venezia durante la sosta del poeta in quella città nel 1479-80. Si veda in
proposito P. G. MOLMENTI, *Venezia. Nuovi studi di storia e d'arte*, Firenze, 1897, p. 177;
Idem, *La storia di Venezia nella vita privata dalle origini alla caduta della Repubblica*, Parte
II, Bergamo, 1906, pp. 312-313; come osserva Molmenti, questi spettacoli furono analoghi a
quelli, terrestri, che ebbero luogo in altre città, come Firenze e Milano, e il lettore ricorderà
la lunga ed intima familiarità del Poliziano con gli spettacoli della Firenze laurenziana.
L'ipotesi di datazione della Tissoni Benvenuti viene rinforzata dall'affermazione dello stesso
Branca (con la quale concordo) per cui gli interessi del Poliziano dopo la congiura dei Pazzi
divergono dal neoplatonismo ficiniano e si concentrano invece nello studio di Aristotele e
nella filologia (*Poliziano e l'umanesimo della parola*, pp. 13-16).

[17] I. MAÏER, *Ange Politien. La formation d'un poète humaniste (1469-1480)*, Genève, 1966, p.
419.

[18] A. F. VERDE, *Lo studio fiorentino 1473-1503. Ricerche e documenti*, 4 voll., Firenze, 1973-
1985, vol. 1, pp. 312-355 *passim*, vol. 2, pp. 26-27.

[19] Si veda, ad esempio, la nota 1 alla p. 412 nel mio, «Le thème d'Orphée dans les oeuvres
latines d'Ange Politien», *Bulletin de l'Association Guillaume Budé*, XXXIX (1980), pp. 408-
419. Fu il Poliziano a scoprire l'ortografia classica del nome del poeta augusteo.

[20] BRANCA, *Poliziano e l'umanesimo della parola*, (n. 16) pp. 13-16.

poetico – ma per ora, negli anni '70, mentre trascorre la sua gioventù diventando un familiare nella casa di Lorenzo, il Poliziano sarà profondamente influenzato dal neoplatonismo di Ficino[21] (come lo fu peraltro lo stesso Lorenzo in quest'epoca). I due uomini – forse tutti e tre – volano sulle ali delle idee neoplatoniche e dell'interpretazione poetica ed allegorizzata (ma non moralizzata) dei miti classici. Il Poliziano paragona il Ficino ad Orfeo, perché ha risuscitato Platone come Orfeo riportò in vita Euridice (adottando l'originale lieto fine del mito[22]), e allude all'interpretazione ficiniana di un Orfeo fondatore di tutti i misteri neoplatonici, o addirittura di tutta la teologia greca.[23] Né possiamo dimenticare la parte avuta da Lorenzo: egli si impegna attivamente, basando la sua *Altercazione* o *De summo bono* sulla lettera a lui indirizzata da Ficino (*Quid est felicitas?*, databile intorno al 1473-1474).[24] Poco dopo, Poliziano scrive le sue *Stanze per la giostra*, i cui elementi neoplatonici sono stati riconosciuti da molto tempo,[25] e, con tutta probabilità, scrive anche l'*Orfeo*, che mostra stretti rapporti con le *Stanze*.

---

[21] Su cui si vedano, ad es.: P. O. KRISTELLER, *The Philosophy of Marsilio Ficino*, New York, 1943, ristampa Gloucester, Mass., 1964 (ed. ital. con indice più completo e con le citazioni in latino: *Il pensiero filosofico di M. F.*, Firenze, 1988²); G. SAITTA, *Marsilio Ficino e la filosofia dell'Umanesimo*, Bologna, 1954; A. CHASTEL, *Art et Humanisme* (n. 3); M. J. B. ALLEN, *The Platonism of Marsilio Ficino*, Berkeley, 1984; J. HANKINS, *Plato in the Italian Renaissance*, Leiden, 1990.

[22] Si trova nell'*Alcesti* di Euripide, che Poliziano conosceva: cfr. il mio «Le thème d'Orphée» (n. 19), p. 408, n. 4. Su questa versione: J. HEURGON, «Orphée et Eurydice avant Virgile», *Mélanges d'Archéologie et d'Histoire*, XLIX (1932), pp. 6-60; C. M. BOWRA, «Orpheus and Eurydice», *Classical Quarterly*, N. S. II (1952), pp. 113-126; P. DRONKE, «The Return of Eurydice», *Classica et Mediaevalia*, XXIII (1962), pp. 198-215; M. O. LEE, «Orpheus and Eurydice: Myth, Legend, Folklore», *Classica et Mediaevalia*, XXVI (1965), pp. 402-412.

[23] D. P. WALKER, «Orpheus the Theologian and Renaissance Platonists», *Journal of the Warburg and Courtauld Institutes*, XVI (1953), pp. 100-120, ristampato nel suo volume, *The Ancient Theology. Studies in Christian Platonism from the Fifteenth to the Eighteenth Century*, London, 1972, pp. 22-41; E. WIND, *Pagan Mysteries* (n. 3), p. 162 (ed. ital., p. 24, n. 13; p. 47).

[24] M. FICINO, *Epistolarum Liber I*, in *Opera Omnia*, Basel, 1576 (ristampa in 2 voll., Torino, 1962), I, pp. 662-665; cfr. L. DE' MEDICI, *Scritti scelti*, a cura di E. Bigi, Torino, 1965, p. 49; cfr. anche A. BUCK, *Der Einfluss des Platonismus auf die volkssprachliche Literatur im Florentiner Quattrocento*, Krefeld, 1965, p. 21.

[25] Si vedano E. H. GOMBRICH, «Botticelli's Mythologies», (1945), nelle sue *Symbolic Images* (1985: n. 3), pp. 31-81, 199-217, soprattutto le pp. 66-75 (ed. ital., pp. 47-116; 280-302); A. CHASTEL, *Marsile Ficin et l'art*, Genève, 1954, 1975, p. 121; e per un'analisi particolare, P. M. J. MCNAIR, «The Bed of Venus: Key to Poliziano's *Stanze*», *Italian Studies*, XXV (1970), pp. 40-48.

È dunque nel contesto del neoplatonismo fiorentino che dobbiamo prendere in considerazione le favole mitologiche, e ciò, nonostante il fatto che tutte le altre favole che derivano dall'*Orfeo* polizianesco provengano dalle corti dell'Italia settentrionale (Milano, Mantova, Ferrara), e nonostante il legame che si riscontra in alcuni dei manoscritti tardi tra l'*Orfeo* e la corte di Mantova, tramite l'ode saffica in latino indirizzata al cardinale Francesco Gonzaga.[26] Il contesto fiorentino dell'origine di queste favole mitologiche ci permette almeno una parziale comprensione della scelta di particolari miti, dato che tutte contengono degli elementi importanti nel simbolismo neoplatonico, e in particolare quello della teoria dell'amore neoplatonico. Per di più, è possibile seguire l'evoluzione di elementi neoplatonici nello sviluppo di queste rappresentazioni mitologiche, anche dal punto di vista cronologico; e in alcuni casi tale evoluzione si può collegare ad avvenimenti, a testi o ad oggetti specifici (siano intellettuali, letterari o artistici), per cui abbiamo prove concrete.

\*   \*   \*

Un fenomeno interessante, a questo riguardo, è la scelta dei libri stampati in Italia durante gli ultimi decenni del Quattrocento. Presenterà un certo interesse esaminare brevemente questi titoli, prima di prendere in considerazione le rappresentazioni stesse. Cruciale per il presente discorso è la comparsa nel 1471, a Bologna, dell'*editio princeps* delle opere di Ovidio, curate da Francesco Dal Pozzo, il Puteolano.[27] L'edizione fu dedicata allo stesso cardinale Francesco Gonzaga, nominato allora legato pontificio a Bologna, al quale sarà indirizzata successivamente l'ode saffica appena menzionata, e il cui nome è stato per questo motivo avanzato come possibile mecenate di una rappresentazione della favola per la corte dei Gonzaga.[28] Seguirono molte

---

[26] L'ode fu, con tutta probabilità, aggiunta durante i preparativi di una rappresentazione mantovana mai realizzata. Le indagini per identificare riferimenti ad una tale rappresentazione, fatte da parte di chi scrive e da altri per più di un secolo negli archivi di Mantova e di Firenze, sono rimaste senza esito.

[27] Cfr. l'*Indice generale degli incunaboli* (IGI), a cura di E. Valenziani, E. Cerulli, 6 voll., Roma, 1943-1981, vol. IV, p. 165, no. 7041; *Catalogue of Books Printed in the XVth Century now in the British Museum* (BMC), vol. VI, London, 1930; ristampa del 1963, p. 798; L. F. T. HAIN, *Repertorium Bibliographicum* (H), 2 voll. in 4 parti, Milano, 1948, no. 12136. Si vedano le osservazioni di E. J. KENNEY sulla superiorità dell'edizione contemporanea fatta da Bussi per Sweynheym e Pannartz: *The Classical Text. Aspects of Editing in the Age of the Printed Book*, Berkeley, Los Angeles, London, 1974, p. 13; TISSONI BENVENUTI in *Teatro* (n. 1), p. 37.

[28] Si veda sopra, n. 26.

edizioni dell'Ovidio, alcune basate sull'iniziativa del Puteolano, altre no, ed alcune illustrate, anche con delle xilografie che appaiono in diverse edizioni dell'opera. La prima traduzione in italiano, di Giovanni Bonsignore, è uscita a Venezia nel 1497. [29] Ma è la prima edizione di Bologna che viene associata con maggiore plausibilità all'origine delle favole teatrali di cui stiamo parlando, e questo appare tanto più vero se si considera che una delle prime due favole, quella basata sul tema di Cefalo e Procri, si rappresenta a Bologna solo quattro anni più tardi, nel 1475. [30] Né possiamo trascurare le prime edizioni della *Genealogia deorum gentilium* del Boccaccio, stampata prima a Venezia nel 1472, poi altre tre volte in Italia (Reggio Emilia, 1481; Vicenza, 1487; e Venezia ancora, 1494-1495) [31] – tutte edizioni che precedono la rappresentazione del 1496 della *Danae* del Taccone, che sembra basarsi appunto sulla versione di quella favola nella *Genealogia*. [32]

Due anni prima dell'*editio princeps* di Ovidio, nel 1469, era apparsa l'edizione di Apuleio di Sweynheym e Pannartz. Non mi pare senza significato il fatto che furono inclusi nel volume una traduzione latina dell'*Asclepius* di «Hermes Trismegistus» ed un'epitome del *De doctrina Platonis* di Alcinous (tradotta da Ficino). [33] Non c'è bisogno di sottolineare l'importanza di quest'edizione per qualsiasi studio della letteratura neoplatonica ed ermetica del Quattrocento – soprattutto come indice della rapida diffusione, per non

---

[29] Stampata da Giovanni Rosso: H 12166; BMC V, 1924, p. 419; IGI 7128.

[30] Quest'idea è confortata dal legame diretto tra l'editore dell'Ovidio, il Puteolano, e un'altra rappresentazione teatrale scritta da lui per la stessa occasione; cfr. F. CAVICCHI, «Rappresentazioni bolognesi nel 1475», *Atti e memorie della R. Deputazione di Storia Patria per le Provincie di Romagna*, ser. III, vol. XXVII (1908-1909), pp. 71-85, a p. 73.

[31] La prima stampa è di Vindelino da Spira: *Gesamtkatalog der Wiegendrucke* (GW), 8 voll., Leipzig, poi Stuttgart, Berlin e New York, 1925-1978, no. 4475; H *3315; BMC V, p. 162; IGI 1796. L'edizione del 1481 a Reggio è di Bartholomaeus de Bruschis: H *3319; GW 4476; BMC VII, pp. 1085-1086; IGI 1798. L'edizione del 1487 a Vicenza è di Bevilacqua: H *3316; GW 4477; BMC VII, p. 1051; IGI 1799. L'edizione veneziana del 1494-1495 è di Bonetus Locatellus: H *3321; GW 4478; BMC V, p. 444; IGI 1800. Abbiamo inoltre un'edizione del 1473 fatta a Colonia (IGI 1797) ed una veneziana del 1497 di Manfredus de Bonellis de Monteferrato: H *3324; GW 4479; BMC V, pp. 504-505; IGI 1801.

[32] PYLE, *Politian's «Orfeo»* (n. 1), p. 183 (i capitoli della *Genealogia* sono erroneamente indicati 22 e 23 anziché 32-33).

[33] H *1314; GW 2301; BMC IV, p. 6; IGI 769. Cfr. M. D. FELD, *The First Roman Printers and the Idioms of Humanism*, numero speciale del *Harvard Library Bulletin*, XXXVI, 1 (Winter, 1988), pp. 23-26, 42-43. Sui MSS della traduzione di Alcinous: P. O. KRISTELLER, «Spigolature ficiniane», nei suoi *Studies in Renaissance Thought and Letters*, Roma, 1969, pp. 158, 165 e *passim*; sull'edizione parigina del 1561: *Platon et Aristote à la Renaissance. XVIe Colloque International de Tours*, Paris, 1976, p. 542.

dire della moda, di questo nuovissimo interesse –; benché sia, significativa-
mente, solo dopo l'edizione milanese di Leonhard Pachel del 1497 dell'Apuleio[34] che possiamo constatare un eventuale effetto diretto sulle favole mitologiche settentrionali, con la composizione da parte di Galeotto del Carretto
de *Le noze di Psiche e Cupidine* (ca. 1499-1502). Questo è vero malgrado
esista una traduzione o parafrasi in italiano delle *Metamorfosi* di Apuleio fatta da Matteo Maria Boiardo nel 1479 e dedicata, nel manoscritto, al marchese di Mantova nel 1481;[35] benché certamente conosciuta nelle cerchie corti-
giane di Milano e della Val Padana, tale traduzione non fu stampata fino al
1516 e poi, in redazione riveduta, nel 1518.[36]

Anche le opere di Ficino hanno avuto una diffusione manoscritta,[37] e
un'attenzione ancora maggiore dopo le prime edizioni a stampa, quando le sue
idee incominciarono a trasferirsi nella cultura volgare, come vedremo. La prima edizione della sua *Theologia Platonica* si stampò a Firenze presso Antonio
Miscomini nel 1482;[38] accanto alle interpretazioni e ai commentari, la sua traduzione in latino delle opere di Platone apparve a Firenze nel 1484, in un'edizione che includeva pure il suo commento al *Simposio*, cioè il *De amore* (fatto
nel 1469).[39] Queste opere furono di nuovo stampate insieme a Venezia nel
1491,[40] un fatto che ha reso ancora più facile la possibilità che uno dei nostri
drammaturghi, Gaspare Visconti, le incontrasse negli anni '90, quando, sulla
base del *De amore* del Ficino, compose il suo trattato frammentario.[41]

---

[34] T. ROGLEDI MANNI, *La tipografia a Milano nel XV secolo*, Firenze, 1980, p. 110; H 1318;
GW 2304; BMC VI, p. 782; IGI, 772. Ci furono altre due edizioni, tra quella romana e
quella milanese: Vicenza, 1488 (GW 2302) e Venezia, 1493 (GW 2303).

[35] G. REICHENBACH, *Matteo Maria Boiardo*, Bologna, 1929, p. 160.

[36] REICHENBACH (n. 35), p. 158; cfr. G. W. PANZER, *Annales Typographici ab Anno MDI ad
Annum MDXXXVI...*, vol. VIII, Nuremberg, 1802, p. 437, no. 832 e p. 451, no. 937.

[37] P. O. KRISTELLER, *Supplementum Ficinianum*, 2 voll., Firenze, 1937 (ristampa 1973);
Idem, *Marsilio Ficino and his Work after Five Hundred Years*, Firenze, 1987.

[38] KRISTELLER, *Supplementum* (n. 37), I, p. LX; H *7075; GW 9881; BMC VI, p. 637; IGI
3867.

[39] L'edizione fu stampata da Laurentius (Francisci) De Alopa, Venetus: cf. KRISTELLER, *Supplementum* (n. 37), I, pp. LX-LXI; H *13062; BMC VI, p. 666; IGI 7860. Sulla datazione
dell'opera, P. O. KRISTELLER, «The First Printed Edition of Plato's Works and the Date of
its Publication (1484)», in *Science and History. Studies in Honor of Edward Rosen*, Wroclaw,
1978, pp. 25-35; J. A. DEVEREUX, «The Textual History of Ficino's *De amore*», *Renaissance
Quarterly*, 28 (1975), pp. 173-182.

[40] Da Bernardinus de Choris de Cremona: cfr. KRISTELLER, *Supplementum* (n. 37), I, p. LXI;
H *13063; BMC V, p. 465; IGI 7861.

[41] Si vedano i capitoli IV e V di questo volume.

\*    \*    \*

Possiamo incominciare l'analisi della rappresentazione delle favole mitologiche con il frammento che, accettando la nuova datazione dell'*Orfeo* polizianesco già menzionata, risulta pressoché coevo con quest'ultimo: mi riferi-
sco al *Cefalo* di Tommaso Beccadelli, del 1475, rappresentato per un matrimonio Pepoli-Rangoni a Bologna.[42] L'azione si base sull'ultima scena della
favola ovidiana di Cefalo e Procri (*Metamorfosi*, VII, 694-758 e 796-862),
presentata come ammonimento contro certe passioni nocive al matrimonio.
Si ricorderà che Procri è guidata dalla gelosia (ispirata da Aurora, desiderosa
di suo marito, Cefalo) a spiare il marito nel momento in cui invoca l'«aura»,
cioè la brezza; Cefalo intravvede un movimento nei cespugli e, pensando che
si tratti di una fiera selvatica, lancia l'asta infallibile offertagli da Aurora,
ferendo mortalmente la moglie Procri. Malgrado l'occasione nuziale, il finale
della rappresentazione bolognese è luttuoso: la gelosia di Procri viene presentata come *exemplum*, e si lamenta la sua morte con una canzone (che fece
piangere tutti i presenti, ma che non si potè riprodurre perché «fu robata»
prima che il copista la potesse trascrivere). È difficile collegare questa, una
delle prime rappresentazioni mitologiche in volgare, con delle correnti che
vadano al di là dell'inizio di una moda che si concentra sulle favole d'amore
ovidiane – moda probabilmente collegata, come abbiamo detto, all'*editio
princeps* di Francesco Dal Pozzo delle opere di Ovidio (Bologna, 1471).[43]
Colpisce il fatto che l'autore non abbia sentito l'obbligo – né intellettuale, né
sociale, né estetico – di aggiungere un lieto fine. L'austerità della favola sembra infatti riflettere il gusto piuttosto realistico dell'epoca che precede la congiura dei Pazzi (che, avvenuta nel 1478, ebbe ripercussioni in tutta la peniso-
la, incrinando il diffuso sentimento di sicurezza); in seguito il senso di tali
rappresentazioni sarà risolutamente ottimistico.

*La fabula di Orfeo* di Angelo Poliziano, più o meno contemporanea, è
pure senza un lieto fine nel senso stretto della parola.[44] Questa, che è la più

---

[42] Cfr. F. CAVICCHI, «Rappresentazioni bolognesi nel 1475», (sopra, n. 30); PIRROTTA, *Music and Theatre* (n. 10), p. 10 (ed. ital., pp. 11-12); PYLE, *Politian's «Orfeo»* (n. 1), p. 170;
testo in *Teatro* (n. 1), pp. 35-44; si veda pure M. BREGOLI RUSSO, «La rappresentazione
bolognese del 1475: Tommaso Beccadelli solo attore o anche autore?», *Studi e problemi di
critica testuale*, 36 (1988), pp. 93-102.

[43] Si veda la nota 27, sopra.

[44] La conclusione, benché non felice, è di una baldoria ebbra. Questo è chiaramente dovuto in
gran parte alla conoscenza che il Poliziano aveva delle rappresentazioni satiriche della Grecia
antica, a lui note tramite il *Ciclope* di Euripide, che qui imita: si veda TISSONI BENVENUTI,
*L'Orfeo* (n. 1), pp. 92-103. Per il dramma satirico, si veda R. SEAFORD, *Introduction* a EURI-
PIDES, *Cyclops*, Oxford, Clarendon Press, 1984, pp. 1-48. L'altro motivo per una tale

famosa delle favole, ci pone a confronto con un tema (se non proprio con un'azione drammatica[45]) pieno di *nuances* filosofiche, in particolare neoplatoniche.[46] L'*Orfeo* si collega al movimento neoplatonico in forza di diversi motivi: l'epoca della sua composizione (come le *Stanze* appartenente al periodo giovanile, caratterizzato dal neoplatonismo), la *patria* adottiva dell'autore (una Firenze guidata da un uomo di stato - poeta, la cui poesia e il

---

conclusione deriva dall'occasione per la quale credo la rappresentazione sia stata creata: il carnevale (di un anno sempre da precisare); cfr. il mio «Il tema di Orfeo, la musica e le favole mitologiche del tardo Quattrocento», in *Ecumenismo della cultura*, II, *La parola e la musica nel divenire dell'Umanesimo*, Firenze, 1981, pp. 121-139, dove però l'etimologia data per la parola è quella popolare, anziché *carnem levare*, considerata quella corretta.

[45] Quando anni fa scrivevo del tema di questa *fabula*, non intendevo suggerire che la *fabula* stessa avesse un impegno filosofico. Infatti, il tema di Orfeo e l'azione drammatica della *fabula* sono due cose diverse, di cui la seconda dipende dalla prima. Il tema – anche il tema filosofico e «storico» – faceva senz'altro parte dell'ambiente intellettuale e culturale del Poliziano e dei suoi contemporanei fiorentini. Questo ambiente, che ho cercato di lumeggiare in diversi scritti, come aveva già fatto un mio illustre predecessore, non ha influito *direttamente* né sul tema scelto per la favola, né sul suo sviluppo in relazione con l'azione drammatica, ma invece forma la matrice in cui si sviluppano le idee, per altro precoci, dell'autore. Non è necessario (né possibile) vedere delle implicazioni filosofiche nella *fabula* stessa, ma invece mi sembra necessario, come è sembrato ad altri, vedere quelle implicazioni come formatrici dell'*habitus* mentale e delle scelte fatte dal Poliziano. Si tratta, ancora una volta, di un tentativo (forse mal chiarito da parte mia) di inserire il teatro nella sua cultura e, viceversa, di leggere la cultura nel teatro, in un modo che chiamo «iconologico». Le differenze di opinione stanno al livello di *quanto* e *come* questa matrice intellettuale avrà influito sull'uso del tema da parte del Poliziano: se in modo superficialmente simbolico, o in modo già rappresentativo di interessi più profondi. La datazione negli anni '70 della *fabula* importa molto in questo discorso, date le fasi di sviluppo intellettuale (platonica la prima ed aristotelica la seconda) già menzionate. Importa anche la precocità della mente in questione, sicuramente capace di affrontare questioni profonde a un'età giovanile. Per quanto riguarda il baccanale finale, credo che la mia ipotesi di un'occasione carnevalesca (ipotesi basata sulla trama della *fabula* e sul concetto dell'Orfeo cristiano, e sostenuta inoltre dal canto carnascialesco finale) sia sempre valida, ma nel senso di un'evocazione basata sull'occasione, e non di un rito cristiano recitato sul palco. Un altro vantaggio di quest'ipotesi sta nel suo riunire in modo plausibile il fine non lieto della *fabula* (che il Poliziano non evita – anzi sottolinea, introducendo una baccante che riporta la testa di Orfeo sul palco) con un'occasione chiaramente festiva (ancora da identificare, ma la cui esistenza è provata dallo stesso canto carnascialesco, oltre che dal fatto stesso che la *fabula* drammatica sia stata composta). Si veda anche la nota seguente.

[46] R. CODY in *The Landscape of the Mind. Pastoralism and Platonic Theory in Tasso's 'Aminta' and Shakespeare's Early Comedies*, Oxford, 1969, pp. 30-43, sostiene in modo convincente l'esistenza di elementi neoplatonici nell'*Orfeo* del Poliziano. Altre implicazioni filosofiche della scelta di tale tema sono trattate nel mio «Il tema di Orfeo» ([n. 44]; benché nell'arti-

cui pensiero sono imbevuti di idee neoplatoniche, e con cui il Poliziano ha un rapporto privilegiato), e infine la materia dell'opera (il mito di Orfeo, un Orfeo che sarebbe stato nello stesso tempo compositore di inni magici e teurgici, incluso quello al Cosmos).

Per sostenere quest'ultimo legame col neoplatonismo, basterà riferirci al già menzionato fatto che Ficino, capo del movimento neoplatonico, riteneva che tutti i misteri neoplatonici derivassero dall'Orfeo «storico», creatore dei summenzionati testi mistici e teologici.[47] Accanto a questo, l'Orfeo mitico era pure il suonatore che incantava gli uccelli, le fiere e la natura inanimata col suo canto. Insieme con la figura di Orfeo e la centralità del neoplatonismo, nel pensiero e nella vita di Ficino sta l'importanza della musica di per se stessa, soprattutto degli inni orfici, che cantava improvvisando sulla lira, come sappiamo dal *Carmen ad Fontium* del Poliziano[48] e dai suoi scritti tardi.

---

colo si segua per la datazione l'ipotesi del Picotti); cfr. E. GARIN, «L'ambiente del Poliziano», in *Il Poliziano e il suo tempo*, Firenze, 1957, pp. 17-39 (soprattutto la p. 37); PYLE, «Le thème d'Orphée» (n. 19); Eadem, *Politian's «Orfeo»*, 1976, pp. 63-81; N. PIRROTTA, *Music and Theatre* (n. 10), p. 15 (passo aggiunto all'edizione inglese); N. BORSELLINO, «La voce e lo sguardo. Orfeo nella Fabula del Poliziano» in *Orfeo e l'orfismo. Atti del Seminario Nazionale (Roma-Perugia 1985-1991)*, a cura di A. Masaracchia, Roma, 1993, pp. 309-317; M. MARTELLI, «Il mito d'Orfeo nell'età laurenziana», *Ibid.*, pp. 319-351. (Per rispondere alle osservazioni di quest'ultimo, alle pp. 322-325, sottolineo che la mia citazione del fondamentale articolo di Garin, citato sopra, è alla *pagina 25* e alla nota 2, non solo alla nota; e che il collegamento tra la potenza della filologia e quella della poesia – quest'ultima incarnata nella figura di Orfeo – era appunto l'elemento essenziale che cercavo di mostrare citando sia quella pagina, sia il brano dell'Introduzione all'edizione di A. POLIZIANO, *Miscellaneorum Centuria Secunda*, a cura di V. Branca e M. Pastore Stocchi, Firenze, 1972, I, p. 58. Però, se mi è sembrato di vedere nell'*Orfeo* polizianesco un significato univoco attorno al 1980, ora non mi sembra più tale, ma piuttosto, d'accordo con Martelli, collegato strettamente col movimento neoplatonico ficiniano.) Inoltre ricordo che Thomas M. GREENE, *The Light in Troy*, New Haven e London, 1982, pp. 162-170, ha ragione di pensare a motivi politici per certi interessi del Poliziano, però la nuova ipotesi per la datazione (sopra, n. 16) mi sembra obblighi a un riesame della tesi relativa alle implicazioni connesse, per il Poliziano, col motivo generico dello smembramento: piuttosto che vedere un Poliziano ossessionato dal tema in conseguenza dello smembramento da parte del popolo fiorentino degli assassini di Giuliano de' Medici nel 1478, il tema, in quanto un aspetto della morte e specificamente della morte di Orfeo, l'avrà affascinato da tempo, anche negli anni di gioventù (avendo vissuto la morte violenta del padre all'età di nove anni).

[47] WIND, *Pagan Mysteries* (n. 3), p. 162 (ed. ital., p. 24, n. 13; p. 47); WALKER, «Orpheus the Theologian» (n. 23, sopra).

[48] Soprattutto dai vv. 181-188: «Saepe graves pellit docta testudine curas / Et vocem argutis suggerit articulis, / Qualis Apollinei modulator carminis Orpheus / Dicitur Odrysias allicuisse feras. / Marmaricos posset cantu mulcere leones / Quasque niger tigres semper Amanus

Per Ficino, la mente viene elevata sulle arie musicali verso «le cose sublimi e Dio»; la musica «ristabilisce la consonanza delle parti dell'anima».[49]

Ma non si tratta solo di dimostrare a noi oggi i legami tra il pensiero neoplatonico e la musica; nel Quattrocento questo rilievo spirituale e filosofico della musica ha senz'altro favorito, almeno in buona parte, il ruolo preminente della musica in queste favole mitologiche (che si presentano, attraverso il tempo, in forma progressivamente neoplatonica, come si vedrà). Col diffondersi nel Cinquecento della moda delle allusioni neoplatoniche, constatiamo pure il loro effetto sulle prime rappresentazioni teatrali pienamente musicate, le primissime opere. È chiaro però che i semi per questo sviluppo vennero posti nel teatro volgare del quindicesimo secolo.

*  *  *

La più influente tra le favole mitologiche del quindicesimo secolo, *La fabula di Orfeo*, venendo dalla penna del giovane umanista, aderiva nello spirito come nella lingua ai suoi modelli classici, Ovidio (*Metamorfosi*, X, 1 – XI, 66) e Vergilio (*Georgiche*, IV, 281-558). In breve, la favola ben nota racconta la doppia perdita della sposa di Orfeo, Euridice, la prima volta in seguito al morso velenoso di un serpente, e la seconda, dopo che Orfeo è riuscito a riconquistarla avendo incantato (in senso letterale) l'Ade, a causa della sua disubbidienza al comandamento di Plutone che imponeva di non guardare la sposa prima di aver raggiunto la luce del giorno.

Essendo stato scelto come tema in gran parte sulla base delle sue implicazioni musicali e filosofiche, il mito di Orfeo si presta ad una preminenza della musica nella sua rappresentazione scenica. Ben metà della favola è scritta per essere cantata, e una nota in alcuni dei manoscritti ci informa che la parte di Orfeo fu recitata da Baccio Ugolini, uno degli inviati più fidati della cerchia di Lorenzo de' Medici, e musicista e cantore riconosciuto.[50] La mu-

---

habet. / Caucaseo traheret duras e vertice cautes / Saxaque Sicaniis condita gurgitibus». Il carme data da prima del 1481: KRISTELLER, *Supplementum* (n. 37), II, pp. 281-283; la citazione incomincia dal v. 155. Cfr. il mio «Il tema» (n. 44), pp. 122-123.

[49] KRISTELLER, *The Philosophy of Marsilio Ficino* (n. 21), pp. 307, 308 (ed. ital., p. 332: «Mentem ad sublimia Deumque pro viribus erigam», «Partium animae consonantiam ... restituit»; traduzioni mie); FICINO, *Opera omnia* (n. 24), I, p. 651. Sul ruolo della musica, cfr. TOMLINSON, *Music in Renaissance Magic* (n. 15), soprattutto le pp. 67-188.

[50] Pirrotta, *Music and Theatre* (1982: n. 10), pp. 24-25; cfr. PYLE, «Il tema di Orfeo» (n. 44), pp. 133-134: la mia proposta che anche il lamento di Orfeo, «Qual sarà mai sì miserabil canto», fosse musicato, è confortata dall'articolo di F. W. STERNFELD, «The Lament in

sica così ha un ruolo importante nel teatro volgare profano fin dall'inizio.

L'importanza della musica nella rappresentazione delle favole ci ricorda l'espressione «poesia lirica», usata prima.[51] I metri poetici adoperati nelle favole mitologiche sono infatti quelli che si chiamano «lirici»; i brani cantati sono in forma di strambotti, di frottole, di ballate e di canti carnascialeschi – tutte forme che si cantano accompagnati dalla lira (e da altri strumenti nel caso dei balli). Poiché una tradizione di poesia rappresentativa come questa, composta «all'improvviso» e trasmessa oralmente, ci offre poco su cui basare la nostra ricostruzione e comprensione, siamo ostacolati, nel periodo che precede la notazione musicale (soprattutto di canzoni volgari), nei nostri tentativi di visualizzare (o tantomeno ascoltare) gli accorgimenti tecnici impiegati nel rappresentare queste favole teatrali liriche. Sappiamo, però, che i cantari in volgare (le storie cantate in ottava rima nelle piazze e nelle corti) avevano stretti rapporti con le favole mitologiche,[52] e abbiamo delle xilografie che accompagnano le edizioni a stampa di cantari, le quali rappresentano un cantore che suona un liuto o, più raramente, una lira.

Non mi sembra impossibile che la poesia (di tutti i tipi) recitata senza musica potesse colpire il pubblico rinascimentale come più insolita rispetto a una recitazione con musica; questa possibilità riceve peso dalla menzione esplicita che si fa, nel testo del *Cefalo* del 1475, del fatto che il prologo venne recitato «*non cantando*». È forse valida anche la considerazione dell'eventuale presenza di un accompagnamento musicale per la recita di altri poemi in ottava rima, come quelli epico-cavallereschi di Ariosto e di Tasso, soprattutto quando si consideri il già menzionato documento messo in rilievo da Nino Pirrotta, che descrive la produzione vocale di una recitazione come intermedia tra quella cantata e quella parlata.[53]

* * *

Poliziano's *Orfeo and Some Musical Settings of the Early 16th Century*» in *Arts du spectacle et histoire des idées. Recueil offert en hommage à Jean Jacquot*, Tours, 1984, pp. 201-204. Su Baccio Ugolini si veda il mio studio «L'entrée de Charles VIII dans Paris (1484) racontée par Baccio Ugolini à Lorenzo di Pierfrancesco de' Medici», *Bibliothèque d'Humanisme et Renaissance*, LIII (1991), pp. 727-734.

[51] È utile rammentare qui che sia la tradizione medioevale che quella rinascimentale della poesia lirica hanno elementi neoplatonici molto chiari.

[52] G. CARDUCCI, *Le Stanze, l'Orfeo e le Rime di Messer Angelo Ambrogini Poliziano*, Firenze, 1863, pp. LXIX-LXXVI; cfr. l'Appendice al capitolo VIII di questo volume.

[53] *Music and Theatre* (nn. 10, 13), p. 36 (ed. ital., p. 36). Potrebbe confermare questa ipotesi il fatto che si riconoscesse la poesia dell'Ariosto adatta ad essere musicata: cfr. C. V. PALISCA, «The Alterati of Florence, Pioneers in the Theory of Dramatic Music», nei suoi *Studies in*

Come abbiamo visto, l'*Orfeo* del Poliziano venne con tutta probabilità composto negli anni '70 del Quattrocento, ed è dunque probabile che sia stato composto a Firenze, malgrado la mancanza di prove di una rappresentazione in quella città, e malgrado l'ode indirizzata al cardinal Francesco Gonzaga, che appare come variante in alcuni dei manoscritti più tardi. Il *Cefalo* bolognese del luglio 1475 l'avrà forse preceduta, ma le due favole successive, la *Representazione di Dafne* del della Viola e la *Fabula de Cefalo* del Correggio,[54] furono scritte dopo la pubblicazione dell'*editio princeps* della *Theologia platonica* di Marsilio Ficino (Firenze, 1482) e del suo *De amore* (in *Platonis opera omnia*, Firenze, 1484). Questo fatto è importante perché, come abbiamo già visto (nel capitolo V), esiste una prova concreta almeno dello studio del *De amore* fra i poeti delle corti settentrionali, che discuteremo più avanti. Inoltre, le altre favole mitologiche nascono in un'epoca di instabilità crescente (in seguito all'assassinio di Galeazzo Maria Sforza a Milano nel 1476 ed alla congiura dei Pazzi del 1478, che ha avuto, come abbiamo già detto, delle ripercussioni in tutta l'Italia) — in un'epoca, cioè, in cui il conforto di pensieri ed esperienze armoniosi e lieti sarà stato particolarmente gradito.

La *Representazione di Dafne* di Gian Pietro della Viola (scritta per la corte dei Gonzaga nel 1486 circa) racconta con la musica prima la storia bellicosa della sconfitta del mostro Pitone da parte di Apollo, aggiungendo poi quella della punizione di un Apollo vanaglorioso da parte di Cupido, che lo colpisce con l'amore per la driade Dafne, figlia del fiume Peneo (*Metamorfosi*, I, 416-567); alla fine dell'inseguimento amoroso di Apollo, Dafne viene mutata in lauro, e perduta così dal dio come oggetto del suo desiderio.[55]

---

*the History of Italian Music and Music Theory*, Oxford, 1994, pp. 408-429, alle pp. 427-428. A proposito di altre forme poetiche, si veda la lettera indirizzata da Michel DE MONTAIGNE a Mme. de Grammont, contessa di Guissen, che introduce la pubblicazione dei 29 sonetti di La Boétie: «et puis, qu'il n'en est point qui la puissent rendre vive et animée, *comme vous faites par ces beaux et riches accords* dequoy, parmy un million d'autres beautez, nature vous a estrenée», *Essais*, cap. XXIX, in *Oeuvres complètes*, a cura di A. Thibaudet e M. Rat, Paris, 1962, p. 194 (il corsivo è mio).

[54] Non parleremo qui delle due rielaborazioni dell'*Orfeo* polizianesco, l'una convertita in una tragedia di cinque atti, l'altra pure in cinque atti e allungata con l'aggiunta della cornice della favola vergiliana di Aristeo e le api ed altro materiale mitologico:*Orphei tragoedia*, in *Teatro* (n. 1), pp. 171-198; *La favola di Orfeo e Aristeo: Festa drammatica del secolo XV*, a cura di G. Mazzoni, Firenze, 1906.

[55] L'importanza di Apollo, dio del sole, nelle immagini neoplatoniche e nel pensiero del Ficino, si può documentare, come si è documentata quella della figura di Orfeo: si veda P. CASTELLI, «Orphica», in *Il lume del sole. Marsilio Ficino medico dell'anima* ([Mostra], Figline Valdarno,

Una delle mode che abbiamo ricordato è quella del lieto fine. Come nel-l'*Orfeo* (la cui struttura è ripresa dalla *Dafne*), a prima vista sembrerebbe che questo tipo di conclusione non fosse stata apposta alla favola. A ben vedere, però, si può notare che Dafne viene trasformata non in un albero deciduo, ma in uno sempre verde, il lauro: essa diventa così immortale, destinata ad essere il simbolo eterno di Apollo. Il titolo completo dell'*opus magnum* fici-niano, ricordiamolo, è *Theologia platonica de immortalitate animorum*, il che mette in rilievo un tema fondamentale nel pensiero neoplatonico del Rinasci-mento: l'immortalità dell'anima. Mi sembra che la forte presenza di questo tema nelle correnti intellettuali del tempo possa aver contribuito alla scelta di un mito che si conclude con una chiara allusione all'immortalità. L'autore della *Dafne* sembra inoltre voler creare un'atmosfera positiva, in contrasto sia con il *Cefalo* frammentario, sia con *La fabula di Orfeo*. Può darsi che questo fatto sia dovuto all'occasione per cui fu scritta la favola (la festa cri-stiana dell'Ascensione), benché, come abbiamo visto, l'occasione altrettanto festosa delle nozze del 1475 non abbia prodotto una simile conclusione. An-che altri motivi, questa volta politici, possono stare dietro il sottile cambia-mento di moda percepibile in questo testo. Un nuovo senso del bisogno di stabilità politica sembra farsi più forte all'inizio di un periodo segnato nel-l'Italia settentrionale da un crescente numero di dispute interne, che in breve diverranno anche esterne coll'arrivo nel 1494 delle truppe francesi sul suolo italiano. L'azione drammatica della *Representazione di Dafne* inizia con la violenza del confronto di Apollo col Pitone, passa attraverso l'inseguimento che Apollo fa dell'oggetto del suo più grande desiderio (Dafne/lauro), e fini-sce con la serena accettazione, da parte del dio, del lauro come suo simbolo eterno. La risoluzione, tramite l'amore e la musica, è quella della pace.

Le correnti politiche, religiose ed intellettuali che influiscono sul tipo di conclusione atteso, unite alla crescente importanza che assumeva l'ascesa del-l'anima nel pensiero di Ficino, ci potranno fornire la chiave anche della pre-senza di un'altra caratteristica comune alle favole mitologiche, soprattutto da

---

18 maggio-19 agosto, 1984), Firenze, 1984, pp. 51-64, dove si ricorda che i due personaggi mitici vengono a volte addirittura fusi (pp. 54-56). Gli studi fondamentali sul mito sono: W. STECHOW, *Apollo und Daphne*, Leipzig-Berlin, 1932; Y. F.-A. GIRAUD, *La fable de Daph-né. Essai sur un type de métamorphose végétale dans la littérature et dans les arts jusqu'à la fin du XVII$^e$ siècle*, Genève, 1969. Altro simbolismo apollineo viene discusso in B. R. HAN-NING, «Glorious Apollo: Poetic and Political Themes in the First Opera», *Renaissance Quarterly*, XXXII (1979), pp. 485-513, e, più recentemente, in M. E. BARNARD, *The Myth of Apollo and Daphne from Ovid to Quevedo: Love, Agon and the Grotesque*, Durham, 1987.

questa favola in poi, cioè il risalto dato al contatto tra divinità ed esseri mortali. Nella *Representazione di Dafne*, questi temi sono rafforzati, se non addirittura suggeriti, dall'occasione della festa cristiana dell'Ascensione. Nei puri termini teatrali, una tale motivazione sincretista è conforme agli effetti scenografici spettacolari che sono in evidenza per tutto il secolo quindicesimo nelle sacre rappresentazioni, svolte su due livelli diversi, con discese ed ascese di angeli, e con i «cieli» ruotanti con i loro putti. [56] Questi effetti, che furono anche trasferiti nella commedia umanistica della prima metà del secolo, [57] poi apparvero nella discesa e nell'ascesa del messaggero degli dèi polizianesco, Mercurio, per culminare, almeno in quel secolo, con la scenografia leonardesca della *Danae* di Baldassare Taccone del 1496, in cui la comunione tra la terra e il cielo si realizzerà non solo con la discesa di un dio (ancora Mercurio), ma anche con l'ascesa di un mortale, Danae, tra le stelle immortali, sotto forma di una torcia fiammeggiante. Ma circa un decennio prima della *Danae*, già nella scena finale della *Dafne*, dopo la trasformazione della ninfa in albero, il pubblico veniva visualmente trasportato nel regno degli dèi, in questo caso un cielo, probabilmente posto ben al di sopra del palco che rappresentava la terra. Lì Apollo implora Giove che il suo lauro resti per sempre verde. Segue un dibattito tra gli dèi a proposito dei compiti e dei poteri di Apollo e di Cupido, con allusioni a quelli di Venere, Marte e Nettuno. Giove porta la concordia fra gli dèi, assegnando loro i rispettivi regni, e così una conclusione conviviale si sostituisce a quella altrimenti molto più sottilmente positiva dell'immortalità di Dafne. Questa festa degli dèi, che probabilmente preannunziava un vero banchetto svoltosi in occasione della rappresentazione della favola, prefigura altre feste divine successive, che si sarebbero evolute negli intermezzi e grandi spettacoli elaborati nei secoli XVI e XVII – nei quali, dobbiamo aggiungere, gli elementi neoplatonici non sono sfuggiti all'attenzione degli studiosi. [58]

---

[56] Si vedano, ad esempio, *Il luogo teatrale a Firenze. Brunelleschi, Vasari, Buontalenti, Parigi*, catalogo della mostra «Spettacolo e musica nella Firenze Medicea. Documenti e restituzioni. 1», Milano, 1975, pp. 59-66; *Le tems revient* (n. 6), pp. 214-219.

[57] Già nel 1432 la rappresentazione in latino di Tito Livio Frulovisi, *Claudi Duo*, esibisce due livelli di scenografia, di cui quello superiore rappresenta l'Olimpo: cfr. BATTISTI, «La visualizzazione della scena classica» (n. 6), p. 108.

[58] Si vedano, ad esempio, *Les fêtes du mariage de Ferdinand de Médicis et de Christine de Lorraine. Florence 1589*, a cura di D. P. Walker e con un saggio di J. Jacquot, Paris, 1963; i tre volumi curati da J. Jacquot, *Les fêtes de la Renaissance*, Paris, 1956, 1960, 1975; A. M. NAGLER, *Theatre Festivals of the Medici 1539-1637*, New Haven e London, 1964; MOLINARI, *Le nozze degli dèi* (n. 6); R. STRONG, *Art and Power. Renaissance Festivals 1450-1650*.

Si potrebbe proporre l'idea che gli elementi che stiamo studiando siano stati imposti deliberatamente per creare un sentimento di armonia presso il pubblico, e che queste rappresentazioni siano state addirittura degli strumenti politici, rivelando uno scopo utilitaristico nella rappresentazione di feste di corte sempre più elaborate. Una tale ipotesi diventa, sì, più plausibile quando ci avviciniamo alla Firenze tardocinquecentesca dei duchi, mentre una prova sicura non è ancora stata fornita per queste istanze quattrocentesche. Più verosimile sembra la possibilità di una autoimposizione, da parte degli autori delle favole, dei segni di armonia cui abbiamo accennato, benché forse per le stesse ragioni di base che avrebbero motivato la loro imposizione da parte dei ceti superiori. Rimane sempre possibile che gli autori fossero sensibili alle reazioni dei principi alle loro rappresentazioni (sappiamo, ad esempio, che una *Callisto* di Niccolò da Correggio non piacque ai Gonzaga), e che siano stati via via sempre più inclini verso un teatro di tendenze neoplatoniche, verso una maggiore comunicazione tra gli dèi e i mortali, e verso una maggiore presenza della musica e del lieto fine, mettendo in ombra rappresentazioni più austere, come l'*Orfeo* polizianesco. Ad ogni modo, tali sfumature politiche non negano, almeno per il Quattrocento, gli interessi culturali dimostrati da personaggi di spicco educati secondo i principi umanistici, il cui mecenatismo, spesso illuminato e sempre entusiasta, è stato tanto significativo nel creare e nell'esprimere i gusti dell'epoca.

*   *   *

Passiamo ora al *Cefalo* ferrarese del 1487 di Niccolò da Correggio, e infine alle ultime tre favole da prendere in considerazione, che mostrano sempre più chiaramente l'influsso delle correnti neoplatoniche. *La fabula de Cefalo* tratta dell'intera leggenda di Cefalo e Procri così come appare nelle *Metamorfosi* di Ovidio (VII, 694-758, 796-862); al pari di quella bolognese, anteriore di poco più di un decennio, viene rappresentata in occasione di un matrimonio.[59] Parzialmente musicata come le altre favole teatrali, offre agli

---

Woodbridge, 1984; e adesso J.M. SASLOW, *The Medici Wedding of 1589. Florentine festival as* Theatrum Mundi, New Haven, 1996 (non visto). Per il rapporto tra banchetti e teatro: PIRROTTA, *Music and Theatre* (n. 10), pp. 8-12, 46-47 e *passim* (ed. ital., pp. 10-13, 57-59 e *passim*); Idem, «Intermedium», in *Die Musik in Geschichte und Gegenwart*, VI, Kassel, 1957, coll. 1310 ss.

[59] *Diario Ferrarese di Bernardino Zambotti (anni 1476-1504)*, a cura di G. Pardi, *Rerum Italicarum Scriptores*, XXIV, Parte VII², 1928-1933, p. 178. La maggior parte degli storici ha confuso quest'occasione con quella delle nozze di Annibale Bentivoglio con Lucrezia d'Este, che

sposi gli stessi avvertimenti contro la gelosia visti nella favola bolognese. Incontriamo però un nuovo e importante sviluppo: dopo che la lancia di Cefalo ferisce mortalmente sua moglie Procri, la casta Diana, dea della caccia, si impietosisce per la sorte della coppia e scende, *dea ex machina*, per far rivivere Procri. Così, il matrimonio di Cefalo e Procri è ricomposto per il resto delle loro vite: viene quindi apposto alla favola, normalmente tragica, un lieto fine.

Anche qui possiamo fermarci per considerare più accuratamente le implicazioni presenti nel testo. Ci colpisce, per prima cosa, così come ci colpiva nel mito di Apollo e Dafne, l'importanza della comunicazione tra il cielo e la terra; notiamo in secondo luogo la compassione insolita per lo stato matrimoniale da parte della sorella nubile di Apollo, e in terzo luogo il fatto stesso del matrimonio. Panofsky[60] ha incluso nel concetto rinascimentale di un amore «più alto, spirituale e sacro», l'amore matrimoniale (insieme con l'amore «platonico» e quello cristiano), e ha dimostrato la validità di quest'idea tramite esempi tratti dalle arti visive. L'interpretazione è sostenibile anche nel caso delle favole mitologiche che furono in parte scritte per nozze; l'idoneità del neoplatonismo al contesto matrimoniale viene evidentemente dall'idea dell'unione dell'amante con l'amata, che implica pure l'arrivo dell'anima nell'al di là – la completa fusione – e la pace. Il matrimonio ideale può ritenersi il tipo più profondo (o, volendo, più alto) di lieto fine.

Già in modi relativamente diretti, troviamo dunque indicazioni di una conoscenza crescente della teoria neoplatonica dell'amore, e un'applicazione di essa nel lavoro di uno dei poeti più importanti delle corti dell'Italia settentrionale. Dopo qualche anno Correggio scriverà *La fabula de Psiche*, un poemetto basato sulla favola d'amore apuleiana, chiaramente neoplatonica, che dedicherà ad Isabella d'Este Gonzaga, committente e «programmatrice» entusiasta di altri programmi iconografici, come quelli dipinti da vari artisti per il suo studiolo nel palazzo ducale a Mantova.[61]

* * *

---

ebbero luogo alla stessa data, all'incirca. Il matrimonio è identificato con quello di Julio Tassone con Ippolita dei Contrarii nel mio *Politian's «Orfeo»* (n. 1), p. 170; questa identificazione viene accettata in *Teatro* (n. 1), p. 205. Si veda l'analisi della favola nel mio lavoro cit., pp. 169-180; bisogna aggiungere un riferimento all'importante articolo di Irving LAVIN, che collega l'iconografia dei dipinti di Bernardo Luini e di altri autori posteriori sul tema di Cefalo alla rappresentazione teatrale del Correggio e a quella operistica più tarda del Chiabrera: «Cephalus and Procris. Transformations of an Ovidian Myth», *Journal of the Warburg and Courtauld Institutes*, XVII (1954), pp. 260-287, tavv. 35-43.

[60] PANOFSKY, *Studies in Iconology* (n. 3), p. 126 (ed. ital., p. 177).

[61] Cfr. *Le studiolo d'Isabella d'Este Gonzaga*, (Musée du Louvre, «Les dossiers du Départe-

Gli autori settentrionali, benchè non siano giunti alle altezze del Poliziano e del Ficino, furono nondimeno influenzati dalla poesia del primo e dal pensiero del secondo. Mentre il Poliziano imitò, con grande arte, lo stile e le locuzioni delle fonti classiche,[62] i poeti settentrionali imitarono lui: echi del suo *Orfeo* sono una costante in tutte le favole successive. Per quanto riguarda il pensiero del Ficino, recenti ricerche hanno messo in luce un testo in cui il poeta lombardo Gaspare Visconti (in rapporti stretti con Correggio e con gli altri poeti settentrionali qui considerati), traduce in italiano brani da varie parti del *De amore* di Ficino (soprattutto dai libri I e III), rimodellandoli, con aggiunte minori, in un breve trattato sulla nobiltà, sulla grandezza, sull'utilità e sul potere unificatore dell'amore: un testo che non deriva dalla versione italiana del Ficino stesso, *Sopra lo amore*, ma costituisce una traduzione e una rielaborazione indipendenti.[63] Visconti esprime questi concetti anche nella lettera dedicatoria del canzoniere (1495-1496) indirizzata alla sua patrona e anima affine, Beatrice d'Este Sforza;[64] la lettera contiene una chiara e sistematica difesa dell'amore e delle sue «virtù» contro i teologi, i falsi profeti e tutti quegli stolti i quali dicono che l'amore nasce ignobilmente e porta con sé le conseguenze di tale origine. Inoltre occore notare che questi due lavori (lettera prefatoria e rielaborazione in volgare di Ficino) si situano nel periodo in cui il Visconti probabilmente compose la favola *Pasithea*: 1493-1497.[65]

Visconti fu un uomo di grande erudizione, educato alla maniera umanistica, conoscitore del greco, del latino e dell'ebraico, e un uomo che amava pensare profondamente. Non può stupire, allora, che la *Pasithea* mostri gli

---

ment de la Peinture»), Paris, 1975; W. LIEBENWEIN, *Studiolo. Die Entstehung eines Raumtyps und seine Entwicklung bis um 1600*, Berlin, 1977, soprattutto la fine del terzo capitolo, alle pp. 103-127, 215-229, e le tavv. 55-77 (non ho visto la traduzione italiana fatta da C. Cieri Via, Modena, 1988); C. M. BROWN, *La grotta di Isabella d'Este. Un simbolo di continuità dinastica per i duchi di Mantova*, Mantova, 1985; e per una bibliografia aggiornata: S. BOORSCH, K. CHRISTIANSEN, D. EKSERDJIAN, «Le studiolo d'Isabella d'Este et les derniers thèmes», in *Andrea Mantegna, peintre, dessinateur et graveur de la Renaissance italienne*, Milano, 1992, pp. 429-479; S. FERINO-PAGDEN, «*La prima donna del mondo*». *Isabella d'Este Fürstin und Mäzenatin der Renaissance*, Wien, 1994, pp. 385-432.

[62] PYLE, «Le thème d'Orphée» (n. 19), p. 412, n. 1; TISSONI BENVENUTI, *L'Orfeo* (n. 1), pp. 133-167, *passim*.

[63] Si veda il capitolo V di questo volume.

[64] Pubblicata da Paolo Bongrani in G. VISCONTI, *I canzonieri per Beatrice d'Este e per Bianca Maria Sforza*, Milano, 1979, pp. 4-7.

[65] Cfr. il mio *Politian's «Orfeo»* (n. 1), pp. 187-190, e il capitolo VIII di questo volume, anche per l'argomentazione che segue.

effetti della sua erudizione e dei suoi interessi più profondi. Il nome stesso della sua protagonista, «Pasithea» (benché la leggenda sia quella ovidiana di Piramo e Tisbe: *Metamorfosi*, IV, 51-166), viene dalle *Stanze* del Poliziano, alle cui allusioni neoplatoniche abbiamo già accennato. Come scrive il Poliziano (*Stanze*, II, 22), Pasithea è una delle Grazie, e, se guardiamo al suo nome, *Pasi-thea Calē*, è la «dea bella a tutti» – come ben sapeva il Poliziano, che infatti la chiama la più bella delle Grazie.[66] Non occorre sottolineare il significato della bellezza nel pensiero del tardo Quattrocento: in uno dei cicli neoplatonici, precisamente nel *De amore* del Ficino (che il Visconti conosceva profondamente, come abbiamo visto), l'Amore deriva dalla Bellezza e viene trasformato in Gioia celeste (*Voluptas*): «Amor ... in voluptatem a pulchritudine desinit».[67] Sarebbe allora una contraddizione in termini, in questo mondo delle corti quattrocentesche, se una bellezza come quella di Pasithea fosse destinata a morire per la stessa spada che fu strumento del suicidio del suo amante. Il doppio suicidio infatti avrà luogo, come accade in Ovidio e nella fonte diretta del Visconti, un cantare del XIV secolo,[68] ma ancora una volta incontriamo l'intervento divino, questa volta nella persona di Apollo – egli stesso inevitabilmente conquistato dalla bellezza di Pasithea – che soccorre i due amanti con una generosità uguale a quella esibita dalla sorella Diana nel *Cefalo* di Niccolò da Correggio, e li resuscita, permettendo così l'ormai atteso lieto fine, che comprende il matrimonio di Dioneo e Pasithea (Piramo e Tisbe).

*    *    *

Nella favola successiva, *Danae*, scritta dall'amico del Visconti, Baldassare Taccone, incontriamo la leggenda tradizionale (probabilmente, come abbiamo visto, presa dalla *Genealogia* del Boccaccio, II, 32-33[69]) di Danae tenuta prigioniera dal padre Acrisio, per evitare la realizzazione di una profezia secondo la quale sarebbe stato ucciso dalla progenie della propria figlia. Ma

---

[66] Sulle Grazie nel Quattrocento, GOMBRICH, «Botticelli's Mythologies» (n. 25), pp. 56-60.
[67] M. FICIN, *Commentaire sur le Banquet de Platon*, cura e trad. di R. Marcel, Paris, 1978, p. 146 (*De amore*, II, ii); cfr. WIND, *Pagan Mysteries* (n. 3), pp. 43, 51 (ed. ital., pp. 55, 63-64). A questo proposito un confronto con il *De voluptate* di Lorenzo Valla sarebbe utile; cfr. l'edizione curata da M. de Panizza Lorch: L. VALLA, *De vero falsoque bono*, Bari, 1970. Cfr. anche la n. 92.
[68] Si vedano nel capitolo VIII, sopra, la n. 22 e l'Appendice.
[69] Si veda la n. 32, sopra.

Giove scorge la bella fanciulla (la cui bellezza viene particolarmente sottolineata nella favola del Taccone) e, sconvolto dall'amore (tormentato, secondo le sue stesse parole, quasi da morire![70]), si accosta a Danae sotto forma di una pioggia d'oro. Tutto questo è rappresentato nel palazzo di Gian Francesco Sanseverino, il conte di Caiazzo, a Milano il 31 gennaio 1496, con la scenografia di Leonardo da Vinci.[71] La scena include un luminoso «cielo» (che ricorda quello della *Dafne* e quello creato dallo stesso Leonardo per *La Festa del Paradiso* di Bernardo Bellincioni nel 1490[72]) «con infinite lampade in guisa de stelle», e il suono di «tanti instrumenti che è cosa inumerabile e incredibile». Lo spettacolo dev'essere stato abbagliante.

Consono all'epoca, e legato ad un'interessante tradizione medievale di Danae come simbolo della carità virtuosa (alla quale si associano alcune allusioni alla Immacolata Concezione),[73] un fenomeno del tutto nuovo si aggiunge alla favola alla fine del quarto atto: una volta scoperta la sua gravidanza, Danae è destinata, sì, ad essere consegnata al mare, ma prima di esser rinchiusa nella «corba» da abbandonare alle onde, recita cantando (io credo: cfr. *Orfeo*, vv. 165-166) una supplica a Giove. Mostrando indulgenza, Giove ricompensa la virtù ed il sacrificio della fanciulla, convertendola in una stella fiammante – una stella *immortale* – che sale lentamente nel cielo con suono di trombe e di pifferi squillanti (per cui pareva «che 'l pallazzo cascasse», secondo la didascalia). Questo spettacolare punto culminante di ispirazione neoplatonica viene commentato da Apollo – «con la lyra» – in un lungo capitolo che, insieme con un coro introduttivo di ninfe e un brano recitato da parte di Hebe, «*dea de la immortalità*» (sospesa a mezz'aria), costituisce il quinto atto della favola. Hebe restituisce ad Acrisio la sua giovinezza, suggerendo così il dono anche a lui dell'immortalità, e l'informa che sua figlia è fra le «alme

---

[70] «Giove è chi parla, che si strugge e chiama / te sola,... / Quei crini, quella boca, quei sembianti, / che sempre inanti al cor posti se vede, / gli dan tra vita e morte dubia spene». (*Danae*, III, 24-25, 28-30; il testo è in *Teatro* (n. 1), pp. 291-334)

[71] M. HERZFELD, «La rappresentazione della *Danae* organizzata da Leonardo», *Raccolta vinciana*, XI (1920-1922), pp. 226-228; K. T. STEINITZ, «Le dessin de Léonard de Vinci pour la représentation de la *Danae* de B. T.», in *Le lieu théâtral à la Renaissance*, a cura di J. Jacquot, Paris, 1968, pp. 35-40 e tavv. 1-2; PYLE, *Politian's «Orfeo»* (n. 1), 1976, pp. 181-187. I disegni di Leonardo si trovano nel Metropolitan Museum of Art di New York, e nell'Ambrosiana di Milano.

[72] K. T. STEINITZ, «Les décors de théâtre de Léonard de Vinci», *Bibliothèque d'Humanisme et Renaissance*, XX (1958), pp. 257-265.

[73] S. SETTIS, «Danae verso il 1495», *I Tatti Studies. Essays in the Renaissance*, I (1985), pp. 207-237 e tavv. 25-57.

serene» (V, 14): in altre parole, Danae ha realizzato l'ideale neoplatonico, raggiungendo infine la pace nell'immortalità. Il canto di Apollo rafforza il messaggio della beatitudine di Danae e della sua quasi santità: ella infatti, come una santa cristiana, pur essendo assunta in cielo, non abbandona la cura dei mortali e del mondo terreno. In questo finale cristianizzato, Giove diventa un dio che ama «con perfecto core» (V, 52); Danae diventa sia una martire (dell'Amore) sia un *exemplum* che dà testimonianza dell'idea che il servizio fedele procura la gloria. [74] Questa mescolanza di temi cristiani e platonici, temi sia pure semplificati e venati di eventuali interessi politici, non può non rammentarci ancora una volta il sincretismo ficiniano a cui abbiamo già accennato.

E chi meglio di Leonardo da Vinci per realizzare la scena di un tale spettacolo, come già aveva fatto per *La festa del Paradiso*? Leonardo fu, lo sappiamo bene, educato nel fermento fiorentino del neoplatonismo degli anni sessanta e, se è vero che fu probabilmente il suo lato pratico che lo attirò a Milano nel 1482, non può avere completamente abbandonato la sua formazione fiorentina e neoplatonica, come ha sottolineato Augusto Marinoni soprattutto riguardo alla sua collaborazione matematica con Luca Pacioli. [75]

*    *    *

Un altro membro di questo gruppo di poeti cortigiani, Galeotto del Carretto (1455?-1530), si è spinto ancora più avanti nell'utilizzare il neoplatonismo risorgente, e ha basato la sua favola drammatica sulla leggenda di Cupido e Psiche come appare nelle *Metamorfosi* (o *L'asino d'oro*, IV, 28 – VI, 24) di Apuleio di Madaura, lo scrittore e filosofo platonico del secondo secolo della nostra era. Mentre le opere filosofiche di Apuleio, soprattutto *De Platone et eius dogmate* e *De deo Socratis*, furono studiate nell'alto Medioevo – da figure come Giovanni da Salisburgo, Vincenzo da Beauvais, e forse Alberto Magno –, le allusioni alle *Metamorfosi* spariscono dopo Marziano Capella e

---

[74] «Vedete che di grazia eterna è il manto, / vedete come sua bella persona, / doppo la crudeltà del padre e 'l pianto / in cielo è facta degna di corona! / E tra quelle alme lucide e immortale / non altro che di lei più se ragiona. / Costei proposta fia ad ogni animale / e comendata assai più che natura / poi che può sopra gli altri andar senza ale. / Sola costei de tutto el mondo ha cura / e del ciel la possanza in lei si serra / preposta al giorno et alla nocte oscura. / ... / Exempio da costei per nui sia tolto / che servendo con fe' se acquista gloria; / chi fa bona semente ha bon racolto». (*Danae*, V, 53-64, 77-79).

[75] A. MARINONI, *Introduzione* a Leonardo DA VINCI, *Scritti letterari*, Milano, 1952, pp. 11-12 (1974, pp. 16-17).

Fulgenzio nei secoli V e VI. Esse rimangono nel buio finché il Boccaccio – che a quanto sembra ne possedeva un manoscritto molto prima che Zanobi da Strada scoprisse il codice di Montecassino attorno al 1360-1370 – comincia a trarre da questo testo spunti sia di lingua che di sostanza per il *Decameron* (V, 10 e VII, 2), per l'*Ameto* e per la *Genealogia deorum gentilium*. Boccaccio adopera anche le opere filosofiche di Apuleio nella sua *Genealogia* I, 5; I, 15, e XIV, 9,[76] ma più importante nel nostro contesto è la sua versione della leggenda di Cupido e Psiche in *Genealogia*, V, 22, con l'aggiunta della solita interpretazione allegorico-moraleggiante, in questo caso con l'accento sulla divinità dello stato matrimoniale.[77] Questo accento s'intreccia con l'idea sopra espressa del significato neoplatonico dello stato matrimoniale, e inoltre con l'uso fatto da Galeotto del Carretto di questa particolare leggenda.

La traduzione delle *Metamorfosi* di Apuleio fatta da Boiardo (1478-1479, probabilmente basata sulla parafrasi parziale del nonno, Feltrino Boiardo) è già stata menzionata.[78] Dedicata nel 1481 al Marchese di Mantova, Federico Gonzaga, la sua presenza nelle corti di Mantova e di Ferrara non può che aver rinforzato una conoscenza crescente delle favole di Apuleio, soprattutto quella di Cupido e Psiche; rafforza questa supposizione il fatto, già ricordato, che Niccolò da Correggio dedica alla cugina Isabella d'Este Gonzaga nel 1491 il poemetto in ottava rima, *Psiche*,[79] nel quale Amore stesso narra, come *exemplum* a un pastore innamorato, la storia del suo amore per Psiche. Galeotto del Carretto crea a sua volta la favola che ci interessa qui, anch'essa probabilmente scritta per Isabella, circa un decennio più tardi.

*Le noze de Psiche e Cupidine* contengono virtualmente tutti gli elementi iconografici (cioè le immagini verbalmente evocate) della teoria neoplatonica dell'amore che circolavano all'epoca. Come le altre favole fu musicata, alme-

---

[76] C. MORESCHINI, «Sulla fama di Apuleio nel Medioevo e nel Rinascimento», negli *Studi filologici, letterari e storici in memoria di Guido Favati*, a cura di G. Varanini, P. Pinagli, 2 voll., Padova, 1977, II, pp. 457-476; Idem, *Apuleio e il platonismo*, Firenze, 1978, pp. 259-266.

[77] «Tandem penitens et amans, perniciem sororum curat astutia, easque adeo opprimit, ut adversus rationem nulle sint illis vires, et erumnis et miseriis purgata presumptuosa superbia atque inobedientia, *bonum divine dilectionis atque contemplationis iterum reassumit, eique se iniungit perpetuo*, dum perituris dimissis rebus in eternam defertur gloriam, et ibi ex amore parturit Voluptatem, id est delectationem et letitiam sempiternam»: G. BOCCACCIO, *Genealogie deorum gentilium libri*, ed. V. Romano, Bari, 1951, I, pp. 260-261. (Il corsivo è mio).

[78] Si vedano sopra, le note 35 e 36.

[79] Cfr. N. DA CORREGGIO, *Opere*, a cura di A. Tissoni Benvenuti, Bari, 1969, pp. 47-96.

no in parte, e in questo caso noi abbiamo la musica per una canzone, quella di Pan, probabilmente scritta da Bartolomeo Tromboncino (o da Marchetto Cara). [80] I due musicisti, al pari del poeta, lavoravano spesso per la corte mantovana dei Gonzaga (i quali avevano degli interessi politici nel Monferrato, patria di Del Carretto e feudo dei Paleologi, a cui la famiglia Gonzaga si sarebbe legata con un matrimonio nel 1517-1518). Isabella Gonzaga, quale figlia di Ercole d'Este, mantenne stretti legami anche con la corte ferrarese, committente di quegli affreschi di Cupido e Psiche a Belriguardo che devono essere stati uno dei nostri tesori d'arte, ora perduti. [81] Questi affreschi possono essere stati dipinti nello stesso momento, all'incirca, in cui Niccolò da Correggio scrisse e dedicò la sua *Psiche* ad Isabella, cioè nel 1491 circa, benché la data sia solo una congettura. [82] Gli affreschi esistevano, ad ogni modo, nel 1497, l'anno della descrizione dettagliata fattane da Sabadino degli Arienti. [83] Raccontavano visualmente, con poche alterazioni, l'intera favola (l'amore di Cupido per Psiche; la curiosità di Psiche, stimolata dalle sorelle malvagie, per le sembianze dell'amante; la soddisfazione della sua curiosità, che provoca le fatiche assegnatele da Venere; e infine il matrimonio di Cupido con Psiche), in modo corrispondente alla favola di Del Carretto, scritta forse nel 1499. [84]

Mentre né il ciclo degli affreschi descritti da Sabadino né la nostra favola teatrale (che, essendo un testo, procede linearmente nel tempo) avranno creato una rappresentazione gerarchica e non-lineare della leggenda come quella più tarda di Giulio Romano, [85] l'argomento stesso sarà bastato a soddisfare un pubblico sempre più abituato, se non ad interpretare l'allegoria

---

[80] PIRROTTA, *Music and Theatre* (n. 10), pp. 73-75 (ed. ital., pp. 83-84). Il testo della favola si legge in *Teatro* (n. 1), alle pp. 611-725.

[81] W. L. GUNDERSHEIMER, *Art and Life at the Court of Ercole d'Este: The «De triumphis religionis» of Giovanni Sabadino degli Arienti*, Genève, 1972, pp. 19-22, 62-65; Idem, *Ferrara. The Style of a Renaissance Despotism*, Princeton, 1973, pp. 258-261.

[82] GUNDERSHEIMER, *Ferrara* (n. 81), p. 261.

[83] GUNDERSHEIMER, *Art and Life* (n. 81), pp. 21 e 62-65.

[84] È possibile che sia questa la favola a cui si riferiscono quattro lettere di Galeotto e Isabella scritte tra il novembre del 1499 e il gennaio del 1500: A. TISSONI BENVENUTI, *Introduzione* a due commedie di G. del C., in *Teatro* (n. 1), pp. 560, 564-565; cfr. G. TURBA, «Galeotto del Carretto tra Casale e Mantova», *Rinascimento*, ser. II, XI (1971), pp. 95-169, soprattutto le lettere XXVIII, XXIX, XXXI, XXXIII, alle pp. 117-118, 121-123.

[85] Circa venticinque anni più tardi Giulio Romano dipingerà un ciclo nel Palazzo del Te a Mantova, che è stato collegato a diversi commentari neoplatonici apuleiani, incluso quello di Filippo Beroaldo; ciclo che si sviluppa nello spazio non linearmente, ma gerarchicamente,

neoplatonicamente, almeno ad essere immerso in allusioni neoplatoniche. È sintomatica, ad esempio, l'evoluzione dei nomi dei personaggi principali: mentre i genitori della Psiche apuleiana sono un re e una regina innominati, Marziano Capella chiama la madre «Entelechia» (Attuazione) e il padre «Sol» (l'Elemento Creatore[86]), nome che il Boccaccio riprende (Genealogia, V, 22), chiamando il padre «Apollo». Galeotto del Carretto, però, si muove in un altro senso, chiamando il padre «Cosmo». Oltre all'allusione ovvia al primo patrono delle idee neoplatoniche, Cosimo de' Medici, ci colpisce la corrispondenza con un passo di una lettera del Ficino: «Quid enim gratius quam in Charegio, hoc est gratiarum agro, una cum Cosmo gratiarum patre versari?».[87] Che Galeotto conoscesse o no la lettera (e sarebbe stato facilissimo che la conoscesse, perché si stampò dal 1495 in poi), un tale epiteto sarebbe potuto divenire corrente entro le cerchie letterarie, e di conoscenza comune prima della fine del secolo.

Benché Psiche non sia specificamente una Grazia, in tutti i testi è chiaramente bella come la più bella delle Grazie (fin dalle Stanze del Poliziano identificabile con Pasithea) e così, nel mondo duttile delle triadi neoplatoniche, ha il diritto, da questo punto di vista più che da quello offertole dal suo ruolo nella favola, di prendere il posto della Grazia e di impersonare la Bellezza. La bellezza di Psiche (come quella di Pasithea) è infatti leggendaria e determina il punto cruciale della leggenda, perché incita la gelosia di Venere, dea dell'amore. Che Cupido, il figlio di Venere che rappresenta il Desiderio e l'Amore, dovesse innamorarsi della bellezza di Psiche è, neoplatonicamente parlando, inevitabile (per Platone stesso, l'amore è il desiderio provocato dalla bellezza); ma questo fatto non acquieta Venere: Psiche diviene oggetto dell'invidia delle sorelle e, spronata da esse, cerca di vedere l'amante (ormai anche il suo amore) che mai aveva visto.

---

nel senso che le immagini sono disposte più o meno in alto sulle pareti e sul soffito a seconda della loro valenza simbolica; cfr. F. HARTT, «Gonzaga Symbols in the Palazzo del Te», Journal of the Warburg and Courtauld Institutes, 13 (1950), pp. 151-188, soprattutto le pp. 163-173. Un'ascesa concettuale è evidente anche nel nostro testo, come si vedrà. L'intera questione rimane da approfondire.

[86] Cfr. Martianus Capella and the Seven Liberal Arts, vol. II, trad. e cura di W. H. Stahl e R. Johnson, New York, 1977, pp. 6-7, n. 16.

[87] Cito da M. FICINO, Epistolarum Liber I, in Opera (n. 24), I, p. 608 (il corsivo è mio). Cfr. WIND, Pagan Mystenes (n. 3), p. 39 (ed. ital., p. 50). La prima edizione delle lettere di Ficino fu stampata a Venezia nel 1495 (H *7059; GW 9873; BMC V, 486; IGI 3863: cfr. KRISTELLER, Supplementum [n. 37], I, p. LXVII), e fu dunque disponibile per Galeotto del Carretto dopo quella data.

Tutto questo non può non ricordarci che, in termini quattrocenteschi, si può rinunciare alla visione per ottenere la gioia ultima, con lo spostamento dell'attenzione d'amore dalla bellezza alla gioia, come si vede nella medaglia coniata per Pico, che mostra la triade *Pulchritudo-Amor-Voluptas*:[88] una concretizzazione della dichiarazione del Ficino, citata sopra, che muovendo dalla Bellezza, l'Amore si volge verso la Gioia.[89] Inoltre, nelle parole del Pico stesso, «Ideo amor ab Orpheo sine oculis dicitur, quia est supra intellectum».[90] L'oggetto dell'amore invisibile diventa così ancora più prezioso di quello visto. Nella leggenda, quando Psiche vede, il suo amore le è tolto, ed ella deve sopportare le penitenze inflitte da Venere. Ecco l'espressione perfetta, ma rovesciata, del motivo di Cupido cieco enunciato da Pico nel passo precedente, che venne tanto usato nel corso del periodo rinascimentale.[91]

Proprio come avviene nel testo di Apuleio, Psiche supera le prove con l'aiuto dell'intervento divino, e alla fine la coppia si riunisce. Psiche (l'Anima) è resa immortale da Giove; Cupido (il Desiderio, l'Amore) sposa Psiche (la Bellezza, l'Anima), e la loro progenie è Voluptas (la Gioia).[92] Ora il Desiderio può godere la Bellezza immortale nell'Amore – e, non a caso, nella pace che è l'ideale del matrimonio, e che trae origine dall'unione dell'amante con l'amata. Tutto questo, nella nostra favola teatrale, è accompagnato da un coro nuziale finale di imitazione catulliana, e da una grande esultanza, che probabilmente in questa, come nelle altre favole mitologiche, suscitava una esultanza generale anche fra il pubblico.[93]

\* \* \*

---

[88] G. F. HILL, *A Corpus of Italian Medals of the Renaissance before Cellini*, 2 voll., London, 1930, no. 998; cfr. WIND, *Pagan Mysteries* (n. 3), p. 43 (ed. ital., pp. 55-56); cfr. GOMBRICH, «Botticelli's Mythologies» (n. 25), p. 56 (ed. ital., p. 82), che cita Warburg alla n. 84.

[89] Cfr. sopra, n. 67.

[90] Giovanni PICO DELLA MIRANDOLA, *Conclusiones secu(n)dum propriam opinionem numero LXII. in doctrinam Platonis...*, no. 6, in *Opera*, Venezia, 1557, fol. 157ᵛ, e *Opera Omnia*, Basel, 1573, p. 96. Cfr. WIND, *Pagan Mysteries* (n. 3), p. 51 (ed. ital., p. 64).

[91] PANOFSKY, *Studies in Iconology* (n. 3), pp. 95-128 (ed. ital., pp. 135-183); cfr. WIND, *Pagan Mysteries* (n. 3), pp. 53-80 (ed. ital., pp. 67-100).

[92] Il cui significato per Ficino è testimoniato dal trattato giovanile *De voluptate* (in *Opera*, I [n. 24], pp. 986-1012); ma l'approfondimento di questo tema particolare va oltre i limiti del presente lavoro. Cfr. anche la n. 67.

[93] È alquanto interessante che lo sviluppo delle favole mitologiche comincia e finisce (o piuttosto sfocia in altre forme drammatiche) con leggende i cui elementi essenziali comprendono il potere distruttivo dello sguardo dell'amante verso l'oggetto del suo amore. Il potere magico

Vediamo così ampliarsi, nella breve evoluzione di queste favole mitologiche, l'iconografia e il simbolismo neoplatonici (in armonia iconologica con la scelta delle favole d'amore prese da Ovidio, da Apuleio e da Boccaccio), con l'uso crescente del lieto fine e della musica, e con l'espansione dell'importanza in scena della comunicazione tra i mortali e gli dèi immortali.

Inoltre, questi stessi medaglioni teatrali possono anche essere visti, conformemente ai requisiti di uno studio iconologico enunciati all'inizio di questa trattazione, come indici delle tendenze culturali dell'epoca, in questo caso, della diffusione da Firenze della teoria neoplatonica dell'amore e delle sue ripercussioni culturali più generali, soprattutto nella nuova cultura volgare. Questa diffusione e la crescente popolarità dell'iconografia neoplatonica si possono anche collegare alle incertezze sociali e politiche a cui si è accennato brevemente. Nei momenti difficili, se rimane una struttura sociale e finanziaria sufficiente alla produzione dell'arte, gli esseri umani amano volgersi verso pensieri di pace, di armonia musicale ed artistica, e verso la speranza di una risoluzione armonica nella pace della mente e dell'anima.[94] Il neoplatonismo ha offerto una tale pace a colui che lo ha richiamato in vita, Marsilio Ficino, e alla sua cerchia; ed espandendosi in un raggio crescente da Firenze al nord dell'Italia (e gradualmente oltre i suoi confini), chiaramente rispondeva ai bisogni di una sfera sociale che si andava ampliando, e si stabilizzava.

Alla fine del Quattrocento, il simbolismo neoplatonico abbandona a poco a poco la forma coerente dei tentativi drammaturgici, per essere usato in modi sempre più fantastici nei «grandi spettacoli» menzionati all'inizio di que-

---

di questo sguardo, che si vede operante sia in Orfeo che si volge verso la moglie (come rileva Nino Borsellino nell'articolo citato [n. 46]), sia nell'illuminazione da parte di Psiche del viso del consorte, crea nei due protagonisti uno squilibrio emotivo, intellettuale e perfino fisico. Nel caso di Psiche, lo sguardo necessita di una purificazione tramite le fatiche, e nel caso di Orfeo crea le circostanze che portano alla perdita dell'integrità del corpo e infine della vita per mano delle baccanti.

[94] Ricordo che la politica conciliatrice di Caterina de' Medici quale reggente, descritta da Frances Yates, fu rinforzata dall'adozione dei simboli della pace e dell'armonia nelle cerimonie di stato, come l'insediamento del figlio, Carlo IX: cfr. F. A. YATES, Astraea. The Imperial Theme in the Sixteenth Century, London e Boston, 1975, soprattutto le pp. 133-137; cfr. anche STERNFELD, «The Birth of Opera» (n. 9), p. 34 (bisogna ricordare, però, che la parola «politique» nel testo della Yates si riferisce ad un partito cattolico e legittimista). Non è certo casuale che Caterina fosse italiana, imbevuta di pratiche sociali, politiche ed artistiche italiane.

sto saggio – fino alla fine del secolo successivo, quando tutti questi elementi e motivi si radunano di nuovo, concentrandosi su alcune delle favole amorose e sul loro significato musicale e neoplatonico, nelle mani dei creatori del melo-dramma. [95]

---

[95] Si vedano soprattutto: A. SOLERTI, *Gli albori del melodramma*, Milano, 1905; N. PIRROT-TA, «Temperaments and Tendencies in the Florentine Camerata», e «Monteverdi and the Problems of Opera», nel suo *Music and Culture* (n. 15), pp. 217-253, 418-422; Idem, *Music and Theatre* (*Li due Orfei:* n. 10); PALISCA, *Studies* (n. 53), pp. 346-363; 389-466; HAN-NING, *Of Poetry and Music's Power* (n. 15); G. TOMLINSON, *Monteverdi and the End of the Renaissance*, Oxford, 1987; STERNFELD, *The Birth of Opera* (n. 1); sui «grandi spettacoli»: MOLINARI, *Le nozze degli dèi* (n. 6); cfr. anche la n. 58.

# CHAPTER X

## Three Renaissance Women's Soliloquies
## Written by Men

In the history of Renaissance Italian theater, the fact that authors, audience and actors were predominantly male leads one to enquire into their
portrayal of female characters. Recent feminist criticism has in fact discussed
the depiction of women by men and emphasized the bias built into such roles
– a bias which would create characters that satisfied a male view of the social
hierarchy, in which women are in essence used for men's purposes. [1] On this
premise, the creation of dramatic characters to reinforce such a status quo,
even in subtle ways that are not immediately evident, could be expected.

That said, I wish to examine here three specific soliloquies in Italian
Renaissance drama, not for their bias, but for their realistic portrayal of what
may be called the female condition – in itself a non-negligible feat, which
has, I believe, been underestimated. [2] For, in the final analysis, apart from
the question of maintaining the status quo, the creation by men of believable

---

[1] See, for example, F. I. ZEITLIN, «Playing the Other: Theater, Theatricality, and the Feminine in Greek Drama», in *Nothing to Do with Dionysos? Athenian Drama in Its Social
Context*, eds. J. J. Winkler and F. I. Zeitlin, Princeton, 1990, pp. 63-96. The norms and
constructs of Renaissance society with regard to women, such as the Aristotelian acceptance
of their inferiority (physiological and intellectual) and their lack of power in most realms of
public life (judicial, political, ecclesiastical), are here taken for granted; on them, see
especially R. DE MAIO, *Donna e Rinascimento*, Milano, 1987.

[2] Except in the study of M. LEFKOWITZ, *Women in Greek Myth*, London, 1986; see especially
pp. 37-42.

female roles for theater demonstrates the common humanity of men and
women, and the ability of men to empathize with (if not always to alleviate,
or even wish to alleviate) women's situation.

Spanning a period of just over a century in Italy are three plays containing
substantial soliloquies by their female protagonists. The first is the Latin
humanistic comedy *Poliscena* written in 1433 by Leonardo della Serrata (no
longer attributed to Leonardo Bruni),[3] the second is Gaspare Visconti's
*Pasithea* of 1493-1496,[4] and the third is Giambattista Giraldi Cinzio's *Orbecche* of 1541.[5] The remarkable thing about these three speeches, given

---

[3] *Poliscena* has been dated and the author identified by Enzo Cecchini in the introduction to
his critical edition of E. S. PICCOLOMINI, *Chrysis* (Firenze, 1968; pp. xvi-xvii, n. 13). Giorgio
Nonni went on from there to document the life of the author and to make a preliminary
edition of the play in two articles brought to my attention by Paul Oskar Kristeller: G.
NONNI, «Documenti intorno all'umanista vercellese Leonardo della Serrata», *Giornale italiano di filologia*, XXVI, N.S. 5, (1974), pp. 278-294; «Contributi allo studio della commedia umanistica: La *Poliscena*», *Atti e memorie dell'Arcadia*, 6 (1975-76), pp. 393-451. Prior
to their work, the play had been attributed to Leonardo Bruni from the time of the first
edition, Schussenried, 1478 (H *1595; GW 5610). Cf. I. SANESI, *La commedia*, 2 vols., Milano, 1911, 1954², vol. I, ch. 2; A. STÄUBLE, *La commedia umanistica del Quattrocento*,
Firenze, 1968, pp. 12-16; A. PEROSA, *Teatro umanistico*, Milano, 1965, pp. 19-20; D.
RADCLIFF-UMSTEAD, *The Birth of Modern Comedy in Renaissance Italy*, Chicago, London,
1969, p. 33; J. P. PERRY, «*Poliscena*», *a Latin Humanist Comedy of the Early Renaissance*,
Ph.D. dissertation, Harvard University, 1975 (not seen); L. BRUNI, *The Humanism of Leonardo Bruni. Selected Texts*, tr. and intro. G. Griffiths, J. Hankins, D. Thompson. Binghamton, N.Y., 1987, p. 393. An English translation based on the Schussenried edition was
made and supplied to me by the late Jon Perry, copyright 1988; when he wrote, Perry did
not yet know of the work by Cecchini and Nonni, but I hope his lively translation will soon
find a suitable editor for revision and publication.

[4] Dated in my *Politian's «Orfeo» and other Favole Mitologiche in the Context of Late Quattrocento Northern Italy*, Ph.D. Dissertation, Columbia University, 1976, pp. 187-190; the play
was first edited there at pp. 207-261; cf. chapter VIII, above, and P. BONGRANI, «Lingua e
stile nella *Pasitea* e nel teatro cortigiano milanese», *Interpres*, V (1983-84), 163-241 (reprinted in his *Lingua e letteratura a Milano nell'età sforzesca. Una raccolta di studi*, Parma,
1986, pp. 85-158). The text also appears in *Teatro del Quattrocento. Le corti padane*, eds. A.
Tissoni Benvenuti and M. P. Mussini Sacchi, Torino, 1983, pp. 335-396.

[5] *Orbecche* was first printed in Venice in 1543 by the sons of Aldus. Besides numerous 16th
century editions, it appears in two editions of the anthology, *Teatro italiano antico*, London,
1787, vol. 4, pp. 85-240 and Milano, 1809, vol. 4, pp. 115-247. There is an expurgated
version in *La tragedia classica dalle origini al Maffei*, ed. G. Gasparini, Torino, 1963 pp.
135-215, and a full version in *Il teatro italiano*, II. *La tragedia del Cinquecento*, ed. M. Ariani, 2 tomes, Torino, 1977, t. I, pp. 79-184. Cf. A. ANGELORO MILANO, *Le tragedie di Giambattista Cinthio Giraldi nobile ferrarese*, Cagliari, 1901; F. NERI, *La tragedia italiana del Cinquecento*, Firenze, 1904, esp. pp. 59-63; E. BERTANA, *La tragedia*, Milano, [1906?], pp.

their content, is that they were all written by men. They constitute a foil (which has other manifestations in the literature of the time, such as the treatises on the equality or superiority of women[6]) to the *topos* of misogyny current from classical antiquity on.[7]

---

40-47; F. DELLISANTI, *L'«Orbecche» del Giraldi e il «Tieste» di Seneca ed altri studi giraldiani*, Barletta, 1933; P. R. HORNE, *The Tragedies of Giambattista Cinthio Giraldi*, London, 1962, pp. 16, 21, 48-62; R. BRUSCAGLI, «G. B. Giraldi: drammaturgia ed esperienza teatrale», *Atti e Memorie della Deputazione Provinciale Ferrarese di Storia Patria*, Ser. III, Vol. XV (1972); R. MERCURI, parag. 60, in N. BORSELLINO and R. MERCURI, *Il teatro del Cinquecento*, Bari, 1973 (Letteratura Italiana Laterza, IV, 21), pp. 88-96; M. ARIANI, *Tra classicismo e manierismo. Il teatro tragico del Cinquecento*, Firenze, 1974, pp. 115-178; C. LUCAS, *De l'horreur au «lieto fine». Le contrôle du discours tragique dans le théâtre de Giraldi Cinzio*, Roma, 1984.

[6] For example, the treatise of 1487 dedicated to Eleonora d'Aragona d'Este by Bartolomeo Goggio, that of 1500-1501 offered to Margherita Cantelma by Mario Equicola, and the similar contemporary work by the cleric Agostino Strozzi, all discussed by Conor Fahy in a pioneering article, «Three Renaissance Treatises on Women», *Italian Studies*, 11 (1956), pp. 30-55. On Goggio, cf. W. GUNDERSHEIMER, «Bartolomeo Goggio: A Feminist in Renaissance Ferrara», *Renaissance Quarterly*, XXXIII (1980), pp. 175-200. Equicola's treatise was a source for Cornelius Agrippa's stress on upbringing and custom in *De nobilitate et praecellentia de foemina* (1509). Besides the indispensable Droz critical edition and translation of this well-known treatise (*De nobilitate et praecellentia foeminei sexus* [based on the first edition of Antwerp, 1529], eds. R. Antonioli and C. Béné, transl. O. Sauvage, Genève, 1990), there is another recent French translation by B. Dubourg (*De la supériorité des femmes (1509)*, Paris, 1986). See too Henry Care's 1670 English translation in *The Feminist Controversy of the Renaissance*, intro. D. Bornstein, Delmar, N.Y., 1980. There is further an Italian translation of 1549 taken from an early French translation and attributed to Angelo Coccio: *Della nobiltà et eccellenza delle donne... Con una oratione di M. Alessandro Piccolomini*, Venezia, Gabriel Giolito de Ferrari, 1549. A rare converse example in drama – in a *commedia sacra* by the nun Beatrice del Sera – of a male character created by a woman and defending women (criticizing men for treating women like «pictures to hang on the wall») is mentioned by E. WEAVER, «Spiritual Fun. A Study of Sixteenth-Century Tuscan Convent Theater», in *Women in the Middle Ages and the Renaissance. Literary and Historical Perspectives*, ed. M. B. Rose, Syracuse, N.Y., 1986, pp. 173-205, pp. 193-4 (the whole play is analyzed at pp. 185-197). The women in Ovid's *Heroides* (including Medea) do not seem to me to be integrated characters in the way the protagonists considered here are (cf. n. 12).

[7] And not just from patristic times; cf. the introduction to *The Feminist Controversy* (n. 6), p. v. Marilyn French believes Western culture to be founded on misogyny (*Shakespeare's Division of Experience*, New York, 1981, p. 341 and *passim*). While one can see that misogyny may have a practical function in maintaining the status quo of social structures, it seems possible that other fundamental elements of Western culture are not so charged. LEFKOWITZ, *Women in Greek Myth* (n. 2, pp. 112-113) believes that Greek men did not fear Greek women for their sexuality, but were wary of the effects of passion (to which they believed women even more subject than men) on «reason, judgment and accordingly on action». She adduces the example of Helen, for whom the Trojan War was waged, and who is respected mainly for her «direct intelligence» (p. 135).

*Poliscena* is a fairly typical humanistic comedy with an amorous intrigue, having six characters including the two young lovers, their parents, and two older servants, one an interesting strong nurse/tutor. It is however distinguished by its articulate female protagonist. [8] The play begins with a moralizing prologue, spoken by the author as a student, about imprudent mothers, corrupt servants, indulgent parents and old people who behave inappropriately. The only two characters the audience encounters before Poliscena are Graccus, the young spendthrift lover, and his servant Gurgulio, in Scene 1 (there is no division into acts). Graccus declares his love, curses Poliscena's mother for being so watchful over her daughter, and the two men meet to begin plotting a means to the obvious end of seduction. Poliscena's soliloquy comprises Scene 2. Poliscena laments her own state from within her house, perhaps at the window or doorway of a simple «mansion», blaming «them», her elders, for her treatment:

Nisi me honestatis quedam religio et patria pietas cohiberet, profecto in ipsos effreni ore sermonem prorumperem, sibique haut aliter ac par est succenserem. Qui quo pacto nos puellas potius quam mares intra domus parietes opprimant ignoro; nisi id in consuetudinem, quin immo in corruptelam potius, deduxerunt, propterea quod autumant nos pusillanimes, negotiis familiaribus defatigatas, domique inclusas neci dedere, et sic nostra hereditatis in fraudem iurisconsultorum debita portione privare. Posthac asserunt se istuc facere pudicitie nostre conservande gratia: quod quantum sit a veritate absonum non me latet. Nonnumquam tamen nos delubra deorum pedetentim ducunt visere, fratrum audire confabulationes, portenta superorum inferorumque in pulpito proclamatium. Sed aliud quidem nos maius intus cruciat et quod magis magisque execro. Cum viam ita pudice ambulamus circumquaque caput ipsum velo abdite, adolescentium turba nos contemplari moliuntur. At cum eius rei locus sublatus sit, nos ultro mimos carnisprivii chachinando susurrant; quo satius plurimum nos mortem obire censeo, quam istam vitam lugubrem atque infelicem ducere, quis haut licet hisce frui voluptatibus quas fert huiuscemodi hilaris etas ac suciplena. Sed, perpol, me hoc totum macerabo tempus, neque quicquam faciam operis neque nebo neque lectulos sternam neque suppellectilem abstergam neque vestes resarciam, donec illum ipsum visam adolescentulum qui me hodie pre amore exanimatam effecit.

*Poliscena*, I, 2[9]

---

[8] Her name is based on that of Polyxena, the heroic daughter of Priam and Hekabe of Troy, who goes nobly to her death to expiate the death of Achilles in Euripides' *Hekabe*. She is mentioned in BOCCACCIO, *Genealogia deorum gentilium*, VI, 21 (ed. V. Romano, Bari, 1951), and in various catalogues of noble women.

[9] The text is that of NONNI, «Contributi» (n. 3), pp. 428-429. RADCLIFF-UMSTEAD (n. 3) also noticed the interest of this speech at p. 33. It should be pointed out, however, that the bawd-like character, Taratantara, is not a mere servant but the young Graccus' nurse and

This young woman, though a well-enough born female protagonist (perhaps she can be considered of the merchant class), has character. This of course is a change from the classical models of Plautus and Terence, whose young female protagonists are usually not even seen on stage, and where strong character is reserved for older women, servant women and prostitutes. Poliscena is respectful of her elders, though deeply resentful of her confined condition. She makes the point that such confinement is more likely to result in the very situation it seeks to avoid. She sees her predicament as the result of legalities (which is the truth: a woman is kept away from men before marriage to enable the clear establishment of paternity[10]). She bitterly laments the lack of freedom to indulge the passions that torment her just as they do young men. As a thinking being, she resents the demeaning situation of being paraded before young men to whet their appetites, and essentially regarded as the mere object of men's desire. She even steps ironically apart from her dramatic role for a moment to suggest that during processions to church such as the one she experienced, young ladies are regarded as nothing more than actresses, mimes upon a stage, women whose way of life she disdains. And she resolves to do something about it: she will waste away (a threat often resorted to by young women, turning anger and frustration inward) and do no more work until she can once again see the object of *her* desire.[11]

With the help of another, but expectedly, strong female character, the go-between and Graccus' old nurse, Taratantara, the plot overcomes the mother's resistance (though not before she has buckled momentarily under the weight of gold). The young man has his (and Poliscena's) way, and the situation is finally resolved in matrimony, to everyone's satisfaction.

Poliscena's soliloquy, although written by a young man in a goliardic context for a male audience, does not really seem to argue the male cause, belaboring as it does men's ogling of young women and treatment of them as objects. Then too, rather than representing a suitably demure female stage

---

tutor (she is termed «*lepidam alumnam*» by Graccus in scene 9, l. 449), educated (see her learned dissertations in scenes 5 and 9), and a member of his father's household; this accounts for her sympathetic presentation of Graccus' case and for other differences between her and Roman bawds. Her role indicates the existence of such educated females, analogous to governesses, in early Quattrocento society.

[10] See the further exploration of the ramifications of chastity in FRENCH, *Shakespeare's Division* (n. 7), pp. 126-129.

[11] This could recall Sappho's fragment 102 (*Poetarum Lesbiorum Fragmenta*, eds. E. Lobel, D. Page, Oxford, 1955, p. 84). But Sappho's young woman does not deliberately renounce her chores like Poliscena, she is too overcome with desire to perform them.

character, it appears to show us a full-blooded woman with similar desires to a young man's (although this could of course be seen in part as the creation of a willing female character, pleasing above all to men). This is not a unique instance of the drawing of a flesh-and-blood female character in Renaissance Italian literature. We have the evidence of Boccaccio's *novelle*, and indeed of the whole novellistic tradition, along with that of *contrasti* and semi-popular poetry in Italy – all of which feed directly into the theatrical tradition of the fifteenth and sixteenth centuries – to vouch for the explicit display of female desire among all classes of women in Italian letters of the period. The occurrence of such characters in men's writing bespeaks a down-to earth view of women, which seems to coexist (even in the same author, such as Boccaccio) with both the idealization of women's roles (e.g. Castiglione's *Cortegiano*) and misogyny. Italian culture of the fourteenth, fifteenth and sixteenth centuries, in other words, appears to allow considerable development of integrated female characters.[12] Yet none can so engage our sympathy as a female dramatic character, of necessity drawn with a depth not required of other literary genres, in order to evoke the audience's participation in the dramatic action. This will be further evident in the two other examples treated here.

Visconti's *Pasithea*, a mixed vernacular drama written for the court of Milan some sixty years later, offers a similar reading of a young woman's desire in the context of an essentially tragic plot, that of Pyramus and Thisbe, rendered technically comedic by the intervention of Apollo at the end to revive the two lovers from their double suicide. The protagonist (who could, like Poliscena, be of the merchant or professional class) exhibits her spunky yet modest character in three soliloquies. The first, in *terza rima*, and thereby set off from the bulk of the text as a *capitolo* (which itself seems to correspond to the Plautine *canticum* style of dramatic discourse[13]), reveals that character assaulted by the contrary winds of love:

> Hei me, che non fu mai nel mar galea
> Sì combattuta da contrari venti,
> Come è il dolente cuor di Pasithea.

---

[12] Looked at from the context of French's masculine/feminine principles, the women in these plays and in contemporary *novelle* are whole people, incarnating both French's «inlaw» and «outlaw» female principles, being gentle, nurturing and morally righteous, as well as sexual and willful. While French finds such an integrated female character in Shakespeare only in Beatrice of *Much Ado About Nothing*, her prototype seems to exist in Italy much earlier.

[13] PYLE, *Politian's «Orfeo»* (n. 4), pp. 84, 195-196; and above, chapter VIII, n. 24.

Milli desiri più che fiamma ardenti
   Me assaltano il penser cum tanta forza,
   Che stretta son cerchar farli contenti.
Da l'altra parte, questo foco amorza
   Timor d'infamia e gran desio d'honore,
   E nel contrario suo ragion mi sforza.
Poi subito rinasce il van furore
   Che me respinge ne la prima strada,
   E cercha alcun soccorso a tanto ardore.
Da poi convien che questo anchor reccada,
   E una altra volta l'altro a me ritorni:
   Vero è che l'un de lor più assai mi aggrada.
Che debb'io fare in questi primi giorni
   De la nostra florente giovenezza,
   Che son del vivere i piu dolci e adorni?
Questa sì chara giovenil bellezza
   Qual fumo et ombra in un momento passa;
   Né a retenerla vale arte o fortezza.
Né altro che pentimento dietro lassa
   De non haver saputo usar ben gli anni
   A chi fu stolta e cum la mente bassa.
Convene adunque che mi stessa inganni,
   E che del mio pentir io sia cagione,
   Cerchando me medesma i proprij danni?
Lasserò usar el fil de la ragione
   A i doctor de collegio, o a quelle vechie
   Che a l'opere d'amor più non son bone.
Forza è che a contentarme i' me apparechie,
   Et a colui, il qual tanto amo hormai,
   Porga benigne et ben pietose orechie.
Oi me, mia matre, se lo intenderai,
   Più non havrà la vita mia remedio;
   O se pur viverò, viverò in guai.
Viverò in vita che mi serà tedio,
   E meglio seria il colpo aspro e mortale,
   Che star di tanti affanni in tanto assedio.
Or su, io temptarò per mancho male
   Se'l mio Dioneo me vol tuor per moglie,
   Ben che non sia a lui di roba equale.
Così contentarò tutte mie voglie,
   Né la vechia haverà donde se indiavoli;
   E volterò in piacer mie pene et doglie,
Conservando però la capra e i cavoli!

*Pasithea*, III, 3, 81-126[14]

---

[14] The text throughout is a modified version of my edition of 1976 (*Politian's «Orfeo»* [n. 4], pp. 207-261), taking into account the edition in *Teatro* (n. 4), pp. 335-396.

We see in Pasithea a young woman in the throes of love's passion, to the point of throwing cares to the winds, and conscious of her fleeting youth (a *topos* which was surely particularly dear to the author, already in his thirties). She is determined, in spite of social constraints, to use these years to the fullest, with nods to the dictates of decency and matrimony. Her only fear is that her mother (the guardian of her chastity) might learn of her imprudence and confine her, in which case death would be a preferable fate. She hopes however to have her cake and eat it too by convincing her lord and master to marry her before she becomes his. This is not the order in which things took place in *Poliscena*, but the order is the only difference in terms of result. This embellished telling of the tragic fable of Pyramus and Thisbe ends, through the artifice of a *deus ex machina*, with the classical comic norm and resolution of marriage.

Pasithea's character becomes further known to us in two other soliloquies, recited in the normal *ottava rima* stanzas of the bulk of the play rather than given the discursive flow and probable musical emphasis of *terza rima*. In Act IV, scene 1, she expresses the positive effects on her of love:

> Mirabil fiamma è certo l'amorosa
> Che muta una persona in un momento.
> Solea tremar per ogni pichol cosa,
> Qual canna di palude o foglia al vento;
> Et hor son facta audace et animosa
> Per ubedir a un sol comandamento;
> E di pecora son facta leone:
> A tanto ardir Cupido mi dispone.
>
> Vado la nocte come uno homo d'arme,
> Sempre alevato nei passavolanti.
> E così, sola, esser sicura parme
> Come era in la mia casa poco avanti;
> Amore è meco il qual promette darme
> Il merto e il contracambio dei mei pianti.
> Ma già son gionta al loco del reposo
> Che m'ha insegnato el mio signor e sposo.
>
> Quanto mi piace d'esser gionta imprima!
> A ciò che paia più di lui ch'io avampi!
>
> *Pasithea*, IV, 1, 1-18

Modesty is thrown to the winds under the empowering effects of Cupid, the god of love. Pasithea has been given courage equal to a man's, as though she had been brought up among the accoutrements of little boys' war-games (fifteenth-century Italy too could see that upbringing made crucial differences in the behavior of the sexes[15]), and passion surpassing that of her beloved. (Dioneo in fact oversleeps and arrives late, to find the veil Pasithea had dropped when frightened by a wild beast. As in the tale of Pyramus and Thisbe, the veil, bloodied by a lion, leads Dioneo to believe Pasithea has been killed, precipitating, first his suicide, then hers in turn).

But it is her third soliloquy, again in *ottava rima*, which flies in the face of tradition. Returning to the spring from where she fled in fright, a disillusioned Pasithea realizes her beloved is late in arriving and that to return home now, so near to dawn, will mean dishonor.

> Quanto è meschina donna che se fida
> In homo e creda a un simulato riso.
> Però che benché in vista talhor rida,
> Altro ha nel cuor che quel che monstra in viso.
> Manda uno amante sì pietose strida
> Spesso, che par ch'el cuor li sia diviso,
> E par che avampi d'uno inmenso foco,
> Et poi non ama et altri piglia in gioco.
>
> *Pasithea*, IV, 3, 105-112

No one likely to be reading or hearing these lines in Italy in the 1490s or today could have failed or fail to recognize in this passage a counter-imitation of the misogynistic passage in Angelo Poliziano's famous *Stanze per la giostra*:

> Ah quanto è uom meschin, che cangia voglia
> per donna o mai per lei s'allegra o dole!
> e qual per lei di libertà si spoglia
> o crede a sui sembianti, a sue parole!
> Ché sempre è più legger ch'al vento foglia,
> e mille volte el dì vuole e disvuole:
> segue chi fugge, a chi la vuol s'asconde,
> e vanne e vien come alla riva l'onde.
>
> *Stanze*, I, 14[16]

The passage so fascinated Poliziano that he used it in the nearly contemporary *Orfeo*, which he wrote for the stage and which was printed at the same

---

[15] This is evident too in Equicola's and others' treatises on women.

[16] The text is from A. POLIZIANO, *Rime*, ed. N. Sapegno, Roma, 1967, pp. 13-14; cf. chapter VIII, above. Even in Pasithea's second soliloquy, above, Visconti had the passage in mind, using one of its similes in a positive fashion to indicate Pasithea's innocent timidity: «Solea tremar ... qual ... foglia al vento».

time as the *Stanze*, in Bologna on August 9, 1494 – that is, close to the time
to which *Pasithea* can be dated. [17] Poliziano calls that man a fool who is bent
by woman one way or another, who believes her expression or her speech; he
terms woman of light conscience and fickle, interested only in the unattain-
able man, disdainful of one who loves her. Visconti counters this with a true
reading, in the battle of the sexes, of woman's plight: she is a fool to trust a
man or believe his smiles, when his heart has other interests; she must not
believe his exaggerated cries of torment and ardor, for he can let her drop in
an instant and turn his attentions elsewhere. The riposte counters Poliziano
point-by-point, and is particular to a woman's experience – just as Poliziano's,
besides being a *topos*, must have seemed to him appropriate to a
man's.

That we should find a poet of the Sforza court countering the misogynistic *topos* of the fickle woman in the mid-1490s is cause for some interest.
The explanation in this case doubtless lies partly in the fact that Visconti
certainly wrote the play for a woman, Beatrice d'Este Sforza, wife of Ludovico il Moro. But patronage, while it may explain a slant, cannot alone explain away the poet's clear empathy with a young woman's plight at the
hands of carefree men. Visconti was one who thought about life, as can be
seen in all he wrote; he was also the father of two daughters. [18]

In 1541 Giambattista Giraldi Cinzio embarked on his career as tragedian
with *Orbecche*, a powerful Senecan tragedy – perhaps even more powerful in
ways, or at least more cathartic, than its principal classical model, Seneca's
*Thyestes*. The situation is fully tragic, besides being replete with elements
from the Italian novellistic tradition, and in fact parallelling Cinzio's own
*Hecatommiti* II, 2 and, like it, perhaps suggested in part by Boccaccio's story

---

[17] *Cose vulgare del Politiano*, fols. E i – [F iii] (A. POLIZIANO, *Opera Omnia*, 3 vols., ed. I.
Maïer, Torino, 1971, vol. III, pp. 63-83). Fifteen years later, Poliziano would praise a
woman, Cassandra Fedele, for her learning with the same sort of limpid poetic images he
had used in these earlier works to disown her sex: «At vero aetate nostra, qua pauci quoque
virorum caput altius in literis extulerunt, unicam te tamen existere puellam, quae pro lana
librum, pro fuso calamum, stylum pro acu tractes, et quae non cutem cerussa, sed atramento
papyrum linas, id vero non magis usitatum, nec minus rarum, aut novum, quam si de glacie
media nascantur violae, si de nivibus rosae, si de pruinis lilia». The text is in POLIZIANO,
*Opera Omnia, cit.*, I, pp. 38-39. Of course the contrast between Cassandra and other
women can hardly be said to provide a brief for womankind in general.

[18] Cf. chapters IV and V, above.

of Ghismonda, *Decameron*, IV, 1.[19] The daughter of an elderly cruel tyrant of the Persian city Susa has married Oronte, a foreign member of the court (from the legendary Medea's Colchis, East of the Black Sea, but Northwest of Susa), without her father's knowledge, and the couple have two children. The king has now decided on a royal mate for his daughter, and this event propels the action of the play. The daughter Orbecche's tragic dilemma permits the author to dilate on a woman's position in greater depth than either of the two writers of comedies (be they technically comedic, through divine intervention, or truly so). Orbecche contemplates her state:

> ...io veggio
> ch'altro esser non mi fa trista e infelice,
> che l'esser donna. O sesso al mondo in ira,
> sesso pien di miserie e pien d'affanni,
> e a te stesso, non che ad altri, in odio!
> Non credo (se lo stato miser guardo
> di noi donne) ch'al mondo si ritruovi
> sorte sì trista, tra l'umane cose,
> che la nostra infelice non l'avanzi.
> Noi spesso sin nel ventre de la madre,
> (pel primo don ch'a noi dà la natura,
> madre a ogn'altro animale, a noi madrigna)
> semo dal padre istesso avute in odio.
> E ove nasce ogn'animale in terra,
> per vil ch'egli si sia, libero e sciolto,
> (don che prezzar si dee più che la vita)
> noi, lassa, noi a le catene, ai ceppi,
> oimé nascemo, e a servitù continua.
> Perché sì tosto che conoscer nulla
> possiamo, benché tenere fanciulle,
> com'a perpetuo carcere dannate,
> sotto l'arbitrio altrui sempre viviamo
> con continuo timor, né pur ne lece
> volger un occhio in parte, ove non voglia
> chi di noi cura tiene. E dopo quando

---

[19] The resemblance to Boccaccio's story, widely accepted since at least 1901 (cf. ANGELORO MILANO, *Le tragedie di G. B. C.* [n. 5], p. 37), is actually rather slim. There the princess is a childless widow who, not remarried due to her father's jealousy, takes a lover. The only resemblances are the humble birth of the lover and his nobility of soul, as well as the determined spirit of the princess. More likely is a resemblance based on a common folkloric motif. Furthermore HORNE (n. 5), pp. 57-59, argues that the version we have of Giraldi's *novella* is in fact based in part on directions taken by his play, rather than the other way around as has been thought.

> pur devremo spirar alquanto e avere
> almen marito a nostra scelta (ancora
> che non mutiam per ciò sorte, né stato,
> ma sopponiamo il collo a novo giogo)
> la madre, il padre, od il fratello, od altri,
> al cui severo arbitrio semo date,
> legan il voler nostro e ne conviene
> prender marito a lor volere e ch'essi
> contenti siano. E noi, che con la dote
> comperiamo i mariti, e abbiam con loro
> viver fin a la morte, a tal siam date
> che più che 'l dispiacer, sempre ne spiace.
> E se forse da noi prendiam marito,
> e vogliam far nostro desir contento,
> stiamo a sentenza dura e proviam bene,
> con sommo nostro mal, che cosa importi
> uscir de l'altrui voglie. E chi nol crede
> in me si specchi e la mia sorte attenda.
> A me regno non giova o real sangue,
> né porpora, né scettro, né corona
> esser mi fa di questa sorte fuori.
> Anzi quanto maggior veggio il mio stato,
> tanto più grave la sentenza aspetto.
> Deh, non foss'io nel cieco mondo nata,
> o morta fossi in un momento in fasce,
> più tosto ch'a sì reo stato esser giunta!
> Ma a che vo pur giungendo pianto a pianto
> e querele a i lamenti? In van sospiro,
> e quanto più penso isfogare il core,
> tanto più da dolere anco m'avanza.
> Però, chiudendo il mio dolor nel petto,
> attenderò quel ch'i contrari fati
> disporranno di me misera e trista.

*Orbecche*, II, 4, 47-104[20]

This third soliloquy (taking Pasithea's interventions collectively as witness to her character and situation), in the mouth of a princess, bespeaks wisdom and insight to a degree appropriate for such a regal figure.[21] Her

---

[20] The text is from *Il teatro italiano. II. La Tragedia del Cinquecento* (n. 5), t. I, pp. 111-113. The first part of the speech appears in Appendix I.

[21] On the attributes of a royal woman, who should comport herself as a ruler, rather than as a woman, see I. MACLEAN, *The Renaissance Notion of Woman. A Study in the Fortunes of Scholasticism and Medical Science in European Intellectual Life*, Cambridge, 1980, pp. 61-62.

elevated rank lends weight to the thoughts she expresses, as it does in Greek tragedy. And these thoughts are, one after the other, worthy of consideration. In the course of the full speech (Appendix I), Orbecche first remarks on her conflicted state, owing devotion to her cruel father as his only offspring, yet sure of her (secret) husband's worthiness; in tragic fashion, she imitates epic similes, depicting herself as a helpless duck fallen prey to the goshawk. She touches on the contrast of nobility of soul to nobility of birth or wealth, a topic of discussion in Italian letters at least from Dante forward. She even raises the concept of freedom (current since the fifteenth century revival of the Brutus theme mentioned in chapter I). Her invective against materialism could have been (and has been) written today. But it is her statement of a woman's plight that holds our attention.

Orbecche's complaints are also those of women in various parts of the world today, some of which have had to be rediscovered to be enunciated. Yet here they are, nearly five hundred years earlier, given voice – and with evident sympathy – by a man. She laments the contempt in which the birth of a female child is held by its father. She decries the subjugation of a young woman's character to the will of others, especially in the choice of a husband. She comments clear-sightedly on the function of a dowry, to buy a husband to whom, pleasing or not, the woman is then bound until death. She points out that even her regal position does not alter these facts; if anything it exacerbates them by heightening her public duty. And she concludes in great anguish that it would have been better not to have been born at all, or to have died an infant.[22]

The main point to be made is one which I think bears emphasis. In creating theatrical characters by art (in the sense of *techne*), that is, in this case, by the techniques of rhetoric and characterization, a writer must be able to enter the mind of his creation, and must so thoroughly understand it that he makes it live for us on stage or in a reading. Giraldi Cinzio here transcends the usual catalogue of classical characters available. Instead, he taps two sources for this portion of Orbecche's soliloquy: Cornelius Agrippa's *De nobilitate et praecellentia foeminei sexus* (1509, *ed. princ.* 1529) and the famous first

---

[22] Gian Giorgio Trissino's *Sofonisba* (1524) uses very similar words: «Deh foss'io morta in fasce» (*Il teatro italiano, II. La tragedia del Cinquecento* [n. 5], p. 22, l. 308). Trissino's theme of courageous women in servitude resembles that of Euripides' *Hekabe* (later translated by Matteo Bandello: cf. A. C. FIORATO, *Bandello entre l'histoire et l'écriture. La vie, l'expérience sociale, l'évolution culturelle d'un conteur de la Renaissance*, Firenze, 1979, pp. 432-444).

speech of Euripides' Medea to the women of Corinth. [23] Like Medea, Orbecche is a wife and mother and is royally born, though unlike her, she does
not possess supernatural or heroic powers; nor is she a foreigner, although
she has wed a foreigner. The corresponding points between the two speeches
are several: that women are the most wretched of creatures; that women must
in effect buy their husbands with their dowries, and then become possessions
of their husbands; if the marriage fails for one reason or another, death is the
preferable end. In imitation of the great psychological playwright of ancient
Greece, Cinzio enters the mind of a woman and explores it with a sympathy
not usually acknowledged in the men of his time. [24]

---

[23] Euripides, *Medea*, ll. 214-266. This Greek source, of considerable interest for a consideration of Giraldi's work and thought, does not seem to have been recognized in the studies
and editions I have consulted (n. 5). Most critics are of the opinion of DE MAIO (n. 1, p. 78):
«Garnier e Racine su Fedra sviluppano i grandi pensieri di Euripide. All'inizio della tragedia rinascimentale non fu così. Rucellai, Speroni, Giraldi Cinzio, Gregorio Correr presero
da Seneca il dettaglio orripilante e nulla dai greci». Euripides' *Medea*, available in the Greek
Florentine incunabulum of 1495 (HAIN *6697; GW 9431), was first published in the Latin
translation of the Zurich scholar «Dorotheus Camillus» (Rodolphus Ambuel Collinus) in
Basel in August, 1541.
On *Medea*, see the insightful essay by B. KNOX, «The *Medea* of Euripides», *Yale Classical
Studies*, XXV (1977), pp. 193-225; reprinted in his *Word and Action. Essays on the Ancient
Theater*, Baltimore and London, 1979, pp. 295-322. Medea's speech is rhetorically constructed on Sophistic precepts: cf. P. MAZON, «De quelques vers d'Euripide (*Médée*, 214-
229)», *Revue de philologie*, XXVII (1953), pp. 119-121. Although the princess Orbecche's
soliloquy is constructed (if not as effectively) on rhetorical bases, it has been noted that
Leonardo Bruni in his humanistic curriculum for a noblewoman specifically omits rhetoric,
because a woman will never enter the forum (M. L. KING, *Women of the Renaissance*, Chicago and London, 1991; Italian tr. by L. Nencini, Bari, 1991, p. 225; cf. BRUNI in *Il pensiero
pedagogico dell'Umanesimo*, ed. E. Garin, Firenze, 1958, pp. 154, 155). Other sources for
portions of Orbecche's speech include at least one passage from AGRIPPA (n. 6: 1990, p. 87;
see Appendix II). This is cited in MACLEAN (n. 21, p. 80), yet there termed a «rhetorical
exercise in declamation».

[24] HORNE, *The Tragedies* (n. 5), notes the compassion in Giraldi's own character (p. 62), which
further supports my reading of this soliloquy. This speech in fact makes of Orbecche a
deeply human character, with whom one can indeed sympathize; without it, her character
would be far more shallow. Given the appearance of Euripides in Latin in August of 1541,
and the publication date of *Orbecche* two years later, it may be in order to ask if portions of
Orbecche's speech were indeed recited on stage early in 1541, or if they might not instead
have been added for the first (Aldine) printed edition of 1543 (despite the dedicatory letter
in which, as has been noted by others, Giraldi eschews the Greek tragedians in favor of the
Latin: *Orbecche tragedia di M. Giovanbattista Giraldi Cinthio da Ferrara*, Venezia, 1543, fol.
2). This should lend further impetus to the study of Giraldi's relationship with the Greeks

But it is well for us to note that this degree of sympathy existed in 1541, and that, in the form of Orbecche's soliloquy, it was at least possibly presented on stage in Giraldi's own home, almost certainly before a mixed audience, including the male dedicatee, Duke Ercole II d'Este of Ferrara; certainly it was published two years later. Furthermore, as our other examples attest, sympathetic depiction of some of the complexities of a female protagonist's situation by a man of the Renaissance exists at least as early as 1433 (55 years before the earliest treatise discussed by Fahy and by Gundersheimer) and recurs in the mid-1490s in direct response to the tradition of misogyny. The three genres, comic, mythological-comic, and tragic, and their concomitant implications of social class and education, account for the differences of effect among the three speeches: Poliscena's and Pasithea's speeches are more straight-forward and immediate, less philosophical or weighty than that of the royal Orbecche, based as it is on Greek tragedy.

These soliloquies are different from the feminist treatises of the time. The treatises, even when filled with historical examples and thought through with care, contained elements of condescension, simply by virtue of being apologies written by those in stronger positions to defend women against exploiters, or discussions of their education to be of use in a world dominated by people with particular interests not always coincident with those of women.[25] Even in the two comedies discussed above, there can be felt a nugget of condescension because of the comic context.

However, in Giraldi Cinzio's *Orbecche*, as in Euripides' *Medea*, the words sting and gnaw as if they had been written by a woman in great agony. They convey disagreeable truths, with no redemption. The tragic situation allows this, and the author indulges fully the complaints of a noble, deeply respectable and greatly to be pitied woman. Not only is her character made

---

and their language. And cf. his *Discorsi ... intorno al comporre dei Romanzi, delle Comedie, e delle Tragedie, e di altre maniere di Poesie*, Venezia, 1554, pp. 222-223. Interestingly, Orbecche's reference to «la natura / madre a ogn'altro animale, a noi madrigna», corresponds to a passage in Lactantius' *De opificio Dei* (III, 2), which was published in French translation by J. Breche, Tours, 1543, the year of publication of *Orbecche*; cf. chapter XI, n. 53, below.

[25] Diane Bornstein calls them «in part a rhetorical game»: D. BORNSTEIN, «Introduction» to *The Feminist Controversy* (n. 6), p. xii. Timothy Reiss says, «however 'equal' women's reason might be, it was to be used in a masculine world» (T. REISS, «Corneille and Cornelia: Reason, Violence, and the Cultural Status of the Feminine. Or, How a Dominant Discourse Recuperated and Subverted the Advance of Women» [1987], in *Renaissance Drama as Cultural History: Essays from Renaissance Drama 1977-1987*, ed. M. B. Rose, Evanston, Illinois, 1990, pp. 171-209, p. 175). On categories of treatises, C. JORDAN, «Feminism and Human-

clearer to the audience by this powerful statement, but the author's own character and depth of understanding is itself distinguished in the process.

It is furthermore worth emphasizing that the dramatic setting permits –
even obliges – the straight-forward statement of a character's innermost
thoughts. To create believable characters, the dramatist must face certain
bald facts on stage that cannot be acceptably dealt with in a treatise, essay or
letter, let alone in the rarified atmosphere of a dialogue on manners, however
philosophical.[26] An analogous phenomenon has been recognized with respect to linguistic usage, where, for example, Plautus gives us a more collo-
quial Latin than we find elsewhere.[27] But it is true for other levels of expression as well. Despite the necessity of adherence to norms of staging and dramatic development, plays can be cultural «spies» (to borrow an Italian
phrase) offering us unvarnished clues to social realities. Here we see three
women created by men yet expressing themselves frankly and thoughtfully on
issues we are surprised to find men of the time (or of any time until very
recently) sensitive to. We have an obligation to add the evidence of these
three women's soliloquies written by men to our growing picture of the situation of women in the Renaissance.[28]

---

ists: The Case of Sir Thomas Elyot's *Defence of Good Women*», *Renaissance Quarterly*,
XXXVI (1983), pp. 181-201, esp. pp. 181-184. There were, however, treatises dealing with
the equality or superiority of women, written for women patrons, and adducing substantial
arguments testifying to an appreciation of woman's intellect and character: see AGRIPPA
(and the preface to the 1990 critical edition by R. ANTONIOLI, pp. 7-38), FAHY, GUNDERS-
HEIMER (n. 6). (A hyperbolic and derivative «Oratione in lode delle donne», offered to the
Accademia degli Intronati of Siena by the playwright Alessandro Piccolomini, accompanies
the 1549 Italian translation of AGRIPPA [*Della nobiltà*, n. 6; fols. 29-36], but is in no way
equivalent to it in tone or learning; instead it is flattery of the most obsequious sort, and
thus uninteresting, even in its adducing of Neoplatonic principles to laud womankind near
the end, undoubtedly derived from Agrippa).

[26] One thinks of course of Baldassare Castiglione's *Libro del Cortegiano*, published in 1528 (cf.
B. CASTIGLIONE, *Il libro del Cortegiano con una scelta delle opere minori*, ed. B. Maier,
Torino, 1964).

[27] Cf. W. M. LINDSAY, *Syntax of Plautus*, Oxford, 1907; New York, 1936, *passim*.

[28] It is of further, contemporary, interest that a short soliloquy of similar moment to Orbecche's, by the character Santilla in Bernardo Dovizi da Bibbiena's *Calandria* of 1513 (IV,
5), is also omitted by its modern English translator, raising questions about present-day
norms compared with those of the Italian 16th century. As seen above (n. 5), such omissions
occur in 20th century texts prepared for schools. Cf. B. DOVIZI DA BIBBIENA, *La Calandria*, in
*Commedie del Cinquecento*, ed. A. Borlenghi, 2 vols., Milano, 1959, p. 135 (with a source in
Boccaccio, *Decameron*, IX, 9); Idem, *The Follies of Calandro*, in *The Genius of the Italian
Theater*, ed. E. Bentley, New York, 1964, p. 85. Fulvia's monologue (III, 5) including similar ideas, however, is translated (pp. 67-68).

## Appendix I

*Orbecche*, II, 4, 1-47:

Par che chi miser è poco dia fede
a speme alcuna, e sempre il peggio tema,
poi pare ancor che quel, ch'egli più brama,
aver pur debba il disiato fine.
Così da questi due contrari anch'io
mi trovo combattuta: da una parte,
l'essere unica figlia al re Sulmone
e l'esser tanto caro a lui Oronte,
quanto figliuol gli fosse, e la pietade
ch'egli m'ha sempre mostro, ancor ch'ei sia
via più d'ognun crudele, e l'alte lodi,
ch'egli ha palesemente a Oronte date,
mi dan qualche speranza. Ma da l'altra,
l'essere Oronte di vil sangue nato,
(seguendo l'openion del vulgo sciocco,
che gentil crede sol chi ha copia d'oro)
e potendomi dar a un re per moglie
il re mio padre, a tal timor me induce,
ch'io tremo, come l'anitra, che vede
sovra sé il fier astor per divorarla.
È vero ben che s'ei volesse a pieno,
co lo intiero giudicio, a parte a parte
considerare 'l giusto e non volesse
che più potesse in lui l'oro e la sete
del regno e de l'aver, che la virtute,
io son sicura che non pur errore
non giudicheria il mio, ma di gran loda
mi terria degna, che più tosto avessi
voluto un uom, il qual non cieco errore,
o desio folle, ma giudicio certo
sceglier m'ha fatto tra mill'altri illustri.
Quantunque pover sia, ch'un re possente,
atto più tosto ad ogni vil ufficio,
che lo scettro real tenere in mano,
ancor che paia questi al padre mio,
cui ha velato gli occhi il costui stato,
il primo re, che mai corona avesse.
Quasi ch'egli non sappia, ch'assai meglio
è a donna avere un uom, cui sia mestieri
d'oro, che l'or cui sia mestier d'un uomo.
Ma la fame d'aver tant'è cresciuta,
che non s'istima al mondo altro che l'oro.
Povera e nuda va la virtù istessa:

ahi, sciocca oppenïon del vulgo errante!
ahi, grave error, ch'i mortali occhi appanna,
quant'altri in ciò s'inganna! Ma lasciando
questo da parte, e a me tornando, …

# Appendix II

C. Agrippa, *De nobilitate et praecellentia foeminei sexus*, Genève, 1990, p. 87 (cf. n. 25):

Sed uirorum nimia tyrannide contra diuinum ius naturaeque leges praeualente, data mulieribus libertas iam iniquis legibus interdicitur, consuetudine usuque aboletur, educatione extinguitur. Mulier namque mox ut nata est, a primis annis domi detinetur in desidia, ac velut altioris prouinciae incapax, nihil praeter acus et filum concipere permittitur. Ubi exinde pubertatis annos attigerit, in mariti traditur zelotypum imperium, aut uestalium ergastulo perpetuo recluditur.

# PART V
*Conclusion: Milan and Beyond*

# CHAPTER XI

## Democritus and Heracleitus:
## An Excursus on the Cover of this Book

The woodcut on the cover of this book first appears in 1506 as the frontispiece to the first edition of Antonio Campo Fregoso's *Riso de Democrito*.[1]
Representing two philosophers, Heracleitus weeping and Democritus laughing over the human situation, with a terrestrial globe between them, it embodies a number of themes and reflects a number of circumstances touched
upon in the essays here collected. The study of these themes reveals the uni-
versality of concerns of fifteenth and early sixteenth century Milan, and
demonstrates their diffusion into sixteenth century Europe, and into the
thought, literature and art of later ages.

Heracleitus (ca. 535 – ca. 475 BC) was the earliest of the extant Greeks to
enunciate concepts that would become fundamental to later philosophical
systems, such as the conflict of opposites which he saw as the core of nature's
unity; nature itself being a constant stream of change.[2] Democritus (ca. 460
– ca. 370 BC) was a follower of Leucippus and is our first extant exponent of
atomism (according to which there existed only atoms and the void); he was
interested in physical science, well-travelled, and is considered by some to

---

[1] *Riso de Democrito composito per il Magnifico / Caualere Phileremo .D. Antonio Fregoso. //*
COLOPHON [fol. e:] *Impressum Mediolani p(er) Petrum / Martire(m) de Mantegatiis dictum /
Cassanum. Anno.D(omi)ni.M.D.vi. / Die.xx.Augusti.*

[2] The texts that survive are commented and translated in: HÉRACLITE, *Fragments*, ed. M. Conche,
Paris, 1986 (rpt. 1991).

have been the most knowledgeable philosopher before Aristotle. [3] Heracleitus' ethical thought is based on a goal of understanding the self and nature;
Democritus' ethics were those of moderation and reasonableness in pursuit
of happiness (ideas which would be espoused by Epicurus and his followers).
Over the centuries there grew around these two figures the legend that
termed Heracleitus the weeping and Democritus the laughing philosopher,
thus juxtaposing them in what can itself be seen as a Heracleitan opposition,
or unity. [4]

The theme is alluded to, among other places, in the works of Seneca, who
vacillates between neutrality with regard to the two approaches and a preference for Democritus' venting of the milder emotion over what he sees as
Heracleitus' «weakness» in caring too much (De tranquillitate animi, XV; De
ira, II, 5). Juvenal can understand Democritus' laughing censure of mankind, but not Heracleitus' tears (Satura X, 28-53); Lucian sees merit in both
philosophers' approaches (On Sacrifices, 15; but see his Philosophers for Sale,
13-14, in which the pair are not purchased, but passed over).

Among the non-classical sources are Sidonius Apollinaris, who describes
the facial expressions of the two philosophers as they appeared in the gymna-
sia of the Areopagus and in the prytanea in Athens, and is the probable
source for future artists' renderings (Epistulae, IX, ix, 14); the Greek Anthology (IX, 148[5]); and separate entries for the two philosophers in the Suidae

---

[3] The surviving texts appear in H. DIELS, Die Fragmente der Vorsokratiker, ed. W. Kranz, 3
vols., Berlin, 1951-1952⁶, II, pp. 81-230, no. 68 [55], and are translated (from the fifth
edition) in K. FREEMAN, Ancilla to the Pre-Socratic Philosophers, Cambridge, Mass., 1948
(rpt. 1983), pp. 91-120.

[4] The theme cries out for a rigorous exposition on its own grounds by a classicist. See the short
but penetrating essay by C. E. LUTZ, «Democritus and Heraclitus», The Classical Journal,
49 (1953-1954), pp. 309-314. Z. STEWART, «Democritus and the Cynics», Harvard Studies in
Classical Philology, LXVIII (1958), pp. 179-191, dates the emergence of the juxtaposition at
Seneca's teacher Sotion (fragment in I. STOBAEUS, Anthologii Libri duo Posteriores, Berlin,
1894, I, p. 550). Studies currently available in which the theme is ancillary to the main
argument of the book include A. M. GARCIA GOMEZ, The Legend of the Laughing Philo-
sopher and its Presence in Spanish Literature (1500-1700), Cordoba, 1984 and T. RÜTTEN,
Demokrit – Lachender Philosoph und sanguinischer Melancholiker. Eine pseudohippokratische
Geschichte, Leiden, 1992. On the theme's appearance in Renaissance humanism, see A.
BUCK, «Democritus ridens et Heraclitus flens», in Wort und Text. Festschrift für Fritz
Schalk, Frankfurt am Main, 1963, pp. 167-186.

[5] The Greek Anthology, tr. W. R. Paton, 5 vols., vol. 3, Cambridge, Mass. and London, 1958,
pp. 76-77; Anthologie grecque, ed. P. Waltz, tr. G. Soury, VII, Paris, 1957, p. 59. Cf. J. A.
SYMONDS, Studies of the Greek Poets, 2 vols., London, 1893, vol. II, pp. 282-343; J. HUT-

*Lexicon.*[6] In the Renaissance, the theme was alluded to by Francesco Petrarca in his most popular work (*De Remediis Fortunae*, II, 89[7]); by Cristoforo Landino, who identifies Democritus' *euthymia* with the Christian concept of peace and the highest good (*Disputationes Camaldulenses*, II[8]), and, rather mechanically after Sidonius, by Pietro Crinito (*De Honesta Disciplina*, XI). Later in the Renaissance, it is alluded to by Montaigne, in his essay «De Democritus et Heraclitus» (*Essais*, I, 50), in which he favors Democritus' approach (for what might be called its «sprezzatura») over that of Heracleitus, contrary to Petrarca who believed Heracleitus to have the correct demeanor regarding mankind and this world. Not everyone took sides overtly, as we shall see; some deemed it wiser to consider the two philosophers' attitudes as two extremes, both of which were to be eschewed for a moderate approach. Others saw the underlying unity of the conflict and considered the two as representing two sides of a coin.[9]

The theme of the two philosophers appealed to the Renaissance Platonist Marsilio Ficino enough that he made it a central theme in the fresco decoration of his own «gymnasium» or academy,[10] as Ficino says in a letter to

---

TON, *The Greek Anthology in Italy to the Year 1800*, Ithaca, N.Y., 1935; A. CAMERON, *The Greek Anthology from Meleager to Planudes*, Oxford, 1993. This epigram was known to the humanists since it was included in the Planudean portion, compiled in the 10th century though representative of various ages of Greek literature. It is termed «late» by LUTZ (cf. n. 4, above). And see the final paragraphs of this chapter.

[6] 10th cent.; first Greek and Latin ed., 2 vols., Genève, 1619; 2nd ed., Coloniae Allobrogum (Genève), 1630, I, pp. 680, 1196-1197 (in both editions). The are also treated separately by Diogenes Laertius in the early 3rd century.

[7] Cf. N. MANN, «Petrarch and Humanism: The Paradox of Posterity», *F. P. Citizen of the World*, Padova and Albany, 1980, p. 289.

[8] C. LANDINO, *Disputationes camaldulenses*, ed. P. Lohe, Firenze, 1980, p. 59.

[9] In the words of LUTZ, «Democritus and Heraclitus» (n. 4), p. 312. In discussing a painting by Rembrandt in which the artist depicts himself as Democritus painting a portrait of Heracleitus, her lucid conclusion is that «Democritus-Rembrandt was looking into a mirror and painting the Heraclitus that he saw there[.] For surely the real significance of the legend is that Heraclitus and Democritus are one» (p. 313). This point seems implicit too in the woodcut in Sebastian Brant's *Stultifera Navis*, Paris, 1498 (first published in German in 1494), at fol. [q5]ᵛ, where Heracleitus is replaced by Diogenes. Each philosopher has a fool behind him, sporting the opposite demeanor from his own. D. F. DARBY, «Ribera and the Wise Men», *The Art Bulletin*, XLIV (1962), pp. 279-307, points to the Stoic character of Heracleitus and the Epicurean character of his counterpart Democritus (p. 284).

[10] A common usage of the word «gymnasium» also occurring, e.g., in Cicero, *Tusculanae disputationes*, II, iii, 9.

several friends first discussed by Arnaldo della Torre.[11] In this, Ficino may have taken his cue, directly or indirectly, from Sidonius Apollinaris' mention of the paintings on the Areopagus. This letter of Ficino's, the one preceding it and the one following it form an essay, «Stultitia et miseria hominum», in which Ficino explores in some depth, using the theme of the two philosophers as a springboard, the contrasts inherent in mankind's cultivation of those things external to himself at the expense of the cultivation of his soul. His syncretistic conclusion appears in the third letter, addressed to Cristoforo Landino: while Socrates wished to cure us of our tendency to become falsely happy and truly miserable, only God can cure mankind; the one solution to the problem posed by Democritus and Heracleitus is to rise above mankind and to commend oneself to God and to love God.[12]

Yet another motivation for Ficino's interest in Heracleitus and Democritus, or at least support for it, may have come from Book I of Cicero's *De divinatione*, where Cicero has his brother Quintus espouse the cause of *furor divinus*, which became one of Ficino's most important contributions to the poetic theory of his day, one version being taken up by Angelo Poliziano (who may have converted the idea into his own «subitus calor», closer to Statius' concept[13]). It may not have mattered to Ficino, as it seems not to

---

[11] A. DELLA TORRE, *Storia dell'Accademia platonica di Firenze*, Firenze, 1902, pp. 639-640. Cf. P. O. KRISTELLER, *Il pensiero filosofico di Marsilio Ficino*, ed. riveduta con bibliografia aggiornata, Firenze, 1988, pp. 315-317 (*The Philosophy of Marsilio Ficino*, New York, 1943, pp. 293-294); also his *Marsilio Ficino and his Work after Five Hundred Years*, Firenze, 1987, p. 11 and pl. 22.

[12] «Denique, ut mihi videtur, quoniam falso virtutes, vitia vero revera exercemus, iccirco, quantum in nobis est, falso felices, revera miseri evademus.

«Hec risit Democritus, hec deploravit Heraclitus, curare voluit Socrates, curare potest Deus. O quam miserum animal homo est, nisi aliquando evolet super hominem, commendet videlicet se ipsum Deo, Deum amet propter Deum et cetera propter ipsum: hec unica problematum illorum solutio est requiesque malorum». M. FICINO, *Lettere, I. Epistolarum familiarum liber I*, ed. S. Gentile, Firenze, 1990, p. 115.

[13] A. TISSONI BENVENUTI, *L'Orfeo del Poliziano. Con il testo critico dell'originale e delle successive forme teatrali*, Padova, 1986 (Medioevo e Umanesimo, 61), pp. 5-10, discusses Poliziano's heat of inspiration in terms of Statius, separating it from Ficino's *furor*. I believe the difference between the two phenomena is less clear-cut and that indeed they are intimately linked, albeit with slightly different nuances of emphasis. On the other hand, it may well be that Poliziano was not as inspired as the greatest poets, that he was too constrained by elegance (the *lima* Tissoni Benvenuti refers to), and perhaps the difference between *furor* and *subitus calor* can be identified in precisely that way. But that makes it a question of level, not of kind. On poetic madness, see further M. J. B. ALLEN, *The Platonism of Marsilio Ficino. A Study of his «Phaedrus» Commentary, its Sources and Genesis*, Berkeley and Los Angeles, 1984, pp. 41-67.

have mattered to Landino, that Cicero argues against his brother's advocacy of *furor* in Book II of *De divinatione*; the important precedent was Plato's *Phaedrus*. The direct link to our theme lies in the fact that Cicero has Quintus cite Democritus as a further precedent in favor of *furor* as a necessary condition for poetic creation. [14]

Although the fresco from Ficino's house is lost, there is plausible speculation that Leonardo da Vinci may have executed it. [15] This hypothesis is lent weight by Leonardo's clear interest in Platonism, referred to several times in the above chapters. Leonardo moved to Milan in 1482-1483, and, like other Tuscans attracted to Ludovico il Moro's court, he took with him elements of Tuscan culture. It is entirely likely, as suggested in correspondence between Paul Oskar Kristeller and Carlo Pedretti, that the theme of the laughing and the weeping philosophers was one of those elements. In this case the theme may have arrived in Milan well before the publication of Ficino's letters in Venice in 1495. It is the theme of an extant fresco (see Frontispiece) painted by Bramante for the home of Gaspare Visconti, whom we have met in his political, poetic, dramaturgic and philosophical guises earlier in this book (chapters IV, V, VIII and *passim*), and who may have hosted Bramante in his home for several years in the 1480s.

Pedretti proposed years ago[16] that the likenesses of the two philosophers in Bramante's fresco were those of Leonardo (as Heracleitus) and Bramante himself (as Democritus). This theory is bolstered not only by the similarity of features between this Heracleitus and the widely accepted self-portrait of Leonardo in the Biblioteca Reale in Torino, but also by the equally widely accepted portraits of Leonardo and Bramante by Raffaello in his «Disputa»

---

[14] *De divinatione*, I, xxxvii: «Atque etiam illa concitatio declarat vim in animis esse divinam. Negat enim sine furore Democritus quemquam poëtam magnum esse posse, quod idem dicit Plato. Quem, si placet, appellet furorem, dum modo is furor ita laudetur, ut in *Phaedro* Platonis laudatus est». Cicero may argue vehemently against this position in Bk. II, but he espouses quite similar ideas himself in *Orator*, xxxvii, 130 and xxxviii, 132; Cicero's position is complex and varied, however: cf. *De oratore*, III, lvii, 215-217.

[15] See the correspondence between C. PEDRETTI and P. O. KRISTELLER, reprinted in *Achademia Leonardi Vinci*, VI (1993), pp. 144-145. I thank Prof. Pedretti for calling my attention to it.

[16] C. PEDRETTI, «The Sforza Sepulchre», *Gazette des Beaux-Arts*, 89 (1977), pp. 121-131, esp. pp. 123-125, nn. 11-20 and figs. 4-5. On the association and friendship between Bramante and Leonardo, see C. PEDRETTI, «The Original Project for S. Maria delle Grazie», *Journal of the Society of Architectural Historians*, 32 (1973), pp. 30-42 (esp. pp. 30-33) and «Newly Discovered Evidence of Leonardo's Association with Bramante», *Ibid.*, pp. 223-227.

and «School of Athens» frescoes in the Stanze della Segnatura of the Vatican. [17] These two frescoes were executed between 1508 and 1511. In the «Disputa», the figure thought to be Bramante is seen at the left, leaning on a balustrade and consulting earthly knowledge in a book (which, in one interpretation, Raffaello here opposes to the revealed truth of the Church fathers). In the «School of Athens» Bramante is again thought to be depicted, this time as Euclid, leaning over at the right to measure a geometric figure. [18] If we accept the Torino drawing as Leonardo's self-portrait, Leonardo was clearly the model for the central figure of Plato (further supporting

[17] On the portrayals of Bramante: E. MÜNTZ, *Histoire de l'art pendant la Renaissance*, 3 vols., vol. II, Paris, 1891, pp. 393 (plate), 394, n. 1; cf. P. DE VECCHI's notes and references, including those to the work of André Chastel, in *The Complete Paintings of Raphael*, New York, Milan, 1966, pp. 100-103, esp. p. 102. But cf. M. WINNER, «Disputa und Schule von Athen», in *Raffaello a Roma. Il convegno del 1983*, Roma, 1986, pp. 29-45 and plates XI-XX, esp. p. 37 and figs. 13, 19. For a contrary opinion on the Torino drawing, see H. OST, *Das Leonardo-Porträt in der kgl. Bibliothek Turin und andere Fälschungen des Giuseppe Bossi*, Berlin, New York, 1980. I am grateful to Philipp Fehl for these two references.

[18] This identification also concords with that of Bramante as the author of the small book, *Antiquarie p(ro)spetiche / Romane Co(m)poste per / prospectiuo Melanese / depictore*, s.n.t. (Roma, dated variously from 1493 to 1500; HAIN-COPINGER-REICHLING 987; IGI 602; I am grateful to Dott.a Panetta of the Biblioteca Casanatense, Rome, for allowing me to study the unique copy). Bramante's authorship was first proposed by G. DE ANGELIS D'OSSAT, «Preludio romano del Bramante», *Palladio*, XVI (1966), pp. 83-102 (esp. pp. 92-94), and reinforced by D. D. FIENGA, *The Antiquarie Prospetiche Romane composte per prospectivo melanese Depictore: A Document for the Study of the Relationship between Bramante and Leonardo da Vinci*, Dissertation, University of California at Los Angeles, 1970, pp. 61-74 (at p. 68 she relates the woodcut on the first folio to two Vitruvian dicta) and by C. PEDRETTI, «Newly Discovered Evidence» (n. 16), pp. 224-225 and nn. 5, 6; cf. A. BRUSCHI, *Bramante*, Bari, 1985, p. 106. The bald nude in the woodcut, identified as Bramante, is measuring geometric shapes with a compass, like the Euclid of Raffaello's fresco. Pedretti also noticed this similarity in his *Leonardo architetto*, Milano, 1969, pp. 116-121, where he reproduces photographically the woodcut and text from the small volume, pp. 116-117 (as does Fienga at pp. 32-36, with an English translation at pp. 37-59). Note too that the figure in the woodcut holds in his right hand a celestial armillary sphere, which may be worth recalling in our later discussion of the terrestrial globe in Bramante's fresco, along with the real *mappamondo* inventoried in Visconti's house (Chapter IV, above), and cf. P. MURRAY, «'Bramante milanese': the P[a]intings and Engravings», *Arte Lombarda*, VII, 1962, 25-42, p. 29, where Murray notes that Fra Sabba da Castiglione terms Bramante a cosmographer. (There is a seventeenth century armillary sphere held by a satyr kneeling in exactly the same position in the Istituto e Museo di Storia della Scienza, Firenze, Sala VII). For a contrary opinion, see D. ISELLA, «I sonetti delle calze di Donato Bramante», in *Operosa parva. Per Gianni Antonini*, eds. D. De Robertis and F. Gavazzeni, Verona, forthcoming (not seen); I am grateful to Paolo Bongrani for this reference.

the idea of an interest on his part in Platonism); the features of the Torino drawing also correspond, abstracting away from the beard, to those of Heracleitus in Bramante's fresco. Furthermore, the paintings by Raffaello were executed either roughly ten or roughly twenty years after the Bramante fresco (dated at 1486-1487 by Grazioso Sironi, but to the late 1490s by Germano Mulazzani[19]), and the models' faces have aged correspondingly. (Interestingly, the figure tentatively but convincingly identified as Bramante, who was born in 1444 and was thus older than Leonardo by eight years, looks younger in both sets of portraits. This is in keeping with Bramante's easy temperament and Leonardo's apparent tendency to appear older than his years[20]). It may be worth pointing out Eugène Müntz's conviction that Bramante's architecture shows early familiarity with Florentine churches, and thus indicates a likelihood of his presence in Florence as a young man in the early- to mid-1470s, when Ficino's letter was written, and before Bramante's own arrival in Lombardy in 1477.[21] This possibility would theoretically permit of Bramante's participation in some capacity in, or at least his knowledge of, Ficino's fresco; but the possibility remains in the realm of conjecture, along with that of Leonardo's participation.

If the hypothesis concerning the portraits in the Milan fresco is correct, however, as I believe likely, the presence of Leonardo in the fresco in Gaspare Visconti's house allows us to postulate friendly relations between these two men. The thought receives further support both from their common friendship with Bramante, and from a common interest in Ficino's Platonic love theory (cf. above, chapters V and IX).

---

[19] G. SIRONI, «Gli affreschi di Donato D'Angelo detto il Bramante alla Pinacoteca di Brera di Milano: chi ne fu il committente?», Archivio storico lombardo, ser. X, IV (1978), pp. 199-207; confirming the hypothesis of P. MURRAY, «'Bramante milanese'» (n. 18), p. 33. See below, n. 42. G. MULAZZANI, «Apparati critici e filologici» in L'opera completa di Bramantino e Bramante pittore, Milano, 1978, pp. 82-85, here, p. 84.

[20] For B.'s personality, MÜNTZ (n. 17), II, pp. 360-361, 392, and especially G. VASARI, Le vite de' più eccellenti pittori, scultori ed architettori scritte da G. V. pittore aretino, ed. G. Milanesi, 9 vols., Firenze, 1906, vol. IV, pp. 145-174, esp. pp. 163-164. W. SUIDA, Bramante pittore e il Bramantino, Milano, 1953, p. 9, brings more contemporary evidence to bear for B.'s generosity of spirit, from Giovanni Caporali di Perugia's 1536 edition of Vitruvius. On the similarity of expression between a weeping and a laughing face, see L. B. ALBERTI, De pictura, II, 42, in his Opere volgari, ed. C. Grayson, 3 vols., vol. III, Bari, 1973, pp. 72-73; C. PEDRETTI, Leonardo da Vinci on Painting. A Lost Book (Libro A) Reassembled from the Codex Vaticanus Urbinas [latinus] 1270 and from the Codex Leicester. With a Chronology of Leonardo's «Treatise on Painting», London, 1965, p. 61 and n. 71.

[21] MÜNTZ (n. 17), II, p. 360; for the date: SUIDA, Bramante pittore (n. 20), p. 13. Cf. MURRAY, «'Bramante milanese'» (n. 18), n. 14.

Bramante's fresco (Frontispiece) is of no small interest in itself. [22] Besides heralding the growth and diffusion of a Renaissance *topos* in art and letters, as we shall see, it includes elements of other significant traditions. The frieze above the heads of the two philosophers embodies one such tradition, that raised to a high level by Bramante's mentors Piero della Francesca and Andrea Mantegna, who, in concert with the antiquarianism of their age, depicted classical stone reliefs and inscriptions with convincing monochrome technique in their paintings. The frieze here is in fact also telling in its subject-matter. Mulazzani has related the frieze to Plato's *Republic* and *Laws*, suggesting that the two halves represent, respectively, Temperance holding the reins and Justice seated (compare Raffaello's depictions of these themes in his Stanze della Segnatura). Besides being compatible with one message of the legend of the two philosophers, that of moderation or the *via media*, such a framing concept is compatible in even deeper ways with other contemporary, and specifically Platonic, currents.

However, another reading suggests itself, one with an even clearer Platonic basis, leading us to believe that Bramante's fresco may indeed adhere in close detail to that which once appeared in Ficino's gymnasium. The left-hand portion of the frieze depicts a charioteer attempting to direct two pairs of horses, one heading back into the frieze, the other in conflict, with the farther horse heading out toward the viewer, the nearer heading into the frieze. This portion in fact might appear to be a linear depiction of the Phaedran charioteer, attempting to guide between two extremes his *quadriga*, or four-horse chariot, a type of chariot which is explicitly associated with the Phaedran myth in Ficino's *Theologia Platonica*, published in 1482. The chariot in this, as in other myths and legends, represents the soul. [23]

---

[22] Cf. L. BELTRAMI, «La sala dei Maestri d'Arme nella Casa dei Panigarola in San Bernardino (ora Via Lanzone) dipinta da Bramante», *Rassegna d'arte*, II (1902), pp. 97-103 and Tav. facing p. 104; G. MULAZZANI's notes in *L'opera completa* (n. 19) and references therein; G. MULAZZANI, M. DALAI EMILIANI, S. MATALON, P. BRAMBILLA BARCILON, A. GALLONE, *Donato Bramante: Gli uomini d'arme*, Firenze, 1977 (Quaderni di Brera, 3); and G. FERRI PICCALUGA, «Gli affreschi di casa Panigarola e la cultura milanese tra Quattro e Cinquecento», *Arte lombarda*, n.s., 86-87 (1988, 3-4), pp. 14-25; most recently, P. MARANI, «Eraklitos och Demokritos», *Leonardos Broar*, ed. C. Pedretti, Firenze, 1994, (in Swedish, not seen; reference kindly supplied by the author). I am grateful to Dr. Pietro Marani, Director of the Pinacoteca di Brera, for having enabled me to see the fresco in its storeroom.

[23] *Opera Omnia*, 1576, p. 389 (reprint, 1962, p. 419), as noted by ALLEN, *The Platonism of Marsilio Ficino* (n. 13), p. 88, n. 3. Allen points out the numerous uses, eastern and western, of the ascent of chariots to represent the ascents of the soul in *Marsilio Ficino and the Phaedran Charioter*, Berkeley and Los Angeles, 1981, pp. 3-4 and n. 6 at pp. 29-30. For Ficino chariot, charioteer and horses seem to be analogous to parts of the soul.

But there is a further allusion here, again in close keeping with Ficino's thought and knowledge. That is an allusion to a source as venerable as Plato himself: the poet and philosopher Parmenides (fl. ca. 450 BC). In Parmenides' *Poema*, which Ficino knew from Sextus Empiricus (acquired in Italy by Francesco Filelfo after 1427[24]), a chariot is described, the vehicle for Parmenides' own spiritual ascent and passage through «the gates separating the ways of day and night, enclosed by a lintel and a threshold of stone. The ethereal gates themselves are covered with big wing-doors, of which Dike, whose vengeance is stern, possesses the rewarding keys».[25] The horses proceed through the «gaping chasm» of the open doors, and the goddess receives Parmenides gladly and takes in her hand his right hand, and welcomes him to her abode and that of immortal charioteers. She welcomes him, for he has been sent forth by right and justice.

The fresco is badly damaged, and difficult to read in places, but the gist would seem to be there. The figures behind (to the left of) the chariot appear to be female ones, corresponding to the daughters of the sun, Parmenides' escorts. The scene in the right portion of the frieze would seem to be – or to be created in analogy with – the welcoming scene in Parmenides, especially since Sextus identified the unnamed goddess with Dike. In fact, the figure seated on a throne resembles strongly the ancient iconography of the personification of *Roma* or *Virtus*: a woman clothed in a hunting chiton and buskins. Specific attributes of this «Amazon» type of the goddess *Roma* correspond to Bramante's goddess: a full, rounded chin, curving down-turned mouth, heavy-lidded eyes, and holding an orb of dominion (which in our frieze may appear under the goddess's right hand or may be replaced by the central globe of the fresco, discussed below). The figure makes a gesture of clemency in keeping with the Roman emperors' gestures of meting out forgiveness to the conquered. This prototype, which would have been known from triumphal monuments like the arch of Septimius Severus, has here come to stand for

---

[24] R. SABBADINI, *Le scoperte dei codici latini e greci ne' secoli XIV e XV*, Firenze, 1905 (reprint Firenze, 1967), p. 48; see L. FLORIDI's forthcoming article on Sextus in the *Catalogus Translationum et Commentariorum: Medieval and Renaissance Latin Translations and Commentaries. Annotated Lists and Guides*, ed. V. Brown, P. O. Kristeller, F. E. Cranz, Washington, D.C., 1960-, kindly furnished to me by the author.

[25] L. TARÁN, *Parmenides. A Text with Translation, Commentary, and Critical Essays*, Princeton, 1965, pp. 8-9, 18. The image was recognized by Andrea Cavaggioni, to whom I am most grateful.

Dike, who in our text welcomes Parmenides (or in Platonic terms, the soul) among the other charioteers and their horses. Behind the seated goddess is the figure of a bearded philosopher, leaning on a crutch and with one foot crossed in front of the other, again in conformity with classical iconography, and here representing the particular philosophical tradition identified. [26] Because Ficino received this important fragment of Parmenides through Sextus, he was subject to Sextus' interpretation, which was thoroughly Platonic. It is thus that the chariot can at one and the same time resemble both Parmenides' chariot and the Phaedran chariot, so dear to Ficino.

This interpretation also helps us to understand the enigmatic symbol between the two halves of the frieze. It has been variously read as the numeral 60 or 40, or as the word *Lex*, with overtones of the Christian *nomen sacrum* alluded to by Peter Murray. Given the source as Parmenides and the Renaissance context, a composite reading seems plausible, one in which both *Lex* and *Lux* are referred to, along with the Greek *chi* representing the *nomen sacrum*. (This in turn might be ciphered into a numeral 60, or 40, which, for the person to whom it referred or for whom it was significant, would then hold all the above overtones). The «XL» is in the exact center of the frieze and above the terrestrial globe, itself skewed slightly to the right – Democritus' side, which would seem to jibe with Edgar Wind's ideas concerning the Renaissance preference for a Christian Democritus. [27] The iconography of the frieze as a whole would thus allude to the coming of the soul into the light, where justice will be accorded it, in keeping with the truth of philoso-

---

[26] R. BRILLIANT, *The Arch of Septimius Severus in the Roman Forum*, Roma, 1967 (Memoirs of the American Academy in Rome, XXIX), pp. 143-146 and pl. 44, identifies the specific attributes of the goddess listed. Cf. P. P. BOBER, R. RUBINSTEIN, *Renaissance Artists and Antique Sculpture*, London, 1987, pp. 217-218; C. C. VERMEULE, *The Goddess Roma in the Art of the Roman Empire*, Cambridge, Mass., 1959, pp. 65-68; E. GOMBRICH, «Icones Symbolicae», in his *Symbolic Images. Studies in the Art of the Renaissance II*, London, 1978, pp. 123-195, 228-235, esp. pp. 175-176. The philosopher's pose and garb are analogous to the type represented by the famous fresco in Boscoreale (unknown until 1900), on which see G. SAURON, «Nature et signification de la mégalographie énigmatique de Boscoreale», *Revue des études latines*, 71 (1993), pp. 87-117 (esp. pp. 92-93, 104-105), which proposes an interpretation for Boscoreale in ways analogous to that proposed here for our frieze. I thank Karin Einaudi for identifying the imperial gesture of clemency and the figure of the philosopher behind the goddess, and for the first and last of these references.

[27] E. WIND, «The Christian Democritus», *Journal of the Warburg Institute*, I, 1937, pp. 180-182, points to Landino's equation of Democritean *euthymia* with Christian peace; see also nn. 8 and 28, here.

phy, under the aegis of Christ or the Christian religion. [28] The reading is furthermore eminently compatible with Ficino's three letters «Stultitia et miseria hominum», mentioned earlier.

The terrestrial globe between the two philosophers, besides symbolizing the world over which Parmenidean-Platonic-Christian justice is to hold sway, is of interest in other ways too. Around the earlier possible date of execution of Bramante's fresco and in any case before the execution of the woodcut on our cover (1506), the tip of Africa was circumnavigated by Bartolomeu Dias, in 1488. [29] Whereas the continent extends beyond the horizon in the painting, the water south of the continent is clearly visible in the woodcut. [30] As has been noted, there was often a palpable lag between geographical discoveries and their divulgation and acceptance, as is true with most discoveries in any field. Of further interest is the fact that Leonardo too was particularly interested in projections related to the earth's surface, and while he may not have actually drawn a *mappamondo*, this interest makes the globe's juxtaposition between him and Bramante (whose interest in the physical sciences is also known, and may be referred to in his depiction of himself in the woodcut previously alluded to[31]) appropriate, as it is appropriate to the scientific interests of the two philosophers represented.

The frescoed globe, which also formed a part of Ficino's fresco as described in the letter mentioned earlier, here includes an excellent rendering of the Mediterranean basin, well known from portolans of the time. Pedretti has noted that the mountains, African and European, are evocative of Leo-

---

[28] These thoughts are lent weight by the occurrence of a similar, if simpler, suggestion in Cornelis Cornelisz of Haarlem's *Democritus and Heracleitus* of 1613, where the laughing Democritus holds the sceptral globe and cross, symbolizing Christ's dominion over the world. See W. WEISBACH, «Der sogenannte Geograph von Velazquez und die Darstellungen des Demokrit und Heraklit», *Jahrbuch der preuszischen Kunstsammlungen*, 49 (1928), pp. 141-158, pp. 152-153, fig. 10; and cf. WIND, *op. cit.*, p. 181 and Pl. 24 d.

[29] Cf. D. KIANG, «The 'Mappamondo' in Bramante's *Heraclitus and Democritus*», *Achademia Leonardi Vinci*, V (1992), pp. 128-135, figs. 1-7. The fresco also figured in the exhibition «Circa 1492» on the basis of its globe; cf. *Circa 1492. Art in the Age of Exploration*, ed. J. A. Levenson, Washington, New Haven, London, 1991: Catalogue entry no. 128 by J.-M. MASSING. The woodcut of 1506 is clearly based loosely on the fresco, which it reverses.

[30] Interestingly, in the *mappamondo* of Fra Mauro of the mid-fifteenth century (1459), water is already visible below Africa, which could be due, as has been suggested, to the cartographer's expectation that this was so, and to his wish to promote such a view and consequent explorations by his patrons: cf. *Il Mappamondo di Fra Mauro*, ed. T. Gasparrini Leporace, Presentazione di R. Almagià, Roma, 1956.

[31] See above, n. 18.

nardo's style of mapmaking, [32] and that the globe also includes the first modern depiction in a painting of Scandinavia. [33] In all of this, we see the burgeoning interest in scientific matters, such as geography, and we recall that an inventory made after Gaspare Visconti's death describes a *mappamondo* in a room adjacent to Visconti's bedroom. Although it has been proposed that the mappamondo was there for the use of his presumed house-guest, Bramante (see above, chapter IV), it is unnecessary to exclude an interest on the part of Visconti himself in the exciting scientific developments of their age. Visconti's library also included Pier Candido Decembrio's *De Cosmographia*, testifying further to his own scientific (in the broadest sense of the word) bent, and, incidentally, linking across time two of the major protagonists of this book. [34]

The *topos* of the two philosophers and the globe continued to appear in art over the next three centuries, and was addressed by such painters as Rubens and Velazquez. [35] It also borders on the history of another *topos*, that of the world as theater, not irrelevant to our discussion of theatrical phenomena of this time. This *topos* is explicitly juxtaposed to that of Democritus and Heracleitus at the beginning of Book I of Pierre Boaistuau's *Le théâtre du monde*, published in 1558. [36] Frances Yates explored the *topos*, relating it on philosophical as well as concrete grounds to the work of John Dee and

---

[32] PEDRETTI, «The Sforza Supulchre» (n. 16), p. 124.

[33] PEDRETTI, «Leonardo in Sweden», *Achademia Leonardi Vinci*, VI (1993), p. 203.

[34] The two men's lives overlapped by sixteen years; Decembrio in fact entered briefly into correspondence with Visconti's friend and fellow poet Niccolò da Correggio during the latter's childhood. See the biographical sketch of Correggio in my *Politian's «Orfeo» and Other «Favole Mitologiche» of Late Fifteenth Century Northern Italy*, Dissertation, Columbia University, New York, 1976, pp. 10-19; cf. P. FARENGA, «N. da C.» in *Dizionario Biografico degli Italiani*, 29, Roma, 1983, pp. 466-474. On Decembrio, see chapters II and III, above.

[35] WEISBACH, «Der sogenannte Geograph von Velazquez» (n. 28); cf. DARBY, «Ribera and the Wise Men» (n. 9), pp. 284-288; O. FERRARI, «L'iconografia dei filosofi antichi nella pittura del sec. XVII in Italia», *Storia dell'arte*, 57 (1986), pp. 103-181 and figs. 1-87, pp. 120-123 and *passim*. I am grateful to Ines Aliverti for the last reference, and see her article, «An Unknown Portrait of Tiberio Fiorilli», forthcoming in *Theatre Research International* (not seen).

[36] Crit. ed. by M. Simonin, Genève, 1981, p. 66; cf. J. JACQUOT, «*Le théâtre du monde* de Shakespeare à Calderón», *Revue de littérature comparée*, 31 (1957), pp. 341-372, esp. p. 348 and most recently, J.M. SASLOW, *The Medici Wedding of 1589. Florentine Festival as Theatrum Mundi*, New Haven, 1996 (not seen). According to Jean Jacquot, the «theater of the world» *topos* itself harks back to a fragment by none other than Democritus. I am unable to find such a passage among his extant fragments, however.

Robert Fludd and ultimately to the choice of the name and the motto, as well as the structure (which she sees as deeply and consciously Vitruvian), of the Globe Theatre of Shakespeare's company.[37] We are thus brought close to the idea of «Theater as Mirror» which is the heading of Part IV of this book. (Clearly, the juxtaposition of the laughing comic and frowning tragic masks is analogous to that of the laughing Democritus and the weeping Heracleitus, if not even more closely connected).

The fresco of the two philosophers was conceived and executed as part of a larger scheme including seven large frescoes of men of arms, documented by Gian Paolo Lomazzo in the late 16th century.[38] The original disposition of the frescoes is uncertain.[39] The late 18th century collector Venanzio De Pagave – whose acquaintance Count Borri, the owner of the house, moved the frescoes, cutting some in half – leaves us a second-hand narrative of their original disposition, including the statement that the *Uomini d'Arme* had been in a nearby (rather than the same) room.[40] Bramante had executed other similar commissions, notably that for the Palazzo della Ragione or del Podestà in Bergamo, where in 1477 he painted seven monumental philosophers on the outer wall. The men of arms in the so-called Casa Panigarola (actually Casa Visconti at the time which interests us) are related to a long iconographical tradition of «Uomini Famosi», themselves not unrelated to Petrarca's *Triumph of Fame*.[41] Their connection with the fresco of the two

---

[37] F. YATES, *Theatre of the World*, London, 1969; see too E. R. CURTIUS, *European Literature and the Latin Middle Ages*, tr. W. R. Trask, London, 1953, pp. 140-141, where he relates the Globe Theatre's motto directly to John of Salisbury.

[38] G. P. LOMAZZO, *Trattato dell'arte della pittura, scoltura et architettura* (1584), in his *Scritti sulle arti*, 2 vols., ed. R. P. Ciardi, Firenze, 1973, II, p. 335.

[39] See BELTRAMI, «La sala dei Maestri d'Arme» (n. 22); PEDRETTI, «The Sforza Sepulchre» (n. 16); MULAZZANI, *L'opera completa* (n. 19; the disposition of the frescoes is reversed in the lower two diagrams at p. 85).

[40] PEDRETTI, «The Sforza Sepulchre» (n. 16), p. 129, n. 11; cf. FERRI PICCALUGA, «Gli affreschi» (n. 22), p. 20, n. 8. On Venanzio De Pagave, see the introduction by A. SCOTTI to *La collezione De Pagave (Le stampe dell'Archivio di Stato di Novara)*, Novara, 1976, pp. 5-16. De Pagave's life of Bramante, «Dialogo fra un forestiero e un pittore che si incontrano nella Basilica di S. Francesco Grande in Milano» is in MS C VI 28 of the Biblioteca d'Arte in the Castello Sforzesco, Milano, shelf-mark D 221 (the text referred to by Pedretti, *loc. cit.*, is at pp. [*sic*] 478-480 of the MS). This would seem to be De Pagave's working draft as Scotti assumes, although there are references throughout to «folios» with Roman numerals that do not correspond at all to the pagination of this MS, but could correspond to an earlier draft.

[41] T. MOMMSEN, «Petrarch and the Decoration of the Sala Virorum Illustrium in Padua», *The Art Bulletin*, XXXIV (1952), pp. 95-116, figs. 3-40; M. M. DONATO, «Gli eroi romani tra

philosophers under discussion is primarily through authorship and patronage, besides being related to the topical juxtaposition of the warrior and the
philosopher so perfectly adapted to Gaspare Visconti's life and character.
Due to these associations, it may be appropriate to wonder whether, along
with the portraits among these frescoes, identified (albeit a full century later)
by Lomazzo as Pietro Suola il Vecchio, Giorgio Moro da Ficino and Bel-
tramo, some of the faces of the *Uomini d'Arme* depicted were not members
of Gaspare Visconti's own family, even including the poet, philosopher and
man of arms Gaspar Ambrogio himself (see chapter IV). Two of the figures
are crowned with laurel, one of these being clad in armor as well. If the frescoes were painted in about 1486-1487, as Grazioso Sironi has suggested,
seconding the hypothesis of Peter Murray,[42] Gaspare Visconti would have
been 25 or 26; he might then be identifiable with the younger of the two
laureates, the blond «Cantore» (or, perhaps more appropriate to the setting
and context, the «Oratore»). If instead, as Germano Mulazzani has suggested,[43] they were painted after 1495, Gaspar Ambrogio would have been
in his mid-thirties, that is, a possible age for the older «Uomo Laureato». It
is not unknown for figures representing personages of the past to be modelled on contemporary ones, thus, in the spirit of *imitatio*, enriching the evo-
cations of the past with those of the present (and simultaneously flattering
the contemporary models). Given the strong arguments for the faces of the
two philosophers being portraits of Leonardo and Bramante, the possibility
that Gaspare Visconti's portrait is among the *Uomini d'Arme* seems to me
eminently plausible, though it cannot be ascertained without documentation. Certainly, however, the three men identified by Lomazzo as portrayed
in the frescoes must have been friends of our poet and playwright to be depicted in his house.

---

storia ed *exemplum*. I primi cicli umanistici di Uomini Famosi», *Memoria dell'antico nel-
l'arte italiana*, ed. S. Settis, Torino, 1985, II, pp. 99-152, figs. 75-93; cf. also MURRAY,
«'Bramante milanese'» (n. 18). Mulazzani sees the *Uomini d'Arme* as separate from the
*Uomini Famosi* tradition, however: «Lettura iconologica», in G. MULAZZANI, *et al., Donato
Bramante: Gli Uomini d'Arme* (n. 22), p. 9. I am grateful to Lilian Armstrong for the first
two references.

[42] SIRONI, «Gli affreschi» (n. 19), p. 201; MURRAY, «'Bramante milanese'» (n. 18), p. 32. Sironi's hypothesis is advanced on the basis of documents proving ties between Visconti and
Bramante. While I remain convinced of his primary hypothesis that Visconti was the patron
of the frescoes, the documents Sironi transcribes leave open both the date of execution of
the frescoes and Bramante's residence in Visconti's house (chapter IV, n. 24, above).

[43] MULAZZANI, *L'opera completa di Bramantino e Bramante pittore* (n. 19), p. 84.

Returning now to the larger context of the *topos* of the two philosophers
and its tradition, let us look at a significant literary work written in Milan
just a few years after the death in 1499 of the fresco's patron, Gaspare Visconti, issuing from the pen of his friend Antonio Campo Fregoso «Il Fileremo» (or Lover of Solitude). This is the double poem in *terza rima*, *Riso de
Democrito* and *Pianto di Heraclito*, the first portion published in 1506, joined
by the second in the edition of [1507].[44] Campo Fregoso is the author of the
lament on the death of Gaspare Visconti, «Chi darà a gli ochi mei d'acqua
mai tanto?» (clearly echoing the famous lament of Angelo Poliziano on the
death of Lorenzo de' Medici, «Quis dabit?», set movingly to music by Hein-
rich Isaac.[45]) The fortune of the pair of poems bespeaks their importance to
the reading public of the age, for they were reprinted fourteen times in Milan
and Venice in the fifty years following the edition of [1507], and translated
into French (1547) and Spanish (1554), thus being assured of a European
diffusion which, through the French, would have reached England in the
mid-16th century.

The poems pick up the theme of the laughing and the weeping philosophers, developing the logical ramifications of the two in an allegorical fan-
tasy which Gabriella Ferri Piccaluga has related convincingly to Francesco
Colonna's *Hypnerotomachia Poliphili*, printed in the famous edition by Aldus
in 1499, and to the *topos* of *melancholia*.[46] The latter theme was of course
depicted by Dürer in his complex and beautiful woodcut of 1514, which
Dürer himself juxtaposed to his own «St. Jerome in his Study», also of 1514,
by offering the two together in a further Heracleitan opposition of

---

[44] A. FILEREMO FREGOSO, *Opere*, ed. G. Dilemmi, Bologna, 1976 (Collezione di opere inedite
o rare pubblicate dalla Commissione per i Testi di Lingua, vol. 135); this valuable critical
edition should be the one used by scholars discussing the works of Fregoso. The date of the
second, complete, edition is established on the basis of watermarks by Dilemmi in his introduction, pp. xxxvi-xxxvii. The first two editions were printed by Pietro Martire Mantegazza.
Our cover is taken from the 1506 edition, and this woodcut establishes the original intention
of the author to write about both philosophers, as it is logical to assume he would have
intended. I discern no break in narrative continuity alluded to by some critics under the
impression that a gap of six years separated the two poems (the next dated edition of both
poems is from the press of Scinzenzeler in 1511: on Milanese printers, see chapter I).

[45] Fregoso's lament is at pp. 6-8 of Dilemmi's edition. Cf. A. POLIZIANO, *Prose volgari inedite
e poesie latine e greche edite e inedite*, ed. I. Del Lungo, Firenze, 1867, pp. 274-275 (reprinted as vol. II of A. POLITIANUS, *Opera Omnia*, ed. I. Maïer, 3 vols, Torino, 1970):
«Quis dabit capiti meo / Aquam, quis oculis meis / Fontem lachrymarum dabit, / Ut nocte
fleam? / Ut luce fleam? ...»

[46] Cf. FERRI PICCALUGA, «Gli affreschi» (n. 22), pp. 16-19.

melancholy and what may be seen as a kind of *euthymia*. [47] This is a theme rich in significance for all times, including our own, as recognized in another context by Klibansky, Panofsky and Saxl. [48] Not only the contrast between a humorous and a tragic view of the same (or sometimes slightly different) human plights, but the ambiguities of each – the melancholic view, with its inherent conflict between discipline and passion and its by-product of artistic expression, and the comic view, with its clear and constant undercurrent of the tragic – fascinate thinkers, writers and artists as they always have and will.

Fregoso's two allegorical poems had great success, yet their apparent impact on the culture of 16th century Europe is perhaps underestimated, being noticed only with respect to the two translations (which clearly were vehicles of transmission – but a work must excite interest to be translated in the first place). Their poetic value is not high, except in certain of the images evoked and in that the author makes a valiant and progressively successful attempt to express his ideas in the meter of Dante, *terza rima*, with many echoes of Petrarca and Poliziano; but their philosophical and intellectual interest is great and lasting.

The author diverges from Dante's choice to let theology be his guide, opting instead explicitly for philosophy and earthly knowledge and wisdom, even creating with skillful images a Palace of Knowledge (built of philosophers' stone!) surrounded by four seasonal gardens (clearly Burgundian in inspiration), as the *locus amoenus* for a gathering around Plato. The poet is steered away from the vast questions being raised there by his guide (his «Demonio Bono»), toward the more manageable one of how to know oneself (the very question associated with this topos by Ficino in his epistolary essay on the foolishness and the misery of men). He drinks of the comforting,

---

[47] It is impossible not to conceive a relation (albeit one of type arising from common insights into a way of life) between the figures of Democritus, the book-loving solitary, good-humored figure and the similarly disposed St. Jerome; and see below for the common attributes between Fregoso's Heracleitus and Jerome. On the joint offering of the two prints: E. PANOFSKY, *Albrecht Dürer*, 2 vols., Princeton, 1948, vol. I, p. 156; cf. A. DÜRER, *Schriftlicher Nachlass*, ed. H. Rupprich, 3 vols., vol. I, Berlin, 1956, pp. 154, 156, 157 (all Aug.-Sept., 1520), cf. pp. 265 (no. 59, 1520), 295 (no. 9, 1515); *The Complete Engravings, Etchings and Drypoints of Albrecht Dürer*, ed. W. L. Strauss, New York, 1973, p. 168, n. 11.

[48] Cf. R. KLIBANSKY, E. PANOFSKY, F. SAXL, *Saturn and Melancholy. Studies in the History of Natural Philosophy, Religion and Art*, London, 1964, esp. pp. 234-235 on the contradiction of humor and melancholy, which ties in perfectly with the opposition of our two philosophers (and has implications for tragedy and comedy).

sweet water issuing from the statue of Philosophy's breast, then moves on to the small house of Democritus where he meets the philosopher capable of laughing not only at the fools of the world, but at himself (VII, 74-75). Democritus instructs Fregoso on the types of delusion that give rise to mankind's foolishness (hope, love, bravado, greed), which he sees in the human occupations of the hunt, of war, of burial practices. The philosopher expresses the opinion that animals are less stupid about their needs than mankind, who is superior to them only by virtue of his immortal soul (XII). Fregoso leaves, having been instructed to laugh, not only at the world, but at himself, and not only in derision, but also in compassion.[49]

The second poem, of the same length (15 *capituli* of 91 lines each[50]), after invoking the Muses and Apollo, carries the poet on the crest of his great desire to learn, into the domain of the lachrimose Heracleitus, some distance from the Palace of Knowledge, in a small dwelling on a rugged peak of the mountain. His new guide is an angel, Dianeo, son of *Otium* and Solitude (prerequisites for poetic work), sent by his first and principal guide, his *genio*. This angel, created from the minds of miserable mortals, has large wings (as will Dürer's *Melencolia*), by which to serve those endowed with worthy and elevated spirit, and to loft Fregoso to the height of Heracleitus' dwelling (like Dante's Geryon, only here the poet's fear is displaced by the enormous pleasure of flying). The poet drinks of the river swelled by Heracleitus' «lacrime pietose»[51] and finds it bitter. Heracleitus is here the hermit in a cave, surrounded by books and a skull – the attributes of St. Jerome – who counsels a «vita solitaria»[52], far from the madding crowd. Contemplating the skull, Heracleitus echoes Lactantius' contrast (*De opificio Dei*, III, 2), saying that Nature is stepmother rather than mother to humanity (a note that will

---

[49] Jean JEHASSE relates this capacity to laugh (in jest, in ridicule, and critically) specifically to the rise of the critical spirit as it affects intellectual and scientific inquiry (though emphasizing French thought and letters, in which this tendency appears well after its appearance in Italian humanism and its offshoots, including the present poems): «Démocrite et la renaissance de la critique», *Etudes seizièmistes offertes à Monsieur le Professeur V.-L. Saulnier par plusieurs des ses anciens doctorants*, Genève, 1980, pp. 41-64. He brings new classical and medieval sources to his discussion.

[50] The first *capitulo* of *Riso de Democrito* has only 88 lines in Dilemmi's edition, but it is the only exception. There are thus 909 *terzine* in all, rather than the expected 910.

[51] Democritus in the first poem had no trace of the Christian Democritus eyoked by Wind; Heracleitus here has compassion, though it will be mingled with a disdain for the world not unlike that of Democritus.

[52] Petrarca (author of *De vita solitaria*) had in fact favored Heracleitus over Democritus in his *De remediis*, as was seen (n. 7).

again be echoed in the middle of the century in Orbecche's soliloquy, discussed in chapter X, and in Boaistuau's *Théâtre du monde*).[53] Mankind is subject to the ills both of intellect, understanding his plight and struggling with it, and of the passions, subject to blind Cupid's damage. Mankind is created to contemplate Nature and to understand its workings, the creation of «il gran Rettore» (X, 41), «'l summo Architettor» (XI, 84), yet he does not do so. Instead he follows *Voluptas* (for Fregoso clearly not a balanced pleasure or Valla's *summum bonum*), neglecting Reason («la luce ch'è infinita»), the study of physics or of law, and seeking instead ephemeral pleasures (which are like «nebbia al vento o al sol la brina»).

Fregoso leaves Heracleitus, vowing to flee the crowd and live in solitude (as his knickname, Fileremo, implies) but Dianeo counsels against this, suggesting instead a moderate way, of life in the city, but among learned and modest friends. Near the beginning of the first poem, and here at the end of the second, Timon the misanthrope is evoked (as he will be in the same context by Boaistuau and by Montaigne later in the century), as one who did not know the way of moderation, and sank into despair, in contrast with both philosophers whose wisdom is being tapped as beings able to see the evils of the world, yet not be overcome by them.

The first edition of the *Riso de Democrito* is preceded by several epigrams and poems, including one by Bartolomeo Simonetta, the brother of Cicco (see chapter I). Fregoso had grown up in the Simonetta household and retained close contacts with the family, as did his friend Gaspare Visconti through his wife, Cicco's daughter (chapter IV). Bartolomeo's epigram is a direct translation of an anonymous one (IX, 148) from the *Greek Anthology*, the Planudean version of which had already been printed twice, in 1494 and 1503, at the time of the first editions of Fregoso. It is more than apt to the subject, and further reinforces our impression of Fregoso's intention to expand his poem to include Heracleitus:

> Bartholamei Simonett(a)e Epigra(m)ma in imagines
> Heraclyti & Democriti.
>
> Defle hominum uitam plusq(uam) Heraclyte solebas
>     In lachrymas totos solue age nunc oculos:
> Concute maiori splenem Democrite risu

---

[53] In both our poems Nature is seen as the dominant force over Art. Animals are born better equipped for the world than helpless infants (as in *Orbecche*: see chapter X, above).

Et toto resonans ore cachinus hiet:
Vita fuit nunq(uam) post condita saecula mundi
Et risu pariter dignior & lachrymis.[54]

The same epigram is translated several years later for his *Emblematum liber* by the Milanese jurist and man of letters Andrea Alciati as Emblem 152 (*olim* 151), «In vitam humanam» (also usually accompanied by a woodcut showing the two philosophers, most often in a pastoral setting), which Henry Green conjectures was contained in the lost Milanese (MS) copy of 1522. Alciati had already produced a version of his book during the «Saturnalia» (December 17) of 1521, as he states in a letter of that month. Nine epigrams were then translated by him for Johannes Soter's *Epigrammata graeca* of 1528 (in which this epigram appears in Latin translations by two other authors), and 153 epigrams for Janus Cornarius' *Selecta epigrammata graeca* of 1529.[55] Cornarius' collection included our epigram in both Simonetta's and Alciati's translations, the latter of which then appears two years later as «In vitam humanam» at fol. E7 of the first printed edition of Alciati's own *Emblematum liber* (Augsburg, Steyner, 28 Feb., 1531):

Plus solito humanae nunc defle incommoda vitae,
   Heraclite: scatet pluribus illa malis.
Tu rursus (si quando alias) extolle cachinnum
   Democrite: illa magis ludicra facta fuit.
Interea haec cernens meditor, qua denique tecum
   Fine fleam, aut tecum quomodo splene iocer.[56]

---

[54] I give the epigram as it appears beneath the woodcut reproduced on the cover of this book, to complete the picture of the first folio (a) of the book. GARCIA GOMEZ (n. 4), p. 101, correctly points out the preponderance of attributions to various classical and medieval Latin sources for Simonetta's epigram, at the expense of the clearly direct transmission from the *Planudean Anthology* (at least to Simonetta, the first modern Latin writer to use it). Cf. n. 5, above.

[55] Cf. A. SAUNDERS, «Alciati and the Greek Anthology», *The Journal of Medieval and Renaissance Studies*, XII (1982), pp. 1-18; the letter of 1521 is published by H. MIEDEMA, «The Term *Emblema* in Alciati», *Journal of the Warburg and Courtauld Institutes*, 31 (1968), pp. 234-250, at pp. 236-237, including n. 15. The first edition of Alciati's *Emblematum liber* may have been illustrated without his approval (cf. MIEDEMA, p. 243); the similar case of Ripa's *Iconologia*, first published without illustrations in 1593, will be recalled from chapter IX, n. 5. Even the early modern use of the terms «emblema» and «icones» in other words, was not that of today, but seems to have referred to the text alone.

[56] Text transcribed from the edition of Lyon, 1550. Cf. H. GREEN, *Andrea Alciati and his Book of Emblems. A Biographical and Bibliographical Study*, London, 1872 (reprint, New York, n.d.), pp. 103-115, 322. For facsimiles of various editions and translations of the epigram, see A. ALCIATUS, *The Latin Emblems. Indexes and Lists*, ed. P. M. Daly, V. W. Callahan, S. Cuttler, 2 vols., Toronto, 1985.

By 1534 there was a Paris edition of Alciati, and the rapid and wide diffusion of this popular work is legendary. The revived *topos* of the laughing and
the weeping philosophers, largely diffused by impulses from Milan, was
catching the fancies of the lettered in all the countries of Western Europe.
Those it spoke to would include Montaigne (*Essais*, I, 50), and many artists.
Because of the richness and complexity of its implications, and the many
areas of human thought it touches, from the sciences to the visual, aural and
verbal arts and theater, it is a theme worthy, not only of deeper study, but of
further use in the arts and the thought of today.

# INDICES

# INDEX OF NAMES

# INDEX OF MIYTHOLOGICAL AND FICTIONAL CHARACTERS

# INDEX OF MANUSCRIPTS